Film Reboots

Screen Serialities

Series editors: Claire Perkins and Constantine Verevis

Series advisory board: Kim Akass, Glen Creeber, Shane Denson, Jennifer Forrest, Jonathan Gray, Julie Grossman, Daniel Herbert, Carolyn Jess-Cooke, Frank Kelleter, Amanda Ann Klein, Kathleen Loock, Jason Mittell, Sean O'Sullivan, Barton Palmer, Alisa Perren, Dana Polan, Iain Robert Smith, Shannon Wells-Lassagne, Linda Williams

Screen Serialities provides a forum for introducing, analysing and theorising a broad spectrum of serial screen formats – including franchises, series, serials, sequels and remakes.

Over and above individual texts that happen to be serialised, the book series takes a guiding focus on seriality as an aesthetic and industrial principle that has shaped the narrative logic, socio-cultural function and economic identity of screen texts across more than a century of cinema, television and 'new' media.

Titles in this series include:

Film Reboots
Edited by Daniel Herbert and Constantine Verevis

Reanimated: The Contemporary American Horror Remake
By Laura Mee

Gender and Seriality: Practices and Politics of Contemporary US Television
By Maria Sulimma

Film Reboots

Edited by Daniel Herbert and
Constantine Verevis

EDINBURGH
University Press

Edinburgh University Press is one of the leading university presses in the UK. We publish academic books and journals in our selected subject areas across the humanities and social sciences, combining cutting-edge scholarship with high editorial and production values to produce academic works of lasting importance. For more information visit our website: edinburghuniversitypress.com

© editorial matter and organisation Daniel Herbert and Constantine Verevis, 2020, 2022
© the chapters their several authors, 2020, 2022

First published in hardback by Edinburgh University Press 2020

Edinburgh University Press Ltd
The Tun – Holyrood Road, 12(2f) Jackson's Entry, Edinburgh EH8 8PJ

Typeset in 11/13 Ehrhardt MT by
IDSUK (DataConnection) Ltd

A CIP record for this book is available from the British Library

ISBN 978 1 4744 5136 9 (hardback)
ISBN 978 1 4744 5137 6 (paperback)
ISBN 978 1 4744 5138 3 (webready PDF)
ISBN 978 1 4744 5139 0 (epub)

The right of Daniel Herbert and Constantine Verevis to be identified as the editors of this work has been asserted in accordance with the Copyright, Designs and Patents Act 1988, and the Copyright and Related Rights Regulations 2003 (SI No. 2498).

Contents

List of Figures and Tables vii
Notes on Contributors ix

    Introduction: Film Reboots 1
    Daniel Herbert and Constantine Verevis

Part I Industry and Commerce

1 Rethinking the 'Supersystem': Film Reboots and the *Teenage Mutant Ninja Turtles*
    Daniel Herbert 19

2 Live Long and Prosper: Rebooting *Star Trek* and Reimagining Fandom 33
    Erin Hanna

3 The Many Reboots of the Batman 47
    Eileen R. Meehan

Part II Structure and Narrative

4 The Edge of Reality: Replicating *Blade Runner* 65
    Constantine Verevis

5 Gender, Genre and the Reboot: From *Ocean's 11/Eleven* to *Ocean's 8/Eight* 81
    Jennifer Forrest

6 Understanding *Twin Peaks: The Return* as a 'Film Reboot' via Anti-Franchise Discourses Within Media Franchising 97
    Matt Hills

7   All This Has Happened Before: Mythic Repetition in the
    Film-to-Television Reboot   111
    Nicholas Benson and Jonathan Gray

Part III Politics and Identity

8   Resistance and Empire: *Star Wars* and the Social Justice Reboot   127
    Derek Johnson

9   Rebooting the Politics of the Sports Melodrama: *Creed* vs *Rocky* 143
    Chuck Tryon

10 Ghost Girls: *Ghostbusters*, Popular Feminism and the
    Gender-Swap Reboot   157
    Claire Perkins

Part IV Fans and Audiences

11 Reboot, Requel, Legacyquel: *Jurassic World* and the
    Nostalgia Franchise   173
    Kathleen Loock

12 World-building, Retconning and Legacy Rebooting:
    Alien and Contemporary Media Franchise Strategies   189
    James Fleury

13 Anticipating the Reboot: Teasing *Top Gun 2*   205
    Paul Grainge

14 A Dark Knight on Elm Street: Discursive Regimes of
    (Sub)Cultural Value, Paratextual Bonding, and the Perils of
    Remaking and Rebooting Canonical Horror Cinema   219
    William Proctor

Index   233

Figures and Tables

FIGURES

2.1	An objectifying shot of Uhura as she removes her top, *Star Trek* (2009)	41
2.2	A shot of Kirk in bed with a woman, her face and body obscured by shadow, appears between two suggestive shots of Uhura in the film's trailer, *Star Trek* (2009)	41
2.3	A shot of Uhura and Kirk's first meeting is taken out of context in order to suggest a sexual relationship between the two characters, *Star Trek* (2009)	41
4.1	Deckard emerges from the shadows, *Blade Runner 2049* (2017)	68
4.2	Rachael replicated, *Blade Runner 2049* (2017)	76
4.3	Deckard finds his daughter, *Blade Runner 2049* (2017)	77
5.1	Danny Ocean appears before a New Jersey parole review board, *Ocean's Eleven* (2001)	83
5.2	Keeping it in the family, Debbie Ocean appears before another New Jersey parole review board, *Ocean's Eight* (2018)	84
11.1	Gray's View-Master expresses *Jurassic World*'s (2015) self-understanding as a nostalgia-driven reboot	180

11.2 Serial progression: Gray and Zach's 'Gyrosphere' ride echoes and surpasses the View-Master's immersive experience *Jurassic World* (2015) — 183

11.3 Backward-gazing temporalities of the nostalgia franchise: *Jurassic World* (2015) privileges ideas of white, middle-class heteronormativity — 185

13.1 Artefacts of *Top Gun* nostalgia, photo by author — 207

TABLES

3.1	Budget and revenues for WCI's *Superman* films	56
3.2	Budget and revenues for WCI's *Batman* films	57
3.3	Budget and revenues for TWI's *Batman* films	58

Notes on Contributors

Nicholas Benson is Visiting Assistant Professor in the Department of Communication Studies at Augustana College, Illinois. His work has appeared in *Critical Studies in Television* and *Quarterly Review of Film and Video*.

James Fleury is a lecturer in Film and Media Studies at Washington University in St Louis. He received his PhD in Cinema and Media Studies from UCLA in 2019. He is the co-editor of the anthology *The Franchise Era: Managing Media in the Digital Economy* (2019). His publications have appeared in *Mediascape* (2012, 2015), the *South Atlantic Review* (2015), and the edited collections *James Bond and Popular Culture: Essays on the Influence of the Fictional Superspy* (2014) and *Content Wars: Tech Empires vs. Media Empires* (forthcoming). He is currently preparing a monograph based on his doctoral dissertation, which analyses the history of video game development and licensing at Warner Bros.

Jennifer Forrest is Professor of French at Texas State University. She is the co-editor with Leonard Koos of *Dead Ringers: The Remake in Theory and Practice* (2002), the editor of *The Legend Returns and Dies Harder Another Day: Essays on Film Series* (2008) and *Decadent Aesthetics and the Acrobat in Fin-de-Siècle France* (2019). Her media-related publications in journals and book chapters centre on remakes and seriality in cinema and television.

Paul Grainge is Professor of Film and Television Studies at the University of Nottingham. His books include *Promotional Screen Industries* (co-authored with Catherine Johnson, 2015), *Ephemeral Media: Transitory Screen Culture from Television to YouTube* (ed. 2011), *Brand Hollywood: Selling Entertainment in a Global Media Age* (2008), *Film Histories: An Introduction and Reader* (ed. 2007), *Memory and Popular Film* (ed. 2003) and *Monochrome Memories: Nostalgia and Style in Retro America* (2002).

Jonathan Gray is Hamel Family Distinguished Chair in Communication Arts and Professor of Media and Cultural Studies at University of Wisconsin–Madison. He is author of *Watching with The Simpsons: Television, Parody, and Intertextuality* (2006), *Television Entertainment* (2008), *Show Sold Separately: Promos, Spoilers, and Other Media Paratexts* (2010) and (with Amanda D. Lotz) *Television Studies* (2012), and co-editor of numerous collections including *A Companion to Media Authorship* (2013) and *Keywords for Media Studies* (2017). He is also Chief Editor of the *International Journal of Cultural Studies*.

Erin Hanna is an assistant professor of Cinema Studies at the University of Oregon. She is the author of *Only at Comic-Con: Hollywood, Fans, and the Limits of Exclusivity* (2019), and her work also appears in *CineAction*, *Television and New Media* and the *Journal of Fandom Studies*.

Daniel Herbert is an associate professor in the Department of Film, Television, and Media at the University of Michigan. He is author of *Film Remakes and Franchises* (2017) and *Videoland: Movie Culture at the American Video Store* (2014), the co-author (with Amanda Lotz and Aswin Punathambekar) of *Media Industry Studies* (2020) and co-editor (with Derek Johnson) of *Point of Sale: Analyzing Media Retail* (2020).

Matt Hills is Professor of Media and Film at the University of Huddersfield. He has published widely on fandom and cult media, beginning with the book *Fan Cultures* (2002), and including *The Pleasures of Horror* (2005), *Triumph of a Time Lord* (2010) and *Doctor Who: The Unfolding Event* (2015). Matt is working on a follow-up to *Fan Cultures* for Routledge, *Fan Studies*, and has published on *Twin Peaks* in the Palgrave edited collection *Return to Twin Peaks* (2016) as well as in 'American TV Series Revivals', a themed special issue of *Television and New Media* (2017).

Derek Johnson is a professor of Media and Cultural Studies in the Department of Communication Arts at the University of Wisconsin–Madison. He is the author of *Media Franchising: Creative License and Collaboration in the Culture Industries* (2013) and *Transgenerational Media Industries* (2019). He edited *From Networks to Netflix: A Guide to Changing Channels* (2018) and co-edited *A Companion to Media Authorship* (2013), *Making Media Work: Cultures of Management in the Media Industries* (2014), as well as *Point of Sale: Analyzing Media Retail* (2020).

Kathleen Loock holds a postdoctoral position in American Studies at the University of Flensburg (Germany), where she works as Associate Editor of the journal *Amerikastudien/American Studies*. She has co-edited *Film Remakes, Adaptations, and Fan Productions: Remake/Remodel* (with Constantine Verevis, 2012), edited the special issues 'Serial Narratives' for *LWU: Literatur in Wissenschaft und Unterricht* (2014) and 'American TV Series Revivals' for *Television and New Media* (2017), and co-edited the special issue 'Exploring Film Seriality' for *Film Studies* (with Frank Krutnik, 2017). Her other publications include journal articles and book chapters on film remakes and seriality in film and television. She is currently finishing her second book, *Hollywood Remaking*.

Eileen R. Meehan is a political economist interested in how the structure of trans-industrial and trans-sectoral media conglomerates shapes media content and merchandising. She is the author of *Why TV Is Not Our Fault* (2005) and has published research on the *Batman* and *Star Trek* franchises. She is a professor emerita at Southern Illinois University in Carbondale.

Claire Perkins is Senior Lecturer in Film and Screen Studies at Monash University, Melbourne. She researches primarily on American independent cinema and contemporary 'quality' television, with a focus on the gendered discourses of each. She is the author of *American Smart Cinema* (2012) and co-editor of six collections including *Indie Reframed: Women's Filmmaking and Contemporary American Independent Cinema* (2016), *Transnational Television Remakes* (2016) and *Film Trilogies: New Critical Approaches* (2012). Her writing has also appeared in journals including *Camera Obscura*, *Continuum: Journal of Media and Cultural Studies*, *The Velvet Light Trap*, *Celebrity Studies* and *Critical Studies in Television*. She is (with Constantine Verevis) series co-editor of *Screen Serialities* for Edinburgh University Press.

William Proctor is Principal Lecturer in Comics, Film and Transmedia at Bournemouth University. He is the co-editor of *Transmedia Earth: Global Convergence Cultures* (with Matthew Freeman, 2018) and *Disney's Star Wars: Forces of Production, Promotion, and Reception* (with Richard McCulloch, 2019). William is a leading expert on the history and theory of reboots, and is currently preparing his debut monograph, *Reboot Culture: Comics, Film, Transmedia*. He has also published widely on a broad array of subjects including Batman, James Bond, Stephen King, Star Trek, Star Wars, and other forms of popular culture. William is also co-editor on the forthcoming edited collection, *Horror Franchise Cinema* (with Mark McKenna).

Chuck Tryon is a professor of English at Fayetteville State University and is the author of three books: *Political TV* (2016), *On-Demand Culture: Digital Delivery and the Future of Movies* (2013) and *Reinventing Cinema: Movies in the Age of Media Convergence* (2009). He has also written essays for *Screen*, *Convergences* and *Media Industries Journal*.

Constantine Verevis is Associate Professor in Film and Screen Studies at Monash University, Melbourne. His publications include *Film Remakes* (2006), *Second Takes* (2010), *Film Trilogies* (2012), *Film Remakes, Adaptations and Fan Productions* (2012), *Australian Film Theory and Criticism, Vol. I: Critical Positions* (2013), *Transnational Television Remakes* (2016), *Transnational Film Remakes* (2017) and *Flaming Creatures* (2020). With Claire Perkins, he is series editor of *Screen Serialities* for Edinburgh University Press.

For Charlie and Noel – DH

For Deane – CV

Introduction: Film Reboots

Daniel Herbert and Constantine Verevis

In an illuminating analysis from 1972, Umberto Eco notes that the character of Superman operates in an unusual textual and cultural space characterised by a contradictory temporality. Eco describes how figures from classical myth, such as Hercules, exist in a kind of 'always time' because their stories are already completed and known by audiences in advance of narration (Eco 1972: 15). It is always and already true, for instance, that Perseus defeats Medusa. Alternatively, contemporary novelistic or 'romantic' narratives unfold while the story is told and feature characters and story worlds that are subject to change (1972: 15). Thus, for instance, it is possible for Sam Spade – and readers or viewers – to discover unexpectedly that the Maltese Falcon is a fake. There is no changing this after the fact and the world moves on.

But the Superman of comic strips, and also of television series and a number of movies, such as *Man of Steel* (Snyder, 2013), operates somewhere between these two narrative and cultural worlds. On the one hand, he is physically impervious and embodies specific moral and ideological values, aligning him with mythic figures and temporalities. His meaning is eternal, to some degree. On the other hand, Superman participates in stories in the everyday world. He alters his world by accomplishing goals and defeating villains. In this manner, Superman's time is consumed to some degree, even while Superman's mythic character remains inconsumable (Eco 1972: 16). This places Superman, and other 'mythological characters from comic strips' (1972: 15), in a paradoxical temporal situation, where narrative events occur over time and yet the character remains unchanged. Eco notes that writers must resolve this narrative paradox in some fashion, and lists a number of storytelling devices that seek to do so, including time travel, as in the case of *Star Trek* (Abrams, 2009), as well as portraying worlds that have 'hazy' senses of chronology, such as *Mad Max: Fury Road* (Miller, 2015) (see Verevis 2019).

The post-millennial film and television industries appear to have addressed this otherwise confusing paradox, between 'forever' and 'historical' temporalities, with something called 'the reboot' – and not only for superhero stories. Resembling both the remake and the sequel, the film reboot is a complex case of 'industrial intertextuality', where an individual film is linked to an existing film or film series by commercial design (Herbert 2017; Hunting and Gray 2018; cf. Kinder 1991), and yet also deviates from those previous texts to some degree in an attempt to generate a new cycle of cinematic productions. *Batman Begins* (Nolan, 2005), *Casino Royale* (Campbell, 2006), *Battlestar Galactica* (2004–9) and many more movies and television programmes appearing in the 2000s were deemed 'reboots' in the press, apparently because they returned to the beginning of a story that had been told in existing texts and started these narratives anew. How many times have we seen Bruce Wayne's parents killed? How many times has Peter Parker been bitten by a radioactive spider, or Kal-El been adopted by Jonathan and Martha Kent?

In the intervening years, critics, scholars, fans and media producers have used the term 'reboot' in a much looser fashion, to include works that might otherwise be understood as remakes, such as *RoboCop* (Padilha, 2014), or sequels, like *Blade Runner 2049* (Villeneuve, 2017). The reboot, as a category, came to stand in for a wide range of recycled and/or serialised media, and related terms like 'legacy-quel' (Singer 2015) and 're-quel' (Pinkerton 2016: 34) cropped up as well. Yet, even if the word 'reboot' has proven somewhat slippery in popular and scholarly discourses, it seems clear that it holds meaning and power within contemporary media culture. And for all that reboots raise issues of temporal stasis, continuity and change, the film reboot appears as a defining element of media within the current historical moment. Beyond issues of time and temporality, the film reboot asks us to consider the complexities of seriality, intertextuality, industrial practice, audience engagement and discursive formations.

DEFINING THE FILM REBOOT

There is considerable academic enquiry centring on issues of serial film and media production (Forrest 2010; Henderson 2014; Herbert 2017; Jess-Cooke 2009; Jess-Cooke and Verevis 2010; Kelleter 2017; Klein and Palmer 2016; Loock 2017; Loock and Verevis 2012; Perkins and Verevis 2012; Smith and Verevis 2017; Verevis 2006). Studies specifically looking at film reboots have been less common. Although this collection presents a relatively open definition of reboots, the existing scholarship on this topic has made considerable contributions toward defining and analysing this cinematic form and its cultural significance. Perhaps the most notable is that of William Proctor, who in two essays and forthcoming work has sought to provide rigorous and precise definitions of the reboot. Although not always in agreement, the numerous references to Proctor's essays in the following chapters of this collection attest to the importance of the work to the study of reboots. As Proctor writes:

> a film remake is a singular text bound within a self-contained narrative schema; whereas a reboot attempts to forge a series of films, to begin a franchise anew from the ashes of an old or failed property. In other words, a remake is a reinterpretation of one film; a reboot 're-starts' a series of films that seek to disavow and render inert its predecessor's validity. (Proctor 2012: 4)

Proctor's definition simultaneously makes claims regarding film reboots' textual features, their intertextual approach toward other texts, their industrial intentions and their cultural ambitions. Yet, for all that in this, and in subsequent work (Proctor 2013, 2017), where Proctor discusses reboots' industrial and cultural meanings, he is strict in his definition of reboots as a particular textual, intertextual and formal cinematic category. In addition to distinguishing the reboot from the remake, Proctor writes:

> a reboot is not the same as a prequel as it strives to disconnect itself, in a spatio-temporal sense, from the earlier incarnation in a quest for autonomy. Concurrently, a reboot is not a sequel as this would, once again, imply an adherence to continuity. *A reboot wipes the slate clean and begins the story again from 'year one', from a point of origin and from an alternative parallel position.* (Proctor 2012: 5, emphasis added)

Proctor's primary endeavour, then, is to distinguish the reboot as a particular kind of cinematic narrative with a specific intertextual relationship to prior texts; to this extent we might see his work as textualist. Proctor strives to maintain clear differentiations between the reboot and other serial formats – the remake, the sequel and so on – in what is perhaps an 'exclusive' approach toward genre and classification more generally (Altman 1999: 216–17). Proctor's comment – that *Batman Begins* is 'a quintessential reboot' (Proctor 2012: 8) – suggests not only a hierarchy of the form but also an ideal instance of the reboot that other examples may not match.

However textual and prescriptive Proctor's work may be, it is not naive regarding issues of industry, audience and media culture. For instance, Proctor acknowledges that while a reboot may seek to wipe a narrative or diegetic space clear for new stories, no reboot can wipe a cultural space clear (2012: 14).

Media texts may appear side by side in the world and offer conflicting versions of the same characters and, most certainly, audiences will remember multiple and sometimes contradictory texts as they consume new ones. For us, this suggests that the reboot is more of a discursive entity than it is a purely textual one. Indeed, in a study of horror film reboots in particular, Joe Tompkins offers an explicitly discursive approach toward reboots, generally (Tompkins 2014: 382). For Tompkins, reboots operate as a media industrial practice with a particular approach toward audiences. He writes 'Reboots function as a critical industrial practice . . . a means of activating and sustaining discourses of aesthetic value and distinction that provide fan-consumers with officially sanctioned interpretive frameworks for legitimating subcultural investments in a given franchise' (2014: 382).

In this formulation, Tompkins offers a definition of reboots that signals their industrial function and, as part of this, the powerful role that is played by '*extratextual* practices' of branding, marketing, advertising and other promotional activities on the part of the media industries (Tompkins 2014: 382). Industrial and promotional 'paratexts' (Gray 2010), in other words, help to define the reboot as such and, crucially, seek to distinguish the reboot as formally distinct and culturally valuable. Tompkins' analysis – of *Halloween* (Zombie, 2007) – is particularly insightful as it relates to a film genre – horror – which has been culturally devalued.

Although there are commonalities across the wide range of discourses in which the reboot has been defined and analysed – Chuck Tryon (2013), for instance, examines how reboots can be used to accommodate new technologies, looking specifically at the role of 3-D in *The Amazing Spider-Man* (Webb, 2012) – it also appears that this keyword has raised multiple issues regarding contemporary serialised media production, circulation and consumption. Moreover, Daniel Herbert has asserted the importance of reboots across all three of these zones, stating: 'reboots bring together industrial pressures to create new productions, textual elements that can be "open" to further elaboration, and audience desires for novelty within a familiar frame' (Herbert 2017: 39). In this respect, reboots are not a single thing, as the term has been used variously (some might say irresponsibly!) by different people and, just as important, gains different meanings and significance in the separate but interrelated spheres of production, textuality, circulation and reception. This collection upholds this 'inclusive' approach towards reboots as a kind of genre (Altman 1999: 216–17) in an effort to contribute to a rich and wide-ranging conversation about serial media formats and contemporary media culture. Although individual chapters will offer varying definitions of the reboot, as editors we align with Tompkins' view of reboots as a discursive category, allowing for and even appreciating breadth and diversity among conceptions of this cultural form.

When we refer to film reboots as a 'discursive category' we mean to invoke a Foucauldian notion of 'discourse', elaborated in *The Archaeology of Knowledge* (1972). Thus, we see reboots as a contingent locus of multiple discourses, themselves characterised by variability and even contradiction. As a model for understanding popular media culture, in particular, we see the reboot similarly to the way that Jason Mittell, also following Foucault (1972), conceives of genres as 'cultural categories' and 'discursive clusters' (Mittell 2001). In Mittell's formulation, genres come about through the discursive activities of multiple constituencies, including media producers, audiences, critics and scholars. Such discourses describe a corpus of cultural texts – a genre – in historically specific contexts, although there may be variations in the way the term is used (2001: 11). To this extent, genres are sites of meaning, to be sure, but the definitions of a genre and its meanings are always in potential flux and contestation. No one 'owns' a genre or cultural category, and while there may be consistencies in different peoples' and groups' definition of a genre, no single definition is absolutely correct or timeless.

So it is with film reboots. As the following chapters show, the reboot relates to many different, related forms of cinema, such as the remake, the sequel, the series and so on, and people's investments in calling something a 'reboot' rather than – or in addition to – some other kind of serial format or intertextual form of cinema relate to their position within media culture and their desire to affect some sort of meaning within it. As editors, we recognise that the slippages of meanings might be confusing, or even frustrating, to some readers. Our goal with this book is to provide analyses of some of the most notable films (and some television programmes) to have gained attention in the press and popular discourses as 'reboots', from *Batman Begins* in the first instance through to *Ocean's Eight* (Ross, 2018) and *Top Gun: Maverick* (Kosinski, 2020) in the most recent. Given this inclusive approach to the category, then, it might be less useful to ask 'what is a reboot?' but rather to inquire '*why* is a reboot'?

WHY 'REBOOT'?

If we shift away from issues of definition towards assessing the cultural contexts in which the reboot gains significance, it seems especially notable to us that the 'reboot' occurs as a category of film and media after the turn of the millennium (Verevis 2017: 163). In this regard, the reboot marks a historical shift in discourses regarding cinematic seriality and intertextuality, even if in reality reboots resemble other kinds of serial media formats and the discourses around reboots recycle issues and meanings previously attached to other cinematic categories and genres. But how and why might this be the case? Constantine Verevis contends with reboots, in fact, as part of his intervention into the history of the *remake*, when he analyses changes among remakes, and the new conditions within which the remake operates, in the post-millennial moment (Verevis 2017). As Verevis indicates, new millennial remakes are distinguishable in several ways: they are intermedial, transnational, post-authorial and are characterised by proliferation and simultaneity (2017: 149–61; cf. Verevis 2016).

This last point prompts Verevis' discussion of reboots, but his larger impulse – to understand the changing conditions of film remakes in the post-millennial moment – implicates a broader context that helps us situate the importance of the film reboot. Specifically, it seems notable that the reboot draws upon an analogy with computers in an age when digital technologies became more commonplace and, simultaneously, internalises franchising as a dominant logic for serialised media production. These two factors – the rise of digital technologies and the dominance of franchising – characterise conglomerate Hollywood (Schatz 2009; Elsaesser 2012), of course, and also set the stage for film reboots.

As Proctor also notes in his genealogy of the concept, 'reboot' appears first as a term to describe phenomena related to computing:

> the term reboot, in its original context, is 'used to describe the process of restarting a computer or electronic device [in order] to recover from an error' ('Reboot Definition' 2010) . . . Shutting down the computer . . . and rebooting it, resets the hardware and, hopefully, restores the unit to optimum functionality. As with a computer's internal memory, rebooting the system does not signify total loss of data. (Proctor 2012: 5)

Proctor goes on to draw an analogy between the clearing of the short-term memory in computers and the more recent iterations of a franchise. Indeed, in multiple essays Proctor likens franchises and audiences' interests to 'systems' akin to computer systems.

Yet, given the looseness of the computer 'system' analogy and the multiplicity of texts that one might call 'reboots', we would like to emphasise the broader historical importance regarding the adoption of this term to describe cultural products. Since the 1980s, and especially since the spread of the World Wide Web in the 1990s, we have entered an era when computers and other digital technologies appear ubiquitously across the social landscape in many parts of the world. It would be quite correct, then, to think of the reboot as a kind of 'remediation' of film and television in light of the impact of digital technologies (Bolter and Grusin 1999). With this in mind, calling a film a 'reboot' rather than a 'remake' or 'sequel' or something else suggests the general adoption of computer and digital metaphors to describe a wide range of cultural activities and objects. Computers and so-called 'new media' have a language (Manovich 2001; cf. Stenport and Traylor 2015), it seems, and as a culture we have transplanted digital logics into other spheres of culture just as these technologies have insinuated themselves into many aspects of our individual and social lives.

What does it mean to think of cultural production – and audience consumption – according to the logics of digital technologies, however much our construction and understanding of these logics may be hazy at best and ignorant at worst? In the case of the reboot, in particular, it seems that the overall assumption is that film and television is produced by a complex system defined by two kinds of memory, the short-term memory of the RAM and the long-term memory of the ROM. Mind you, 'memory' serves as a anthropomorphic metaphor for the ways in which computers store and retrieve data. Thus both RAM and ROM represent inhuman forms of memory, suggesting that the reboot metaphor also implies that the 'system' behind cultural production is also inhuman to some degree. Whatever other values the reboot may have, it seems to hold meaning because of our trust in computerised systems in general. The irony is, of course, that contemporary Hollywood really has been digitised over the last several decades, from the cameras used to record moving images, to the processes of editing, to the generation of special effects and animation, to the projectors, televisions and other devices that play these texts for audiences far and wide. In a common day-to-day experience, one goes through the process of unplugging, and then plugging back in, a digital television in order for it to reconnect to the internet and access a streaming platform, such as Netflix. If carried out recently, then this would likely find *The Dark Crystal: Age of Resistance* (2019) prominently placed on the home screen, echoing – in cultural form – the technological process of rebooting just completed.

As Proctor details, the first uses of 'reboot' to describe a kind of cultural text appeared not in relation to film and television but rather within comic book culture (Proctor 2017: 226). Further, Proctor shows how comic books developed rebooting as an approach towards clearing a narrative space for future iterations of already serialised texts (Proctor 2012: 5–7). We might then think that the rise of the reboot is connected to the increasing industrial importance and cultural popularity of movies and television programmes based on comic book characters. This rings true, to a degree. Yet we would also connect the rise of comic book cinema and television – and the reboot – to a greater, even more pervasive shift in contemporary media culture, namely the dominance of media franchising (see Fleury et al., 2019).

As Proctor describes, the DC comic book universe, featuring characters like Wonder Woman, Batman and Superman in a shared narrative world, was 'rebooted' in the 1980s with the *Crisis on Infinite Earths* series, which restarted the narratives of many major characters in such a way as to maintain the diegetic coherence of all previous stories (Proctor 2012: 5–7). The DC 'hyperdiegesis'

(Hills 2002: 137) had become too complex and even contradictory over the years, evidently, and yet the publisher aimed to maintain the pseudo-mythical meanings of certain characters in this story world. As these and other comic book characters figured centrally within movie and television franchises of the 1980s and 1990s, it appears that major studios, such as Warner Bros. and others, faced similar issues. In an endeavour to continue making stories with established characters – to continue exploiting specific intellectual property (IP) – with new actors, in new diegetic worlds and with the utility of new technologies, and yet without necessarily contradicting previous iterations, the studios appealed to rebooting strategies.

But comic books were not the basis of all media franchises, nor were they the source for all reboots appearing in the new millennium. Indeed, we might posit that the pseudo-mythical status that Eco attributes to Superman was now held by all sorts of characters appearing in serialised audiovisual media, from James Bond to Number 6 from *The Prisoner* (1967, 2009). And it seems to us that the kind of recycled, serialised textual proliferation generated through media franchising is more at the root of the post-millennial reboot phenomenon than the adaptation of comic book characters, specifically, into films and television. Indeed, whatever disagreements there may be among critics and scholars over just what a 'reboot' may be, it seems universally understood that the reboot operates within the overall logic of franchises and franchising as an industrial practice. As Herbert has written:

> within the logic of a franchise, a specific intellectual property gets manifested as multiple consumer products, from movies and television programs to books, comic books, toys, video games, clothing, and so on. Franchises are generative, as franchise logic dictates that a copyright holder exploits that copyright in myriad ways, spreading a single property as far and wide as is profitable. (Herbert 2017: 13–14)

This is an ideal scenario, of course, and many franchises appear 'merely' within a single medium, such as with a film series or as a television brand or portable formula.

Moreover, franchises do not just appear spontaneously, generated easily and automatically by some computer. Franchises come about through the industrial practices of franchising, which take effort and collaboration. Derek Johnson, in particular, has provided the most rigorous and detailed analysis of media franchising as an industrial practice (Johnson 2013). Although practices of industrial serialisation, intertextuality and licensing occurred throughout the twentieth century (Santo 2015), Johnson notes that it was not until the 1980s that 'franchising' became a common way of understanding 'the multiplied replication of culture from intellectual property resources' (Johnson 2013: 6).

Further, franchising entails 'the shared exchanger of content resources across multiple industrial sites and contexts of production operating in collaborative but contested ways through networked relation to one another' (2013: 7). Thus, while franchises may appear as a cluster of texts spread across popular culture, Johnson's work highlights the historical and industrial contingency of such serialised and intertextual forms of media. Indeed, it seems notable that 'franchising' became a common way of thinking of industrial intertextuality during the same historical period that computers and other digital technologies proliferated across culture.

Franchising has become so common among the major Hollywood entertainment conglomerates that many, if not all, of the biggest, most expensive, most lucrative and most popular films and television programmes occur as elements within larger media franchises. The reboot appears amidst this proliferation of franchised texts and, as so many critics and scholars have described and analysed, respond to their larger franchises in particular ways. Indeed, we can and should see the narrative, intertextual and paratextual qualities of film reboots as entirely bound up with the industrial imperatives and hopes that a conglomerate has regarding a particular franchise. We can see this in the effort invested by *Batman Begins* in wiping a narrative space clean, in *Star Trek* using time travel to re-do without re-writing, in *Prometheus* (2012) returning to the *Alien* universe most 'authentically' under the direction of Ridley Scott and in *The Force Awakens* (Abrams, 2015) aiming to reawaken excitement in *Star Wars* properties. In all these cases and more, the reboot seeks to recalibrate a franchise: the reboot is the singular textual embodiment of this effort.

FILM REBOOTS IN THEORY AND PRACTICE

We do not live in the forever time of myth, and we have one and not infinite Earths. But film reboots offer multiple points of entry into the seemingly timeless and infinite story worlds that make up post-millennial, franchised media culture. *Film Reboots* brings together a host of notable scholars to provide in-depth analyses – and multiple vantages – from which to examine some of the most important reboots to appear over the last two decades, offering rich insights into this contemporary serial formatting practice. How does something like *A Nightmare on Elm Street* (Bayer, 2010) call back to the original film (Craven, 1984), expand upon it and also clear a space for future textual production? In what ways is *Blade Runner 2049* simultaneously a sequel and a reboot, as it draws from a wide range of related intertexts? How does *Jurassic World* (Trevorrow, 2015) operate within the *Jurassic Park* universe: as sequel, as remake, in both of these ways and more? Although centred on cinema, this collection examines film reboots in relation to other adjacent and interlocking cultural forms, including television. What are the strategies used in rebooting a movie into a television series? Is *Twin Peaks: The Return* (2017) a television programme or a single, long film? This book also considers reboots in relation to changing industrial practices, audience and fan activities, as well as issues related to cultural life and social identities, most particularly gender and race. What does it mean to rework the plots of *Oceans 11* (Soderbergh, 2001) or *Ghostbusters* (Reitman, 1984) with female actors taking the lead roles? Does the casting of a film constitute a progressive political agenda, such as in films like *Creed* (Coogler, 2015) or *The Force Awakens*? By investigating a variety of case studies and locating them within current debates surrounding cinematic seriality and intertextuality, industry and culture, *Film Reboots* provides distinctive new models for understanding the film reboot and contemporary movie culture.

The collection is divided into four parts, each of which represents a defining aspect of film and media culture. We begin with three essays that consider issues of 'Industry and Commerce'. In the first of these, 'Rethinking the "Supersystem"', Daniel Herbert draws upon Marsha Kinder's (1991) theorisation of the media 'supersystem' – that is, an intertextual, industrialised transmedia network – to examine the *Teenage Mutant Ninja Turtles* franchise, specifically the television (2012–17) and film (Liebesman, 2014; Green, 2016) reboots produced following Nickelodeon's acquisition of the IP in 2009. Building upon his account of New Line Cinema's twentieth-century innovations in franchising – which included not only *Teenage Mutant Ninja Turtles* but also the *Nightmare on Elm Street* and *Critters* series (Herbert 2019) – Herbert describes the way in which the post-2009 Turtles rebooted a supersystem, one characterised by textual mutability and overlapping forms of intertextuality, to create new versions of the Turtles and provide opportunity to expand the franchise. Herbert's 'rethinking' of the supersystem demonstrates the ways in which rebooting creates a major 'event' in the serial life of a property: one that appeals to new audiences and generates fresh merchandising possibilities. In the second essay, 'Live Long and Prosper', Erin Hanna looks to *Star Trek*, a reboot that employed a time travel narrative to simultaneously cast the *Star Trek* universe as a new continuity and strategically recast iconic characters in a parallel timeline. For Hanna, the reinvention of the *Star Trek* property as a twenty-first-century blockbuster required an investment not only in its narrative strategies, but also in a discursively reimagined audience, one that included both pre-existing and future fans. Appealing to her recent investigation of the relationship between media industries and fans (Hanna 2019), Hanna demonstrates the way in which *Star Trek* highlights the intersecting logics of the film reboot and the mainstreaming of fandom in popular culture, both of which grow out of serial strategies designed to exploit new and established markets. In the final essay of Part I, 'The Many Reboots of the Batman', Eileen Meehan revisits her influential work from *The Many Lives of Batman* (1991) to inquire into the industrial background to, and subsequent rebooting of, the filmed property from the 1940s. This includes the initial 'pop art' rebooting of Batman as a television series (1966–8), and subsequently as a film blockbuster (Burton, 1989) and transmedia franchise (1989–97 and 2005–12). Focusing on the ways that different industrial structures and corporate relationships have shaped Batman over the decades, Meehan explores the political economy of Batman to illuminate both the routines of corporate creativity and the particular contributions of media artists and professionals working to generate rebooted versions of Batman that are at once completely new and totally familiar.

Part II, 'Structure and Narrative', begins with Constantine Verevis' 'The Edge of Reality', a chapter that describes *Blade Runner 2049* as a 'reboot-sequel' for the way it retraces its precursor(s) at the same time as it extends them. In making this point, Verevis argues that *Blade Runner 2049* – a film that might be seen as a 'true sequel' to *Blade Runner* (Scott, 1982) – can be understood as a film that reboots a entire franchise. That is, Blade Runner – its multiple versions (1982, 1992, 2007) and many transmedia paratexts – is characterised as a serialised property, one that operates according to the protocols of both organic and, following the work of Jason Mittell (2018), operational seriality. In the next chapter, 'Gender, Genre and the Reboot', Jennifer Forrest extends her interest in film remakes (Forrest and Koos 2002) and series (Forrest 2008) to investigate the case of the *Ocean's* film series – *Ocean's 11, 12* and *13* (Soderbergh, 2001–7) – and its *Ocean's 8* reboot. As in the case of some other new millennial reboots (discussed in Part III), *Ocean's 8* is a 'gender reversal' reboot of (in this case) a typically male-oriented heist genre that reinterprets collaboration to emphasise feminine bonding. In addition to marking out the film's gender transformation, Forrest outlines the intricate textual and intertextual network that exists among the series of films – including its unofficial 'reboot', *Lucky Logan* (Soderbergh, 2017) – to describe *Ocean's 8* as an auteur-reboot, one that playfully absorbs commercial imperatives into the structure and narrative of each instalment. In 'Understanding *Twin Peaks: The Return*', Matt Hills argues for the status of the long-awaited 'third season' of Twin Peaks – *The Return* – as film reboot. Drawing upon Johnson's (2013) work on franchising, Hills explores the extent to which *The Return* is positioned via 'anti-franchising' discourses at the very same time that it is contradicted by a logic of franchising. Outlining David Lynch's discursive ownership of the eighteen-part 'movie', Hills writes that *The Return* offers up a 'twin challenge': an imperative to interpret it as an auteurist anti-franchise but one that simultaneously invests in the brand reinvigoration of conventional franchising. In the final chapter, 'All This Has Happened Before', Nicholas Benson and Jonathan Gray look more deliberately to television, in this case to consider the phenomenon of film-to-television reboots. Noting that television has increasingly become a space for expanding and reinvigorating pre-existing story worlds of feature films, Benson and Gray inquire into the intertextual and narrative strategies that are employed when comparatively limited texts are extended and serialised for television screens. Taking the pilots of television reboots of high-profile feature films – *Fargo* (Coen, 1996) and *The Exorcist* (Friedkin, 1973) – as their case studies, they argue that the strategy of adaptation is to uncover the 'mythic' qualities and structures of the source material in order to build their respective televisual narratives upon these foundations. For Benson and Gray, the development of the mythic value of these original texts is essential for the film-to-television reboot.

In Part III, 'Politics and Identity', contributors look at the ways in which film reboots can at once embrace nostalgia for an earlier film while also functioning as a comment upon the original's politics. In the first chapter, 'Resistance and Empire', Derek Johnson builds upon important work on media franchising (Johnson 2013) to attend to recent instalments in the *Star Wars* series as 'social justice' reboots. Johnson employs this term to describe those properties – not only *Star Wars*, but also series such as *Ghostbusters*, *Ocean's* and *Creed/Rocky* – in which industrial and commercial priorities of reproduction (sameness) mediate imperatives to address the inequities of access and representation (difference). Attending to *The Force Awakens* and *Rogue One* (Edwards, 2016), Johnson demonstrates how parent companies Disney and Lucasfilm judiciously balance repetition and innovation so as to maintain a franchise in which social justice itself is rebooted as a marketable output of serialisation. In the next chapter, 'Rebooting the Politics of the Sports Melodrama', Chuck Tryon describes *Creed* as a sequel-reboot which functions as a politically ambivalent, but textually reverent, reboot of the *Rocky* franchise (1976–90). For Tryon, *Creed* is a film that at one and the same time celebrates the franchise's deployment of the tropes of the boxing picture and male melodrama, while also updating the racial and sexual politics of the series. Developing ideas on the way film reboots mediate the tension between familiarity and novelty (Tryon 2013), Tryon demonstrates how *Creed* rewrites aspects of the original *Rocky* films so as to create a new political narrative, one that explicitly challenges stereotypes of African-American athletes. In the final chapter of Part III, 'Ghost Girls', Claire Perkins appeals to recent debates on 'popular feminism' to attend to the politics of the 'gender-swap' reboot, *Ghostbusters* (Feig, 2016). As Perkins points out, *Ghostbusters* – and other gender-swapped properties (such as the *Ocean's* series, discussed in Part II) – take the recasting of the sexual politics of their predecessors as their point of departure but, she argues, the promise of revisionism communicated by the film's narrative image is contradicted by its storyline and attitude. Situating the gender-swap reboot at the intersection of popular feminism and popular misogyny, Perkins performs a close reading of *Ghostbusters* to demonstrate the ways in which its feminist message – of gender equality in Hollywood – is ultimately compromised by a 'comedic tone' that suggests that this issue is *not* to be taken seriously.

Part IV of the book focuses on 'Fans and Audiences'. In the first chapter, 'Reboot, Requel, Legacyquel', Kathleen Loock turns her attention to the 'nostalgia' reboot (Loock 2016), a serial form that restarts a franchise at the same time that it preserves and celebrates its past. Loock identifies films like *The Force Awakens* and *Creed* as new films in these nostalgia franchises, but specifically investigates the case of *Jurassic World*, a film that summons its (pre-historic) past and employs nostalgia as its method of renewal. Describing the nostalgia reboot as evidence of a type of Hollywood remake practice that invests in sequelisation strategies that preserve long-term continuity, Loock outlines nostalgia-driven pleasures and multi-generational appeal of those reboots that maintain continuity and facilitate immersion in an ongoing, already familiar story world. In the next chapter, 'World-building, Retconning, and Legacy Rebooting', James Fleury extends his work on transmedia franchising (Fleury et al. 2019) to examine reboot efforts within the *Alien* franchise during the 2010s. Looking particularly at *Prometheus* and *Alien: Covenant* (Scott, 2017), as well as several video games, Fleury analyses how various promotional materials and narrative devices have taken variable approaches toward rebooting this franchise, including retconning and legacy rebooting. Given that the *Alien* universe 'has not necessarily followed a systematic, planned path' according to Fleury, he shows how the franchise's IP holder (first 20th Century-Fox, now Disney) devised variable ways to appeal to potential audiences. In 'Anticipating the Reboot', Paul Grainge builds upon his work on Hollywood branding (Grainge 2008) to interrogate the ways in which *Top Gun*'s (Scott, 1986) status as filmic reference point for Hollywood 'high concept' of the 1980s has informed speculation around its new millennial reboot, *Top Gun: Maverick*. With the new film still unreleased at the time of writing, Grainge's essay focuses not on the reboot (or even its promotional materials) but on the anticipation of the reboot as 'discursive project'. Attending to the paratextual arrays that inform and prefigure media events, Grainge focuses on the period in the mid-2010s leading up to the first official publicity still for *Top Gun: Maverick* to investigate the dynamics of speculation and nostalgia that accompany the 'anticipation' of Hollywood reboots. In the book's final chapter, 'A Dark Knight on Elm Street', William Proctor builds upon his substantial work on film reboots (Proctor 2012, 2013, 2017) to analyse *A Nightmare on Elm Street* as a remake of the 1984 film and a reboot to the Elm Street franchise. Part of this rebooting entailed establishing a complex authorial identity for the film, aligning it with Christopher Nolan's work with the Batman reboots and Wes Craven, whose own status as auteur had changed since directing the original Elm Street film. Further, Proctor shows how paratexts situate the reboot as a return to the scariness of the original Elm Street film, disavowing the later more comic films in the series, in such a way that likewise aligns the reboot with Nolan's Batman films.

In their totality, the essays in this collection provide astute and diverse analyses of the film reboot in theory and practice, and of the significance of this serial format within post-millennial film and media culture.

REFERENCES

Altman, Rick (1999), *Film/Genre*, London: BFI/Palgrave Macmillan.
Bolter, Jay David and Richard Grusin (1999), *Remediation: Understanding New Media*, Cambridge, MA: MIT Press.
Eco, Umberto (1972), 'The Myth of Superman', *Diacritics*, 2: 1 (Spring), 14–22.
Elsaesser, Thomas (2012), *The Persistence of Hollywood*, London: Routledge.
Fleury, James, Bryan Hikari Hartzheim and Stephen Mamber (eds) (2019), *The Franchise Era: Managing Media in the Digital Economy*, Edinburgh: Edinburgh University Press.
Forrest, Jennifer (ed.) (2008), *The Legend Returns and Dies Harder Another Day: Essays on Film Series*, Jefferson, NC: McFarland.
Forrest, Jennifer and Leonard R. Koos (eds) (2002), *The Remake in Theory and Practice*, Albany, NY: State University of New York Press.
Foucault, Michel (1972), *The Archaeology of Knowledge and the Discourse on Language*, trans. A. M. Sheridan, New York: Pantheon Books.
Grainge, Paul (2008), *Brand Hollywood: Selling Entertainment in a Global Media Age*, London: Routledge.
Gray, Jonathan (2010), *Show Sold Separately: Promos, Spoilers, and Other Media Paratexts*, New York: New York University Press.
Hanna, Erin (2019), *Only at Comic-Con: Hollywood, Fans, and the Limits of Exclusivity*, New Brunswick, NJ: Rutgers University Press.
Henderson, Stuart (2014), *The Hollywood Sequel: History & Film, 1911–2010*, London: BFI/Palgrave Macmillan.
Herbert, Daniel (2017), *Film Remakes and Franchises*, New Brunswick, NJ: Rutgers University Press.
Herbert, Daniel (2019), 'Evil Spawn or Good Business? New Line Cinema, *Critters*, and Film Franchising at the Margins', in James Fleury, Bryan Hikari Hartzheim and Stephen Mamber (eds), *The Franchise Era: Managing Media in the Digital Economy*, Edinburgh: Edinburgh University Press, pp. 52–74.
Hills, Matt (2002), *Fan Cultures*, London: Routledge.
Hunting, Kyra and Jonathan Gray (2018), 'Disney Junior: Imagining Industrial Intertextuality', in Derek Johnson (ed.), *From Networks to Netflix: A Guide to Changing Channels*, New York and London: Routledge, pp. 197–207.
Jess-Cooke, Carolyn (2009), *Film Sequels: Theory and Practice from Hollywood to Bollywood*, Edinburgh: Edinburgh University Press.
Jess-Cooke, Carolyn and Constantine Verevis (eds) (2010), *Second Takes: Critical Approaches to the Film Sequel*, Albany, NY: SUNY Press.
Johnson, Derek (2013), *Media Franchising: Creative License and Collaboration in the Culture Industries*, New York: New York University Press.
Kelleter, Frank (ed.) (2017), *Media of Serial Narrative*, Columbus, OH: Ohio State University Press.
Kinder, Marsha (1991), *Playing with Power in Movies, Television, and Video Games: From Muppet Babies to Teenage Mutant Ninja Turtles*, Berkeley, CA: University of California Press.

Klein, Amanda Ann and R. Barton Palmer (eds) (2016), *Cycles, Sequels, Spin-Offs, Remakes, and Reboots: Multiplicities in Film and Television*, Austin, TX: University of Texas Press.
Loock, Kathleen (2016), 'Retro-Remaking: The 1980s Film Cycle in Contemporary Hollywood Cinema', in Amanda Ann Klein and R. Barton Palmer (eds), *Cycles, Sequels, Spin-Offs, Remakes, and Reboots*, Austin, TX: University of Texas Press, pp. 277–98.
Loock, Kathleen (2017), 'The Sequel Paradox: Repetition, Innovation, and Hollywood's Hit Film Formula', *Film Studies*, 17: 1 (Autumn), 92–110.
Loock, Kathleen and Constantine Verevis (eds) (2012), *Film Remakes, Adaptations and Fan Productions: Remake-Remodel*, Basingstoke: Palgrave Macmillan.
Manovich, Lev (2001), *The Language of New Media*, Cambridge, MA: MIT Press.
Meehan, Eileen R. (1991), '"Holy Commodity Fetish, Batman!": The Economics of a Commercial Intertext', in William Uricchio and Roberta E. Pearson (eds), *The Many Lives of Batman: Critical Approaches to a Superhero and His Media*, London: BFI/Routledge, pp. 47–65.
Mittell, Jason (2001), 'A Cultural Approach to Television Genre Theory', *Cinema Journal*, 40: 3, 3–24.
Mittell, Jason (2018), 'Operational Seriality and the Operation of Seriality', in Zara Dinnen and Robyn Warhol (eds), *The Edinburgh Companion to Contemporary Narrative Theories*, Edinburgh: Edinburgh University Press, pp. 228–38.
Perkins, Claire and Constantine Verevis (eds) (2012), *Film Trilogies: New Critical Approaches*, Basingstoke: Palgrave Macmillan.
Pinkerton, Nick (2016), 'The Rise of the Reboots', *Sight and Sound* (March), 32–5.
Proctor, William (2012), 'Regeneration and Rebirth: Anatomy of the Franchise Reboot', *Scope: An Online Journal of Film and Television Studies*, 22 (February), 1–19.
Proctor, William (2013), 'Beginning Again: The Reboot Phenomenon in Comic Books and Film', *Scan: Journal of Media Arts & Culture*, 9: 1, <http://scan.net.au/scan/journal/display.php?journal_id=163>.
Proctor, William (2017), 'Reboots and Retroactive Continuity', in Mark J. P. Wolf (ed.), *The Routledge Companion to Imaginary Worlds*, New York and London: Routledge.
Proctor, William (forthcoming), *Reboot Culture: Comics, Film, Transmedia*, London: Palgrave Macmillan.
'Reboot Definition' (2010), *Computer Hope*, <http://www.computerhope.com/jargon/r/reboot.htm>.
Santo, Avi (2015), *Selling the Silver Bullet: The Lone Ranger and Transmedia Brand Licensing*, Austin, TX: University of Texas Press.
Schatz, Thomas (2009), 'New Hollywood, New Millennium', in Warren Buckland (ed.), *Film Theory and Contemporary Hollywood Movies*, London: Routledge, pp. 19–46.
Singer, Matt (2015), 'Welcome to the Age of the Legacyquel', *ScreenCrush*, 23 November, <http://screencrush.com/the-age-of-legacyquels/>.
Smith, Iain Robert and Constantine Verevis (eds) (2017), *Transnational Film Remakes*, Edinburgh: Edinburgh University Press.
Stenport, Anna Westerdahl and Garrett Traylor (2015), 'The Eradication of Memory: Film Adaptations and Algorithms of the Digital', *Cinema Journal*, 55: 1, 74–94.
Tompkins, Joe (2014), '"Re-imagining" the Canon: Examining the Discourse of Contemporary Horror Film Reboots', *New Review of Film and Television Studies*, 12: 4, 380–99.
Tryon, Chuck (2013), 'Reboot Cinema', *Convergence: The International Journal of Research into New Media Technologies*, 19: 4, 432–7.
Verevis, Constantine (2006), *Film Remakes*, Edinburgh: Edinburgh University Press.
Verevis, Constantine (2016), 'The Cinematic Return', *Film Criticism*, 40: 1 (January), <https://quod.lib.umich.edu/f/fc/13761232.0040.134/--cinematic-return?rgn=main;view=fulltext>.

Verevis, Constantine (2017), 'New Millennial Remakes', in Frank Kelleter (ed.), *Media of Serial Narrative*, Columbus, OH: Ohio State University Press, pp. 148–66.

Verevis, Constantine (2019), 'Another Green World: The *Mad Max* Series', in Felicity Collins, Jane Landman and Susan Bye (eds), *A Companion to Australian Cinema*, Hoboken, NJ: Wiley Blackwell, pp. 133–48.

Part I
Industry and Commerce

CHAPTER 1

Rethinking the 'Supersystem': Film Reboots and the *Teenage Mutant Ninja Turtles*

Daniel Herbert

The 'reboot' appears as a kind of discursive mutant, able to shift and morph to take on different meanings in different circumstances. For William Proctor, for instance, the reboot operates intertextually much like a remake but aims to generate additional cultural texts within the same 'hyperdiegesis' or story world shared among characters across multiple texts (Proctor 2012: 4, 6; Hills 2002: 137). Although Proctor's is primarily a text-based definition of reboots, it is important to note that it invokes industrial activities, namely the perpetuation of a franchise. Alternatively, Joe Tompkins (2014) defines reboots as a discursive phenomenon, and he directly highlights their industrial function. By Tompkins' reckoning, reboots aim to build discourses of value around a text so as to invite audiences to invest or reinvest themselves into an existing franchise.

Both these accounts, and many others, suggest that reboots occur as a kind of 'industrial intertextuality', where the links across cultural texts occur by industrial design (Herbert 2017: 9–10, 23–4). From this view, one can think of intertextuality not only as a matter of textual form or interpretive practice but also as a mode of cultural production. In addition to my work on the topic, Kyra Hunting and Jonathan Gray have also developed the idea of industrial intertextuality in their study of Disney Jr. They show how the channel used textual connections across a number of programmes to create a 'multidirectional' industrial intertextual network aimed at 'connect[ing]' viewers to the sprawling corporate network that is Disney' (Hunting and Gray 2018: 198). The television network, in other words, fundamentally consists of an intertextual network.

Similar to the way that reboots often return to a character's origin to begin an old tale anew, my interest in reboots prompts me to return to an earlier theorisation of industrial intertextuality. This chapter looks back at the idea of the media 'supersystem' theorised by Marsha Kinder (1991), which stands as one of the rare cases that rigorously examines both intertextual and industrial aspects of popular culture simultaneously. My goal is to assess how this theory might help us understand contemporary rebooting practices or, alternatively, if reboots might require us to rethink the idea of the supersystem.

For Kinder, the Teenage Mutant Ninja Turtles serve as *the* primary example of a supersystem. The Turtles were especially popular at the time she was writing, with the characters appearing in a weekly cartoon, a popular feature film, and as action figures and other merchandise. Following Kinder's interest in the Turtles, this chapter examines the television (2012–17) and film reboots (2014, 2016) of the Turtles produced after Nickelodeon acquired the underlying intellectual property (IP) in 2009. Ultimately, this case demonstrates two things. First, contemporary reboots do not require us to rethink Kinder's 'supersystem' very much at all. Instead, something like the reverse is true, as her theory allows us to see rebooting as a kind of industrial 'rethinking' of a supersystem. Like Tompkins, I believe film reboots function as industrial and discursive entities that allow for an established supersystem to be reconceived by media producers and audiences alike. Second, the case of the Turtles demonstrates that reboots do not always aim to wipe a narrative space clean for future cultural production in a clearly linear narrative and intertextual chain. Rather, like some 'new millennial remakes', the post-2009 *Turtles* reboots reveal an intertextual logic of overlap and even simultaneity (Verevis 2017: 158–64). In this regard, these reboots fittingly built upon the Turtles' existing intertextual network, which was already inconsistent and palimpsestuous. The *Turtles* reboots are somewhat unusual in this regard, as other reboots and reboot discourses aim to evoke a stable 'essence' for their characters and story worlds. The Teenage Mutant Ninja Turtles, as characters and as a supersystem, prove to have no essence, essentially, but rather are subject to the transformations of a changing media industry.

THE SUPERSYSTEM AND THE TURTLES

Within a larger effort to understand children's media culture of the 1980s and early 1990s, Kinder identified the 'supersystem of entertainment' as a new and important cultural phenomenon. She lists a number of elements that characterise a supersystem, summarised as follows:

1. Consists of an intertextual network
2. Is built upon figures from popular culture (can be real or fictional)
3. Cuts across different media forms
4. Appeals to a broad audience/multiple demographics
5. Fosters collectability through merchandising
6. Grows rapidly to become a 'media event'. (Kinder 1991: 122–3)

Kinder's model anticipates a number of subsequent theories of industrialised media culture. For instance, her observation that supersystems cut across media forms precedes Henry Jenkins' analysis of 'transmedia storytelling' (Jenkins 2006: 20–1). Although Kinder's model of 'transmedia intertextuality' (Kinder 1991: 1) is looser than the tightly interlinked narrative structures that Jenkins examines, particularly in *The Matrix* franchise, it is also true that most franchises, including the *Teenage Mutant Ninja Turtles*, have a looser intertextual structure than *The Matrix* texts.

Kinder's supersystem theory also intersects with notions of media franchises, as it accounts for intertextuality across texts and products that solicit engagement from diverse consumers (Herbert 2017: 13–15). As I have asserted elsewhere, media franchises 'entail the exploitation of an intellectual property across multiple cultural texts and consumer products' with the aim of expanding 'as far and wide as possible' (Herbert 2017: 85–6). In his account of franchising, Derek Johnson engages with Kinder's work directly, but finds that it cannot help us fully understand 'franchising as an industrial structure, set of social relations, and cultural imaginary' (Johnson 2013: 31). Indeed, Johnson's sophisticated treatment of franchising as industrial practice contributes significantly to our understanding of media supersystems. Rather than simply looking at 'franchises' as clusters of texts, he conceives of franchising as a process made up of multiple creative communities. Here, the intertextual network is a network of creative resources and communities, and our consideration of supersystems should likewise account for the inter-firm relationships that make them possible. Further, Johnson shows that franchises can be heterogeneous and flexible arrangements, thus refuting the notion that franchises are monolithic or invincible.

With these additional considerations in mind, Kinder's theoretical model helps us understand the post-2009 *Turtles* reboots as attempts at rethinking this supersystem, industrially and intertextually. The Turtles first appeared in a small, independent comic book written by Kevin Eastman and Peter Laird and published by Mirage Studios in 1984. The characters gained mainstream popularity after Laird and Eastman licensed the Turtles to Playmates Toys in late 1986, which was a relatively small company at the time. Playmates helped create an animated series based on the characters, which first aired in 1987 and eventually entered regular, syndicated broadcast in 1988. The show made a number of alterations to the characters, including the origin story of how they became teenage ninjas. Other aesthetic changes aimed to make the Turtles more child-friendly, such as a reduction in grittiness and violence and the addition of catchphrases like 'cowabunga!' As one reviewer of the programme stated, 'The designers have softened the bold lines of the comic book figures and made the Turtles look like muscular Muppets' (Solomon 1987: 11).

A plethora of toys and merchandise featuring the Turtles appeared in stores simultaneously with the programme's premiere (Solomon 1987: 11). This first wave of toys and merchandise maintained the brighter aesthetic of the cartoon, apparently to make the characters more appealing to younger consumers. By the summer of 1989, 'Turtlemania' was in full effect and the characters appeared on 'lunch boxes, backpacks, calendars, drinking straws, decals, shampoo, toothbrushes and, of course, the obligatory Nintendo video game' (Logan 1989). The television show also inspired a new comic book, *Teenage Mutant Ninja Turtles Adventures*, published by Archie Comics, which ran parallel to the original comic but featured the more kid-friendly version of the Turtles found in the cartoon. This comic mirrored some plotlines from the cartoon, but created new and different narratives as time went on.

A live-action *Turtles* film followed in 1990, produced by Hong Kong-based studio Golden Harvest and released in March by American independent distributor New Line Cinema. The film earned more than $133 million over the course of 1990, making it the most successful independent film for many years ('The Numbers Page: Top Twenty Boxoffice Performers' 1991). Another wave of Turtles merchandise accompanied the film, including 'T-shirts, posters, caps, buttons, bumper stickers [and] trading cards', among other items (Smith 1990). The Turtles were clearly an industrial success and achieved widespread cultural popularity, making them obvious examples of a supersystem.

The variability across these different Turtles texts came to define the Turtles supersystem more generally. Whereas the original comic was 'dark' and 'gritty', the cartoons and action figures featured bold primary colours. The feature film mixed these two versions of the Turtles to create a third iteration that aimed to balance child-friendliness with more mature grittiness. And, as mentioned, there were variations in the characters' origins and backgrounds from version to version. Kinder draws upon theoretical concepts from literary studies to help account for this textual variability. She refers to the Turtles as sliding signifiers, which she defines as 'those words, images, sounds, and objects that ... blatantly change meaning in different contexts and that derive their primary value precisely from this process of transformation' (Kinder 1991: 3). For Kinder, the Turtles are conspicuous in this regard because of their status as mutants, a condition that enables them to transform from turtles into teenage ninjas. Kinder asserts that, as sliding signifiers, the Turtles invite multiple kinds of spectators and, further, invite spectators to see themselves as transformative and adaptable (1991: 135). Kinder's analysis thus makes linkages between the Turtles' diegetic world(s) and the conditions of their industrial production and cultural consumption. Her work offers a model for franchising that allows for variability across the industrial and intertextual network. Further, she indicates that such variability can allow a franchise to expand into different markets or demographic groups.

Two things are important to note here. First, the Turtles' variability across texts and products occurred while the underlying IP remained with Mirage Studios. Thus, the copyright owner(s) allowed the *Turtles* franchise to be defined by aesthetic mutability and diegetic inconsistency (in 2000, Eastman sold his share of the Turtles' rights to Laird and the Mirage Group) ('Shell Corporation' 2009). Second, the Turtles continued to mutate as they proliferated across culture during the remainder of the 1990s and into the 2000s. Another Turtles comic began publication in 1996, from Image Comics, and here the Turtles engaged in levels of violence not seen in the Archie comics. The Turtles appeared in a live-action television programme, *Ninja Turtles: The Next Mutation* (1997–8), which featured a female Turtle not found in other iterations. As a final example (although there are still more versions), another animated series ran from 2003 to 2009, which resembled the original Mirage comics and yet significantly altered course when, in a later season, the Turtles travelled into the future to fight new adversaries.

Thus, from their inception in 1984 through to 2009, so many versions of the Teenage Mutant Ninja Turtles appeared that it would be foolish to claim that they have a clear or singular 'essence'. They were defined by mutability. Although some versions were more popular than others, and while some *Turtles* films and programmes were more financially successful than others, the variability across the texts and products does not appear to have been a weakness of the franchise. Rather, it seems the Turtle supersystem was one in which different iterations and diegetic worlds were allowed to exist side by side or even to overlap as they appeared simultaneously in different media and cultural forms. Indeed, the Turtles' mutability was so notable that it was dramatised in a made-for-television movie, *Turtles Forever* (Burdine, 2009), in which the Turtles from the 2003–9 series teamed up with the Turtles from the first animated series (1987–95).

REBOOTING THE SUPERSYSTEM

Also in 2009, Mirage Studios celebrated the Teenage Mutant Ninja Turtles' twenty-fifth anniversary, and marked the occasion with multiple events at San Diego Comic-Con in July ('TMNT "Shell-Ebrate"' 2009). However, in October of that year, Mirage Studios sold the rights to the Teenage Mutant Ninja Turtles to the Nickelodeon network for around $60 million (Flint 2009: B.3). Multiple kinds of reboots ensued. News articles noted that Nickelodeon planned for a new computer-animated programme as well as a new feature film, with the intention of releasing both by 2012 (Flint 2009; Szalai 2009: 1). These stories also clarified Viacom's larger strategy for Nickelodeon. In her study of the network, written prior to 2009, Sarah

Banet-Weiser analyses how Nickelodeon empowers children, as individuals, as a community and as citizens, through programming strategies and, just as importantly, through its promotion of consumerism (Banet-Weiser 2007: 2–5). She notes that Nickelodeon aimed to serve a broad, diverse population of children and other viewers (2007: 2–3). Heather Hendershot likewise noted that Nickelodeon appealed to a broad audience of both adults and kids (Hendershot 2004: 2–3). However, in the late 2000s, the network was losing viewership among boys between the ages of six and fourteen (Flint 2009), particularly as a result of the success of DISNEY XD and Cartoon Network, which more concertedly appealed to boy audiences (2009).

Thus, by attaining the rights to the Teenage Mutant Ninja Turtles, which was described as 'harder-edged' than other Nickelodeon programmes, the network sought to reboot itself as newly invested in youthful masculinity. News stories presented different pictures of how the Turtles would fit within the network. In one, a Nickelodeon executive stated that 'action adventure has not been part of our DNA', suggesting that the Turtles would allow the network to branch out into a new genre (Flint 2009). Yet in another story, the pairing of the Turtles with Nickelodeon was celebrated as a natural combination, with that same executive stating that the *Turtles* franchise 'shares a comedic sensibility with the Nickelodeon DNA' (Szalai 2009). Given the way in which DNA is central to the Turtles' existence as mutants, this rhetorical slippage conforms to the already-established malleability of the Turtles supersystem. Nickelodeon could use the Turtles' variability as an asset to create a range of associations and meanings as it aimed to reboot itself through them.

Reports also indicated that Paramount Pictures, also owned by Viacom, would produce the feature film reboot (Szalai 2009). This strategy to create synergies between Nickelodeon and the movie studio was somewhat new for Viacom. Previous attempts to do so, such as *The Spongebob Squarepants Movie* (Hillenburg and Osborne, 2004) and *Lemony Snicket's A Series of Unfortunate Events* (Silberling, 2004) were seen as financial failures (Barnes 2010: B.1). Reports also suggested that internal management problems within the different branches of Viacom had hindered previous attempts at synergy between the television network and the movie studio (Barnes 2010). Admittedly, the first product of this new Nickelodeon-Paramount pairing, *The Last Airbender* (Shyamalan, 2010), turned out to be a disappointment. Nevertheless, Viacom held to this attempt at synergy and the Turtles figured centrally within the public rhetoric regarding this strategy. The aim was clear. The corporation could exploit the Turtles IP in multiple ways across divisions. Keeping with Kinder's earlier observations regarding the Turtles' slipperiness as signifiers, the company aimed to produce different kinds of Turtles in different media for potentially different audiences. Whereas the animated series could have an air of comic adventure, the company planned for the new feature film to 'return to the franchise's roots' by having the 'action and humor' of the 1990 film as well as 'the darker tone of the original comics' (Szalai 2009). The differences among these nebulous promotional discourses aligned well to the mutability of the Turtles themselves.

The new animated series appeared as planned in the autumn of 2012. Produced by Nickelodeon Animation Studio for around $800,000–$1,000,000 per episode (Barnes 2012: AR.17), this version featured 3-D computer animation. As with other Turtles stories, and in keeping with the logic of many reboots, this series retold the Turtles' origin story yet again. Here, the characters begin as the pet turtles of a human ninja master, who all get transformed when exposed to an alien 'mutagen' technology. The character April O'Neil appears as a spunky, red-headed teenager in the programme, whereas in other versions she was an adult scientist or television reporter. Aesthetically, the Turtles appear blockier than earlier portrayals and there is more physical variation among them, with Donatello appearing taller and lankier than the others, while Raphael appears short and squat.

Discussed as a reboot and a remake in the press, one review noted that the backstory would be known to most viewers, making the new computer-generated animation the most novel aspect of the series (Gay 2012: B.9). The show was quite successful, with the initial broadcast attracting 2.1 million viewers, 'making it the no.1 kids programme on basic cable' at the time (Cioletti 2012: 33). The Turtles appeared to serve their purpose for Nickelodeon, revitalising the network and allowing it to compete more directly with rivals like the Disney Channel (James 2012: A.17).

Just as important, the new cartoon prompted a storm of new consumer merchandise, as more than fifty companies had licensed the property as the cartoon went on air (Cioletti 2012). Numerous Turtles toys 'debuted' at Toys 'R' Us in the summer preceding the show's premiere, in fact, including new action figures, vehicles and playsets ('Nickelodeon's Teenage Mutant Ninja Turtles Toys' 2012). A press release indicated that Nickelodeon would maintain the longstanding relationship with Playmates for the toys' production and, further, that both companies collaborated with Toys 'R' Us in designing and retailing the merchandise ('Nickelodeon's Teenage Mutant Ninja Turtles' 2012). The press release indicated that the new action figures would adopt the aesthetic of the new series and that the figures would be different sizes to reflect the new differences in height among the characters ('Nickelodeon's Teenage Mutant Ninja Turtles' 2012). This television reboot thus re-energised the merchandising aspect of the franchise, which entailed collaboration among new and established industrial players within the Turtles supersystem.

Although a feature film reboot was announced in 2009, it took a few more years before it was finally released. The narrative of the film, titled simply *Teenage Mutant Ninja Turtles* (Jonathan Liebesman, 2014), maintains many of the story elements found across the Turtles supersystem. Although the film begins with the Turtles already appearing as teenage ninjas that secretly fight crime at night, a flashback provides their origin story. In this version, some turtles and a rat were used in a series of scientific experiments that mutated them, and are released into the sewer by a young April O'Neil. O'Neil appears as an adult television news reporter once again and Shredder remains the primary Turtles villain.

Aesthetically, the movie differs considerably from previous incarnations of the Turtles and, further, the film differs from the contemporaneous animated series as well. Many of the film's formal characteristics, including the rendering of the Turtles themselves, appear strongly linked to the film's attachment to Paramount Studios. At the time, Paramount was known for releasing the *Transformers* series of films (2007–18), which were produced and directed by Michael Bay. Like the *Turtles* reboot, the *Transformers* films were designed to re-ignite a franchise from the 1980s that had similarly tied cartoons with toy sales. In fact, toy manufacturer Hasbro worked to revitalise both the Transformers and the G.I. Joe toy lines through film series in the 2000s. Hasbro CEO Brian Goldner oversaw this strategy when he took control of the company, having previously worked in advertising (Itzkoff 2009). The company had planned to create new animated shows for both *G.I. Joe* and *Transformers* with new characters, narrative lines and toys (Itzkoff 2009). Yet, the explicit aim was to create feature films out of the toys in order to generate a new wave of toy sales.

Intertextuality was a key element of Hasbro's, and later Paramount's, industrial strategy. As one producer said of the G.I. Joe cartoon in advance of the release of *G.I. Joe: The Rise of Cobra* (Sommers, 2009), 'the series "never really killed off any characters . . . so there was a lot of interesting back story and interrelationships"' (Lorenzo di Bonaventura, quoted in Itzkoff 2009). In noting that the stories from the existing cartoons were made in such a way that they might be sampled for future movie narratives, this producer performs some basic but interesting narratological work. Further, he points towards the 'interrelationships' among the characters, implying that the feature films could pick up some elements of this intertextual web and contribute back to it. Indeed, *G.I. Joe: The Rise of Cobra* features many characters from the 1980s cartoon and pits the heroes against the international terrorist organisation Cobra. Notably, this movie depicts some of the G.I. Joe soldiers as pseudo-superheroes, as they wear super-powered suits that allow them to run at incredible speeds, jump extremely high, fall from great heights and so on.

Directed by Michael Bay, the first live-action *Transformers* film (2007) depicted the robots from the 1980s animated series in photo-realistic computer animation. The design of the robots was notably detailed and intricate, while the overall look of the film featured high-contrast, high-saturation imagery. The movie earned over $700 million globally, leading to a sequel, *Transformers: Revenge of the Fallen* (Bay, 2009), which earned over $800 million. The films also generated substantial revenues in ancillary markets. One report estimated that the first *Transformers* movie made $480 million for Hasbro and the second film generated as much as $600 million (Chmielewski 2009: B.1). With *Revenge of the Fallen* appearing in June, and *The Rise of Cobra* being released in August, it seems conspicuous that Nickelodeon purchased the rights to the Teenage Mutant Ninja Turtles a few months later, in October 2009. The success of these two recent, hugely successful film franchises, which paired Paramount Pictures with a toy company, paved the way for Viacom to seek out similar cartoon/toy/film franchises. The company sought to reboot a supersystem.

The same story that noted the exceptional sales of Transformers merchandise also cited the Teenage Mutant Ninja Turtles as a franchise that failed to cross over between success in toy sales and movie ticket sales, mentioning the 2007 *TMNT* film as the prime example (Chmielewski 2009). Another article from 2009 similarly asserted that the Turtles did not have the same historical staying power as the Transformers evidently did (Taylor 2009). Thus, even though it appears logical that Viacom would seek to replicate the success of the *Transformers* and *G.I. Joe* movies by finding and rebooting existing properties that had clear ties to toys and/or animated programming, choosing the Turtles in 2009 was not necessarily a sure bet.

Yet it is possible that the Turtles' lack of contemporary appeal drove the idea of the reboot, with the supersystem appearing especially available for revision. The reboot did revise the Turtles, drawing heavily from the Transformers' playbook in particular. Michael Bay became the producer of the *Turtles* reboot in 2010. Although he did not direct either of the *Turtles* reboots, Bay's role appears critical for both industrial and textual reasons. Bay was credited for much of the look of the *Transformers* films and, industrially, some credited him with making the franchise relevant and viable again (Taylor 2009). Bay's position as producer thus suggested that the Turtles could be made similarly exciting and relevant once again. A further industrial and intertextual link was forged when Megan Fox, who had performed in multiple *Transformers* films, was cast as April O'Neil in the new *Turtles* film.

The style of the 2014 *Turtles* film also owed a lot to both the *Transformers* and *G.I. Joe* movies. Like the *Transformers*, the *Turtles* reboot featured incessantly mobile camerawork, consistent flashes and lens flares, high-contrast imagery with intense colour saturation, as well as a rapid editing style with the intermittent use of slow motion during key action moments. The Turtle characters' physical design also resembled the style of both *G.I. Joe* and *Transformers*. These Turtles appeared taller, bulkier and more intensely muscular than previous incarnations, matching the hyper-masculine, hyper-muscular representations of Transformer robots and super-suited G.I. Joe soldiers.

Public discourses about the new *Turtles* film before its release help show how it operated as a reboot and as part of a supersystem within a wider cultural arena.

Despite the fact that the Turtles supersystem entailed an overlapping, inconsistent form of intertextuality for many years, there were public discussions during the reboot's development about how it should represent the characters appropriately. Specifically, fans expressed concerns when rumors circulated that the Turtles would appear as aliens in this film, and not as mutated turtles from Earth. This prompted Bay to state publicly that:

> Fans need to take a breath, and chill. They have not read the script. Our team is working closely with one of the original creators of Ninja Turtles to help expand and give a more complex back story. Relax, we are including everything that made you become fans in the first place. (quoted in Rich 2012)

Here, Bay uses rhetoric that is typical of promotional rebooting discourses, particularly regarding fidelity to an imagined 'essence' of the characters or to the franchise as a whole. Invoking the Turtles' 'original creators' signals that this new iteration will both innovate and also have the link to a franchise heritage. Thus, although the existing Turtles supersystem may have been defined by textual mutability, the very rhetoric of the 'reboot' ensnared the new film within a contradictory discourse of authenticity and textual stability.

Reviews of the film were almost entirely negative and similarly framed the film in relation to issues regarding reboots, franchises and supersystems. Franchises and supersystems often seek new audiences by addressing different demographics, yet many reviews of the *Turtles* reboot asserted that it did not clearly appeal to children, or teenagers, or nostalgic adults (Gettell 2014). For critics, it seems that the way in which the film blended the Turtles' intertextual palimpsest with the stylistic idioms of the *Transformers* films did not work. One critic stated the obvious and called the film 'derivative', but another was a bit more astute and stated that the film 'often feels like some sort of corporate seminar in brand management' (Gettell 2014).

The idea of the supersystem allows us to see the relationship between these two criticisms. As a film reboot, appearing alongside but different from a television cartoon reboot, the 2014 *Teenage Mutant Ninja Turtles* sought a new opportunity for the supersystem to grow. Although critics took issue with the film's style, it was a longstanding practice within the Turtles supersystem to create new versions of the characters that were often different from past versions even while they might appear simultaneously alongside them. However much some viewers may have desired a particular depiction of the Turtles, the film reboot actually maintained a fidelity to the mutability of the existing franchise. These critics' concerns appear to be related more to contemporary rebooting practices than they are about the Turtles specifically.

Although these discourses framed the 2014 feature as a (bad) reboot and ignored the tendency for variability within the Turtles supersystem, the film appeared to do much of the industrial work that was intended. It earned over $65 million in its opening weekend and eventually earned nearly $500 million globally. And just as the 2012 animated series initiated a new wave of Turtles merchandise based on that cartoon, so too did the 2014 film reboot set off a new round of consumer products. A press release from Playmates Toys indicated that the new toys would be modelled on the depictions of the Turtles found in the film ('Press Release' 2014). These toys created a momentary surge in the already steady sales of Turtles products, as Playmates had a 40 per cent increase in sales in 2014 over its 2013 performance ('Playmates Toys Announced 2014 Interim Results' 2014). Interestingly, these toys appear to have been slightly less profitable on a per-item basis than previous Turtles figures, due to the detailed modelling required for the Turtles' more defined and muscular look.

This press release also discussed aspects of the new Turtles toys and merchandise that resonate with Kinder's notion of the supersystem. It asserted, 'The range of toys will provide kids and fans of all ages with a one-of-a-kind ninja play experience', and, further, that 'These products . . . will provide hours of play, collectability and deepen our fans' connection to the beloved brand' ('Press Release' 2014). These statements echo Kinder's points that a supersystem should appeal to multiple demographics and foster collectability. They also recall Tompkins' idea that reboots attempt to re-instil fan loyalty into a franchise.

The toys based on the film reboot stood alongside the existing Turtle toys in stores, including those based on the rebooted animated series. This simultaneous, overlapping kind of intertextuality was, in all likelihood, not especially confusing to Turtles fans or shoppers; the Turtles had always already existed merely as 'versions' of themselves, mutating across their larger supersystem. Despite the fact that reboots, as the term is used in many popular and academic discussions, might try and wipe a narrative slate clean, the post-2009 *Turtles* reboots make it clear that reboots do not, in fact cannot, fully clear out a new cultural space. Indeed, this case makes it clear that the companies that produce and distribute reboots can be quite aware of this. It may or may not make sense for an individual film to create a new narrative continuity for a series of films to follow, but franchises almost always exist horizontally, with different manifestations sitting next to one another. This is especially true for the Teenage Mutant Ninja Turtles.

CONCLUSION: TURTLES FOREVER, ALWAYS ALREADY

Based on the success of the 2014 *Teenage Mutant Ninja Turtles* film and the related toy sales, Nickelodeon and Paramount released another film in this series, *Teenage Mutant Ninja Turtles: Out of the Shadows* (Green, 2016). Yet this film earned less than half of the 2014 reboot. According to a report from Playmates, however, sales of toys related to the 2016 film 'provided a meaningful boost to the brand' ('Playmates Toys Announced 2016 Annual Results' 2017). Meanwhile, Nickelodeon began airing a new *Turtles* animated series in 2018, *Rise of the Teenage Mutant Ninja Turtles*, which returned to 2-D animation and ushered in a wave of new toys. And in 2019 producers announced their intention to make yet another *Turtles* feature film that would be separate from the 2014 and 2016 films, rebooting the characters yet again (Evangelista 2019).

Thus, it seems that the Turtles supersystem remains as generative and mutable as ever. Yet at the same time, the contemporary discourse around reboots seems to have impacted this supersystem, as some newer iterations of the Turtles get rhetorically positioned as displacing others, even while they actually just add to the longer, variable, overlapping palimpsest that actually characterises the Turtles supersystem. In light of this ongoing process of industrial and textual proliferation and mutation, the post-2009, Nickelodeon-based *Turtles* reboots help us understand some important aspects of film reboots, entertainment supersystems and industrial intertextuality. First, we see that reboots can provide media producers with opportunities to rethink a media supersystem. The reboot tries to create an 'event' within a franchise's industrial life that seeks a new audience and new merchandising possibilities. Second, we see how a corporation can seek to reboot itself, or parts of itself, through the acquisition and deployment of a particular IP. In taking on the Turtles in 2009, Viacom aimed to change its own system, masculinising Nickelodeon while also seeking synergies between Nickelodeon and Paramount. Third and finally, this example shows how intertextuality in mainstream media is a concerted, although not always tidy, industrial process. The linkages among texts, toys and merchandise take real work. The reboot represents one aspect of that work: an industrial rethinking of a supersystem.

REFERENCES

Banet-Weiser, Sarah (2007), *Kids Rule! Nickelodeon and Consumer Citizenship*, Durham, NC: Duke University Press.
Barnes, Brooks (2010), 'Nickelodeon Tries Again to Move to the Big Screen', *New York Times*, 5 July, B.1.
Barnes, Brooks (2012), 'Half-Shell Heroes Return to Action', *New York Times*, Late Edition, 30 September, AR.17.
Chmielewski, Dawn (2009), 'Retailers' New Toy Story: Blockbuster Summer Films', *Los Angeles Times*, 13 July, B.1.
Cioletti, Amanda (2012), 'Global Toy Trends', *License! Global* (November/December), 32–3.
Evangelista, Chris (2019), '"Teenage Mutant Ninja Turtles" Reboot Coming From Producers of Previous "Teenage Mutant Ninja Turtles" Reboot', *Slashfilm*, 14 January, <https://www.slashfilm.com/ninja-turtles-reboot>.

Flint, Joe (2009), 'Nickeldeon to Shell Out for "Turtles"', *Los Angeles Times*, 22 October, B.3.
Gay, Verne (2012), 'Cowabunga! the Mutant Turtles are Back', *Newsday*, Combined Editions, 29 September, B.9.
Gettell, Oliver (2014), '"Teenage Mutant Ninja Turtles" Has an Identity Crisis, Reviews Say', *Los Angeles Times* (blog), 8 August, <https://www.latimes.com/entertainment/movies/moviesnow/la-et-mn-teenage-mutant-ninja-turtles-movies-reviews-critics-20140807-story.html>.
Hendershot, Heather (2004), 'Introduction: Nickelodeon and the Business of Fun', in Heather Hendershot (ed.), *Nickelodeon Nation: The History, Politics, and Economics of America's Only Channel for Kids*, New York: New York University Press, pp. 1–12.
Herbert, Daniel (2017), *Film Remakes and Franchises*, New Brunswick, NJ: Rutgers University Press.
Hills, Matt (2002), *Fan Cultures*, London: Routledge.
Hunting, Kyra and Jonathan Gray (2018), 'Disney Junior: Imagining Industrial Intertextuality', in Derek Johnson (ed.), *From Networks to Netflix: A Guide to Changing Channels*, New York and London: Routledge, pp. 197–207.
Itzkoff, Dave (2009), 'The Movie Industry's New Playthings', *New York Times*, online, 21 June, <https://www.nytimes.com/2009/06/21/movies/21itzk.html>.
James, Meg (2012), 'Turtles to the Rescue', *Orlando Sentinel*, 28 September, A.17.
Jenkins, Henry (2006), *Convergence Culture: Where Old and New Media Collide*, New York: New York University Press.
Johnson, Derek (2013), *Media Franchising: Creative License and Collaboration in the Culture Industries*, New York: New York University Press.
Kinder, Marsha (1991), *Playing With Power in Movies, Television, and Video Games: From Muppet Babies to Teenage Mutant Ninja Turtles*, Berkeley, CA: University of California Press.
Logan, Joe (1989), 'Teen Turtles Make a Splash with Fans', *Philadelphia Inquirer*, 8 July.
'Nickelodeon's Teenage Mutant Ninja Turtles Toys Hit Toys "R" Us® Stores Nationwide this Month' (2012), *PR Newswire*, 18 July.
'The Numbers Page: Top Twenty Boxoffice Performers' (1991), *Boxoffice*, 1 February, 111.
'Playmates Toys Announced 2014 Interim Results' (2014), *Playmates Toys*, 29 August, <http://ir.playmatestoys.com/eng/press/p140829.pdf>.
'Playmates Toys Announced 2016 Annual Results' (2017), *Playmates Toys*, 24 March, <http://ir.playmatestoys.com/eng/press/p170324.pdf>.
'Press Release: Teenage Mutant Ninja Turtles Emerge from the Shadows Onto the Big Screen and into Fans' Hands' (2014), *Dow Jones Institutional News*, 18 June, 2.
Proctor, William (2012), 'Regeneration and Rebirth: Anatomy of the Franchise Reboot', *Scope: An Online Journal of Film and Television Studies*, 22 (February), 1–19.
Rich, Katey (2012), 'Michael Bay Tells Teenage Mutant Ninja Turtles Fans To Chill Out', *CinemaBlend*, 20 March, <https://www.cinemablend.com/new/Michael-Bay-Tells-Teenage-Mutant-Ninja-Turtles-Fans-Chill-Out-30049.html>.
'Shell Corporation' (2009), *Boston Globe*, 14 July, G.22.
Smith, Stacy Jenel (1990), 'Shell Shock', *Los Angeles Times*, 4 February, H.26.
Solomon, Charles (1987), 'TV REVIEWS "Ninja Turtles" Crawls Out, Lands on Back', *Los Angeles Times*, 28 December, 11.
Szalai, Georg (2009), 'Cowabunga! Nick Shells out for Turtles', *Hollywood Reporter*, 22 October, 1, 10.
Taylor, Wes (2009), '"Transformer" Fans Revved up For Return to Big Screen', *McClatchy-Tribune Business News*, 21 June.

'TMNT "Shell-Ebrate" Culmination of Official Anniversary Tour and Look Forward to Next Generation with 2011 Motion Picture' (2009), *Business Wire*, 22 July.

Tompkins, Joe (2014), '"Re-imagining" the Canon: Examining the Discourse of Contemporary Horror Film Reboots', *New Review of Film and Television Studies*, 12: 4, 380–99.

Verevis, Constantine (2017), 'New Millennial Remakes', in Frank Kelleter (ed.), *Media of Serial Narrative*, Columbus, OH: Ohio State University Press, pp. 148–66.

CHAPTER 2

Live Long and Prosper: Rebooting *Star Trek* and Reimagining Fandom

Erin Hanna

When Paramount rebooted its *Star Trek* film franchise in 2009, director J. J. Abrams pitched the new film as '*Star Trek* for moviegoers', adding, 'if you happen to be a *Star Trek* fan you will love it, but you don't have to be to see this movie' (ScreenSlam 2015). In order to negotiate this delicate balance between appealing to fans and the rest of the moviegoing public, the film used a time travel narrative to introduce an entirely new, parallel continuity that reimagined the *Star Trek* universe and recast iconic characters in an alternate timeline. This narrative twist meant that the reboot could capitalise on strategic overlaps, such as the casting of the original Spock, Leonard Nimoy, as the reboot's 'Spock Prime', who provided a thread of continuity between the two timelines. It also allowed for a slew of references to the original television and film series, from staging Kirk's infamous 'Kobayashi Maru' test, first referenced in *Star Trek II: The Wrath of Khan* (Meyer, 1982), to a strategically placed Tribble. However this narrative reboot also provided the freedom to avoid aspects of the original that might not translate to a blockbuster audience, such as Abrams' well-publicised decision to exclude William Shatner (Captain Kirk), in order to ensure the film remained an 'irony-free zone' (Thompson 2008).

Because film reboots like *Star Trek* are oriented towards restoring profitability to waning intellectual properties (IPs), such decisions were as much about promoting the film to moviegoers as reimagining its narrative world (Proctor 2012). Indeed, the very idea of a film reboot might be understood as an industry construct stemming primarily from promotional discourses (Verevis 2017: 280; Tompkins 2014). It comes as little surprise, then, that the rise of the film reboot, beginning around the turn of the twenty-first century, intersects with industrial and promotional discourses that sought to similarly reimagine media consumption by celebrating the increased visibility and mainstreaming of fandom in popular culture (Gray et al. 2017: 2; Hanna 2019: 13–16).

The resulting emphasis on participation and collaboration between fans and media industries, Derek Johnson argues, has yielded a 'discursively imagined audience' that exists to legitimate the authority of producers and reinforce 'the persistently hierarchical institutions and cultures of industrial production' (Jenkins 2006; Johnson 2013: 154, 137). Rebooting and promoting *Star Trek*, however, necessitated a discursively *reimagined* audience that would include both pre-existing and future fans. In this way, the 2009 *Star Trek* highlights the intersecting logics of the film reboot and the mainstreaming of fandom in popular culture, both of which grow out of promotional strategies designed to extract additional profits from something that already exists.

Paramount has long incorporated *Star Trek* fandom in promoting the franchise. But in rebooting *Star Trek* as a twenty-first-century blockbuster, the studio's approach to fans employed only a superficial aura of continuity, much like the narrative of the film itself. Promotional discourses highlighted those fans and fan practices that aligned with the studio's economic goals and largely ignored or marginalised the rest. The goal, ostensibly, was to sell the rebooted franchise to the 'comfortable majority' of viewers that Jonathan Gray calls 'non-fans': those who might still watch the film, but with a lessened level of knowledge and investment in previous iterations of *Star Trek* (Gray 2003: 74–6). However, coming at a time when fandom was being discursively repositioned as a mainstream mode of media consumption, this film – like many other reboots in this period – also worked to reimagine this 'comfortable majority' of media consumers as the next generation of *Star Trek* fans.

'STAR TREK LIVES!'

With its 2009 *Star Trek* reboot, Paramount added yet another text to a franchise that had been steadily expanding since the 1970s. Though the original *Star Trek* television series was cancelled in 1969, after three seasons, its popularity in syndication led to the show's brief revival as an animated series in 1973 (Beerman 1972: 1). This decision was also helped along the way by *Star Trek*'s vocal fanbase, who organised a number of letter-writing campaigns, one of which was credited with saving the original series from cancellation in 1968, and several well-attended conventions beginning with New York's 'Star Trek Lives!' in 1972 (Tulloch and Jenkins 1995: 8–11; 'Radio-Television' 1968; Winston 1979).

While popular discourses about *Star Trek* fans have long marginalised this group as 'social misfits' or 'brainless consumers', even in the 1970s Paramount found ways to reimagine and profit from the visibility of this segment of their audience (Jenkins 1992: 10). Take, for example, a four-page *TV Guide* article, which provided detailed coverage of the 1972 'Star Trek Lives!' convention. While remarking on '*Star Trek*'s fanatic band of fans', the article also included a brief interview with Paramount Television's Shirley Gerstel who said, 'the calls and letters that come into my office are tremendous . . . I keep passing them on to the West coast. I never thought that *Star Trek* would come back, but now there's a rumor that Paramount might start making it again' (Marsano 1972: 18). This rumour, *TV Guide* reported, 'passed from one Trekkie to another, electrifying them' and was further legitimated with a statement from series creator Gene Roddenberry, who was also in attendance: 'I didn't think it was possible six months ago . . . but after seeing the enthusiasm here I'm beginning to change my mind' (Marsano 1972: 18–19). While these accounts connect a possible revival of the show to the enthusiasm of *Star Trek* fans, the article fails to mention that Paramount Television's Shirley Gerstel was likely attending the convention and circulating said rumours in her capacity as a publicist for the studio (Weber 2016). These rumours were also fuelled by advance coverage of the convention in *Variety*. 'If enough interest is sparked,' the trade reported, 'Paramount may very well look to sell a new "Star Trek" series to a network' (Beerman 1972: 69). According to 'Star Trek Lives!' organiser Joan Winston, *Variety*'s coverage of the convention was orchestrated by Paramount vice president Bob Newgard, demonstrating that, even in 1972, fan activities and conventions like this one were also heavily mediated by industry discourses that worked to reimagine and reframe the activities of this audience by highlighting their connection to the industry's economic objectives (Winston 1979: 17).

However, even as Paramount presented itself as a studio attentive to its fan base, 'the very significance of *Star Trek* to its fans', as Eileen Meehan points out, 'encourages Paramount to target the population from which revenues are not guaranteed' (Meehan 2000: 86). *TV Guide*'s story, for example, reaffirmed Paramount's investment in *Star Trek*'s niche audience of 'fanatics', but it also promoted the series to *TV Guide*'s nearly 16.5 million readers (Campbell et al. 2013: 268). So while the interventions of Paramount employees meant that the first *Star Trek* convention was covered in high-profile publications, this coverage functioned primarily as a way to promote the series to non-fans.

While the revival rumours in 1972 were probably tied to the studio's plans for *Star Trek: The Animated Series*, Paramount undertook a more ambitious revival with 1979's *Star Trek: The Motion Picture*, launching the ten-film franchise that it would ultimately reboot in 2009. In the years that followed, the *Star Trek* universe continued to grow as a transmedia franchise, spawning five television spin-offs (including the animated series) between 1969 and 2009, not to mention a vast and expanding market of games, comics, novels and collectables. *Star Trek* fans may have played a significant role in the decision to produce the first feature film, but equally important was the success of *Star Wars* in 1977, which demonstrated that science fiction films were viable box office blockbusters that could capitalise on the consumer habits of fans and non-fans alike. From the very beginning, then, *Star Trek*'s successes (and failures, such as the cancellation of the original series) were less a reflection upon the franchise's diehard fans, and more accurately centred on the abstracted and homogenised mass audience that fuelled television ratings in the network era and propelled New Hollywood's blockbuster model (Ang 1991; Schatz 1993). And, as the coverage of 'Star Trek Lives!' in 1972 suggests, promoting *Star Trek* to fans was less about imagining them as constituents of this mass audience and more accurately about reimagining fans as vehicles for publicity that could then be aimed at the broader moviegoing public.

'WE'RE ALL TREKKIES NOW'

As I argue in *Only at Comic-Con* (Hanna 2019), the reimagining of fans as promotional vehicles has happened on a much larger scale in the twenty-first century, as discourses connecting fans to the popularity and profitability of Hollywood's business model seem to be propelling fandom into the mainstream, blurring the line between fan and non-fan. Such discourses both construct and deconstruct an aura of exclusivity by suggesting that fans are powerful tastemakers, even as they paint a picture of fandom that is so broad as to be indistinguishable from the modes of media consumption that are actively encouraged of all viewers under conglomerate Hollywood's blockbuster and franchise model (Hanna 2019; Jenkins 2006; Schatz 2008; Balio 2013).

Capturing this sentiment, *Newsweek*'s cover story of 4 May 2009, published just before *Star Trek*'s 8 May release, declared, 'We're All Trekkies Now', arguing that '"Star Trek" is way cool' thanks to the fans 'who knew the product better than the people who made it' and 'push[ed] what had been marginal movie-genre ephemera – science fiction, fantasy, costumed-superhero stories – into the mainstream' (Daly 2009). Kim Masters' 7 May article in the *Daily Beast* similarly inquired, 'Is Star Trek Now Cool?' but instead of emphasising the longevity of *Star Trek* fandom, Masters attributed this shift to the film's director, J. J. Abrams, suggesting that he 'may have done the impossible: sex up the ultimate nerd franchise' (Masters 2009). This article also cites Abrams' surprising advice to '*Star Trek* purists . . . "Don't see the movie. You'll just get angry"' (Masters 2009). As these examples suggest, when it comes to articulating the power and influence of *Star Trek* fandom, the discourses surrounding the 2009 reboot were inconsistent, at best. But there was at least one through line connecting these examples: the suggestion that in the process of rebooting *Star Trek* the cultural meanings that long framed *Star Trek* fans as marginal and excessive consumers were also being actively reshaped. In this way, the discourses surrounding the *Star Trek* reboot were also part of a broader discursive thrust captured in Lev Grossman's 2005 headline in *Time* magazine: 'The Geek Shall Inherit the Earth' (Grossman 2005).

In navigating this 'subversion of the hip/square dialectic', Paramount targeted fans with more deferential promotional content, even as it reimagined the *Star Trek* reboot as a 'cool' new take on the franchise (suggesting that previous iterations were decidedly 'uncool') and reassured audiences that this was a film everyone could and should enjoy (Quail 2011: 467). For example, as Leora Hadas notes, references to the show's original creator, Gene Roddenberry, were strategically deployed in promoting the film to fans, but 'in the popular press that addresses those elusive nonfans, who might be interested in the film merely as an action or summer movie, the mentions of Roddenberry all but vanish' (Hadas 2017: 54–5). Paramount publicist Katie Martin Kelley summarised the strategy by directly aligning it with the logic of rebooting: 'There's a core fan base you have to cater to . . . But with a reboot, you have an opportunity to wipe the slate clean' (quoted in Brodesser and Hampp 2009).

FAKING A 'TREKGASM'

Nowhere is this strategy – and its conflicting messaging and implications – more apparent than in the surprise premiere of the 2009 film, which was staged at the South Lamar Alamo Drafthouse in Austin, Texas on Monday, 6 April 2009. The audience was lured to the Alamo that evening with the promise of a free screening of a restored 35 mm print of *Wrath of Khan* followed by 'an exclusive sneak preview of 10 minutes of NEVER BEFORE SEEN footage from the new STAR TREK' (headgeek 2009b). Two stalwarts of Austin's geeky film scene introduced the screening: Alamo Drafthouse's owner Tim League and Austin's well-known movie blogger Harry Knowles of *Ain't it Cool News*.[1] Also present to kick off the festivities were *Star Trek*'s screenwriters Roberto Orci and Alex Kurtzman, and producer Damon Lindelof. While all of the speakers praised *Khan* as a high point, not just in the *Star Trek* franchise but also in cinema history, they were equally, if not more, invested in hyping the exclusivity of the ten-minute sneak preview of the reboot. League gave a strongly worded piracy warning, Knowles reminded the audience that they would get to see the footage several hours before the film's Australian world premiere and Kurtzman told the audience that the trio had opted to skip the world premiere because 'ultimately we made this for the fans and you guys are the fans, so we wanted to be with you tonight' (MightyBest 2009a).

This last statement, that the film was made for the fans, further exemplifies the dual and duelling strategies employed in the promotion of the film, which was to show reverence in fan spaces, like conventions and interviews with fan publications, while disavowing the excessive aspects of *Star Trek* fandom in the popular press (Hadas 2017: 54–5). In the case of the Alamo screening, however, Paramount had essentially constructed its own fan space, one that it could control and repurpose for promotion to both fans and non-fans alike. While the audience that evening certainly included *Star Trek* fans, badge holders of Fantastic Fest, a popular Austin-based genre film festival, got first crack at the tickets. And at least one member of the crowd, Cole Abaius, would later tweet, 'Yes, I'm the guy who's never seen an episode of ST and got to see *Star Trek* tonight' (quoted in Sciretta 2009). As it turned out, Abaius was not a *Star Trek* fan, but a movie blogger who later published a glowing review of the film on the site *Film School Rejects* from the perspective of a '*Star Trek* virgin' (Abaius 2009). In fact, the audience that evening was peppered with Austin-based movie bloggers, as is evident from the slew of reviews that emerged from the event and appeared on sites like *AICN*, *Film School Rejects*, *Cinema Blend*, *Twitch Film* and *CHUD* (headgeek 2009a; Quint 2009; Abaius 2009; Miller 2009; Tyler 2009; Perkins 2009; Clark 2009). As one might suspect, and as one review actually disclosed, these bloggers didn't stumble upon the screening by accident; they were formally invited by a Paramount representative (Tyler 2009).

With the stage set for a nostalgic return to a fan favourite and an invigorating glimpse at the new *Star Trek*, the lights went down and the audience, many of who were about to see *Khan* on the big screen – and in 35 mm – for the first time, settled in for the show. But it quickly became clear that this was far from the restored print they had been promised. The film was reportedly covered in scratches, the image began to warp and then, scarcely two minutes in, the print burned up before the audience's eyes (Admin 2009). Orci, Kurtzman and Lindelof hustled back to the front of the theatre, ostensibly to buy some time while League saw to the damaged print. But when Leonard Nimoy joined the trio onstage, it became clear that the *Khan* screening was just a clever ruse: they were really there to premiere the new *Star Trek* reboot in its entirety.

In staging this elaborate set-up, promoters took the unusual but somewhat pointed step of positioning the new *Star Trek* film as a destructive force, literalising William Proctor's description of the franchise reboot as something that rises 'from the ashes of an old or failed property' (Proctor 2012: 4). In this case, however, Paramount's bait and switch meant that this audience, which had already been discursively reimagined as fans, was compelled to bear witness, not just to the surprise premiere and launch of a 'new' *Star Trek* film franchise, but to the annihilation of the 'old' *Star Trek*, captured both figuratively and literally, through the simulated destruction of cinema's 'old' 35 mm film technology. Under normal circumstances, a company promising one thing and delivering another would prompt a slew of customer complaints. Instead, the reactions that emerged from the screening were largely positive, even glowing, highlighting the power of promotional discourses to reframe and reconstruct audience expectations, particularly when presented in exclusive contexts that appear to bring audiences closer to the industry (Hanna 2019; Gray 2010; Couldry 2000).

At the same time, however, by luring the audience to the premiere under the false pretence of a *Wrath of Khan* screening, Paramount sought to tether its reboot to a very specific text amidst the diverse points of entry into the *Star Trek* universe. While the first instalment in the original film franchise, *Star Trek: The Motion Picture* (Wise, 1979), was commercially successful but panned by critics, *Khan* had been an unequivocal success, making it an ideal 'entryway paratext' through which audiences might be directed to consume the rebooted film franchise (Gray 2010: 35).² Similarly, Leonard Nimoy's appearance at the event signalled the complicated intertextual relationship between the reboot, the original series and *Star Trek*'s original film franchise. However, Nimoy's presence and visibility at the Austin premiere also meant he was absent from the glitzy red-carpet world premiere of the film in Australia three hours later, allowing *Star Trek*'s global launch to highlight the new faces of the film, untethered from the cumbersome legacy of the over forty-year-old franchise.

When Nimoy, before revealing the surprise screening, asked the crowd if they would rather be in Australia for the premiere, he was met with some cheers and applause, but video of the event also captured a resounding chorus of 'noes' (MightyBest 2009b). Upon hearing the audience's mixed response, Nimoy quickly rephrased his question: 'You guys are gonna see, what, ten minutes of the movie? Wouldn't you rather see the whole movie?' This time the crowd got the message and erupted in cheers and applause. Of course, the ambivalence surrounding this surprise announcement did not make its way into the media coverage that emerged after the screening, which might best be captured by *io9*'s headline, 'Star Trek Sneak Explodes in Giant Trekgasm' (MightyBest 2009b; Woerner 2009; Nashawaty 2009; headgeek 2009a; Sciretta 2009).

The framing of this surprise screening as a way of rewarding fans for their loyalty to the *Star Trek* franchise was certainly part of the reboot's larger promotional strategy, or what Matt Hills calls 'fanagement: responding to, and anticipating, fan criticisms, as well as catering for specific fractions of fandom who might otherwise be at odds with the unfolding brand, and attempting to draw a line under fan resistance to diegetic and production changes' (Hills 2012: 410). But was the reboot's premiere really what fans wanted that evening? By all accounts, a free screening of *Wrath of Khan* was, itself, enough to draw audiences to the Alamo that night (Admin 2009; headgeek 2009a). The promise of ten minutes of the new *Star Trek* film was just icing on the cake. However, in framing this surprise preview as an exclusive fan event, both during the screening and in subsequent coverage in the press, Paramount was able to discursively reimagine a real movie audience with a range of investments in the new film, from non-fans to movie buffs to *Star Trek* fans to movie bloggers whose livelihoods depended on continued access to studio promotion. In doing so, they homogenised the crowd and deployed them as signifiers of fandom that, like the 1972 'Star Trek Lives!' coverage in *TV Guide*, would deliver Paramount's promotional message far and wide. At the same time, however, holding the parallel world premiere in Australia also allowed the studio to promote the film as a global blockbuster designed to attract a mass audience. And, if successful, perhaps this audience would take its place as the next generation of *Star Trek* fandom, one that operated in close alignment with Paramount's economic bottom line.

'NOT YOUR FATHER'S *STAR TREK*'

So what did the next generation of *Star Trek* fans look like? According to a 2009 *Variety* article, Paramount's promotional plan was simple: 'Go young and prosper' (Siegel 2009: 1). While early promotion for the film 'had to be sensitive to old-school fans', as one unnamed marketing executive put it, as the release date grew closer, the studio pivoted away from the older generation of *Star Trek* fans and launched an aggressive marketing campaign targeting a younger demographic who might be less familiar with the franchise (Siegel 2009: 1). Of course, in keeping with the spirit of the film reboot, this strategy was essentially a return to what had made *Star Trek* part of the cultural zeitgeist in the first place. Many of the fans who watched the show during its original run in the 1960s or in syndication in the 1970s skewed younger, too (Shuit 1972: A1; Beerman 1972: 1; Marsano 1972: 19).

In rebooting the film, Paramount hoped that younger audiences would sustain the growth of the new franchise in much the same way. Thus, like the launch of *Star Trek: The Motion Picture* in 1979, rebooting *Star Trek* in 2009 ultimately meant 'turning to the mass audience' (Siegel 2009: 1). In doing so, Paramount promoted the film on parent company Viacom's younger skewing platforms, including a behind-the-scenes feature on MTV and a tie-in with the popular video game *Rock Band*, then owned by MTV Games (Siegel 2009: 1; Brodesser and Hampp 2009; TrekMovie.Com Staff 2009). The studio also partnered with brands like Burger King, which *Variety* described as 'among the edgier of the fast food chains' (Siegel 2009: 1). And, of course, Paramount's selection of J. J. Abrams to direct and produce the franchise was a calculated one as well, as the studio hoped to tap into his following among younger viewers and his 'cool' authorial brand (Hadas 2017).

But nowhere is this generational divide more apparent than in the reboot's tagline, 'This is not your father's *Star Trek*', launched approximately one month before the film's release. The phrase first appeared in a thirty-second TV spot that blasted *Star Trek*'s previous associations with cerebral science fiction into oblivion. Instead, the trailer used a blaring hard rock soundtrack and rapid editing to propel the viewer through James T. Kirk's (Chris Pine) various high-octane adventures, including a car chase, a sky-dive (from space!), a bar brawl and a number of special effects pieces, primarily in the form of spaceships that were either on fire or exploding. But the brief appearance of Uhura (Zoe Saldana), the only female character featured in the trailer – and one of the few to be featured prominently in the film – reveals even more about this marketing strategy, and its ideological implications, when it comes to reimagining *Star Trek* fandom.

LIVE LONG AND PROSPER 41

Figure 2.1 An objectifying shot of Uhura as she removes her top, *Star Trek* (2009).

Figure 2.2 A shot of Kirk in bed with a woman, her face and body obscured by shadow, appears between two suggestive shots of Uhura in the film's trailer, *Star Trek* (2009).

Figure 2.3 A shot of Uhura and Kirk's first meeting is taken out of context in order to suggest a sexual relationship between the two characters, *Star Trek* (2009).

Uhura first appears in the middle of the trailer, beginning with a shot where she removes her top to reveal a white bra and ending with a close-up as she utters a flirty 'I'm impressed', before a reverse shot reveals Kirk's coy half-smile. Sandwiched between these two shots is a fleeting image of Kirk in bed with a woman, her face and body obscured by shadow. While there is a romantic relationship between Uhura and Spock in the film, no such relationship exists between Uhura and Kirk. And yet, the trailer is clearly edited in such a way as to titillate viewers by implying that such a relationship exists and situating it among Kirk's other action-packed conquests. In this way, the trailer also foreshadows the treatment of Uhura (and other female characters) throughout the film (Tudor and Meehan 2013). Though her status as a well-known character from the original series means she dodges the fate of Kirk and Spock's dead mothers (Jennifer Morrison and Winona Ryder), like these two women, her role is primarily concerned with ensuring these male characters remain at the narrative centre of *Star Trek*.

As this example suggests, uniting Paramount's strategic incorporation of fandom and its so-called 'go young and prosper' strategy was what Suzanne Scott describes as the industry's broader 'embrace of the fanboy as a power demographic' (Scott 2019: 51). Drawing on well-worn action tropes and relegating the film's primary female character to the role of sex object, the trailer closed the gap between fans and non-fans by claiming 'this is not your father's *Star Trek*' in order to 'recuperate the fanboy into hegemonic masculinity' (Scott 2019: 51–2). Given Uhura's status as a groundbreaking character of colour in television history, her troubling distillation in the trailer (and film) further suggests Paramount was primarily invested in 'reinforc[ing] Hollywood's ongoing allegiance to sixteen to thirty-four-year-old straight white, cisgender men as their default target audience' (Scott 2019: 51). Confirming this strategy, an unnamed marketing executive described the studio's approach: 'if you are [a] 30-year-old male, you know this film is coming' (Siegel 2009: 1).

Just as the surprise Austin, Texas premiere enabled Paramount to reimagine the assembled audience as a homogeneous group of *Star Trek* fans in service of publicity for the film, the broader promotional campaign's appeal to male fans and non-fans alike worked to decrease the visibility of female *Star Trek* fans in order to serve the industry's economic goals (Scott 2019: 53). As many have noted, women have been particularly significant to the history of *Star Trek* fandom, publishing fan fiction and fanzines, leading letter-writing campaigns and organising the first *Star Trek* conventions (Bacon-Smith 1992; Coppa 2006; Verba 2003; StarTrek.com Staff 2011; Lichtenberg et al. 1975). However, demonstrating the success of Paramount's promotional campaign in discursively reimagining *Star Trek* fandom to align with its ongoing investment in a young, male demographic, when the 'not your father's *Star Trek*' trailer and tagline were released, critics were so busy discussing its apparent affront to *Star Trek*'s voracious fan base and debating if, how, or how much the reboot would, in fact, depart from the original series and films, that few stopped to question if *Star Trek* ever *belonged* to 'your father' in the first place.

CONCLUSION

When *Star Trek* was released on 8 May 2009, it became the top-grossing film in the franchise's history, suggesting that Paramount's strategies in promoting *Star Trek* to non-fans were economically successful, however problematic. While, as this chapter argues, Paramount has long worked to reimagine *Star Trek*'s fan base in ways that centred its utility to the studio's economic bottom line and promoted the franchise to non-fans, the 2009 reboot captures a key moment in this history, where the line between fan and non-fan was growing increasingly blurry. In rebooting *Star Trek*, Paramount further eroded these distinctions by selling the film as a blockbuster for general audiences. But rather than disavow fans altogether, the film's promotion worked to discursively reimagine fandom as a seemingly more accessible and mainstream mode of media consumption. What these discourses actually produced, however, was a considerably narrower vision of *Star Trek* fandom; one that highlighted those practices (the circulation of hype and buzz) and people (young men) that aligned with the studio's economic goals.

Over a decade later, the future of the *Star Trek* film franchise is uncertain, having been outpaced by similarly strategic attempts to reboot popular stories and reimagine fandom, like Abrams' 2015 *Star Wars: Force Awakens* and Marvel's Cinematic Universe (which Paramount also helped to launch in 2008) (Mendelson 2019). However, as these examples demonstrate, the connection between rebooting franchises and reimagining fandom as a mode of mainstream media consumption that benefits the industry has only deepened, and extends well beyond this single case study. More recently, *Star Trek* has been revived in the form of two television spin-offs, *Star Trek: Discovery* (2017–) and *Star Trek: Picard* (2020–), a strategy to draw subscribers to CBS's new streaming service (Johnson 2018). These shows provide very different entry points into the franchise than those offered by the 2009 reboot. But they are also a reminder that rebooting *Star Trek* – and reimagining fandom in the process – continues to be integral to industrial strategies designed to ensure that the franchise lives long and prospers.

NOTES

1. Both Tim League and Harry Knowles have been under increased scrutiny in recent years, with Knowles stepping away from *AICN* in light of allegations of sexual harassment and League facing criticism for his failure to act on these and other allegations of harassment and assault levelled against his employees and close associates (Abramovitch 2017).
2. Like *Khan*, the *Star Trek* reboot places a heavy emphasis on the relationship between Kirk and Spock. The connection between *Khan* and the rebooted franchise was further established in the sequel, *Star Trek: Into Darkness* (Abrams, 2013), which featured *Wrath of Khan*'s titular villain, Khan Noonien Singh (Ricardo Montalbán/Benedict Cumberbatch).

REFERENCES

Abaius, Cole (2009), 'Review: Star Trek', *Film School Rejects*, 7 April 2009, <https://web.archive.org/web/20090413020218/http://www.filmschoolrejects.com/reviews/review-star-trek.php>.

Abramovitch, Seth (2017), 'Alamo Drafthouse in Crisis: Allegations of Sexual Assault and Harassment Mount', *Hollywood Reporter*, 26 September, <https://www.hollywoodreporter.com/news/alamo-drafthouse-crisis-allegations-sexual-assault-harassment-mount-1043207>.

Admin (2009), 'Leonard Nimoy beamed into the South Lamar Alamo', *Alamo Drafthouse*, 7 April, <https://drafthouse.com/news/leonard-nimoy-beamed-into-the-south-lamar-alamo>.

Ang, Ien (1991), *Desperately Seeking the Audience*, New York: Routledge.

Bacon-Smith, Camille (1992), *Enterprising Women*, Philadelphia, PA: University of Pennsylvania Press.

Balio, Tino (2013), *Hollywood in the New Millennium*, London: Palgrave Macmillan on behalf of the British Film Institute.

Beerman, Frank (1972), '*Star Trek*: Conclave in NY Looms as Mix of Campy Set and Sci-Fi Buffs', *Variety*, 19 January, 1, 69.

Brodesser, Claude and Andrew Hampp (2009), 'Tale of Two Flicks' Marketing Tactics', *Advertising Age*, 20 April, 4.

Campbell, Richard, Christopher R. Martin and Bettina Fabos (2013), *Media & Culture: An Introduction to Mass Communication*, 8th edn, Boston, MA: Bedford/St. Martin's.

Clark, Greg (2009), 'Star Trek: The Wrath of a Review!', *CHUD*, 7 April, <https://web.archive.org/web/20090410052544/http://chud.com/articles/articles/18883/1/STAR-TREK-THE-WRATH-OF-A-REVIEW/Page1.html>.

Coppa, Francesca (2006), 'A Brief History of Media Fandom', in Karen Hellekson and Kristina Busse (eds), *Fan Fiction and Fan Communities in the Age of the Internet*, Jefferson, NC: McFarland, pp. 41–59.

Couldry, Nick (2000), *The Place of Media Power: Pilgrims and Witnesses of the Media Age*, New York: Routledge.

Daly, Steve (2009), 'We're All Trekkies Now', *Newsweek*, 4 May, 52–5.

Gray, Jonathan (2003), 'New Audiences, New Textualities: Anti-fans and Non-fans', *International Journal of Cultural Studies*, 6: 1, 64–81.

Gray, Jonathan (2010), *Show Sold Separately: Promos, Spoilers, and Other Media Paratexts*, New York: New York University Press.

Gray, Jonathan, Cornel Sandvoss and C. Lee Harrington (eds) (2017), *Fandom: Identities and Communities in a Mediated World*, 2nd edn, New York: New York University Press.

Grossman, Lev (2005), 'The Geek Shall Inherit the Earth', *Time*, 25 September, <http://content.time.com/time/magazine/article/0,9171,1109317,00.html>

Hadas, Leora (2017), 'A New Vision: J.J. Abrams, *Star Trek*, and Promotional Authorship', *Cinema Journal*, 56: 2, 44–66.
Hanna, Erin (2019), *Only at Comic-Con: Hollywood, Fans, and the Limits of Exclusivity*, New Brunswick, NJ: Rutgers University Press.
headgeek (2009a), 'TREK Reviews Pour in from the Drafthouse Screening!', *Ain't it Cool News*, 7 April, <http://legacy.aintitcool.com/node/40679>.
headgeek (2009b), 'Want to See a Stunning Print of STAR TREK II: THE WRATH OF KHAN Plus 10 Exclusive Minutes of the New STAR TREK Here in Austin?', *Ain't it Cool News*, 1 April, <http://legacy.aintitcool.com/node/40613>.
Hills, Matt (2012), '*Torchwood*'s Trans-transmedia: Media Tie-ins and Brand "Fanagement"', *Participations: Journal of Audience & Reception Studies*, 9: 2, 409–28.
Jenkins, Henry (1992), *Textual Poachers: Television Fans & Participatory Culture*, New York: Routledge.
Jenkins, Henry (2006), *Convergence Culture: Where Old and New Media Collide*, New York: New York University Press.
Johnson, Derek (2013), 'Participation is Magic: Collaboration, Authorial Legitimacy, and the Audience Function', in Jonathan Gray and Derek Johnson (eds), *A Companion to Media Authorship*, Malden, MA: John Wiley & Sons, pp. 135–57.
Johnson, Derek (2018), 'CBS All Access: To Boldly Franchise Where No One Has Subscribed Before', in Derek Johnson (ed.), *From Networks to Netflix: A Guide to Changing Channels*, New York: Routledge, pp. 395–407.
Lichtenberg, Jacqueline, Sondra Marshak and Joan Winston (1975), *Star Trek Lives!*, London: Corgi.
Marsano, William (1972), 'Grokking Mr. Spock Or May You Never Find a Tribble in Your Chicken Soup', *TV Guide*, 25 March, 16–19.
Masters, Kim (2009), 'Is Star Trek Now Cool?', *The Daily Beast*, 7 May 2009, <https://www.thedailybeast.com/articles/2009/05/07/the-worlds-smartest-trekkie>.
Meehan, Eileen (2000), 'Leisure or Labor?: Fan Ethnography and Political Economy', in Ingunn Hagen and Janet Wasko (eds), *Consuming Audiences? Production and Reception in Media Research*, Cresskill, NJ: Hampton Press, pp. 71–92.
Mendelson, Scott (2019), 'Paramount Has Canceled "Star Trek 4", And Disney's "Star Wars" Is To Blame', *Forbes*, 10 January, <https://www.forbes.com/sites/scottmendelson/2019/01/10/paramount-has-canceled-star-trek-4-and-disneys-star-wars-is-to-blame/>.
MightyBest (2009a), 'Star Trek World Premiere with Leonard Nimoy Pt 1', *YouTube*, 7 April, <https://www.youtube.com/watch?v=9LLFMmNquNE&t=69s>.
MightyBest (2009b), 'Star Trek World Premiere with Leonard Nimoy Pt 2', *YouTube*, 7 April, <https://www.youtube.com/watch?v=ZddhJTYOAWw>.
Miller, Neil (2009), 'Star Trek Makes Surprise World Premiere in Austin! Read Our First Review', *Film School Rejects*, 7 April, <https://filmschoolrejects.com/star-trek-makes-surprise-world-premiere-in-austin-read-our-first-review/>
Nashawaty, Chris (2009), '"Star Trek": What People Are Saying after the Surprise Screening', *Entertainment Weekly*, 7 April 2009, <https://ew.com/article/2009/04/07/star-treks-snea/>.
Perkins, Rodney (2009), 'Initial Thoughts on J.J. Abrams' STAR TREK', *Twitch Film*, 6 April, <https://web.archive.org/web/20090410053521/http://twitchfilm.net/site/view/abrams-star-trek-thoughts/>.
Proctor, William (2012), 'Regeneration and Rebirth: Anatomy of the Franchise Reboot', *Scope: An Online Journal of Film and Television Studies*, 22 (February), 1–19.
Quail, Christine (2011), 'Nerds, Geeks, and the Hip/Square Dialectic in Contemporary Television', *Television & New Media*, 12: 5, 460–82.

Quint (2009), 'Quint Has Seen JJ Abrams' STAR TREK', *Ain't it Cool News*, 7 April, <http://legacy.aintitcool.com/node/40675>.

'Radio-Television: "Star Trek" Saved from Death Row by Write-In Vote' (1968), *Variety*, 1 February, 32.

Schatz, Thomas (1993), 'The New Hollywood', in Jim Collins, Hilary Radner and Ava Preacher Collins (eds), *Film Theory Goes to the Movies*, New York: Routledge, pp. 8–36.

Schatz, Tom (2008), 'The Studio System and Conglomerate Hollywood', in Paul McDonald and Janet Wasko (eds), *The Contemporary Hollywood Film Industry*, Malden, MA: Blackwell Publishing, pp. 13–42.

Sciretta, Peter (2009), 'Early Twitter Buzz: Star Trek Has Secret Premiere in Austin', *SlashFilm*, 6 April, <https://www.slashfilm.com/early-twitter-buzz-star-trek-has-secret-premiere-in-austin-texas/>.

Scott, Suzanne (2019), *Fake Geek Girls: Fandom, Gender, and the Convergence Culture Industry*, New York: New York University Press.

ScreenSlam (2015) 'Star Trek: J.J. Abrams Offical Interview', *YouTube*, 27 February, <https://www.youtube.com/watch?v=PZ441RT_dNQ>.

Shuit, Doug (1972), 'Living on Reruns: Star Trek: Still Luring a Galaxy of Aficionados', *Los Angeles Times*, 27 June, A1, 3.

Siegel, Tatiana (2009), '"Trek" Plan: Go Young and Prosper', *Variety*, 6 April, 1, 9.

StarTrek.com Staff (2011), 'Bjo Trimble: The Woman who Saved Star Trek', *Star Trek*, 31 August, <http://www.startrek.com/article/bjo-trimble-the-woman-who-saved-star-trek-part-1>.

Thompson, Bob (2008), 'What Simon Says: From Spaced to Space, Pegg Is Ready for the Otherworldly', *National Post*, 25 September, AL1

Tompkins, Joe (2014), '"Re-imagining" the Canon: Examining the Discourse of Contemporary Horror Film Reboots', *Review of Film & Television Studies*, 12: 4, 380–99.

TrekMovie.Com Staff (2009), 'MTV Shows Behind-the-Scenes Star Trek "Featurette" [UPDATED: w/ Kelvin Bridge Shot?]', 21 February, <https://trekmovie.com/2009/02/21/mtv-shows-more-behind-the-scenes-star-trek-clips/>.

Tudor, Deborah and Eileen Meehan (2013), 'Demoting Women on the Screen and in the Board Room', *Cinema Journal*, 53: 1, 130–6.

Tulloch, John and Henry Jenkins (1995), *Science Fiction Audiences: Watching Doctor Who and Star Trek*, New York: Routledge.

Tyler, Josh (2009), 'Early Review of JJ Abrams' Star Trek!', *CinemaBlend*, 7 April, <https://www.cinemablend.com/new/Early-Review-JJ-Abrams-Star-Trek-12650.html>.

Verba, Joan Marie (2003), *Boldly Writing: A Trek Fan and Fanfiction History, 1967–1987*, 2nd edn, Minnetonka, MN: FTL Publications.

Verevis, Constantine (2017), 'Remakes, Sequels, Prequels', in Thomas Leitch (ed.), *The Oxford Handbook of Adaptation Studies*, New York: Oxford University Press, pp. 267–84.

Weber, Bruce (2016), 'The East Village May Change, but the Strudel at Moische's Stays the Same', *New York Times*, 16 March, <https://www.nytimes.com/2016/03/20/nyregion/the-east-village-may-change-but-the-strudel-at-moishes-stays-the-same.html>.

Winston, Joan (1979), *The Making of the Trek Conventions*, Chicago, IL: Playboy Press.

Woerner, Meredith (2009), 'Star Trek Sneak Explodes in Giant Trekgasm', *io9*, 7 April, <https://io9.gizmodo.com/star-trek-sneak-explodes-in-giant-trekgasm-5202449>.

CHAPTER 3

The Many Reboots of the Batman

Eileen R. Meehan

Batman has long been an oddity in the DC universe as the lone superhero without super powers. Instead, he uses his status as a millionaire and his ability to invent gadgets to give him an edge over villains like the Joker or Catwoman. Fortunately for Batman, his highly eccentric foes are mostly human. Originally owned by National Periodicals, Batman debuted in *Detective Comics* #27 in 1939, which led to the *Batman* line of comic books.

Subsequently, Batman was redeployed through different media by various corporate owners to achieve goals typical of capitalist enterprises: generate profits through multiple revenue streams; decrease production costs; and build consumer loyalty to ensure continued revenues. To provide some context for Batman, I first sketch the emergence of the comic book industry and describe Batman's corporate roots in DC Comics. Next, I discuss the character's initial deployment in two film serials during the 1940s and his subsequent reboot for the television series *Batman* (1966–8). I end by focusing on Batman's return to film between 1989 and 1997 and between 2005 and 2012 within the context of media franchises and transindustrial media conglomeration. By focusing on the ways that different corporate structures and corporate relationships shaped Batman and his reboots, we explore the political economy of Batman as a cultural icon and a revenue generator. This illuminates both the routines of corporate creativity and the particular contributions of media artists and professionals working to generate yet another version of Batman that can be promoted as completely new and totally familiar.

BATMAN AND COMIC BOOKS

In the late 1920s and early 1930s, various small firms produced experimental comic books. Perhaps the earliest was Dell Publishing's *The Funnies* (1929): a collection of original comic strips printed in tabloid format and distributed by newspapers (Daniels 1971). In 1933, Eastern Colored Printing repackaged newspaper strips as the comic book *Funnies on Parade*, which was marketed to companies like Kinney Shoes and Proctor & Gamble as an inexpensive reward for consumer loyalty (Daniels 1971). Subsequently, Eastern Color Printing and other publishers experimented with both the comic book format and direct sales to readers through drugstores and newspaper stands (Goulart 1986).

Like most emerging media industries in the early twentieth century, the comic book industry depended on low wages, low budgets and low production costs. That encouraged numerous companies to enter the market. Approximately sixty firms operated between the late 1930s and 1954, publishing comics in genres that ranged from funny animals like Mickey Mouse to superheroes like Superman. Much of the industry's creative process was rooted in imitation and versioning: a successful character for one comic brand inspired artists employed there or by the brand's competitors to generate similar characters and storylines. This type of creative production undergirds our media industries: take the tried-and-true, give it a twist and generate a product that seems totally new yet entirely familiar (Meehan 2007).

Superman's commercial success motivated his owner, National Periodicals/DC Comics, to generate a slew of characters similar to him but with creative twists that made each character different. The first derivative hero was Batman, drawn by Bob Kane and scripted by Bill Finger. While Superman 'passed' as Clark Kent and worked as a reporter for the *Daily Planet* newspaper, he was actually an extraterrestrial with 'powers and abilities far beyond those of mortal men' (*Adventures of Superman*, 1952–8) including extraordinary strength, flight and X-ray vision. In contrast, Bruce Wayne was an ordinary but very wealthy human who funded his own research to produce technologies that allowed him to pass as a superhero. Batman was an alter ego for the real Bruce Wayne just as Clark Kent was the alter ego for the real Superman. Other creative twists on the Superman model generated a plethora of characters including The Flash, Hawkman, Green Lantern, etc. Notable among them is Wonder Woman, the only superhero for whom DC's creative twists involved gender.

Also notable were the limitations on corporate earnings during the Golden Age. The relevant corporations were small, competitive and focused on a single industry. Primary revenues were earned from comic book sales to an audience comprised mostly of children and teenagers. For Batman, secondary revenues from licensing agreements were limited to small companies operating in a single industry, such as the Marx Company which manufactured children's toys that included an inexpensive Batman figure and Batmobile, both cast in lead. The Hollywood film studios also engaged in licensing.

LICENSING BATMAN: THE COLUMBIA SERIALS

In the 1940s, Columbia Pictures licensed Batman from DC Comics for two film serials: *The Batman* (1943) and *Batman and Robin* (1949). Serials were shown prior to the main feature along with cartoons, newsreels, coming attractions and a 'B' movie. That was the standard practice for movie theatres owned by Hollywood's major studios. But Columbia owned no theatres, which made serials a potential source of income. By licensing Batman from DC, Columbia had access to an IP with name recognition, making the serials more likely to be included in a major studio's programme and perhaps attracting some ticket buyers.

In *The Batman*, our hero and Robin struggled to defeat Dr Tito Daka, a Japanese spy who was using traitorous Americans to sabotage the national war effort. Like much commercial media produced during World War II, *The Batman* used racist language and Japanese stereotypes. The serial had fifteen chapters: fourteen ended with Batman and Robin in mortal danger, and in the fifteenth the dynamic duo defeated Dr Daka and his minions.

Columbia followed that serial with *Batman and Robin*, which introduced the villainous Wizard. The character's costume was noteworthy (Maz 2018): a black cowl covered his head, completely masking his face and throat. Black gloves hid his hands while a voluminous black cloak hid the rest of his body. The Wizard controlled a device that disrupted the normal functioning of automobiles and trains, thus drawing the Dynamic Duo into action and repeatedly exposing them to danger. Unsurprisingly, our heroes brought the Wizard to justice and unmasked him in the fifteenth chapter.

In the 1950s, many of these old films, cartoons and serials were recycled through programmes on local television stations (Hollis 2001). In the 1960s, the emergence of new media technologies and new cultural sensibilities brought some old media products back into circulation. For Batman, the key events were Columbia's redeployment of its *Batman and Robin* serial in 1965 to movie theatres and ABC's airing of the *Batman* series produced by William Dozier and 20th Century-Fox in 1966.

COLUMBIA'S *BATMAN AND ROBIN*: NEW REVENUES FROM OLD PRODUCTS

In 1965, Columbia Pictures capitalised on the pop art movement and its camp aesthetic by re-releasing the *Batman and Robin* serial (Rayburn 2014). All fifteen chapters were screened as a single film and the event was packaged as 'Columbia Pictures Presents: An Evening with Batman and Robin'. The lobby advertisement made three key claims:

THE GREATEST SERIAL EVER FILMED ... NOW THE ENTERTAINMENT OF THE YEAR!

Made in '43 ... Discovered in '65!

TWO HIGH-CAMP FOLK HEROES IN A MARATHON OF FIST-FIGHTS, ZOMBIES & RAVENOUS ALLIGATORS!
(Time Magazine)

The first claim plays on *The Greatest Story Ever Told*, United Artists' solemn biography of Jesus Christ. In tandem with the second claim, the ad signals that the screening targets a contemporary in-crowd ready to watch a genuinely bad film from an ironic distance. The quote from *Time*'s review further positions the audience to 'read' the film from a camp perspective and thereby savour the serial's low production values, poor plotting and over-acting.

With the advent of new technologies in the 1980s, Columbia released *The Batman* as well as *Batman and Robin* on VHS tape. It licensed both serials to cable channels including Time Warner's Comedy Channel (1989) and American Movie Classics (early 1990s). To capitalise on the premiere of Time Warner's *Batman Begins* (Nolan, 2005), Columbia repackaged the Bat-serials on DVD and the Turner Broadcasting System featured them on its Turner Classic Movies cable channel. Currently, *Batman and Robin* is also available on YouTube.

In retrospect, Batman's debut in DC Comics and subsequent licensing to Columbia for two cheap movie serials hardly seems the 'stuff' upon which multimedia empires are built. However, over the decades, the cultural impact of the camp and pop sensibilities – plus political and economic changes in the television industry – would enable Batman's corporate owners to transform him into a trans-industrial media franchise. That process began with the *Batman* television programme: DC comics licensed the television rights to ABC, which made a deal with William Dozier's Greenway Productions to design and oversee the programme's production at 20th Century-Fox Television's production facility. As a result of this deal, 20th Century-Fox Television owned *Batman*'s copyright. When Rupert Murdoch took over 20th Century-Fox, *Batman* was among the IPs that he acquired.

BATMAN: TELEVISION'S CAMP CRUSADER

Dozier fully embraced the camp aesthetic of pop art including the use of irony, bright colours, media icons and comic book conventions (Lichtenstein 1963). Pop art was fun, accessible, colourful and often ironic – as was Dozier's *Batman* (1966–8). Indeed, *Batman*'s camp aesthetic differentiated it from every other programme on network television including those that earned high scores in the Nielsen ratings, like *The Beverly Hillbillies* (CBS, 1962–71) or *The Red Skeleton Show* (NBC 1951–3, 1970–1; CBS 1953–70). Given that standard network practice was to stick to genres and formats that earned high ratings, we have to ask: why did ABC take such a risk?

One answer can be found in the document published by the House of Representatives' Special Subcommittee on Investigations (House of Representatives 1963) reporting its in-depth investigation of the broadcast ratings companies. Focusing on both measurement practices and business tactics, the Subcommittee found considerable evidence of fraud across the television ratings industry. In particular, it found that the A. C. Nielsen Company had achieved a monopoly over network broadcast ratings through a combination of anti-competitive business practices and false claims regarding its sample and measurement methods (House of Representatives 1963). The hearings also revealed that Nielsen's television ratings were still based on radio households recruited between 1938 and 1948. When households in the sample notified Nielsen that they had bought television sets, Nielsen installed meters on those sets and used the results to rate television programmes. That radio-based sample explained the television networks' preferences for the genres, character-types and stars from a bygone era (Meehan 1983).

The Special Subcommittee's revelation generated significant pressure for Nielsen to update the sample. That, in turn, encouraged networks to experiment with genres, themes and performers who might appeal to a new Nielsen sample – one projected to be younger, more urban and into contemporary styles (Meehan 1983, 1991, 2007, 2018). Because of the hearings' disclosures, all three networks knew that Nielsen would begin replacing its old households and that the new sample would be fully in place by 1971. Attracting that new sample required changes in programme genres, themes and casting (Meehan 1983, 1991, 2018). All three networks purged their schedules of the old reliable programmes and experimented with programmes that departed from the old norms. In retrospect, *Batman* fits that bill.

In terms of visual style, acting and scheduling, Dozier's *Batman* was a major departure from 'television as usual'. *Batman* mixed garish colours, awkward dialogue, overacting, melodrama, irony, artifice and parody. In this way, Dozier embraced the camp aesthetic theorised by Susan Sontag (1966) and appropriated by Lichtenstein (1963). Pop art was fun, colourful, accessible and often ironic – in a word, it was camp.

Batman's camp aesthetic was most visible in its villains (Newmeyer 2018). Its guest stars used an over the top style of acting that relied on odd speech patterns, notable physical traits and costuming. As the Penguin, for instance, Burgess Meredith adopted a distinctive waddle and punctuated his lines with honking sounds. Dressed in a black tuxedo accessorised by white gloves, a purple tie and a top hat, the Penguin clenched a cigarette holder in his teeth so that his cigarette was at a right angle to his forehead in a manner reminiscent of US President Franklin Roosevelt.

While Meredith's Penguin had clearly moved beyond the realm of television's 'normal bad guys', he seemed subdued in comparison to Cesar Romero's Joker. That character's pasty white face make-up exaggerated Romero's high forehead. Sweeping up from his forehead was a mass of greenish hair styled in a marcel wave. His eyebrows were boldly arched and painted a reddish-brown, providing some contrast to the bright red colour of an exaggerated smile painted around his mouth and extending up his cheeks. His costume was notable: red tuxedo, magenta gloves, floppy black tie and green shirt. On screen, Romero cavorted around the set with a manic energy that suggested some form of mental instability.

The costume and make-up of both Julie Newmar's and Eartha Kitt's Catwoman reflected the 'sexy bad girl' stereotype of the period. Both wore tight, black bodysuits, accessorised with a shiny gold belt and a set of pointy cat ears. They slinked past the camera, exuding a camp sexiness that Batman struggled to resist. Each Catwoman spoke with a low, sexy voice and rolled her 'r's, especially when her plan was working 'purrrrrrrrfectly'.

Adam West and Burt Ward took an ironic and emphatically restrained approach to portraying Batman/Bruce Wayne and Robin/Dick Grayson, respectively: earnest, serious, relatively humorous and dedicated to their work. Bruce Wayne and Dick Grayson dressed as ordinary middle-class European Americans although, as a millionaire, Bruce Wayne donned a tuxedo for high-society events. Batman/Wayne spoke in well-modulated tones; his voice was uninflected and his statements were quite matter-of-fact. Delivered with a straight face, his lines were often comic, as in his explanation of how he detected the presence of a criminal: 'It's obvious. Only a criminal would disguise himself as a licensed, bonded guard yet callously park in front of a fire hydrant'. Or how he faced a deadly threat: 'It's sometimes difficult to think clearly when you're strapped to a printing press' (Armstrong 2015).

In contrast, Robin displayed youthful enthusiasm, reacting with dramatic exclamations: 'Holy hoodwink, Batman!', 'Holy hieroglyphics, Batman!' and 'Holy, uncanny photographic mental processes, Batman!' (GitHub, Inc. n.d.).

Further, ABC's scheduling of *Batman* departed from network norms in its first and second seasons. Although each episode was filmed as an hour-long programme, ABC broadcast *Batman* in half-hour segments on Wednesday and Thursday. Wednesday's instalment ended with a cliffhanger as Dozier's voiceover admonished viewers to 'Tune in tomorrow – same Bat-time, same Bat-channel!' On Thursday, the duo foiled the villain's evil plan and Dozier's admonition was repeated. Because of the scheduling, Nielsen ratings measured each half-hour segment separately, which might have been risky given that viewers could only watch *Batman* when it was broadcast. However, ABC had used the split format successfully in 1964 with *Peyton Place*, which could be watched as a serious soap opera or ironically as an exercise in bad taste – as camp. Initially, this dual scheduling worked for *Batman*. But, by the end of the second season, *Batman*'s ratings were declining and ABC cut back to one thirty-minute programme weekly. Yet low ratings persisted and ABC cancelled *Batman* altogether.

Unfortunately for Dozier and 20th Century-Fox Television, *Batman* didn't have enough episodes for off-network syndication in local markets. Local syndication required five to seven years of episodes in order to run the programme daily. Stations with network affiliations scheduled these reruns after school and before the evening news. Unaffiliated stations had more slots to fill and preferred series like the highly rated and long-running *M*A*S*H* (1972–83) or short-lived programmes like *Star Trek* (1966–9) that had legions of highly vocal and organised fans who watched religiously. *Batman* had neither enough episodes, nor stellar ratings, nor legions of devoted fans. The programme seemed doomed to obscurity.

However, a combination of new technologies and small companies brought *Batman* back to the small screen. Here I focus on two examples: United American Video Company's *Holy Batmania: Special Collector Bat Video* (1989) and Weigel Broadcasting Company's MeTV service which distributed *Batman* using various technologies.

HOLY BATMANIA, BATMAN!

In 1984, the United American Video Company (UAV) was incorporated in Tennessee, then moved to North Carolina and subsequently to South Carolina where it currently operates as the Sterling Entertainment Group. (Given my historical focus on the Dozier-20th Century Fox *Batman*, I will refer to the company as UAV.) In 1975, video cassettes and recorders went on sale to the general public. By 1984, home video recorders were ubiquitous and UAV began copying old media products no longer protected by copyright (Goldstein 1992). These 'new' tapes were priced to encourage impulse buying and sold by Walmart.

Holy Batmania's cover art included a picture of Dozier's Dynamic Duo with a cityscape behind them. Above them, a Bat-signal projected the video's title into the sky. According to the packaging, the tape included 'Coming attractions, Promos, Home videos of all original cast members' as well as 'THE JOKER, THE CAT WOMAN [sic], PENGUIN, RIDDLER, AND SURPRISE GUESTS'.

The cover's bottom right-hand corner had a headshot of *The Green Hornet*'s costumed stars, another Dozier/Paramount collaboration that aired after *Batman* during the 1966–7 season. This was pitched as 'GREEN HORNET footage with BRUCE LEE', capitalising on Lee's posthumous fame as a martial artist and actor. The back panel included images of Batman, Robin and the Bat-signal, a hyperbolic description of the tape's contents and the tape's running time: 37 minutes. UAV later repackaged *Holy Batmania* as a DVD. *Holy Batmania* is now available on YouTube.

Clearly, *Holy Batmania* was an attempt to capitalise on Warner Bros.' release of the expensive and well-publicised *Batman* (Burton, 1989). That film was designed as a blockbuster with a celebrated director (Tim Burton) and major Hollywood stars (Michael Keaton, Kim Basinger and Jack Nicholson). The cultural distance between Burton's noir-inflected film and the unabashedly opportunistic *Holy Batmania* could not be greater.

BATMAN AND NEW TV TECHNOLOGIES

Chicago's Weigel Broadcasting Company (WBC) recycled *Batman* using four technologies: ultra-high frequency television (UHF), low power television, cable television and digital multicast television. In 1964, the company was founded by John J. Weigel, a Chicago radio personality, after Congress mandated that all television sets receive both VHF and UHF broadcasts ('About Us' n.d.). Weigel obtained the licence for UHF channel 26 and began broadcasting as WCIU (McCann 2002). A year later, financial difficulties forced Weigel to sell WCIU to Howard Shapiro, a television retailer and former WCIU advertiser. Under Shapiro, WCIU targeted local audiences with inexpensive programmes such as telenovelas from the Spanish International Network; live coverage of the trading floor at the Chicago Board of Trade; and local programmes like *Kiddie A Go Go* with young children dancing to rock music.

With the advent of low-power broadcasting, WBC launched MeTV as a network providing programming to eighteen television stations across seven states (Feder 2012; 'National Networks' n.d.). WBC next distributed MeTV using cable systems and, by 2010, had expanded MeTV into a digital multicast network. Promoted as 'Memorable Television', MeTV specialised in programmes from the 1950s to the 1980s mixing shows with long syndication histories like *I Love Lucy* (1951–7) and *Hogan's Heroes* (1965–71) with inexpensive, short-lived programmes that traditional syndicators avoided, like *Batman* (1966–8).

WBC licensed programming mainly from CBS and 20th Century Television (owned, respectively, by National Amusements and the Walt Disney Company) and packaged its multicast programming into four brands: MeTV (such as *Batman*), Heroes & Icons (all of the *Star Trek* series), Decades (*The Best of the Ed Sullivan Show*) and Start TV, which targeted women (*Dr. Quinn, Medicine Woman*). Brands were promoted using various themes including MeTV's 'Super Sci-Fi Saturday Night'.

That line-up featured *Batman*, *Star Trek*, *Wonder Woman* (1975–9) and *Battlestar Galactica* (1978–9) plus WCIU's own *Svengoolie*, a 'creature feature' programme running old horror and science fiction movies. Presumably, these cultural artefacts had nostalgic value for MeTV's target audience: baby boomers (Lowry 2012).

The 'Super Sci-Fi Saturday Night' promotional campaign featured Burt Ward, *Batman*'s Robin, in two advertisements. The first referenced *Batman*'s use of recurring shots, such as our heroes using the Bat-rope to climb a high-rise building. In the ad, Ward replicates the sequence but then stands up, revealing the joke: the 'building' is really a floor. Quick clips from *Batman* were then intercut with Ward's pitch for the show.

The second version intercut clips from the Super Sci-Fi programmes with Ward providing Robinesque exclamations:

> 'Holy invisible airplane, Batman!' – *Wonder Woman*
> 'Holy rubber chicken, Batman!' – *Svengoolie*
> 'Holy caped crusaders, Batman!' – *Batman*
> 'Holy Vulcan ears, Batman!' – *Star Trek*
> 'Holy Cylons, Batman!' – *Battlestar Galactica*
> 'Holy Super Sci-Fi Saturday Night, Batman!'

In this way, the ad directly referenced *Batman*'s camp aesthetic. Juxtaposing Ward-as-senior-citizen with the exclamations should resonate with baby boomers (Lowry 2012).

With Disney's acquisition of 20th Century-Fox in 2019, *Batman* and Burt Ward's ads became Disney properties. While Disney is well known for fully exploiting its IPs (Wasko 2001), it seems unlikely that a bevy of camp crusaders will be deployed in Disney's theme parks and attractions. However, the logic of transindustrial media conglomerates might facilitate that just as the logic of copyright law made 20th Century-Fox the owner of Dozier's *Batman*.

'HOLY MASSIVE MEDIA CONGLOMERATE, BATMAN!'

Prior to 1981, legal constraints kept the ownership of television networks and film studios separate but allowed studios to produce programmes for networks, ergo Dozier's use of 20th Century's production facilities for *Batman* (Meehan 2007; Wasko 1994). The Reagan Administration (1981–9) eliminated such legal constraints, launching an era of neoliberal deregulation across the American economy. Deregulation fostered a wave of mergers and acquisitions, producing conglomerates that spanned multiple media industries and multiple continents. By 2017, five companies emerged as global media giants: Comcast, National Amusements, News Corporation, Time Warner and the Walt Disney Corporation. Each had vast capacities to produce, acquire, circulate, repurpose and recirculate their IPs. Historically, several large corporations have owned Batman, and I will sketch each one briefly.

Prior to deregulation, Warner Bros. acquired DC Comics in 1967 as a source of revenues from comic book sales and character licensing (Gritis 1985). Batman and DC's superheroes were routinely licensed to companies generating inexpensive products targeting children, for example Halloween costumes, toy cars and Valentine's cards. In 1972, Kinney Services took over Warner Bros., restructuring it, expanding its media holdings and renaming the combined firms Warner Communications Incorporated (WCI). WCI became Time Warner Incorporated in 1990 after merging with Time Inc. Time Warner was taken over by AT&T in 2018.

Between 1978 and 1983, WCI licensed Superman to International Films Productions (IFP) and Dovemead Limited (DL) for three films starring Christopher Reeve as the Man of Steel. The first, *Superman* (Donner, 1978), was shot on a relatively low budget and was a smash hit. As shown in Table 3.1, profits declined as the series continued, which is typical.

Superman IV (Furie, 1987) had a notably lower budget than previous instalments. Its corporate producers – Golan-Globus Productions, the Cannon Group and the London Cannon Group – were controlled by Menahem Golan and Yoram Globus, who then specialised in lower-budget films like *Enter the*

Table 3.1 Budget and revenues for WCI's *Superman* films.

Title	Budget	Box office worldwide
Superman	$55,000,000	$300, 200,000
Superman II	$54,000,000	$108,185,706
Superman III	$39,000,000	$59, 950, 623
Superman IV	$17,000,000	$11,227,824

Source: 'Box Office History for Superman Movies' (n.d.), *The Numbers*.

Ninja (Golan, 1981) and *The Last American Virgin* (Davidson, 1982). However, *Superman IV* nonetheless lost money and WCI ended the Superman series.

In 1989, WCI launched a Batman film series and hired David Geffen as producer. WCI and Geffen had a long history. In 1975, Geffen joined WCI's management team and co-produced various films. WCI partially funded his Geffen Film Company and also DreamWorks, in which he was a partner. WCI covered all expenses for the Batman films and thus owned their copyrights. Together, Geffen and WCI launched four big-budget Bat-movies: *Batman* (Burton, 1989), *Batman Returns* (Burton, 1992), *Batman Forever* (Schumacher, 1995), and *Batman and Robin* (Schuhmacher, 1997). From 1989 to 1995, the films maintained a serious tone and earned PG-13 ratings from the Motion Picture Association of America.

However, in *Batman and Robin*, director Joel Schumacher and screenwriter Akiva Goldsman lightened the tone à la Dozier's *Batman* (Booker 1999) in order to attract families while still appealing to 'hipster' adults. Lines like 'Holy rusted metal, Batman!' clearly referenced Robin's dialogue in Dozier's *Batman*. Despite its generous budget, *Batman and Robin* had the lowest earnings of the four films ('Box Office History for Batman Movies' n.d.) (see Table 3.2). In response, WCI cancelled pre-production work on the next sequel and plans for a fifth movie.

WCI also used the films to feed its various operations, thereby earning secondary revenues (Meehan 1991). The promotion for *Batman* was particularly intense, involving both licensed and in-house products. The latter included the film's novelisation, the DC comic book version of the film and various Bat-books (such as *Tales of the Dark Knight: Batman's First Fifty Years 1939–1989*). *Batman* also fed WCI's music and cable operations. Warner Brother Records released two albums: Danny Elfman's *Batman: The Original Motion Picture Score* and Prince's *Batdance*. From Prince's album, WCI released a single 'Batdance', which sampled dialogue from the film. The 'Batdance' music video premiered and played in heavy rotation on WCI's MTV cable channel.

WCI also conducted an unprecedented licensing campaign, flooding consumer markets with 214 products including toys, casual clothing, collectibles

Table 3.2 Budget and revenues for WCI's *Batman* films.

Title	Budget	Box office worldwide
Batman	$35,000,000	$411,348,924
Batman Returns	$80,000,000	$226,824,291
Batman Forever	$100,000,000	$336,529,144
Batman and Robin	$125,000,000	$238,317,814

Source: 'Box Office History for Batman Movies' (n.d.), *The Numbers*.

and an adult-sized replica of Batman's costume. Prices ranged from $2 to $576 (Meehan 1991).

Batman also played a role in WCI's merger negotiations with the publishing giant Time Inc. In one scene, photojournalist Vickie Vale and reporter Alexander Knox discussed her coverage of the war in Corto Maltese. That discussion ended with a shot of *Time Magazine*'s cover featuring Vale's photograph. In the second, the Joker examined her photographs of the carnage in his copy of *Time*, which was also identifiable (images Heroes Wiki, n.d.). In 1990, the merger was consummated, making Time Warner the world's largest transindustrial media conglomerate (Fitzgerald 2017).

That achievement put Time Warner under tremendous financial pressure, making it ripe for takeover by AOL in 2000 (Fitzgerald 2017). AOL-Time Warner's combination of new and old media was expected to launch a deluge of profits but, by 2003, AOL-Time Warner was $29 billion in debt and its stock had crashed (Fitzgerald 2017). As a result, AOL-Time Warner sold numerous operations, including AOL.

The new Time Warner Incorporated (TWI) was comprised of Home Box Office, Turner Broadcasting System, Warner Bros. Entertainment and DC Entertainment, which included DC Comics (Fitzgerald 2017). Divisions ran multiple operations across multiple media industries including film production and distribution, cable channels and the CW broadcast network, production and distribution of television programming. While still a transindustrial media conglomerate, TWI's leaner profile reflected an increasing emphasis among major shareholders on financialisation, for example on increasing their share of the company's profits (Fitzgerald 2017).

Between 2005 and 2012, TWI rebooted the *Batman* franchise with three films directed by Christopher Nolan and starring Christian Bale. Packaged as the *Dark Knight* trilogy, these films had neither a tinge of camp nor a sense of humour: their Gotham City was dark and dystopian. Each film was profitable and accompanied by extensive licensing and merchandising deals, which apparently generated 'more than $10 billion in global (retail) sales dollars over the course of time' (Peabody 2011).

The company launched another film series based on DC characters and branded as the DC Extended Universe (DCEU): *Man of Steel* (Snyder, 2013),

Table 3.3 Budget and revenues for TWI's *Batman* films.

Title	Budget	Box office worldwide
Batman Begins	$150,000,000	$359,142,722
The Dark Knight	$185,000,000	$1,001,996,207
The Dark Knight Returns	$100,000,000	$1,084,439,099

Source: 'Box Office History for Batman Movies' (n.d.), *The Numbers*.

Batman v Superman: Dawn of Justice (Snyder, 2016), *Suicide Squad* (Ayer, 2016) and *Justice League* (Snyder, 2017). By moving from a character-specific film series to a DC-branded series, TWI could interconnect its DC IPs while substituting a brand-based fandom for character-specific fandoms. Results were profitable and Time Warner attracted a corporate 'suitor' – AT&T.

AT&T + TWI = TRANS-SECTORAL CONGLOMERATE

In 2018, Batman and TWI were acquired by the telecommunications giant AT&T, which was ranked first among fifty-four telecommunications firms worldwide (Murphy et al. 2019). AT&T's complicated history began with its founding in 1885 as the American Telephone & Telegraph Company (Danielian 1939). From 1877 to 1982, AT&T monopolised telephone service and manufacturing. Through its subsidiary Bell Laboratories, AT&T developed new technologies for corporations, consumers and the US military (Douglas 1985; Takacs 2018). Among those technologies were systems for film projection, high-fidelity sound recordings, radio networking and television transmission. For decades, AT&T's status as *the* telephone monopolist seemed beyond challenge or change. Indeed, that was a comedic trope in the Paramount film *The President's Analyst* (Flicker, 1967) in which The Phone Company's animatronic executives took over the world. Television's *Rowan & Martin's Laugh-In* (1968–73) featured Lily Tomlin as Ernestine the telephone operator 'explaining' AT&T policy: 'We don't care, we don't have to'.

However, in 1974, AT&T attracted the Department of Justice's (DoJ) attention when the company refused to provide telephone service to households owning non-AT&T phones. From 1978 to 1981, the DoJ conducted pre-trial proceedings, culminating in an anti-trust suit in 1982. The suit argued that AT&T's ownership of the national system of telephone interconnection and the regional operating companies (the so-called baby Bells) effectively monopolised the telephone industry. The DoJ won and AT&T spun off its local companies, thus creating seven regional baby Bells. These new companies were limited to local service but could expand into long distance telephony if they could prove that their local markets were competitive. Subsequent mergers among the baby Bells and their entries into long distance telephony sapped AT&T's revenues to the point that AT&T was taken over by one of its progeny: South Western Bell Communications, which renamed itself AT&T.

That new AT&T acquired DirectTV in 2015 with the Federal Communications Commission's approval (Trefis Team 2015). In 2016, AT&T announced its acquisition of Time Warner during the presidential campaigns ('AT&T to Acquire Time Warner' 2016). Both Hillary Clinton and Donald Trump questioned the merger, with Trump focusing on TWI's ownership of CNN. Prior to Trump's election, his senior economic advisor, Peter Navarro, claimed that 'Donald Trump will break up the new media conglomerate oligopolies' (Shabad 2016). After the election, the DoJ's anti-trust division stated that Trump had issued 'no orders, instructions, or directions' regarding the merger (Shepardson 2019). One year later, AT&T completed its acquisition of Time Warner, describing its new corporate structure and synergies thus:

> The new AT&T was comprised by four divisions: mobile, broadband, video, and other communications services to U.S.-based customers and nearly 3.5 million companies . . . (with revenues over) 150 billion . . .
> . . . HBO, Turner and Warner Bros. (with combined) revenues of more than $31 billion . . .
> AT&T International provides mobile services in Mexico . . . plus pay-TV service across 11 countries in South America and the Caribbean (with) revenues (over) $8 billion . . .
> . . . advertising and analytics business provides marketers with (strategies based on data from) . . . AT&T's TV, mobile and broadband services, combined with extensive ad inventory from Turner and AT&T's pay-TV services. ('Annual Report' 2018)

With the acquisition of Time Warner, AT&T now operates in both the telecommunications and entertainment/information sectors of the global economy – making it a trans-sectoral conglomerate. That means AT&T can use Time Warner's entertainment/information products to showcase AT&T products and services. The new AT&T will undoubtedly generate new Bat-films, new lines of Bat-merchandise and perhaps even Bat-phones with Bat ringtones. But will AT&T use its media holdings to advance its political and economic agendas? Perhaps only *Time* will tell.

REFERENCES

'About Us' (n.d.), *Weigel Broadcasting*, <https://www.weigelbroadcasting.com/about/>.
'Annual Report 2018' (2018), *AT&T*, <https://investors.att.com/~/media/Files/A/ATT-IR/financial-reports/annual-reports/2018/complete-2018-annual-report.pdf>.
Armstrong, Tom (2015), 'Adam West's 17 Funniest Quotes as Batman', *Sabotage Times*, <https://sabotagetimes.com/tv-film/adam-wests-17-funniest-quotes-as-batman>.
'AT&T to Acquire Time Warner' (2016), *AT&T*, 22 October, <https://about.att.com/story/att_to_acquire_time_warner.html>.
'AT&T Completes Acquisition of Time Warner Inc.' (2018), *AT&T*, 15 June, <https://about.att.com/story/att_completes_acquisition_of_time_warner_inc.html>.
Booker, Will (1999), 'Batman: One Life, Many Faces', in Deborah Cartmell and Imelda Whelehan (eds), *Adaptations from Text to Screen, from Screen to Text*, London: Routledge, pp. 185–98.
'Box Office History for Batman Movies' (n.d.), *The Numbers*, <https://www.the-numbers.com/movies/franchise/Batman#tab=summary>.

'Box Office History for Superman Movies' (n.d.), *The Numbers*, <https://www.the-numbers.com/movies/franchise/Superman#tab=summary>.

Danielian, N. R. (1939), *A.T.&T.: The Story of Industrial Conquest*, New York: Vanguard Press.

Daniels, Les (1971), *Comix: A History of Comic Books in America*. New York: Bonanza Books.

Douglas, Sarah (1985), 'Technological Innovation and Organizational Change: The Navy's Adoption of Radio, 1899–1919', in Merritt Roe Smith (ed.), *Military Enterprise and Technological Change: Perspectives on the American Experience*, Cambridge, MA: MIT Press, pp. 117–73.

Feder, Robert (2012), 'Howard Shapiro 1926–2012', *Time Out Chicago*, 24 May, <https://www.timeout.com/chicago/tv/howard-shapiro-1926-2012>.

Fitzgerald, Scott (2017), 'Time Warner', in Ben Birkenbine, Janet Wasko and Rodrigo Gomez Garcia (eds), *Global Media Giants*, London: Routledge, pp. 51–71.

GitHub, Inc. (n.d.), 'holy-catchphrase-batman', <https://github.com/empathephant/holy-catchphrase-batman/blob/master/catchphrases.txt>.

Goldstein, Seth (1992), 'Picture This', *Billboard* (home video news section), 28 November, <https://books.google.com/books?id=KRAEAAAAMBAJ&pg=RA1-PA69#v=onepage&q&f=false>.

Goulart, Ron (1986), *Ron Goulart's Great History of Comic Books: The Definitive Illustrated History from the 1890s to the 1980s*, Chicago, IL and New York: Contemporary Books.

Gritis, Phillip S. (1985), 'Turning Superheroes into Super Sales', *New York Times*, 6 January, p. 6.

Heroes Wiki (n.d.), 'Vicki Vale (Burtonverse)', <https://hero.fandom.com/wiki/Vicki_Vale_(Burtonverse)>.

Hollis, Tim (2001), *Hi There Boys and Girls: America's Local Children's TV Programs*, Jackson, MI: University Press of Mississippi.

House of Representatives, United States Congress (1963), 'Hearings: On the Methodology, Accuracy, and Use of Ratings in Broadcastings', Washington, DC: Government Printing Office, <https://babel.hathitrust.org/cgi/pt?id=umn.31951d035053807&view=1up&seq=9>.

Lichtenstein, Roy (1963), *Drowning Girl*, MoMALearning, <https://www.moma.org/learn/moma_learning/lichtenstein-drowning-girl-1963/>.

Lowry, Brian (2012), 'Me-TV Taps into Boomer Base: Classic TV Channel Courts 35-to-64 Demo', *Variety*, 18 July, <https://variety.com/2012/tv/columns/me-tv-taps-into-boomer-base-1118056699/>.

McCann, Tom (2002), 'John J. Weigal, 89', *Chicago Tribune*, 16 December, <https://www.chicagotribune.com/news/ct-xpm-2002-12-16-0212160021-story.html>.

Maz (2018), 'Batman and Robin 1949 Serial Review', <https://thenerdsuncanny.wordpress.com/2018/08/16/batman-and-robin-1949-serial-review/>.

Meehan, Eileen R. (1983), 'Neither Heroes Nor Villains: Towards a Political Economy of the Broadcast Ratings Industry', PhD dissertation. Institute for Communications Research, University of Illinois at Urbana-Champaign.

Meehan, Eileen R. (1991), '"Holy Commodity Fetish, Batman!": The Economics of a Commercial Intertext', in William Uricchio and Roberta E. Pearson (eds), *The Many Lives of Batman: Critical Approaches to a Superhero and His Media*, London: BFI/Routledge, pp. 47–65.

Meehan, Eileen R. (2007), 'Deregulation and Integrated Oligopolies: Television at the Turn of the Century', in Graham Murdock and Janet Wasko (eds), *Media in the Age of Marketization*, Cresskill, NJ: Hampton Press, pp. 11–32.

Meehan, Eileen R. (2018), 'A History of the Commodity Audience', in Aniko Bodroghkozy (ed.), *A Companion to Broadcast History*, Hoboken, NJ: Wiley Blackwell, pp. 349–69.

Murphy, Andrea, Jonathan Ponciano, Sarah Hansen and Halah Touryalai (2019), 'Global 2000: The World's Largest Public Companies', *Forbes*, 15 May, <https://www.forbes.com/global2000/#5e6ffe6b335d>.
'National Networks: MeTV' (n.d.), *Weigel Broadcasting*, <https://www.weigelbroadcasting.com/national/metv>.
Newmeyer, Scott (2018), 'A Visual Guide to All 37 Villains in the Batman TV Series', <http://mentalfloss.com/article/60213/visual-guide-all-37-villains-batman-tv-series>.
Peabody, Amanda (2011), 'Return of the Dark Knight', *License Global*, 1 June, <https://www.licenseglobal.com/return-dark-knight>.
Rayburn, Martin (2014), 'BATMAN's Beginnings on Film', *Warped Factor*, <http://www.warpedfactor.com/2014/11/batmans-beginnings-on-film.html>.
Shabad, Rebecca (2016), 'Where Do Hillary Clinton, Donald Trump Stand on the AT&T-Time Warner Merger?' *CBS News*, 24 October, <https://www.cbsnews.com/news/where-do-hillary-clinton-donald-trump-stand-on-the-at-t-merger/>.
Shepardson, David (2019), 'Democrats Probe Whether White House Interfered with AT&T Time Warner Merger', 7 March, <https://finance.yahoo.com/news/democrats-probe-white-house-interferred-202539080.html>.
Sontag, Susan (1966), 'Notes on Camp', in *Against Interpretation*, New York: Farrer, Strauss, Giroux, pp. 275–92.
Takacs, Stacy (2018), 'Radio, Television, and the Military', in Aniko Brodroghkozy (ed.), *A Companion to the History of American Broadcasting*, Hoboken, NJ: Wiley Blackwell, pp. 257–77.
Trefis Team (2015), 'AT&T Closes DirecTV Acquisition: Reviewing the Concessions and Benefits', *Forbes*, 27 July, <https://www.forbes.com/sites/greatspeculations/2015/07/27/att-closes-directv-acquisition-reviewing-the-concessions-and-benefits/#70dc352352cc>.
Wasko, Janet (1994), *Hollywood in the Information Age*, Austin, TX: University of Texas Press.
Wasko, Janet (2001), *Understanding Disney: The Manufacture of Fantasy*, Malden, MA: Polity Press.

Part II
Structure and Narrative

CHAPTER 4

The Edge of Reality: Replicating *Blade Runner*

Constantine Verevis

> I walk along a thin line darling/
> Dark shadows follow me/
> Here's where life's dream lies disillusioned/
> The edge of reality
>
> 'Edge of Reality' (Giant-Baum-Kaye 1968)

Adapted from Philip K. Dick's novel *Do Androids Dream of Electric Sheep?* (1968), Ridley Scott's *Blade Runner* (1982) was, at the time of its initial theatrical release, a critical and commercial disappointment. In the years that followed, home video formats helped establish *Blade Runner*'s cult following, and by the end of the decade the film's reputation was well enough established for Scott to prepare a tenth anniversary *Director's Cut* (1992) and, subsequently, for its twenty-fifth anniversary, a definitive *Final Cut* (2007). Divested of voiceover and tidy ending, these re-visions added to the mysterious undercurrent of Scott's movie – namely, the question as to whether blade runner Rick Deckard (Harrison Ford) was himself a replicant (a bioengineered human) – and opened the way for a sequel. Co-screenwriter Hampton Fancher reported that a *Blade Runner* sequel had been under consideration from as early as 1986, and while the film generated three sequel novels by K. W. Jeter (beginning with *Blade Runner 2: The Edge of Human*, 1995) and other transmedia tie-ins, the film sequel – *Blade Runner 2049* – did not appear until 2017. Produced by Scott, featuring Ford, directed by Denis Villeneuve and promoted by three short prequel films – *Blade Runner 2022*, *2036* and *2048* – the (near) real-time sequel leaves Deckard's true nature open to debate, to focus instead on 'K' (Ryan Gosling). 'K' is a next-generation blade runner, a NEXUS-9 replicant whose self-awareness and gradually emerging free will provide opportunity to interrogate ideas of artificial consciousness in ways that rework Scott's film and compound the fan speculation regarding Deckard's status as replicant. This chapter looks at *Blade Runner* and its many 'sequels' – the *Blade Runner 2019* 'trilogy' (1982, 1992, 1997), the Jeter trilogy (1995, 1996, 2000), the three prologue sequels and *Blade Runner 2049* – to investigate how these works clarify and extend the problem of human authenticity explored in *Do Androids Dream of Electric Sheep?* More particularly, this chapter shows how *Blade Runner 2049* operates as a 'reboot-sequel', and as such demonstrates how the film retraces its precursor(s) – narratively, stylistically, existentially – at the same time as it *extends* them.

In May 2011, Warner Bros. announced its plans to make both sequels and prequels to Scott's *Blade Runner* (set in November 2019, this total work – the US theatrical release and its revisions – is hereafter referred to as *BR2019*). Overseeing the project for Alcon Entertainment, producers Broderick Johnson and Andrew A. Kosove declared there was no interest in remaking the property, but rather in continuing on with *Blade Runner* as a franchise: 'to be clear . . . we cannot remake *Blade Runner*. As a legal matter, we have not bought the remake rights . . . we can only do prequels or sequels' (quoted in Orange 2011). Premiering some six years later (October 2017), *Blade Runner 2049* (hereafter *BR2049*) was sometimes reviewed in the context of contemporary reboot practice (see, for example, Dry 2017; Tallerico 2017), but was more typically described as a (much belated) sequel. However, any easy distinction between the continuation of a sequel (or series) and the repetition of a remake (or reboot) immediately obscures the fact that the process of continuation – of sequelisation – is always also a process of repetition: of characters and actors, settings and story worlds, plots and scenarios, and (most significantly) titles of properties (Perkins and Verevis 2012: 2). More than this, while the contemporary serial formatting practice known as the 'film reboot' is often distinguished from the remake for the fact that it is (typically) a franchise-specific concept – that is, the remake is singular and the reboot is multiple – *BR2019* here, too, complicates any easy definition, existing (even before the appearance of *BR2049*) as '*a set of multiple film texts* [but, unusually, one] *without cinematic prequels or sequels*' (Hills 2011: 7, emphasis in original). At once a sequel and a remake – a film that simultaneously extends and replays elements of *BR2019* – *BR2049* can be understood as a film that reboots a franchise: that is, a (serialised) property that operates according to the protocols of both organic and (following Mittell 2018) operational seriality.

The first of these terms – organic seriality – accords with the most typical practices and definitions of serial forms: namely, 'an ongoing narrative released in successive parts' (Hayward in Mittell 2018). As Jason Mittell explains, this type of definition points to the two essential components of (organic) seriality – namely, continuity and gaps:

continuity suggests long-form storytelling, repetition and reiteration, consistency and accumulation, historicity and memory, and potentials for transmedia expansion . . . However, 'serial' is not simply a synonym for vast, as the whole must be segmented into installments broken up by gaps, leading to temporal ruptures, narrative anticipation, moments for viewer productivity, opportunities for feedback between producers and consumers, and a structured system for a shared cultural conversation. (2018: 228)

Mittell goes on to note that serial continuity (organic seriality) is typically based around narrative events: 'a text is considered serialised when events accumulate with a degree of consistency' (2018: 231). In the case of *BR2019* this question of 'consistency' is however no simple thing, in part because there is no single, definitive version but (at least) three principal versions (no one of which displaces the others),[1] and the textual engagement with each of these 'cuts' varies not only from one to the other but also over time. Accordingly, *BR2049* picks up narrative events not only after a thirty-year interval (gap) in story time, but also after a real-time feedback loop of thirty-five years during which time fans had interrogated various versions (and different endings) of *BR2019* for what they might reveal about Deckard's status as a replicant, and speculation about his fate upon electing to go rogue and flee with his quarry, Rachael (Sean Young).

At the beginning of *BR2049*, officer 'K' (Ryan Gosling), a NEXUS-9 replicant employed by the Los Angeles Police Department (LAPD) as a blade runner, arrives at a desolate rural farmhouse where he confronts and 'retires' Sapper Morton (Dave Bautista), an earlier model NEXUS-8, taking his serial number-stamped eyeball for the record. As K is leaving the property, he recovers from beneath a gnarled dead tree a military footlocker that contains the bodily remains of a female replicant. Forensic analysis and investigation subsequently reveal that the remains are those of Rachael, the NEXUS-7 replicant who apparently died giving birth to Deckard's child. For fear of the dire consequences of revealing that a replicant was capable of giving birth, K's superior, Lieutenant Joshi (Robyn Wright), moves to destroy the evidence and orders K – who is programmed to obey commands – to find and retire the replicant child. Continuing his investigation back at the farmyard gravesite, K finds a significant date, carved at the base of the tree, that triggers a recurring childhood memory and leads K, and his holographic girlfriend Joi (Ana de Armas), to think that he himself might be the miracle child, a 'real boy' born of woman, rather than manufactured. K's quest to understand if his memories provide evidence of his humanity leads him first to Dr Ana Stelline (Carla Juri), a gifted memory designer, and eventually to Deckard who, missing for the last thirty years, lives in seclusion in a derelict Las Vegas hotel deep in the

Figure 4.1 Deckard emerges from the shadows, *Blade Runner 2049* (2017).

(now) radioactive Mojave desert, surrounded by holographic ghosts of Elvis (and other iconic twentieth-century performers) and haunted by the loss of his beloved Rachael and the absent child whom he gave up years before so as to protect it from detection.

In his first appearance, Deckard emerges from the shadows, grizzled and hostile, his movements led by the double-barrelled pistol he has aimed at K. Deckard provides few answers to K's questions – least of all offering any clues to the (implicit) question of whether he is human or replicant – but Deckard's appearance (a full 100 minutes into the film) nonetheless responds to three decades of (fan) yearning, 'merging the specter of the past with the fears of the future' (Kohn 2017). By contrast, *BR2049* is more forthcoming around the cumulative reasons for the advanced environmental degradation of the Anthropocene, and developments in the mid-twenty-first century manufacture of replicants, providing a capsule summary in its opening text (itself an update to the crawl that opens *BR2019*):[2]

> REPLICANTS
> FOR USE OFF-WORLD. THEIR ENHANCED STRENGTH MADE THEM IDEAL SLAVE LABOR.
> AFTER A SERIES OF VIOLENT REBELLIONS, THEIR MANUFACTURE BECAME PROHIBITED AND TYRELL CORP WENT BACKRUPT.
> THE COLLAPSE OF ECOSYSTEMS IN THE MID 2020s LED TO THE RISE OF INDUSTRIALIST NIANDER WALLACE, WHOSE MASTERY OF SYNTHETIC FARMING AVERTED FAMINE.
> WALLACE ACQUIRED THE REMAINS OF TYRELL CORP AND CREATED A NEW LINE OF REPLICANTS WHO OBEY.

MANY OLDER MODEL REPLICANTS – NEXUS 8s WITH OPEN-ENDED LIFESPANS – SURVIVED. THEY ARE HUNTED DOWN AND RETIRED.
THOSE THAT HUNT THEM STILL GO BY THE NAME . . .
BLADE RUNNER

Aspects of this backstory are further explained across the duration of the film, but a more elaborate account of these events had already been previewed at Comic-Con 2017 (Fine 2017) and also provided in the form of three official *Blade Runner* sequel films (prequels or prologue sequels to *BR2049*) that appeared on the Web (in non-chronological order) in the months leading up to the theatrical release of *BR2049*. The first sequel, the animated short *Blade Runner 2022: Black Out* (hereafter *BR2022*), opens with a title card – 'Los Angeles May, 2022' – and crawl which explains that, with the expiry of the Replicant NEXUS-6 model, the Tyrell Corporation has developed a new NEXUS-8 line of replicants, who now possess open-ended lifespans equivalent to those of regular humans. This causes a massive backlash among the human populace, who use the Replicant Registration Database to find and hunt down the bioengineered humans. In response, an underground replicant freedom movement sets out to destroy the Tyrell Corporation's database of registered replicants, so that they can no longer be tracked. The so-called 'blackout' of their actions (an electro-magnetic pulse detonated somewhere on the West Coast) is addressed in two cards at the end of the film:

> The Blackout, which led to the prohibition of *Replicant* production, sealed the fate of the TYRELL CORPORATION.
> It took over a decade for the WALLACE CORP. to win approval to manufacture a new breed of *Replicants*.

Just five minutes in duration, the second sequel, *Blade Runner 2036: Nexus Dawn* (hereafter *BR2036*) picks up the narrative hook of the final line of text, to look in on a hearing that creator-entrepreneur Niander Wallace (Jared Leto) is called to in order to defend his technically illegal investment (banned after the blackout of 2022) in the manufacture of a new generation of subservient and controllable NEXUS-9 replicants. The third sequel, *Blade Runner 2048: Nowhere to Run* (hereafter *BR2048*), released around five weeks before the premiere of *BR2049*, follows a brooding Sapper Morton (Bautista) through the streets of Los Angeles. Upon witnessing a backstreet assault, Morton savagely beats up the group of thugs, his superhuman strength attracting the unwanted attention of a passerby who reports him to the LAPD as a likely rogue NEXUS-8 replicant. This call to the authorities connects directly to the opening of *BR2049* in which K locates Morton on a secluded protein farm, and (taken together) all three of the sequels dramatise key events that have occurred since *BR2019*, and explain developments in the mythology of both replicants and blade runners.

The serial continuity evident in and through these short films (and the Comic-Con preview notes) relates not only to narrative events, but also to *BR2019*'s future vision. The film's reputation as ground-breaking science fiction much resided in its visual grandeur and dread-filled rendering of an environmentally degraded Los Angeles, as imagined by Scott and his team, including 'visual futurist' Syd Mead; production designer Lawrence G. Paull; art director David Snyder; special effects supervisors Snyder, Richard Yuricich and Douglas Trumball; and cinematographer Jordan Cronenweth. Scott Bukatman comments not only on *BR2019*'s dark dystopian city, but also on the 'brilliance' (in both senses of the word) of its 'visual density', a panoramic vision that offers 'an urban experience of inexhaustible fluidity, endless passage and infinite perceptibility – *a utopian vision* . . . as distinct from *a vision of utopia*' (Bukatman 1997: 56, emphasis in original). *BR2049* works with all of this, not only delivering on spectacle and an enhanced, immersive soundtrack, but also by extending (sequelising) *BR2019*'s signs of greenhouse warming to a future in which climate change has caused sea levels to rise dramatically, requiring that a massive sea wall be built along with Sepulveda Pass to protect the Los Angeles basin. The area south of Los Angeles lies in waste, an endless scrapheap, and to the east Las Vegas, now a ghost town, glows orange with radioactive dust. As in *BR2019*, towering billboards for multinational corporations, such as Sony, continue to dominate the cityscape, though (somewhat eccentrically) K's wedge-shaped spinner (flying car) is from a lesser player in Peugeot. More than this, in making Los Angeles an ongoing link between it and earlier film versions, *BR2049* renders Los Angeles (as Bukatman would have it) as a 'complex, self-similar space – a fractal environment' (Bukatman 1997: 58) through which the disembodied eye, and itinerant consciousness of the viewer, can wander/wonder.

As is evident from the description so far, the temporal gaps that structure the various *Blade Runner* instalments – *BR2019*, *BR2022*, *BR2036*, *BR2048* and *BR2049* – define it as serial storytelling, and the continuity and consistency of its narrative events – its organic seriality – mark out *BR2049* as a 'true sequel' (even if it is not exactly clear which cut of *BR2019* it sequelises). By contrast, a second line of inquiry – the approach Mittell describes as 'operational seriality' – opens up to practices of cinematic rebooting. The latter takes less of an interest in the narrative events and temporal gaps that structure serial storytelling (and which the prologue sequels seek to bridge) to investigate non-narrative continuity, or those ways in which texts that are difficult to term serialised based on their narratives can be understood as 'embedded within cultural practices of seriality outside the narrative realm' (Mittell 2018: 232).

Mittell counts among these practices the proliferation of paratexts that fill serial gaps with extratextual material, typically to extend engagement across media platforms. This paratextual sprawl is often used to augment narrative series and franchises – notably those properties (*Star Wars*, *Star Trek*, *Batman*, Bond) typically described as 'true reboots' – through toys, games, novelisations and the like, but, as Mittell points out, these paratexts can also be found in the case of a 'self-contained' film such as *BR2019* (2018: 234). For Mittell, the several different 'official' versions of *BR2019*, along with numerous other official and unofficial paratexts that extend and augment the film, suggest a 'serialised feedback loop of production and consumption, turning a seemingly [singular] finished film [*BR2019*] into an ongoing conversation' (Mittell 2018: 235).

Mittell's understanding of operational seriality pushes against the continuity of organic seriality (sequelisation) to emphasise instead 'discontinuities and differences . . . [and] trace the ongoing story of [a] film's making and remaking' (2018: 235; see also Verevis 2019). Such an approach is consistent with Matt Hills' assessment that *BR2019* is 'a single film title which has . . . mutated into a franchise by virtue of [its] textual variation[s]' (Hills 2011: 7). Barry Atkins further explains when he writes (in an essay that precedes *BR2049* by more than a decade):

> It has been some time since it was possible to discuss *Blade Runner* as if it were a single and fixed text that might be considered in isolation from its history of multiple prints, or detached from its vast array of intertexts, paratexts, references and allusions . . . Even before the release of Ridley Scott's authorised *Director's Cut* in 1992, the film was already caught in a web of references to other texts, from its credited relationship to Philip K. Dick's *Do Androids Dream of Electric Sheep?* and its appropriation of the term 'blade runner' from William Burroughs' screenplay title, *Blade Runner: A Movie* (1979), [through] to its density of intertextual allusion to a range of cinematic genres. (2005: 79)

Atkins goes on to argue that even *BR2019*'s appearance in 'such an apparently definitive and authorised form' as the 1992 *Director's Cut* does not nullify the fact that *Blade Runner* remains 'a firmly plural text that resists any sense of closure toward the singular' (2005: 80). This is (literally) borne out by the appearance of the 2007 *Final Cut*, a version which is no more or less 'definitive' than any of the others. Moreover, the question of *Blade Runner*'s multiplicity is not only a matter of its various film (and VHS and DVD) versions, but also that its textuality is complicated by the existence of other authorised transmedia paratexts. These include (but are not limited to): the 1982 reprint of *Do Androids Dream of Electric Sheep?*, published as *Blade Runner*, with a note explaining that its pages contain the 'brilliant science fiction novel that became the source of the motion picture' and encouraging readers to 'discover an added dimension on encountering the original work [Dick's novel]'; the 1982 novelisation, *Blade Runner: A Story of the Future* by Les Martin, derived from the Hampton Fancher and David Peoples screenplay (based on the Dick novel) and illustrated with more than sixty stills from the film; the 1982 Marvel Comics adaptation by Archie Goodwin et al.; the (expanded) 1994 Vangelis soundtrack; the 1997 Westwood Studios *Blade Runner* PC game; and (pre-eminently) the three officially licensed K. W. Jeter sequel novels – *Blade Runner 2: The Edge of Human* (1995), *Blade Runner 3: Replicant Night* (1996) and *Blade Runner 4: Eye and Talon* (2000) – which repeat and continue not only *BR2019*'s narrative but also elements of *Do Androids Dream of Electric Sheep?*

In all likelihood prompted by the success of the 1992 *Director's Cut*, Jeter's first sequel novel, *Blade Runner 2: The Edge of Human*, follows on directly from the film, and was apparently intended to form the basis for a sequel film to *BR2019* (C. Gray 2005: 149). In accordance with its generic lineage, it opens with a line of hard-boiled fiction – 'When every murder seems the same, it's time to quit' (1995: 3), and quickly moves to find Deckard who, since the events of *BR2019*, has been living in a remote cabin with Rachael, who lies suspended in a transport sleep module designed to delay the ageing process of replicants during their travel to the off-world colonies. Across the novel, Jeter integrates elements from both *Do Androids Dream of Electric Sheep?* and *BR2019*, and expands the story world into one of templants – that is, 'original' human templates that are the basis of replicant 'copies' – in order to introduce the (new) character of Tyrell's niece, Sarah, who is the templant for (and thus identical to) Rachael. Jeter additionally finds ways to resurrect several characters from *BR2019* – J. F. Sebastian, Pris and Roy Batty – and then sets Deckard and the blade runner Dave Holden (recovered from wounds inflicted in *BR2019*) about hunting for the notorious missing 'sixth replicant' mentioned by Deckard's captain, Bryant, in a detail left over from an earlier script treatment for *BR2019*, and which had allowed fans to speculate that Deckard himself was the extra replicant. The 2007 *Final Cut* had actually corrected Bryant's dialogue, thus invalidating the premise for *The Edge of Human*, but this erasure only seems to underline the fact that the appeal of the film's multiplicity-in-singularity is that it resists the fixity of a definitive and authorised form. Jonathan Gray discovered exactly this through discussions with *Blade Runner* fan communities, which indicated that they valued *BR2019* for its power to immerse them in a detailed fictional world. Significantly, the fans welcomed the idea of a sequel film – or 'side-quel' – that would expand the *Blade Runner* universe and enrich it through additional material, but only upon the condition that any additional instalment preserve *BR2019*'s multiplicity-in-singularity sense of aperture: that is, rather than close down its meanings and resolve its debates, a *Blade Runner* sequel-reboot had to maintain itself as an open whole, especially with respect to the question of whether Deckard was, or was not, a replicant (J. Gray 2005: 114).

All of this is to say that *BR2019*'s variant futures do not lead (organically) to a single authentic version, but rather that *Blade Runner* is a text that becomes 'more legible when treated like an ancient manuscript . . . a palimpsest, with each extant version *layered atop a previous one*' (Westphal 2017, emphasis added). Conventional wisdom suggests that reboots wipe a narrative space clean for future textual production, but *BR2049* reveals another logic at work, creating a new narrative space by adhering to the complicated textual multiplicity that already defined the franchise: that is, *BR2049* does not set out to explicate questions raised in *BR2019*, but rather to compound them. It does this most evidently by introducing K, a blade runner character, and then having him repeat and retrace the narrative events and thematic concerns (around the authenticity of memory and identity) raised in/through the character of Rick Deckard. This is done, however, in an inverted way: Deckard is a human blade runner who, through his interaction with and pursuit of the NEXUS-6 replicants, especially Roy Batty (Rutger Hauer), and his own developing feelings for NEXUS-7 prototype Rachael, comes to realise the ambiguity of human-replicant definition. K, on the other hand, is a replicant blade runner (serial number KD6-3.7) who, through the course of his investigation and tracking of the replicant child, experiences a shift from biosynthetic to human consciousness, one that similarly calls into question the human-replicant divide. Bukatman makes two important observations with respect to this division and the key question: 'Is Deckard a replicant?' (and, conversely, 'Is K a human?'). The first (consistent with the aforementioned fan observations) is that asking the question – and maintaining its ambiguity – is far more important than determining the answer (Bukatman 1997: 80). The second is the observation that *BR2019* develops two oppositions from Dick's novel – human/replicant and human/inhuman – of which (according to Bukatman) only the latter is really important. As he explains, the first raises a philosophical problem: how do know you are human? The second, instead, leads to a moral problem: what does it mean to be human? (Bukatman 1997: 68–9). In *BR2019*, Deckard, '[whose] status as human – physically, psychically, morally – is increasingly in doubt' (1997: 81), recovers his humanity through an empathic response and connection to Rachael; in *BR2049*, the initially compliant and subservient K gradually discovers his humanity and emergent free will through his self-sacrificing actions to spare Deckard and protect the miracle child.

K's moral journey – his quest for identity and meaning – is also an act of detection, beginning with the flower at the base of the dead tree which marks the location of the box of human remains, ceremoniously buried beneath its roots. After visiting the Wallace Corp. archive, which contains a partial audio file of Deckard's Voight-Kampff test of Rachael, K seeks out Gaff (Edward James Olmos) – the LAPD officer who accompanied Deckard in his pursuit of the rogue NEXUS-6 replicants – who tells him Deckard has 'retired', and will not be found. Seeking further clues, K returns to the farmhouse where he discovers the numbers – 6 10 21 – carved at the base of the dead tree. Startled by his find, the numbers immediately provoke in K an involuntary response – a flash of recollection – which he subsequently explains to Joshi is his memory of a toy wooden horse, with an inscription on its base, that he had as a child. K further recalls that, pursued by a group of boys who sought to take the horse away from him, he hid it in a cold furnace. What K does not tell Joshi, though, is of the 'dangerous coincidence': the fact that the inscription on the horse and carving on the tree carry the same numbers: the date, 6.10.21. DNA records in turn lead K to the Morrillcole Orphanage in San Diego (the city now a bleak waste-processing district for Greater Los Angeles) which he recognises as the location of the childhood dream, and where he finds the carved horse, still wrapped in cloth, in the furnace where it was concealed years before. Urged now by his virtual consort, Joi, to accept the fact that he is a 'real boy', K (still cautious) moves to determine how one might differentiate a real from an implanted memory. This leads him to Dr Stelline, a designer of replicant memories (and Wallace Corp. subcontractor), who – upon asking K to picture his memory – is moved to tears, affirming: 'yes, someone lived this . . . This happened.' Now shaken to the core, K responds – 'I know it's real. I know it's real' – and exits the laboratory thinking he is, indeed, the miracle child.

BR2049 begins with a literal act of excavation and, like an archaeological dig, it encourages K, and the film's viewers, to assemble fragments of the past and of the future, to put together pieces of its original(s) and its sequel(s). It does this, as Roland Barthes would have it, by directing the viewer toward the rewritten text: 'not the *real* text, but a plural text' (1974: 16, emphasis in original). This is, at least in part, enabled in and through the figure-matrix of the horse, and its link to the unicorn symbolism of *BR2019*. In the 1982 *U.S. Theatrical* and *International* cuts, the unicorn appears only at the end of the film as a silver origami figure, a calling card left by Gaff to tell Deckard that he has decided to spare Rachael's life. Much of the interest in the lead-up to the release of the 1992 *Director's Cut* was that it would restore, in the sequence that follows Rachael's first visit to Deckard's apartment, Deckard's reverie: a brief, fourteen-second shot of a unicorn ambling through leafy, misty woods. Included too, but differently, in the 2007 *Final Cut* where it comprises two shots and appears as a vision, rather than a dream (see Brooker 2009), the unicorn footage explains why the origami facsimile left on Deckard's doorstep is so significant. It suggests that, just as Deckard proved to Rachael that she wasn't human with the story of the spider outside her bedroom window, Gaff had access to Deckard's own memory banks: in other words, it demonstrates that Deckard, too, is a replicant, probably another prototype NEXUS-7. The (inverted) symbolism of unicorn and horse – one 'proves' Deckard is a replicant, the other that K is a real boy – is further underlined by K's earlier visit to Gaff, which serves no narrative function but during which the latter fashions, in 'homage' to Dick, an origami sheep. In another way, Deckard's reverie, which (at least in the *Director's* and *Final* cuts) is the only glimpse of a natural, green world and is set to the sound of Vangelis' 'Memories of Green', connects Deckard directly to Stelline, first encountered in a verdant, holographic forest (and the only green in *BR2049*). And, finally, it is Doc Badger's (Barkhad Abdi) carbon testing of the toy horse – a reprise of the Cambodian street merchant's analysis of the snake scale Deckard finds in replicant Leon's bathtub – that leads K to Deckard.

For many, Deckard was last seen getting into the lift in his apartment building with Rachael, the doors closing (perhaps) to trap them – both now fugitives – in a world from which they seek to escape. The *U.S. Theatrical* and *International* cuts responded to disastrous sneak previews (March 1982) by revising this bleak ending, adding a coda in which Deckard and Rachael escape the dark city, winding their way by car through a pristine landscape and, in another major adjustment, with an added voiceover narration in which Deckard explains: 'Gaff had been there [to Deckard's apartment], and let her [Rachael] live. Four years he figured. He was wrong. Tyrell had told me Rachael was special. No termination date. I didn't know how long we'd have together . . . Who does?' (see Sammon 337–56). The additional footage – aerial shots of wide mountain vistas – came in the form of out-takes from the opening montage of *The Shining* (Kubrick, 1980) in which Jack Torrance (Jack Nicholson) drives his family to the remote Overlook Hotel, and was at odds with the film's future vision of Los Angeles steeped in endless rain, and of planet Earth in an advanced state of degradation. The *Director's* and *Final* cuts again pared back the ending, leaving Gaff's last words – 'It's too bad she won't live! But then again, who does?' – to resonate, and contribute to the sense that *BR2019* is a film 'saturated in melancholy, overshadowed by death and peopled by ghosts' (Dalton 2016).

BR2049 underlines the discontinuities and differences of operational seriality, working with both endings to show that Deckard has retreated to a remote and deserted Overlook-type hotel where (like Jack Torrance) his company – aside from a (replicant?) dog – is that of ghosts: spectres of Elvis, Marilyn Monroe and Frank Sinatra. When, following their altercation, Deckard and K call a truce and retreat to the bar, the seriality is not linear, nor even 'tabular' (Barthes 1974: 30), but dreamlike – oneiric. This is evident not only in Deckard's recollection of the past – 'her name was Rachael', he tells K – but also in its sketching of a 'large circuit' (see Deleuze 1989; Verevis 2005), recalling Jack Torrance at the Overlook Hotel bar where he discovers to his surprise, for it is an apparition, the bartender Lloyd, played by none other than Joe Turkel, *BR2019*'s Dr Eldon Tyrell.

Figure 4.2 Rachael replicated, *Blade Runner 2049* (2017).

All the while that K has been undertaking his investigation and search for the identity of the child, he has been tracked by Luv (Sylvia Hoecks), a ruthless, robotic replicant, and lieutenant to Niander Wallace, who is desperate to secure the child for what it may reveal about the secret to replicant reproduction which (lost in the 'blackout') has so far eluded him. In the film's final panel, Deckard is apprehended by Luv and taunted by Wallace, who produces a near-identical version of Rachael in a vain attempt to extract from him the whereabouts of the child. Moreover, in a moment that occludes rather than explicates questions of identity, Wallace suggests that Deckard's meeting with Rachael was predestined, that it was an algorithm rather than love that brought them together. Meanwhile, K meets Freysa (Hiam Abbass), leader of the replicant underground, who in telling him that protecting Rachael's daughter is their absolute priority ('dying for the right cause is the most human thing we can do') also brings him to the realisation that he is not the messianic child, that the memory of the wooden horse was real, but that it was Stelline's, not his. In a final altruistic act, K rescues Deckard, dispatching Luv in the process, and (though mortally wounded) takes him to the Stelline Laboratories to be reunited with his long-lost child. In his final moments, K lies down on the steps of the building, holding out his hand to the touch of the lightly falling snow. Significantly, the experience – of snowflakes alighting on his upturned hand – matches that seen earlier in the film when, following his initial visit to Stelline, K left believing, for the first time, that he really is human. The gesture is also matched to a shot of Stelline who stands – hand outstretched – in a virtual drift of snow, just as Deckard enters the building. In these moments – including the final shot of the film in which Deckard, wordless, places his hand on the glass that separates him from Stelline – K's humanity, his human consciousness, is affirmed through sensation, and his affinity with the natural world.

Figure 4.3 Deckard finds his daughter, *Blade Runner 2049* (2017).

The final moments of *BR2049* reprise and retrace – remake as they serialise – those of *BR2019*, in particular Roy Batty's expiry in the rain, with its emphasis (in his famous death soliloquy) on the experiential: 'I've seen things you people wouldn't believe: attack ships on fire off the shoulder of Orion. I've watched C-beams glitter in the dark near the Tannhäuser Gate. All those moments will be lost in time, like tears in rain'. Just as significantly, *BR2049* reprises its precursors' open ending, Deckard's tentative meeting with his daughter – the miracle child – and the coming storm of the replicant uprising, suggesting (but for the fact that, like its precursor, *BR2049* performed well below expectation at the box office) that the film might be the middle instalment in another *Blade Runner* trilogy. In this respect, *BR2049* would also align with those descriptions of reboots which require that the new film (ideally) initiates a whole new series, a revived franchise. As Brooker reminds us, '*Blade Runner* began in 1982 as an older kind of text – a film adaptation of a novel and expanded . . . into a cross-platform phenomenon': 'an unruly multiverse, a map of possible routes, a network of alternatives rather than a single narrative' (2009: 90). At the time of *BR2049*'s release, Villeneuve noted that the film was made from the 'tension' between *BR2019*'s different versions (Westphal 2017), a comment that suggested an understanding of the textual and cultural practices of seriality that characterised the multiplicities of the franchise. This chapter has argued that *BR2049* contributes to this network of versions, describing it as a 'sequel-reboot': a serialised property that operates according to the complementary protocols of linear-organic and tabular-operational seriality. In retracing its multiple pasts, *BR2049* outlines and extends – without diminishing the labyrinth and mysteries of – its possible futures.

NOTES

1. Hills refers to the three most circulated versions of *BR2019* – the *Original Theatrical* release (aka *U.S. Theatrical Cut*, 1982), the *Director's Cut* (1992) and the *Final Cut* (2007) – to suggest 'a trilogy of one film' (2011: 7). Others discuss further versions. See, for instance, Will Brooker's (2009) account of five versions – the three aforementioned, along with the 1982 *Workprint* and 1982 *International Cut* – released on the *Blade Runner: The Final Cut* five-disc Collector's Edition DVD. See also Paul M. Sammon's (2017) exhaustive discussion of these and other versions.
2. The *BR2019* crawl (the same in all versions but the *Workprint*) reads:
Early in the 21st Century, THE TYRELL CORPORATION advanced Robot evolution into the NEXUS phase – a being virtually identical to a human – known as a *Replicant*. The NEXUS 6 Replicants were superior in strength and agility, and at least equal in intelligence, to the genetic engineers who created them.
Replicants were used Off-world as slave labor, in the hazardous exploration and colonization of other planets.
After a bloody mutiny by a NEXUS 6 combat team in an Off-world colony, Replicants were declared illegal on earth – under penalty of death.
Special police squads – BLADE RUNNER UNITS – had orders to shoot to kill, upon detection, any trespassing Replicant.
This was not called execution.
It was called retirement.

REFERENCES

Atkins, Barry (2005), 'Replicating the Blade Runner', in Will Brooker (ed.), *The Blade Runner Experience: The Legacy of a Science Fiction Classic*, New York: Wallflower/Columbia University Press, pp. 79–91.
Barthes, Roland (1974), *S/Z*, trans. Richard Miller, New York: Farrar, Straus and Giroux.
Brooker, Will (2009), 'All Our Variant Futures: The Many Narratives of *Blade Runner: The Final Cut*', *Popular Communication*, 7: 2, 79–91.
Bukatman, Scott (1997), *Blade Runner*, London, BFI.
Dalton, Stephen (2016), '*Blade Runner*: Anatomy of a Classic', *British Film Institute*, 26 October, <http://www.bfi.org.uk/news-opinion/news-bfi/features/blade-runner>.
Deleuze, Gilles (1989), *Cinema 2: The Time-Image*, trans. Hugh Tomlinson and Robert Galeta, Minneapolis, MN: University of Minnesota Press.
Dick, Philip K. ([1968] 1982), *Blade Runner / Do Androids Dream of Electric Sheep?* London: Grafton.
Dry, Jude (2017), 'Denis Villeneuve Says He Was "Flirting With Disaster" on *Blade Runner 2049*', *Indiewire*, 27 December, <http://www.indiewire.com/2017/12/denis-villeneuve-blade-runner-2049-interview-video-1201911379/>.
Fine, Elazar (2017), '*Blade Runner 2049* Timeline Revealed', *The Playlist*, 24 July, <https://theplaylist.net/blade-runner-2049-timeline-20170724/>.
Giant, Bill, Bernie Baum and Florence Kaye (1968), 'Edge of Reality', Belinda Music.
Goodwin, Archie, Al Williamson and Carlos Garzon (1982), *Blade Runner*, Marvel Comics.
Gray, Christy (2005), 'Originals and Copies: The Fans of Philip K. Dick, Blade Runner and K. W. Jeter', in Will Brooker (ed.), *The Blade Runner Experience: The Legacy of a Science Fiction Classic*, New York: Wallflower/Columbia University Press, pp. 142–58.

Gray, Jonathan (2005), 'Scanning the Replicant Text', in Will Brooker (ed.), *The Blade Runner Experience: The Legacy of a Science Fiction Classic*, New York: Wallflower/Columbia University Press, pp. 111–23.
Hills, Matt (2011), *Blade Runner*, London: Wallflower.
Jeter, K. W. (1995), *Blade Runner 2: The Edge of Human*, London: Orion.
Jeter, K. W. (1996), *Blade Runner 3: Replicant Night*, London: Orion.
Jeter, K. W. (2000), *Blade Runner 4: Eye and Talon*, London: Orion.
Kohn, Eric (2017), 'Denis Villeneuve's Neo-Noir Sequel Is Mind- Blowing Sci-Fi Storytelling', *IndieWire*, 29 September, <http://www.indiewire.com/2017/09/blade-runner-2049-review-ryan-gosling-denis-villeneuve-1201881820/>.
Martin, Les (1982), *Blade Runner: A Story of the Future*, New York: Random House.
Mittell, Jason (2018), 'Operational Seriality and the Operation of Seriality', in Zara Dinnen and Robyn Warhol (eds), *The Edinburgh Companion to Contemporary Narrative Theories*, Edinburgh: Edinburgh University Press, pp. 228–38.
Orange, B. Alan (2011), 'Christopher Nolan Wanted for Blade Runner Sequel or Prequel', 4 March, <https://web.archive.org/web/20131104213322/http://www.movieweb.com/news/christopher-nolan-wanted-for-blade-runner-sequel-or-prequel>.
Perkins, Claire and Constantine Verevis (2012), 'Introduction: Three Times', in *Film Trilogies: New Critical Approaches*, Basingstoke: Palgrave Macmillan, pp. 1–31.
Sammon, Paul M. (2017), *Future Noir: The Making of Blade Runner*, New York: HarperCollins.
Tallerico, Brian (2017), 'Blade Runner 2049', *Roger Ebert*, 6 October, <https://www.rogerebert.com/reviews/blade-runner-2049-2017>.
Verevis, Constantine (2005), 'Cinema', in Adrian Parr (ed.), *The Deleuze Dictionary*, Edinburgh: Edinburgh University Press, pp. 44–6.
Verevis, Constantine (2019), 'Another Green World: The *Mad Max* Series', in Felicity Collins, Jane Landman and Susan Bye (eds), *A Companion to Australian Cinema*, Hoboken, NJ: Wiley Blackwell, pp. 133–48.
Westphal, Kyle (2017), 'The Theological Brilliance of *Blade Runner 2049*', *Chicago Reader*, 8 November, <https://www.chicagoreader.com/Bleader/archives/2017/11/08/the-theological-brilliance-of-blade-runner-2049>.

CHAPTER 5

Gender, Genre and the Reboot: From *Ocean's 11/Eleven* to *Ocean's 8/Eight*

Jennifer Forrest

In the sea of series re-imaginings produced in the last ten years or currently in production, one of the most intriguing in terms of classification is Gary Ross's *Ocean's 8* (2018). Is it merely a gender-reversal remake, revival, or is it a new sequel in the *Ocean's* franchise? Or, since twelve years have passed since *Ocean's Thirteen* (Soderbergh, 2007), is it a reboot? Unlike the *Terminator* series that, with *Terminator Salvation* (McG, 2009), masqueraded as a reboot in the elimination of the numerical sequencing of its predecessors, at first glance *Ocean's 8* intimates coyly that it might be a prequel. According to the *Oxford English Dictionary* (2019), a reboot is 'something revived or revitalized, *esp.* a series of films or television programmes restarted with a new cast, script, etc.'. Inherent in this definition is the disruption of intertextual continuity with an originary series in the creation of a new, self-contained one. In this sense, the reboot shares the practice of disavowal reminiscent of many film remakes, differing here only in number: a remake is singular, a reboot is multiple. *Ocean's 8*'s numeric designation deliberately blurs its remake vs reboot status, denying access to what precisely it is acknowledging and will subsequently disavow. In using the Arabic numeral for the DVD case and disc titles, the movie acts like a remake, recalling Lewis Milestone's original *Ocean's 11* (1960). This suggests that it will update Milestone's film's scenario, promising that the new production will offer a fresh approach with its band of fashionably slick female thieves replacing the original's 82nd Airborne brotherhood.

However, instead of distancing itself from Soderbergh's *Ocean's* films, which spell out their numbers, the introductory and closing titles to Ross's film read *Ocean's Eight*.[1] In the spelling of 'eight' the film functions like a reboot, promising to resurrect and reinvigorate the *Ocean's* action, excitement, wit and style through new personnel with the elegant atmosphere surrounding the Metropolitan Museum of Art Gala. The numeric designation 'Eight' (with possible sequels 'Nine' and 'Ten') reflects the logic that with an unwieldy 'Fourteen' (followed perhaps by a 'Fifteen' and a 'Sixteen'), there would be too many cooks/crooks and the broth/heist would be spoiled. This narrative and production rationale, however, throws one more wrench into the works. While *8/Eight*'s taxonomy announces its intention to replicate the Soderbergh series' rich aesthetic engagement with seriality and its celebration of aesthetic collaboration, it also employs that very same model to induce a seismic ripple reconfiguration of cinema(tic practice) through its gender politics.

PLAYING THE NUMBERS

Unlike a straightforward series like *Lethal Weapon*, whose instalments after the initial feature range from #2 to #4, Soderbergh's *Ocean's* movies begin with a remake – *Ocean's Eleven* (2001) – that functions technically as the first in a series, with the subsequent films continuing sequentially with *Ocean's Twelve* (2004) and *Ocean's Thirteen*.[2] While Soderbergh's unorthodox sequencing does not in itself preclude prequels in the manner of the *Star Wars* cycle, *8/Eight* repeats the practice of bucking standard serial progression in favour of numbering the films according to how many heist crew members there are. The number has a dual purpose: determined by internal elements in each film ('eight'), it also behaves through the title like a commercially oriented franchise production ('8'). Through the play of numbers, the movies initiate a tension between the studio's objectives to make a financially successful series and those of the director to create a work of art.

Accordingly, the titles *Eleven*, *Twelve*, *Thirteen* and *8/Eight* ostensibly echo the number of members in Danny Ocean's and Debbie Ocean's crews respectively. Even here, however, relying on the numbers for orientation forces spectators not only to keep track of heist participants but to assess the nature of the assistance provided and how much of that assistance qualifies a character as an official member of the team. Running these numbers ultimately leads down a rabbit hole of generic classification as well, with critics variously identifying Soderbergh's three films as a series or a trilogy, Ross's film as a spin-off and the group of four films as a 'non-sequential franchise' (Armitage 2018). Indeed, Ross follows Soderbergh's practice of the 'non-sequential' sequel as well as the practice of the unreliable crew head count. Spin-off or sequel, in addition to reactivating the basic thematic structure, there is genetic continuity through siblings, since the new heist leader is Debbie Ocean, Danny's younger sister.[3]

Soderbergh's series concludes with *Thirteen* because, as the director stated in a 2018 interview, 'With Bernie Mac being gone, I don't think any of us would want to return to that' (Gilchrist 2018). In the wake of this imposed end to the series, Ross's contribution would be less another instalment in the *Ocean's* franchise than a remake, or, as proposed by Kevin P. Sullivan (2017) and Peter Travers (2018), the first film in a rebooted series. Yet, if it is a remake, which film does it remake precisely? While *8/Eight* replicates the opening sequence of *Eleven* with Debbie appearing like her brother before a parole board, it also aligns itself contextually with *Twelve* in the correspondence of Old World elegance and New World sophistication, as well as structurally with bookend story updates: *Twelve* begins with scenes from each crew member's post-heist existence and *8/Eight* ends with scenes either reflecting or projecting what each woman does/will do with her share of the money. Additionally, *Thirteen* offers a connection to *8/Eight* in Willy Bank's diamond necklaces, anticipating the latter film's Cartier Toussaint. Even though in *Thirteen* Basher claims that 'you don't run the same gag twice', this is apparently not a hard rule. Indeed, *8/Eight* offers Yen in a literal upside-down re-enactment of François Toulour's spectacular athletic skirting of the Galleria d'Arte di Roma's lasers in *Twelve*. Yen parodies the Frenchman's floor routine high in the Met's metal rafters. Rather than remake one film, *8/Eight* borrows bits in a mosaic of all the *Ocean's* movies, including the 1960 original: the advantage enjoyed by both the 82nd Airborne and Debbie's crew is their invisibility, with Danny and his fellow soldiers having no criminal footprint and Debbie and her crew benefiting from the social blindness regarding women's capabilities.[4]

The signs of the remake emerge formally as well, with Ross's appropriation of the flashbacks, the multiple split screens and the wipes associated with Soderbergh's editing in his *Ocean's* movies. While certainly not a shot-for-shot remake, *8/Eight* nevertheless draws enough attention to its borrowings that Luke Y. Thomson (2018), rather than finding fault with the replication of what

Figure 5.1 Danny Ocean appears before a New Jersey parole review board, *Ocean's Eleven* (2001).

Figure 5.2 Keeping it in the family, Debbie Ocean appears before another New Jersey parole review board, *Ocean's Eight* (2018).

'has become a franchise signature', applauded 'Gary Ross's impersonation of the Soderbergh style' as being 'more Soderbergh than the man himself was able to be on the first one'.

Released ten years after *Thirteen*, Soderbergh's *Logan Lucky* (2017) represents more appropriately a new, rebooted beginning. The film declares itself as part of the *Ocean's* universe, obeying the same logic of crew composition with a news report in the film humorously labelling the hillbilly heist as 'Ocean's 7-Eleven'. This designation comments reflexively, of course, on its (the heist's and the film's) more modest resources. As Soderbergh described it, 'Nobody dresses nice. Nobody has nice stuff. They have no money. They have no technology. It's all rubberband technology' (Sullivan 2017). *Logan Lucky*'s band of thieves comes to seven, if one counts Earl, Clyde's bar patron, who plays an important diversionary role. One cannot lose sight of the role of 7 (and 11) as lucky numbers in gambling. The film title is perhaps waiting for the spectator to complete it as *Logan Lucky Number Seven*.[5] Given that *Logan Lucky* signals Soderbergh's return to filmmaking after retirement, this new beginning may function as an auto-reboot (same director), thereby marking *8/Eight* as the second entry in the new franchise.

The question that now poses itself is: are there different types of reboots in the same way that there are varieties of remakes? I would identify William Proctor's description of the reboot as pertaining to the action-genre reboot, one type to which one can add the auteur-reboot, a category that works to redress the imbalance weighted towards the 'profit principle' as the 'pre-eminent driving force behind the immense popularity of the reboot cycle of films' and tip the balance in favour of the director's aesthetic vision (Proctor 2012: 15).[6] This auteur-reboot would not vacate commercial concerns, but rather playfully absorb them into each instalment's very structure and narrative.

THE AUTEUR-REBOOT IN THEORY AND PRACTICE

In many respects, Proctor is correct to discuss almost exclusively the role of audiences (fans) and studios in the conceptualisation and exploitation of the reboot. Their contributions suggest new reception expectations and production models. In the classic Hollywood era, studios learned to mix genres (primarily within B movies) in order to attract fans of each genre and thereby augment audiences. Even in the absence of A and B units, post-1960s practices continued the separation between the two products, with series falling into the B entertainment category. New millennium studios have modified this template to mix, not genres per se, but features of the A (serious) and B (entertaining) movie. They offer a product that will appeal to those seeking a long-term engagement with a core story and its characters (series fans) and to those discriminating filmgoers who seek the quality experience imparted by the presence of stars, high production values and a director possessing sufficient cachet, if not a signature style, and probing thematic preoccupations. This involves a deft juggling in the marketing of contradictory definitions of 'new' within the same product. There is the 'new' serial product for fans called the 'reboot' (basic core story and characters with a fresh beginning). The reboot is also, however, a unique, discrete prestige work for the filmgoer who normally feels cheated by being served recycled material like remakes and series.

While Proctor insists in his distinction between the remake and the reboot that the former is singular and the latter multiple, this does not reflect how fans navigate these practices. The online pages 'Remakes, Reboots and Reimaginings' (*Visual Thesaurus*), 'Continuity Reboot' and 'Sequel Hook' (*TV Tropes*) include in their lists of reboots not only those series that Proctor would acknowledge as reboots, but movies that most film scholars would categorise as remakes. The reboot can also be singular if there is a 'sequel hook' ('Continuity Reboot'). The sequel hook is the suggestion at the end of a film that there might be another film, one that may, however, never materialise. In addition, the entries of *TV Tropes*'s contributors border on the obsessive-compulsive in their creation of a dizzying taxonomy of reboot types and related practices, offering, among others, the 'Continuity Reboot', the 'Alternate Continuity Reboot', the 'Unreboot', and so on. While this extreme attention to precise terminology provides the type of engagement with the cinematic and often related extra-cinematic material that studios encourage in fans, it also supports a classic Hollywood studio practice of linking the singular sequel (as differentiated from series, which comprise a minimum of three films) to A movies: sequels that were not failed series ('true sequels'), too, had big stars, big budgets, high production values and were screened in the better movie houses.[7] Today, if discriminating viewers liked the first film, they might be inclined to see its sequel, which appropriates the air of originality surrounding the first.

So, while Proctor disparages studios for promoting their films as reboots when they clearly are remakes or new instalments in a pre-existing series, studios' exploitation of the term's malleability provides their product with the aura of newness and originality that attracts both the fan and the cultivated filmgoer.

Logan Lucky and *8/Eight* repeat the model of split market appeal: on the one hand, they please fans who want more heists in the mould of *Eleven*, and, on the other, they cater to aficionados of Soderbergh the auteur and the very workmanlike Ross, both of whom approach each film as a unique exercise in filmmaking. The death of Bernie Mac, not fan dissatisfaction with the last instalment, imposed a continuity break with the 2001–7 series. While there can be no return to the crew composition of the earlier series, what does carry over is the dynamic of the ensemble heist.

Logan Lucky and *8/Eight* also work as discrete creations to the discriminating filmgoer, with each entry conceived as an exercise in and an exploration of genre. *Logan Lucky* is a comic hillbilly movie. As for *8/Eight*, it would belong to a new gender-swap genre, following Amanda Hess's remark that 'the gender-swapped remake has expanded from one-off stunt into full-blown genre' (2018).[8] The latter film's gender reversal serves to garner more fans among female viewers to what has been an undeniably male-centred genre and series. The film was also a low-risk investment that paid off for Warner Bros. in the 'repackag[ing]' of older properties, both the 1960s *Ocean's 11* and Soderbergh's 2001 remake (Klang 2015). It may also encourage greater allegiance to the studio's product in its appearance of 'being progressive' (Klang 2015). However one approaches the *Ocean's* reboot, each new entry engages the fan; each one also stands alone.

Both Soderbergh and Ross comment playfully on their participation in this ambiguous split-market production through their play with numbers. Through the unbroken sequence 11–13 and the reboot's 7–8, the numbers act like series instalments, pleasing the fan while also fulfilling the objective of the studio. Through the numbers' reference to the head-count of crew members (no externally imposed sequencing) and the fact that the directors did not plan to create a series, *Twelve*, *Thirteen* and *8/Eight* act like 'true' sequels, that is, like stand-alone productions.

However much Soderbergh and Ross played ball with the studio in participating in a series/reboot, they also found a space for the art of filmmaking. The heist genre provided a format for working with a studio while remaining true to one's aesthetic vision. A notable example emerges in Soderbergh's commentary on the 2009 DVD of *Eleven* where he reveals that he altered the colour of the Warner Bros. logo, bathing the gold lettering and the shield border in the same sky blue of the background. In discussions with studio representatives, no one made any mention of the modification. The implication is that corporate eyes simply did not notice. Soderbergh was not unaware of the history of the logo, since he formally requested to use Saul Bass's 1970s design for use in *Eleven*, but each time he repeated his request, it moved up into a corporate black hole that eventually rejected it (Kenny 2012). He did receive permission to use the Bass design, however, for *Magic Mike* (2012). Given his struggles to obtain permission with *Eleven*, Soderbergh's wilful disobedience signals that he was assuming a playfully adversarial position vis-à-vis the corporate hand that was feeding him. Through the altered logo, Soderbergh introduced the series and reboot template in which the tension between commerce and art plays out both internally and externally. As a result, *Eleven*'s toying with the logo becomes semantically doubly charged: on the one hand, by the symbol's recognition value, it represents the corporate practices of Time Warner, Warner Bros.'s parent company at the time; on the other, in its alteration, this is an act of directorial insubordination and creativity. Not averse to remaking, Soderbergh took the production company's eye to profit and habit of looking to the past for ready-made material and lit upon a fantasy film that mirrored the search for financial backing and the heavy investment and planning involved in the making of a film/heist.[9] Remaking Lewis Milestone's *Ocean's 11* was a natural fit because it straddled both worlds.

The franchise principle is both formally and thematically the plaything of the *Ocean's* universe, and each film in the series and the reboot absorb it and the subversion of it into its narrative. In an interview, Soderbergh called the films windup toys, which would suggest that they have little value outside of entertainment. They were toys, however, that he controlled, and this in ways that his financial backers did not entirely fathom, somewhat like the elaborate flimflams of all the films, including Ross's. In all instances, the heist entails a bait-and-switch in which the mark/film studio gets fake valuables/a money-making entertainment vehicle and the heisters/director absconds with the real goods/a work of art.

The diversionary heist at the heart of Soderbergh's and Ross's *Ocean's* movies is a dual metaphor for talent (criminal and directorial) trumping finance (invisible but palpable corporate power) by making a work of art, and it plays out in two different spaces: diegetically (the diversionary and real heists within the film) and extradiegetically (the film production). A portal opens between the two spaces in a device that Soderbergh and Ross tapped from Milestone's *Ocean's 11*: the permeability of reality and fiction. *Ocean's 11* uses the real names of the actors on the hotel casino marquees while they are still technically in character. In that moment Josh Howard is also Sammy Davis, Jr., Danny Ocean is also Frank Sinatra, Sam Harmon is also Dean Martin and 'Mushy' O'Connors is also Joey Bishop.

While such a portal opens up allowing Julia Roberts as Tess Ocean to impersonate herself in *Twelve*, the blurring of inside and outside the film emerges elsewhere as well. For example, the comments that Rusty, Danny and Linus make regarding acting in *Eleven* ('Did I go too far?'); Danny/Soderbergh's admission that '[w]e go into some place, and all I can do is see the [figurative/literal] angles' for a heist/film in *Twelve*; Roman Nagel's request to Danny and Rusty to give him 'the big picture' (an update on the situation in both heist and film production), the blatant embodiment of crass capitalism in the name of the casino villain Willy Bank and the *mise en abyme* of Virgil's orchestration of a workers' rebellion at the Mexican factory in *Thirteen* (a revolt within a cinematic revolt); the news report nicknaming the motorway heist as 'Ocean's 7-Eleven' in *Logan Lucky*: all are references that straddle both spaces and initiate a shifting of semantic registers from the metaphor ('the big picture') to the register of filmmaking (the production of the movie).[10] We find these semantic shifters equally in *8/Eight* in the closing sequence with Debbie Ocean and her crew in a subway car, with each woman having a flashforward to what she will set up with her money. In her flashforward, Daphne is a film director on set who addresses the camera directly, saying, 'It's not that difficult'. In the same moment, she both comments on the poor performance of her film's starring actress (who bears a remarkable resemblance to Daphne and the actress Anne Hathaway) and on filmmaking. This is not mere self-reflexivity that makes spectators aware that they are watching a film (metafiction), but a performative device that initiates and maintains the process of making a movie.

AESTHETIC COLLABORATION

The permeability between reality and fiction, between the extradiegetic and the diegetic, also occurs between films. In an example from *Twelve*, Rusty asks Reuben and Danny if they remember the scene in the Coen brothers' *Miller's Crossing* (1990) in which bookie Bernie Bernbaum pleads 'Look into your heart!' to mobster henchman Tom Reagan as the latter prepares to kill him. The exchange seems incongruous and yet it is more than a mere self-reflexive device. Ocean's crew's options are diminishing in an encroaching deadline to repay Terry Benedict, and the real possibility that they are facing prison looms. Through a kind of cinematic shorthand, the reference reaches out to *Miller's Crossing*, aurally conjuring the visual image from the film, and positions the Ocean's crew in an equally desperate quandary vis-à-vis Benedict. The quote performatively opens a portal connecting the two films in which the scene in *Miller's Crossing* does the work that conventional dialogue would normally do in communicating the dire nature of the heisters' situation.

It also collaborates aesthetically with *Miller's Crossing*. In his commentary on the DVD for *Catch-22* (1970), Mike Nichols admits to Soderbergh, his commentary partner, a 'crude attempt to recycle a shot from [Leni Riefenstahl's]

Triumph of the Will (1934) to depict a character's growing authoritarianism' (Gallagher 2013: 231). This 'recycling' works like Soviet montage, not in a juxtaposition of images within the same film, but in a juxtaposition in time across two (or more) films in order to endow the moment with greater expressive power. This kind of montage marks any given film's images as not isolated in one particular historical moment, but rather in constant transformation as they interact with the past, the present and the future. To draw from Riefenstahl is to collaborate with her as an artist.

While Soderbergh acknowledges having done the same thing on innumerable occasions, there is one notable example from *Eleven*. In his co-commentary to *Eleven*, scriptwriter Ted Griffin mentions that the opening scene with Danny Ocean appearing before an unseen parole board recalls the first moments in Soderbergh's *Erin Brockovich* (2000), an auto-citation that had not occurred to the director. As for Brad Pitt on the parallel commentary to the same film, he was reminded of the scene that introduces the Sundance Kid in *Butch Cassidy and the Sundance Kid* (Hill, 1969). This hardly exhausts the galaxy of possible visual connections, however. Indeed, there are at least two other memorable films featuring scenes with an authority figure in voice-off posing questions to, in these instances, an emotionally exposed or vulnerable interviewee – a group in which Erin Brockovich belongs as well: François Truffaut's *Les Quatre cents coups* (1959) and Patrice Leconte's *La Fille sur le pont* (1999). The scene with Danny, who plays the rehabilitated convict before the parole board, draws on such cinematic moments to bolster and inflect with greater contradiction (and irony) his act of sincerity. He displays a poker face like the Kid, but he also expresses a scintilla of genuine contrition, since his decision to participate in the crime that landed him in jail was made at a moment of emotional hardship (his wife had left him).

The tapping of cinematic-historical imagery is not limited to particular shots or scenes (aural or visual) from other movies, however, but includes the more intangible styles associated with a director's signature or with entire cinematic periods as well. In the commentary to *Eleven*, the short eavesdropping sequence with Frank Cotton is described as 'very Brian De Palma' (Soderbergh and Griffin 2009). Ted Griffin notes how '[i]t feels like the movie goes through slightly different film eras as it goes along. Like, it kind of gets more classical as it goes along', with the scene between Danny and Tess as 'kind of a Howard Hawksian 40s love-you-hate-you romance scene'. For Soderbergh, too, the final section of the film 'sort of moves bag and baggage into the 30s and 40s, I mean, to what I consider to be like classic studio romantic movies' (Soderbergh and Griffin 2009). To make the casserole richer and more densely layered, he modelled his own approach on the heist movie after the formal construction by 'masters of the genre'.[11] This is not a simple 'remaking' of discrete shots, scenes, stylistic touches. Soderbergh assimilates them in the organic sense of 'to absorb and incorporate' as in the way 'bodily organs convert food into blood, and thence into animal tissue', and in doing so, is always original.[12]

The examples from *Eleven* are representative, not exhaustive, of the practice employed in each *Ocean's* film, series and reboot instalment. In *8/Eight*, Debbie Ocean's interview activates a montage across series and reboot. Ross's engagement with that sequence from *Eleven* was misinterpreted by Thomson (2018) as an 'impersonation' of the Soderbergh 'franchise signature' through his use of that series' 'once avant-garde (scene-overlapping dialogue, split screens moving in different directions)' stylistic devices. Ross is hardly new to the aesthetic assimilation of and collaboration with other movies, however, since he has been moving in that direction easily since his debut feature film *Pleasantville* (1998). In the commentary to the 1999 DVD of that film, he notes that, with the image of David whose arms are stretched upwards in the rain, he had unconsciously recalled the iconic shot of Andy Dufresne from Frank Darabont's *The Shawshank Redemption* (1994). With *The Hunger Games* (2012), he realised that he had transitioned from being a screenwriter who wanted to 'capture the script' to being a director possessing a 'fearless sense of spontaneous reinvention'.[13] That spontaneity involved arriving on the set having prepared everything in advance and then 'burning it down and inventing it at each step of the process'.[14] James Keller describes the narrative of *The Hunger Games* as meta-fictional in the 'ongoing parallel within the film between the storytelling/filmmaking and game-making, between the director of the Hunger Games and the director of the film of the same name' (2013: 23). With *8/Eight*, the meta-fictional component is no longer merely inscribed narratively in the film. It acts performatively, engaging actively with *Eleven*'s opening interview, the transition wipes, the dialogue overlapping and the split screens, using them in juxtapositional montages in an act of aesthetic collaboration. The Banksy-like hoax in the Met involving the placing of a 'founding mothers' version next to Emanuel Leutze's *Washington Crossing the Delaware* is doubly emblematic of this 'revolutionary' use of montage: it literally includes the historically hidden women of all revolutions and it figuratively revolutionises the practice of making art in the twenty-first century. It does not substitute one painting for the other, rather both versions, in occupying space on the same wall, expand historical narrative.

COLLABORATIVE PRODUCTION AND THE ANTI-AUTEUR REBOOT

This transition from intransigent fidelity to the script to filmmaker also moved Ross towards a production model of collaborative filmmaking, one which, beginning with *The Hunger Games*, encouraged the actors to participate in the interpretation and evolution of their characters, and the movie itself 'to be an actor, an independent creator' (Keller 2013: 23). His model of collaboration has expanded to put him in theory and practice in harmony with Soderbergh, at least in terms of the production of a film.

Ross's fingers are hardly in as many industry pies as Soderbergh. Mark Gallagher defines Soderbergh's various collaborative activities as 'benign colonization' by which he means 'a creative or discursive practice involving claims of kinship to an artist or text or even part-ownership of a work' (2013: 221). He also speaks of 'collaborative authorship'. As a producer – particularly with his former production company Section Eight – Soderbergh is a 'steward of narratively stimulating or semi-adventurous contemporary commercial production' (2013: 221). As an executive producer, he is a 'patron and preservationist for key works of American film history and experimental cinema' (2013: 221). While Gallagher's arguments are excellent, the myriad instances of shared creation through trans-filmic montage makes me stop short of making compound terms of Soderberghian collaboration in which 'colonisation', 'ownership', 'authorship' and 'patronage' are the dominant nouns to the qualifying adjective 'collaborative'. 'Collaboration' is the prevailing and operative practice and the *Ocean's* series and reboot provide a convincing demonstration of a collaborative model of film production through the team dynamics of the films' heists. For its part, *8/Eight* reinterprets collaboration along gender lines, displacing woman-against-woman competition (in which Daphne is merely a mule for the Toussaint) with feminine bonding (in which Daphne makes close girlfriends).

Twelve and *8/Eight* oppose in their narratives a model of filmic creation antithetical to the one posited by Soderbergh and Ross, that of the auteur. *Twelve*'s Night Fox (François Toulour) and *8/Eight*'s Claude Becker are soloists/directors who insist on working alone either in order to merit sole credit for their capers/productions (the Night Fox) or because, to them, women are sometimes useful means to an end, but always expendable (Becker). The Night Fox mistakenly relishes anticipating and frustrating the *Ocean's* team's every move, feats for which he demands recognition as the best thief, as the singular expert compared to the multiple crew participants who each possesses a talent that contributes to the successful completion of the heist/film. The Fox is caught in a linear system of powerful precursors in his quest to receive the approval and exceed the exploits of the father of thieves, Gaspar LeMarque. As for the art dealer Claude Becker, he goes solo by framing his partner in love and crime, Debbie, for fraud. The insurance investigator of the Toussaint heist playfully responds to his womanising swagger and smug style by calling him Jean-Claude Van Damme, a humorous association with the qualities belonging to the lone wolf action hero, behind whom one finds, in this instance, a Rat Pack emulator. With each team outperforming the solo artist, the *Ocean's* series and reboot counter the auteur model one characterised by a collaborative cinematic creation.

THE RIPPLE EFFECT OF REBOOTING FILM HISTORY AS FILM HERSTORY

If, on the diegetic level, Debbie Ocean's efforts to have her team fly under the radar bank precisely on society's blindness to the abilities and accomplishments of women, on the extradiegetic level Ross works instead to make them conspicuous. Feminine visibility and agency are the 'year one' to which Proctor refers as a key feature of the reboot, with the 2001–7 *Ocean's* franchise and the historically male-driven heist film serving as the sites of a 'failure', that failure here being the exclusion or devaluation of women (2012: 5, 2). Most of the crew members in F. Gary Gray's *The Italian Job* (2003), for example, claim in so many ways that the only good visible woman is a naked one, with Napster's ambition to buy 'speakers so loud, they blow women's clothes off' being emblematic of that generic mindset. Accordingly, if *8/Eight* clothes its female cast in magnificent gowns for the (cat)walk down the stairs of the Met, it is to exploit that heist-genre blind spot (an echo of the heisters capitalising on a Met security camera blind spot) so that the women blend imperceptibly into the array of other elegantly dressed patrons. Like living purloined letters, they are able not only to walk out openly wearing the dismantled stones of the Toussaint, but also to hack and alter the coding of the heist genre.

Instalment number *8/Eight* restarts not only the *Ocean's* series and the heist genre from 'year one', but film history and production practices as well, and it does so in the lateral split-flap credits at the beginning and end of the film. If the flaps had been numbers instead of blocks of letters in names, we could imagine them resetting to zero, with zero referring to rebooting cinematic practice in the present moment in order to include women and/or turning a 'flap clock' back to the beginning of cinematic history. Ross ties his heroines' fates to the split-flap action that facilitates the flashforwards in the penultimate section of the film. Anne Cohen (2018) sees the flashforwards as a 'clear shift' from films like *The Italian Job* in which we see how frivolously the men spend their money, with *8/Eight* presenting instead women using it to shape their future in positive ways. The split-flap flashforward transitions work perhaps more importantly not as diegetic sequel hooks, but as extradiegetic genre hooks: Constance skateboards around her new loft in a coming-of-age tale reminiscent of thirteen-year-old Josh-in-a-man's-body from *Big* (Marshall, 1988);[15] Amita finds freedom and love in a romantic comedy whose heroine travels to Paris; Nine-Ball figures in a potential pool hall hustle film; Tammy expands her business as a stolen goods fence, upgrading from a suburban garage to a warehouse in a warped domestic comedy; Lou travels across the United States on her motorcycle in a road movie; and in the second-chances category, Rose reboots her career as a fashion designer. Daphne's new direction – film director – is appropriately shown last as a cue that *8/Eight* has shifted to engage film as a medium. Accordingly, Debbie does not need a flashforward, since she belongs to the heist, the central genre from which the others emanate in that subway car that is a fertile genre womb. She literally embodies the gender-swap split flap, arriving at the columbarium dressed in a feminine version of the tuxedo her brother wore at the end of *Eleven*, completed by a similarly undone formal black tie.

In 'A Heist in Heels', the 2018 DVD special feature to *8/Eight*, Ross both avows his film's relation to the commercial *Ocean's* franchise and promotes his contribution as a stand-alone work: 'I wanted it to be joyous. I wanted it to be a celebration of these women coming together. I wanted it to be off-beat or eclectic in the way the previous franchise was, but to have its own identity.'

His is an anti-auteur reboot that celebrates aesthetic collaboration within the film itself, with the Soderbergh series and with other films. In a flip, but uncannily prescient comment about Soderbergh's *Ocean's* series, Claudia Puig (2004) quips that 'At the rate things are going, all of Hollywood will put in a day's work on *Ocean's Seventeen*'. In some ways, much of Hollywood past, present and future has. With *8/Eight*, however, Ross makes certain that women figure so visibly in that equation that it produces a ripple reconfiguration of cinema.

NOTES

1. All subsequent references to Ross's film will carry both the number and its spelling: *8/Eight*.
2. All subsequent references to Soderbergh's *Ocean's* films will carry only their number.
3. Genes and genre are intertwined in *8/Eight*. The insurance investigator responsible for sending both Debbie's father and brother to prison asks her, 'Is it genetic? Are the whole family like this?'.
4. Lou asks Debbie, 'What's wrong with a "him"?', to which Debbie answers, 'A "him" gets noticed; a "her" gets ignored, and for once we wanna be ignored'.
5. This would equally align with Sammy Davis, Jr.'s song 'E-O Eleven' in the original *Ocean's 11*. 'E-O Eleven' is what is announced in craps to distinguish it aurally from '7'. In addition, 8 is a lucky number for wealth and success in Japanese and Chinese cultures. It equally symbolises balance through its shape, which may function in *8/Eight* as an effort to correct the historical imparity between men and women in society and cinema.
6. As Proctor aptly notes, reboots have the ability to 'support the economy of an entire studio' (2012: 1). While Proctor does state that film industry franchises can and do produce works of (commercial) art, he devotes little space to it.
7. For a discussion of classic Hollywood sequels, see Forrest (2010: 31–44).
8. The *Ocean's* series itself represents as well a foray into different subgenres, with *Eleven* being a straightforward heist film; *Twelve* being the elegant continental jewel/art thief movie like Alfred Hitchcock's *To Catch a Thief* (1955), Blake Edwards's *The Pink Panther* (1963) and William Wyler's *How to Steal a Million* (1966); and *Thirteen*, a stylish comic revenge-without-the-violence movie in the vein of John Boorman's *Point Blank* (1967) and Mike Hodges's *Get Carter* (1971), substituting the lone avenger with the team.
9. In the DVD commentary to *Eleven*, Soderbergh refers to himself as the 'king of the remake'.

10. This is an echo as well of Tony Bergdorf's question to his doctor regarding his bad heart in *Ocean's 11*, well before he becomes involved in the heist: 'Is it the big casino?'
11. The list of masters and their films is extensive, but one must certainly start with John Huston's *The Asphalt Jungle* (1950), Jules Dassin's *Rififi* (1955), Jean-Pierre Melville's *Bob le Flambeur* (1956) and Peter Collinson's *The Italian Job* (1969).
12. Definition from the online research resource *Oxford English Dictionary* (2019).
13. Commentary to the 2012 DVD.
14. Ibid.
15. *Big* was Ross's first feature-film screenplay, a reference that works not only as an auto-citation, but as an auto-correction as well.

REFERENCES

Armitage, Hugh (2018), 'Ocean's 8 Review: Is it Fourth Time Lucky for the Non-sequential Franchise?', *Digital Spy*, 18 June, <https://www.digitalspy.com/movies/a859482/oceans-8-review-spoiler-free-cate-blanchett-sandra-bullock/>.

Cohen, Anne (2018), 'Why the Ending of *Ocean's 8* Matters More Than You Think', *Refinery29*, 12 June, <https://www.refinery29.com/en-us/2018/06/201615/oceans-8-ending-anne-hathaway-character>.

'Continuity Reboot' (n.d.), *TV Tropes*, <https://tvtropes.org/pmwiki/pmwiki.php/Main/ContinuityReboot>.

Forrest, Jennifer (2010), 'Of "True" Sequels: The Four Daughters Movies, or the Series that Wasn't', in Carolyn Jess-Cooke and Constantine Verevis (eds), *Second Takes: Critical Approaches to the Film Sequel*, Albany, NY: SUNY Press, pp. 31–44.

Gallagher, Mark (2013), *Another Soderbergh Experience: Authorship and Contemporary Hollywood*, Austin, TX: University of Texas Press.

Gilchrist, Todd (2018), 'Soderbergh: Fourth "Ocean's" Movie Unlikely Due to Bernie Mac's Passing', *MTV Movies*, 15 December, <http://www.mtv.com/news/2431150/soderbergh-fourth-oceans-movie-unlikely-due-to-bernie-macs-passing/>.

Hess, Amanda (2018), 'The Trouble With Gender Flips', *New York Times*, 12 June, <https://www.nytimes.com/2018/06/12/movies/oceans-8-gender-swap.html>.

Keller, James (2013), 'Meta-Cinema and Meta-Marketing: Gary Ross's *The Hunger Games*, an Allegory of Its Own Making', *Studies in Popular Culture*, 35: 2, 23–42.

Kenny, Glenn (2012), 'Argos (and Logos)', *Some Came Running: Enthusiasms and Expostulations, by Glenn Kenny* (blog), 12 October, <https://somecamerunning.typepad.com/some_came_running/2012/10/argo.html>.

Klang, Jessica (2015), 'Examining Hollywood's Gender Swap Trend and Where It Needs to Go Next', *IndieWire*, 2 November, <https://www.indiewire.com/2015/11/examining-hollywoods-gender-swap-trend-and-where-it-needs-to-go-next-107826/>.

Oxford English Dictionary (2019), Oxford: Oxford University Press, <www.oed.com>.

Proctor, William (2012), 'Regeneration and Rebirth: Anatomy of the Franchise Reboot', *Scope: An Online Journal of Film and Television Studies*, 22 (February), 1–19.

Puig, Claudia (2004), 'Forecast for "Ocean's": Splashy and Very Cool', *USA Today*, 9 December, <https://usatoday30.usatoday.com/life/movies/reviews/2004-12-09-oceans-12_x.htm>.

Soderbergh, Steven and Ted Griffin (2009), DVD commentary to *Ocean's Eleven. 4 Film Favorites*: Ocean's Collection: *Ocean's 11, Ocean's Eleven, Ocean's Twelve*, and *Ocean's Thirteen*, DVD.

Sullivan, Kevin P. (2017), 'Steven Soderbergh Compares Comeback Film to *Ocean's* Movie on "Cement Blocks"', *Entertainment*, 21 April, <https://ew.com/movies/2017/04/21/logan-lucky-first-look-steven-soderbergh/>.

Thomson, Luke Y. (2018), 'Blu-Ray Review: "Ocean's 8" Reveals Just How Cliched Male Heists Were Becoming', *Forbes*, 11 September, <https://www.forbes.com/sites/lukethompson/2018/09/11/blu-ray-review-oceans-8-reveals-just-how-cliched-male-heist-movies-were-becoming/#5c57988e2e83>.

Travers, Peter (2018), '"Ocean's 8 Review": Heist Franchises Female Reboot Gives You Stars for a Steal', *Rolling Stone*, 6 June, <https://www.rollingstone.com/movies/movie-reviews/oceans-8-review-heist-franchises-female-reboot-gives-you-stars-for-a-steal-627919/>.

CHAPTER 6

Understanding *Twin Peaks: The Return* as a 'Film Reboot' via Anti-Franchise Discourses Within Media Franchising

Matt Hills

More than obviously, *Twin Peaks: The Return* (Showtime, 2017) is neither a film nor a reboot. It is a returning television series comprising eighteen episodes. It continues the narratives of characters such as FBI Special Agent Dale Cooper (Kyle MacLachlan) and Audrey Horne (Sherilynn Fenn) who were introduced in *Twin Peaks*' original TV run (ABC, 1990–1). It lacks the diegetic resetting of a 'reboot', at least as the term has been defined by William Proctor (2012). For Proctor, a reboot aims 'to begin a franchise anew' and 'wipes the slate clean and begins the story again . . . from a point of origin' (2012: 4–5). It starts over, acting as a kind of diegetic 'reset' – hence the relevance of rebooting: that is, turning a computer off and on to begin again.

Rather than viewing *Twin Peaks: The Return* as a cuckoo in the nest of this collection, however, I want to argue for its status as a film reboot. I will do so in order to open up questions regarding its position as a contemporary media franchise given that, as Proctor rightly notes, rebooting 'is, essentially, a franchise-specific concept' (2012: 4). I'm interested in the extent to which *The Return* is explicitly and implicitly positioned as anti-franchising (via cultural/ auteurist distinctions), even while its anti-franchise discourses are contradicted by concomitant logics of franchising (Herbert 2017: 82). Flickering between anti-franchise discourses and franchise logics enables *The Return* to become readable for fans/critics as part of the 'Lynchverse' (Nochimson 2013: 163) and David Lynch's *oeuvre*, rather than as part of a calculated commercial franchise. Here, franchising is taken to indicate 'popular yet culturally maligned systems of mass production like McDonald's, suggesting familiar, undifferentiated, homogeneous cultural products churned out ad nauseam without innovation or creativity' (Johnson 2013: 33) – the very antithesis of media art such as Lynch's output (Todd 2012: 109).

In what follows, then, I first address *The Return*'s awkward but illuminating position as a film reboot, placing it within the concerns of contemporary franchising, before moving on to analyse its strongly anti-franchise discourses: for example, diegetic attacks on restaurant franchising; the supposedly parodic use of comic book narrative closure in BOB's defeat; and a strenuous sense of anti-nostalgia. I conclude by examining its simultaneous franchise logics: for example, of world-building; struggles between highly legible forces of good and evil; expansion into merchandising; and its very existence as a brand reinvigoration with greater cultural sustainability (Drummond et al. 2018). This splitting, I will suggest, offers up the real 'twin challenge' (Biderman et al. 2019) of *Twin Peaks: The Return* – namely, that we need to interpret it as both a conventional franchise and an auteurist anti-franchise at one and the same time, with both readings being equally significant to the cultural economy of this 'trickster' text (Jenkins 1995).

TWIN PEAKS: THE RETURN AS 'FILM' AND 'REBOOT'

The Return was placed second in *Sight and Sound*'s poll of 'films of the year' for 2017 (Ewins 2018). This ranking, voted for by invited respondents, suggests a critical acceptance of David Lynch's positioning of the text:

> In various interviews towards the launching of *Twin Peaks: The Return*, the filmmaker argued that . . . it had to be seen . . . as made up of 18 parts, rather than episodes . . . [and] should be considered one long movie. . . . [W]hat we have here, as Lynch argues, is a series that is also a movie, a non-series series. By its very existence, it challenges the familiar TV format and calls upon . . . viewers to reorganise their orientation and conventions. (Biderman et al 2019: 179)

By arguing that *The Return* was an eighteen-part 'movie', Lynch asserted his discursive ownership of the text, seeking to align it with his reputation as a film-maker and his cinematic body of work and downplaying the corporate-televisual role of Showtime. Such a swerve also displaced *The Return*, however insecurely, from discussions circling around 'quality TV', elevating this new *Twin Peaks* above such debates even whilst drawing – more directly than usual – on perspectives which had long equated certain kinds of television drama with the 'cinematic' (Newman and Levine 2012: 28, 171). By arguing that he had made one long film, Lynch could symbolically distance *The Return* from its rivals in 'Peak TV' (McAvoy 2019: 97–8; Hills 2018: 322).

Of course, Lynch was also drawing on the fact that boundaries between film and TV have become increasingly porous due to digital culture and 'platform agnostic consumption' (Newman 2014: 87). Digital video renders film and TV texts effectively equivalent in terms of how they can be downloaded/streamed and consumed. As Francesco Casetti has noted, whereas film was once underpinned by specific technologies, grammars and industries, it may now be in danger of losing 'itself in the great sea of audiovisual products . . . To what degree does film succeed in remaining itself?' (2015: 101). For Casetti, film has to fight for its discursive relevance, and distinctiveness, in today's digital culture; cinema thus 'finds itself having to "return" to being cinema' (2015: 112). Yet this need to prove itself against a scenario where audiences confront 'simply the generic presence of moving images displayed on a screen' (2015: 112) also means that film can become an increasingly mobile signifier, tactically mobilised whenever it suits a bid for cultural distinction. For Lynch, describing *The Return* as 'cinematic' would immediately align it with a swathe of 'quality TV' industrially linked to US premium cable; going one further and asserting its coherence as a single 'film' text that merely happens to be distributed in eighteen 'parts' (and not the 'episodes' of TV discourse) instead places *The Return* in a liminal, auteurist class of its own.

In marked contrast, 'reboot' is not a term widely presented in *The Return*'s official paratextual materials. This categorisation does not offer the distinctions of 'film' in such a context – quite the reverse, given that rebooting raises the spectre of commerce and franchising. And although *The Return* lacks a wholesale 'resetting' function in relation to *Twin Peaks*' seasons one and two, it nevertheless both continues the established diegetic world and notably reorients it. This twenty-first-century version is set in a wider narrative world, ranging far beyond the town of Twin Peaks. It also introduces a 'hidden backstory' for the evil figure of BOB (Metz 2017), and ignores 'virtually all of the second half of Season Two prior to the Lynch-directed cliffhanger conclusion, notably omitting meaningful mentions of either Annie Blackburn (Heather Graham) or Windom Earle (Kenneth Welsh)' (Fallis and King 2019: 55–6). Just as the '[o]mnidiegetic . . . world of the surrounding materials, rhetorics and discourses of creators' stresses Lynch's artistic control and *oeuvre* (Atkinson 2014: 7), so too does the diegetic world appear to edit out, or partially 'reset', story strands from the problematic season two, which Lynch was not much involved with. Whilst not restarting *Twin Peaks* from scratch, *The Return* officially 'forgets' prior aspects of *Twin Peaks*' textuality and takes on characteristics of 'second-stage' Lynchian films, as opposed to *Twin Peaks*' original role in Lynch's 'first-stage' works (Nochimson 2013: 8, 13). Martha Nochimson suggests that Lynch's 'first-stage' works create 'representations of *parallel* worlds, but nothing as disturbing to the traditional worldview as what emerges in his later work' (2013: 13, emphasis in original), where 'the dissolution of the external world' is figured through a quantum-mechanical, multiversal perspective (2013: 8; see also Fisher 2016: 53–4).

The Return can thus be viewed as a 'reboot' by virtue of its official auto-poaching of Lynch-approved elements from the original programme, its editing out of non-Lynch materials (Harvey 2015: 97), as well as its pronounced shift from representing parallel worlds (the town/the Red Room) to implicating Dale Cooper/Richard and Laura Palmer/Carrie in multiversal navigations. But it also restarts *Twin Peaks* after a gap of twenty-six years, performatively affirming it precisely as a franchise capable once again of unifying 'the collective gaze' of fans, audiences and critics around a new textual and 'galvanizing cultural moment' (Drummond et al. 2018: 300, 303). As Derek Johnson has observed of media franchises, they are a mode of cultural production

> persisting over time . . . [O]ne could define media franchising in . . . terms of products and intellectual properties extended in an ongoing fashion within the culture industries. Such a definition would include repeatedly reproduced or reinvented franchises . . . Newer properties . . . could be considered emerging franchises. (Johnson 2013: 28)

The Return repositions *Twin Peaks*. No longer languishing as a 'dusty' franchise (2013: 20), it becomes a successfully reinvented and thus temporally extended brand. As a 'reboot', it combines narrative continuation with a sense of retooling the intellectual property (IP), countering Proctor's (2012) binary of story world coherence versus total reset. *The Return* is more akin to Nick Pinkerton's concept of a 're-quel', facilitating 'the baton passage of characters and . . . worlds from one generation to the next' (2016: 34) by combining familiar elements with twists of difference.

What is important here, however, is more than the semantics of 'rebooting'. By thinking of *The Return* as a reboot, it is analytically possible to challenge official paratextual framings of the text as a 'film' which work to render it purely a matter of Lynchian auteurism, vision and artistry. Where such filmic positioning stresses *The Return*'s relations to the 'Lynchverse' (Nochimson 2013: 163), emphasising its reboot status restores an otherwise occluded sense of industrial creativity and logic to the picture. Viewing *Twin Peaks: The Return* as a film reboot is therefore somewhat contradictory or even oxymoronic – it means both accepting and contesting official paratexts, both affirming and challenging this text's claimed cultural distinctions. In fact, my focus on *The Return* as a film reboot captures the 'both/and' logic of my wider argument: that is, that this text needs to be theorised both as anti-franchising (in the guise of Lynchian art) and as an example of franchising (by reproducing established logics of world-building, transmedia expansion, and so on). It is this reformulated 'twin challenge' (Biderman et al. 2019) of *Twin Peaks* that I will now discuss in greater depth, looking first at how *The Return* is dismissive of franchising practices.

TWIN PEAKS: THE RETURN AS A PERFORMANCE OF ANTI-FRANCHISING DISCOURSES

Johnson has pointed out that 'most [film] scholars do not make the explicit connection between media culture and franchise culture' (2013: 32), failing to move 'outside of media studies proper to consider the history of franchising as a means of sharing business formats within the retail industries' (2013: 29). This history has one set of roots 'in the culture of McDonald's . . . and Chicken Delight that emerged in the 1950s and 60s' (2013: 29). Given such a resonance between franchising discourses and fast food, it is perhaps unsurprising that it is restaurant franchising rather than media franchising that explicitly features in *The Return*'s story world. Although it has been argued that the glass box in Part 1 reflexively connotes Lynch's view of current meanings of 'quality' TV spectatorship and fandom (Garner 2017; McAvoy 2019: 91; Hawkes 2019: 153), this remains subtextually implicit at best. By contrast, the Double R Diner – arguably an icon of *Twin Peaks* – is explicitly involved in diegetic discussions of franchising in Parts 13 and 15. Its owner Norma Jennings (Peggy Lipton) has entered into a business partnership with Walter Lawford (Grant Goodeve), and this involves franchising the Double R across multiple stores. As a result, Norma is advised to reduce the quality of her all-natural cherry pie recipe to 'ensure consistency and profitability', as well as changing her establishment's name to something that has tested well. As Film Crit Hulk (2017) remarks in a recap of Part 13 for *Vulture*: 'Pretty quickly, you realize the entire thing doubles as Lynch's criticism of studio notes and probably capitalism at large'. Franchising is shown to place profit over a restaurant's (filmmaker's?) distinctive identity, and delivery of a beloved experience. It consequently comes as no great surprise when a few episodes later, in Part 15, Norma rejects Walter's franchising model and seeks to restore the Double R to independence – in a 'meta' reflection on the brand of *Twin Peaks*, the distinctiveness of its cherry pie is diegetically preserved. Franchising is denotatively shown to be an evil in the world of *Twin Peaks: The Return*, something to be resisted and fought against. Its rejection by Norma comes at the same moment that she is finally united with Big Ed (Everett McGill), making anti-franchise sentiment part of *The Return*'s most explicit instance of fan service via a long-awaited happy ending for these two characters. Such an on-the-nose critique of restaurant franchising doubles as a Lynchian take on franchise discourses more broadly.

And this dismay with franchising is arguably connoted in other ways across *The Return*. Martin Fradley and John A. Riley state that Part 17, which seems to represent the defeat of BOB thanks to a climactic showdown, in fact undercuts this resolution:

> Perhaps the most jarringly dislocated character in *The Return*, Freddie's glove allows him to defeat the hitherto unfathomable threat

of BOB with a few (manifest) destiny-laden punches (3.17). This absurdist parody of the ideological infantilism of contemporary comic book franchises finds its own grimly realistic reflection when Cooper confronts a group of contemporary cowboys in a bland Texas diner (3.18). (Fradley and Riley 2019: 207)

Freddie Sykes (Jake Wardle) is gifted with the capacity to defeat BOB, and his magical green glove – an ordinary, everyday item which itself seems to satirise the accoutrements which typically characterise superheroes in Marvel/DC films – leads to *Twin Peaks*' ongoing narrative of good versus evil being concluded via a few well-placed physical blows. If we accept Fradley and Riley's reading, then *The Return* is implicitly of a piece with recent statements from auteurs such as Martin Scorsese and Francis Ford Coppola (Shoard 2019) othering 'Marvel films' as pure commerce rather than film art. And it would be fair to conclude that the tonality of Part 17's cosmic punch-up with BOB is odd, even for *Twin Peaks*, with narrative ambiguity, openness and irresolution giving way to a bizarre dust-up. But to posit that superhero franchises per se are marked by 'infantilism' hardly seems persuasive. In any case, as I shall go on to argue, *The Return* is equally permeated by concepts of simplistic good versus evil, constructing a new mythology for BOB and Judy versus the Fireman which is no less ideologically 'infantile' than any account of superheroes versus supervillains, given that it implies an epic struggle across time (and across realities) between opposed forces of good and evil (Lowry 2019: 46).

A more convincing interpretation of *The Return*'s anti-franchising discourses comes not thanks to a premature dismissal of Part 17, but instead through analyses of anti-nostalgia across all eighteen parts. Nostalgia has been assumed to act as a bedrock of contemporary franchising (Lizardi 2015), since it typically involves pre-sold IPs, the implication being that fans are sold more of what they already love. Although franchises are not equivalent to genres (Johnson 2013: 29), there is a replaying of genre criticism from an earlier era here (see Neale 1980), with franchises supposedly offering pure repetition – more of the same – in order to profit from fans' affective investments. In fact, scholarly theorisations of franchising almost always concede that – like genre – to be successful franchises must introduce 'discontinuity' (Archer 2019: 61; Hassler-Forest 2012: 22) into repetition. But the commonsense view of franchising as mass-produced repetition lacking in artistry and variation clearly persists, as much in the Scorsese–Coppola axis of distaste as in David Lynch's positioning of *The Return*.

This version of *Twin Peaks* is intent on disrupting any sense of merely offering 'more of the same' to fans allegedly craving coherence and consistency with the 1990s series. It repeatedly engages in what I have referred to as 'fan disservice' (Hills 2018: 317). Agent Cooper, probably the most beloved character from the original *Twin Peaks*, does not dramatically return until Part 16 of 18, despite the actor Kyle MacLachlan playing a version of 'bad' Cooper from the Black Lodge from the outset, known as 'Mr C', as well as a further doppelganger which Cooper's paralysed consciousness has been switched into, Dougie Jones, and the 'true' Cooper trapped in an otherworldly domain. For the majority of *The Return*, fans were thus confronted with alternate constructions of Cooper in place of the 'real' character they wanted back. As Douglas Anderson has observed of the almost catatonic figure of Dougie, who is seemingly only capable of echolalia, and sometimes incapable of controlling his own bodily functions: 'Viewers don't really want to experience the banality of waiting [for Cooper to genuinely return] and so the experience of Dougie is not pleasurable, but punishing' (Anderson 2019: 189). In place of *The Return* immediately gratifying fans after their extremely lengthy wait for a new series of *Twin Peaks*, it offers yet more waiting. Anderson argues that '*The Return* exposes this architecture' of fan nostalgia and anticipation, with 'the discomfort of waiting produc[ing] a conscious viewer aware of the mechanics of storytelling' (2019: 190).

Interpreting *The Return* as anti-nostalgic, and as wilfully disruptive of expected or anticipated fan pleasures, has in fact become a standard scholarly reading: Anderson suggests that the figure of Audrey Horne (Gillan 2016) is also brought back in *The Return* only to frustrate fan expectations and 'punish . . . viewers for taking any pleasure in the nostalgia offered by Audrey's [iconic and much-loved] dance' (2019: 191; see McAvoy 2019: 98; Lim 2018; Halskov 2017). Similarly, Jeffrey Fallis and Kyle T. King note that

> on the rare occasions that *The Return* meets fans' expectations with heart-warming callbacks to the original series – such as when Big Ed Hurley . . . proposes to Norma Jennings . . . and Agent Cooper undergoes an Angelo Badalamenti-scored reawakening in the hospital – the good vibes promptly are dashed by being followed almost immediately with sorrowful scenes of ostensible suicide and familial dissolution. (Fallis and King 2019: 56)

The Return recurrently focuses on familiar material, for example integrating actor Kyle MacLachlan into old footage, so that it can rewrite and rework the diegetic past (and fans' memories) rather than referencing it nostalgically. This process is literalised in the plot twist whereby Agent Cooper is able to travel back in time to prevent Laura Cooper from being murdered. The original series' detective/thriller mystery – who killed Laura Palmer? – thus gets a radically unexpected new answer: nobody. Fallis and King observe how this 'act of unravelling . . . epitomizes the way *The Return* both revives and undermines the original show's established patterns' (2019: 56).

By constantly seeking to evoke its former self at the same time as enacting multiversal echoes and new variations, whether by making subtle changes to the original programme's 'over-design' of red curtains and chevrons (Johnson 2013: 119; Ryan 2017: 3), or by replacing deceased actors/stars with surreal, non-human elements (such as a 'kettle' in place of David Bowie's Agent Jeffries), *The Return* refuses to be positioned as standardised franchise fare. Indeed, David McAvoy (2019: 87) goes so far as to suggest that David Lynch actively 'trolls' long-term fans of *Twin Peaks*:

> [D]esigned to upset the kinds of Peak TV expectations about narrative 'payoff' created by the online fandom of *Twin Peaks*'s original run, *The Return* instead validates the patience it takes to simply sit, marking time's passage as its own fulfilling aesthetic experience . . . But beyond simply a television auteur setting out to upset our expectations, Lynch is more aggressively trollish in his disdain for what fans want from a Peak TV version of *Twin Peaks*. (McAvoy 2019: 98)

Had *The Return* delivered what fans were presumed to want, rather than a patience-testing, slow-paced destabilisation of its own icons and quotable moments, then it would have been recognisable as a nostalgia-affirming commodification of fan tastes; it would have participated in a franchise discourse of 'consistency and profitability'. But by frustrating fan expectations, even to the point where new official tie-in books appeared to problematise narrative continuity, and hence undermine established fan knowledge (McCarthy 2019: 171), *The Return* casts doubt on its title. Although a 'return' can be promised, it cannot be meaningfully delivered. Auteurist creative innovation, in line with 'second-stage' Lynchian cinema, instead becomes the anti-franchise order of the day, as *Twin Peaks* branches into multiple diegetic realities, thus offering discontinuity and surprise rather than wholly familiar brand pleasures (Archer 2019: 61).

Accepting this account means accepting *The Return* purely in terms of Lynchian art, though, subordinating scholarship to official paratextuality. In what follows, I want to counter this possibility by exploring another interpretation, one which collapses into these anti-franchise discourses and complicates their 'omnidiegetic' story. To wit, what if we approach *The Return* as a successful reinvigoration of the *Twin Peaks* franchise at the same time as we identify Lynch's anti-franchise positionings?

TWIN PEAKS: THE RETURN AS A PERFORMANCE OF FRANCHISING LOGICS

If contemporary film franchising is taken to indicate a situation where '*products themselves* have become part of the story' (Kapell 2004: 184, emphasis in original), rather than merchandise simply allowing its 'buyer to re-live the filmed experience' (2004: 184), then *Twin Peaks: The Return* lives up to this definition, for all its auteurist framings. In both *The Secret History of Twin Peaks* (Frost 2016) and *The Final Dossier* (Frost 2017), books published before and after the initial transmission of *The Return*, series co-writer Mark Frost adds significant narrative details to the on-screen world. As Donald McCarthy has noted, *The Secret History of Twin Peaks* prefigures *The Return*'s fragmentation into a multiversal perspective by presenting a version of Twin Peaks' history which alters established continuity: 'For the reader well acquainted with the television show, there will be a number of inaccuracies to spot . . . As Frost was the co-creator and co-showrunner of *Twin Peaks*, these inaccuracies do not seem to be the result of shoddy research' (McCarthy 2019: 171). Instead, Frost's narratively destabilising gambit introduces discontinuity and novelty into the world-building of *Twin Peaks*, preparing fans for the slant taken in *The Return*. And in *The Final Dossier*, Frost confirms vital narrative information which remained ambiguous in Part 8:

> Frost connects Sarah Palmer to a young girl seen in the 1956 sequence in Part 8. In this sequence, the young girl is on a date with a boy, who kisses her goodnight. She returns to her house, puts on the radio, and falls asleep only to have a creature crawl into her mouth . . . [*The Final Dossier*] describes how . . . Sarah Palmer was involved in a strange, borderline supernatural incident . . . [which] tracks with where Part 8 ended, linking together the nameless girl with Sarah Palmer. In this case, Frost is explicitly resolving a question: who is the girl in Part 8? (McCarthy 2019: 180)

This involvement of Sarah Palmer in the newly revealed backstory of evil supernatural forces BOB and Judy (or 'Jouday') makes sense of her powers in *The Return* (Joyce 2019: 24–5), as well as suggesting that she – or rather the energy 'Judy' which seems to inhabit her – is involved in trying to hunt down Laura Palmer/Carrie Page at the very end of Part 18.

Frost also offers up written answers 'to questions left open by the original run of episodes, such as the fates of Annie Blackburn (she is in a mental institute and rarely speaks) and Leo Johnson (dead)' (McCarthy 2019: 180). As such, his books 'complement and expand the world of *Twin Peaks*' (2019: 180) without entirely resolving its mysteries or filling in all its story world gaps. There is a stronger sense of fan service to Frost's publications, in contrast to the fan disservice which marks Lynch's recurrent approach to *The Return*, as if franchising logics of narrative expansion, coherent world-building and fan targeting can be attributed mainly to Frost, leaving Lynch insulated from such 'commercial' concerns.

However, at the very same moment as Lynch is at his most experimental, avant-garde and auteurist – in the much-celebrated Part 8 (Joyce 2019: 13), with its black-and-white imagery of moving inside a nuclear mushroom cloud – *Twin Peaks: The Return* simultaneously engages in rather more conventional franchising by expanding its hyperdiegetic story world without contradicting what has come before (Hills 2002:137–8). It does this via new 'backstory . . . The murder of Laura Palmer has its roots in the creation of American evil, the development of atomic weapons . . . [T]he plot of Twin Peaks emerges from . . . the deployment of nuclear weapons' (Metz 2017). The small-town events of the original *Twin Peaks* are shown to be part of a seemingly timeless, epic struggle between the evil BOB and forces arrayed against him:

> the Giant in Twin Peaks: The Return seems to be an alien whose job it is to intervene in Earthly affairs once the [1945] atomic bomb liberates Killer Bob from the primordial ooze. The unexpected weapon he delivers [to counter BOB] is Laura Palmer, not a heroic figure by any means, but to us a symbol of an American tragedy. (Metz 2017)

The Giant, or, as he is named here, the 'Fireman', seemingly sends Laura Palmer's spirit to Earth in the form of a 'golden orb of light' which Elizabeth Lowry argues connotes a sense of 'love':

> in *The Return*, light signalling love typically turns to gold, suggesting a movement from the bright white of . . . purification to an alchemical apotheosis. For instance, when Carl joins the grieving mother at the side of the road he watches her child's spirit, a yellow light, float into the air (Season 3, Ep. 6). The same golden orb is seen when Dido and the Fireman ostensibly send Laura down to earth. (Lowry 2019: 46)

The world-building set out in Part 8, then, seems to be simplistically Manichean: just as the evil of BOB is loosed into the world by mankind's deployment of the atomic bomb, then the positive 'love' of Laura Palmer is deployed against him. Laura becomes the target of both BOB and the newly revealed female demonic force Jouday/Judy, indicating that both of her parents, Leland and Sarah Palmer, are possessed by evil spirits. Writing in *Sight and Sound* when *The Return* was voted second in its poll of 'The Films of 2017', Michael Ewins astutely pointed out that

> Lynch has always smeared the line between good and evil in his work . . . but they have never been so clearly conceived as interdependent forces as in *The Return*. 'Dougie' and Mr C. personify Good . . . and Evil in a literal, almost parodic fashion. (Ewins 2018: 36)

Laura and Judy/BOB, on the other hand, personify spiritual forces of love versus hate, or good versus evil, in a serious and epic mode rather than as near-parody. To dismiss Part 17's showdown between Freddie Sykes and BOB as an 'absurdist parody of the ideological infantilism of contemporary comic book franchises' (Fradley and Riley 2019: 207) thus misses the fact that *The Return* enacts an earnest 'ideological infantilism' (where this is presumed to characterise contemporary media franchising) by rooting its psychological complexities in a very much non-parodic stand-off between otherworldly forces of 'good' and 'evil'.

Part 8 thus represents a standardised logic of franchising, offering

> a key to the entire Twin Peaks mythology, or at least as close to a key as fans of David Lynch can ever hope to expect. For audiences of Lynch's work, this is what we crave, and Lynch has given us just enough . . . to produce a rabbit hole's worth of fan- and critic-driven rumination. (Joyce 2019: 13)

Such world-building, where narrative threats such as BOB and aspects of 'over-design' such as the Red Room (Johnson 2013: 119) are integrated into an ever more expansive hyperdiegesis (Joyce 2019: 25), also serves another key function for *Twin Peaks* as a franchise. The reinventions of *The Return*, where *Twin Peaks*' televisual past is selectively mined, give rise to a whole new 'cultural moment' for the brand, focusing critics and gatekeepers on its status as auteur-driven content, and providing a 'rallying point . . . necessary to collect consumers, gatekeepers, prosumers, and producers in a profoundly new artifactual event' (Drummond et al. 2018: 303). Successful media franchises that come to possess cultural sustainability need to display a 'cyclical alternation of cultural [i.e., canonical] moments with proliferations' of fan-created versions/readings (2018: 303). These 'moments' work to unify 'the collective gaze once again', providing a new relevance and significance for a franchise which can then feed into a subsequent period of 'fan- and critic-driven rumination' (Joyce 2019: 13). As such, the return of *Twin Peaks* and its carefully protected canonical status – fully involving Mark Frost and David Lynch, and reuniting as many of the original cast as possible – is surely textbook media franchising at work, regardless of the varied anti-franchise discourses that can be implicitly or explicitly linked to Lynchian auteurism.

CONCLUSION

I have resisted the temptation to reproduce official paratextual framings of *The Return*, instead staging a collision between notions of *Twin Peaks: The*

Return as 'film' (art) and as a (franchise) 'reboot'. And in spite of emergent discussions of the 'experimental blockbuster', where auteurist discourses are harnessed to ensure 'difference' or colouration amongst franchised products (Archer 2019: 53), *Twin Peaks* is perhaps unusual in terms of presenting such a powerfully authored franchise. This symbolic equation between David Lynch and the brand's hyperdiegesis is so insistent that a 'No Lynch, No Peaks' campaign arose when it seemed as though Lynch might step away from *The Return* due to disputes with Showtime (Williams 2016). But even the most auteurist of franchises remains caught in the glass box of franchising logics; even the most blatant performances of fan disservice and fandom trolling can still represent 'Brand Lynch' consistency (Todd 2012: 108). Embedded in anti-franchise cultural distinctions and franchise logics, *The Return* remains liminally caught between realities of art/commerce. Little wonder that it finds a multiverse of hyperdiegetic possibilities so tempting; unravelling its own continuity, history and branding by undoing Laura Palmer's death might be one satisfyingly artistic exit. But outdoing season two's cliffhanger via the shattering conclusion of Cooper's final question, 'what year is this?', reinstates the fannish desire for further explanations. The one 'return' that *The Return* is genuinely able to deliver, like all good auteurs and all effective franchises, is the recurrent wish for more.

REFERENCES

Anderson, Donald L. (2019), '"There Is No Return": *Twin Peaks* and the Horror of Pleasure', in Victoria McCollum (ed.), *Make America Hate Again: Trump-Era Horror and the Politics of Fear*, London: Routledge, pp. 177–94.

Archer, Neil (2019), *Twenty-First Century Hollywood: Rebooting the System*, New York: Wallflower Press/Columbia University Press.

Atkinson, Sarah (2014), *Beyond the Screen: Emerging Cinema and Engaging Audiences*, London: Bloomsbury Academic.

Biderman, Shai, Ronen Gil and Ido Lewit (2019), 'Life in the Black Lodge: The Twin Challenge of Watching *Twin Peaks*', in Amanda DiPaolo and Jamie Gillies (eds), *The Politics of Twin Peaks*, Lanham, MD: Lexington Books, pp. 177–91.

Casetti, Francesco (2015), *The Lumiere Galaxy: 7 Key Words for the Cinema to Come*, New York: Columbia University Press.

Drummond, Kent, Susan Aronstein and Terri L. Rittenburg (2018), *The Road to Wicked: The Marketing and Consumption of Oz from L. Frank Baum to Broadway*, Basingstoke: Palgrave Macmillan.

Ewins, Michael (2018), 'The Stars Turn and a Time Presents Itself', *Sight and Sound* (January), 33–6.

Fallis, Jeffrey and T. Kyle King (2019), 'Lucy Finally Understands How Cellphones Work: Ambiguous Digital Technologies in *Twin Peaks: The Return* and Its Fan Communities', in Antonio Sanna (ed.), *Critical Essays on Twin Peaks: The Return*, Basingstoke: Palgrave Macmillan, pp. 53–68.

Film Crit Hulk (2017), '*Twin Peaks* recap: Just You and I', *Vulture*, 6 August, <https://www.vulture.com/2017/08/twin-peaks-the-return-recap-part-13.html>.

Fisher, Mark (2016), *The Weird and the Eerie*, London: Repeater Books.

Fradley, Martin and John A. Riley (2019), '"I Don't Understand How This Keeps Happening... Over and Over Again": Trumpism, Uncanny Repetition, and *Twin Peaks: The Return*', in Victoria McCollum (ed.), *Make America Hate Again: Trump-Era Horror and the Politics of Fear*, London: Routledge, pp. 195–210.

Frost, Mark (2016), *The Secret History of Twin Peaks*, Basingstoke: Palgrave Macmillan.

Frost, Mark (2017), *Twin Peaks: The Final Dossier*, Basingstoke: Palgrave Macmillan.

Garner, Ross (2017), 'What We Learnt from Sam and Tracey: Does the New *Twin Peaks* Differ to Contemporary "Quality TV"?', *CST Online*, 27 May, <http://cstonline.net/what-we-learnt-from-sam-and-tracey-new-twin-peaks-and-contemporary-quality-tv/>.

Gillan, Jennifer (2016), 'Textural Poaching *Twin Peaks*: The Audrey Horne Sweater Girl GIFs', *Series: International Journal of TV Serial Narratives* 2: 2, 9–24.

Halskov, Andreas (2017), 'No Place Like Home: Returning to *Twin Peaks*', *16:9*, 30 May, <http://www.16-9.dk/2017/05/returning-to-twin-peaks/>.

Harvey, Colin B. (2015), *Fantastic Transmedia*, Basingstoke: Palgrave Macmillan.

Hassler-Forest, Dan (2012), *Capitalist Superheroes: Caped Crusaders in the Neoliberal Age*, Winchester: Zero Books.

Hawkes, Joel (2019), 'Movement in the Box: The Production of Surreal Social Space and the Alienated Body', in Antonio Sanna (ed.), *Critical Essays on Twin Peaks: The Return*, Basingstoke: Palgrave Macmillan, pp. 149–68.

Herbert, Daniel (2017), *Film Remakes and Franchises*, New Brunswick, NJ: Rutgers University Press.

Hills, Matt (2002), *Fan Cultures*, London and New York: Routledge.

Hills, Matt (2018), 'Cult TV Revival: Generational Seriality, Recap Culture, and the "Brand Gap" of *Twin Peaks: The Return*', *Television & New Media*, 19: 4, 310–27.

Jenkins, Henry (1995), '"Do You Enjoy Making the Rest of Us Feel Stupid?": alt.tv.twinpeaks, the Trickster Author and Viewer Mastery', in David Lavery (ed.), *Full of Secrets: Critical Approaches to Twin Peaks*, Detroit, MI: Wayne State University Press, pp. 51–69.

Johnson, Derek (2013), *Media Franchising: Creative License and Collaboration in the Culture Industries*, New York: New York University Press.

Joyce, Ashlee (2019), 'The Nuclear Anxiety of *Twin Peaks: The Return*', in Amanda DiPaolo and Jamie Gillies (eds), *The Politics of Twin Peaks*, Lanham, MD: Lexington Books, pp. 13–34.

Kapell, Matthew (2004), 'At the Edge of the World, Again', in Matthew Kapell and William G. Doty (eds), *Jacking into the Matrix Franchise*, New York and London: Continuum, pp. 183–7.

Lim, Dennis (2018), 'Donald Trump's America and the Visions of David Lynch', *The New Yorker*, 29 June, <https://www.newyorker.com/culture/culture-desk/donald-trumps-america-and-the-visions-of-david-lynch>.

Lizardi, Ryan (2015), *Mediated Nostalgia: Individual Memory and Contemporary Mass Media*, New York: Lexington Press.

Lowry, Elizabeth (2019), 'Extraterrestrial Intelligences in the Atomic Age: Exploring the Rhetorical Function of Aliens and the "Alien" in the *Twin Peaks* Universe', in Antonio Sanna (ed.), *Critical Essays on Twin Peaks: The Return*, Basingstoke: Palgrave Macmillan, pp. 37–51.

McAvoy, David (2019), '"Is It About the Bunny? No, It's Not About the Bunny!": David Lynch's Fandom and Trolling of Peak TV Audiences', in Antonio Sanna (ed.), *Critical Essays on Twin Peaks: The Return*, Basingstoke: Palgrave Macmillan, pp. 85–103.

McCarthy, Donald (2019), 'How Mark Frost's *Twin Peaks* Books Clarify and Confound the Nature of Reality', in Antonio Sanna (ed.), *Critical Essays on Twin Peaks: The Return*, Basingstoke: Palgrave Macmillan, pp. 169–81.

Metz, Walter (2017), 'The Atomic Gambit of Twin Peaks: The Return', *Film Criticism*, 41: 3, <https://quod.lib.umich.edu/f/fc/13761232.0041.324/--atomic-gambit-of-twin-peaks-the-return?rgn=main;view=fulltext>.

Neale, Stephen (1980), *Genre*, London: BFI.

Newman, Michael Z. (2014), *Video Revolutions: On the History of a Medium*, New York: Columbia University Press.

Newman, Michael Z. and Elana Levine (2012), *Legitimating Television: Media Convergence and Cultural Status*, New York and London: Routledge.

Nochimson, Martha P. (2013), *David Lynch Swerves: Uncertainty from Lost Highway to Inland Empire*, Austin, TX: University of Texas Press.

Pinkerton, Nick (2016), 'Rise of the Reboots', *Sight & Sound*, 26: 3, 32–5.

Proctor, William (2012), 'Regeneration and Rebirth: Anatomy of the Franchise Reboot', *Scope: An Online Journal of Film and Television Studies*, 22 (February), 1–19.

Ryan, Scott (2017), 'Credit to the Credits', *The Blue Rose Magazine*, 1: 2, 3.

Shoard, Catherine (2019), 'Francis Ford Coppola: Scorsese Was Being Kind – Marvel Movies are Despicable', *The Guardian*, 21 October, <https://www.theguardian.com/film/2019/oct/21/francis-ford-coppola-scorsese-was-being-kind-marvel-movies-are-despicable>.

Todd, Antony (2012), *Authorship and the Films of David Lynch*, London and New York: I. B. Tauris.

Williams, Rebecca (2016), '"No Lynch, No Peaks!": Auteurism, Fan/Actor Campaigns and the Challenges Of *Twin Peaks*' Return(s)', *Series: International Journal Of TV Serial Narratives*, 2: 2, 55–65.

CHAPTER 7

All This Has Happened Before: Mythic Repetition in the Film-to-Television Reboot

Nicholas Benson and Jonathan Gray

Film-to-television reboots are becoming an increasingly popular mode of textual proliferation. In recent years, we have seen television reimaginings of *Parenthood* (NBC, 2010–15), *Teen Wolf* (MTV, 2011–17), *Fargo* (FX, 2014–), *From Dusk till Dawn* (El Rey, 2014–16), *12 Monkeys* (Syfy, 2015–18), *Minority Report* (Fox, 2015), *The Exorcist* (Fox, 2016–18), *Lethal Weapon* (Fox, 2016–19), *Rush Hour* (CBS, 2016) and *Westworld* (HBO, 2016–), among many others. This trend shows no sign of slowing, and is even more fervid amongst children's media, where properties regularly move from film to television series if successful. Television, it seems, has become an attractive space for expanding and reinvigorating pre-existing story worlds. This trend calls for a new set of questions about reboots that centre on medium and consider the limitations and possibilities inherent in transitioning a text or set of texts from film to television. What does a film-to-television reboot offer writers and producers that a film-to-film reboot might not? What common intertextual and narrative strategies are at work across this category of reboot? And, ultimately, what is involved in rebooting a 90-to-120 minute narrative into a serialised, continuing television show?

William Proctor argues that, unlike a remake which seeks to retell a single story, 'a reboot "re-starts" a series of films that seek to disavow and render inert its predecessor's validity' (2012: 2). Though Proctor's insights are specific to film, if, broadly speaking, the difference between a reboot and a remake is the intent to restart an ongoing story, then in theory television provides an ideal space to do just that. Andrew Scahill has pointed to the ways these types of television reboot often position themselves as prequels to the original text. Writing about two other recent film-to-television reboots, *Bates Motel* (A&E, 2013–17) and *Hannibal* (NBC, 2013–15), Scahill argues, 'these programs employ the seriality of television and the inevitability of the programs' "known" conclusion' (2016: 324). Scahill's analysis of the two programmes highlights the ways temporal trajectories and narrative complexity are combined to create intertextual pleasures for audiences.

Building off Scahill, we want to further the discussion of television reboots by considering how they might contribute to the construction and maintenance of a text's mythic qualities. We use the term mythic here not in its Barthesian sense per se as a text's ideological meanings but to gesture towards a story's deeper narrative meanings and thematic bedrock, and we use it as a way to move beyond a superficial interest in which characters or specific moments from a narrative are adapted or rebooted, to consider instead the ways that reboots can approach intertextuality more broadly and holistically. Sarah Cardwell argues that 'adaptations can be regarded as points on a continuum, as part of the extended development of a singular infinite meta-text: a valuable story or myth that is constantly growing and developing, being retold, reinterpreted and reassessed' (2002: 25). How, then, can television series reboot a narrative while continuing and deepening the telling of the myth(s) that undergird this narrative?

To begin to answer this question, we focus here on television programmes derived from *Fargo* (Coen, 1996) and *The Exorcist* (Friedkin, 1973). *Fargo* rebooted a beloved and prestige cult drama for FX, a channel whose brand identity seemed already to hail likely fans of filmmakers Joel and Ethan Coen. *The Exorcist* rebooted a horror film whose fame had crossed into everyday vernacular of twirling heads, projectile vomit and even the concept of exorcism, and did so for a network television series that surely aimed to attract many whose prior engagement with the series was simply at that vernacular level. Each, we argue, adopted a strategy of adaptation that considers the source material as mythic on some level, not transferring specific characters, scenes and motivations as much as digging beneath them to excavate notions of their mythic structures, and building their televisual narratives upon these structures. This strategy, we argue, is perhaps one that is required for a reboot to television. Quite practically, a single film cannot provide enough material for a serial television drama to draw upon continually. This sets up a challenge that is admittedly present with all reboots but that is amplified with film-to-television reboots, namely that the writers must find sustaining ways to move beyond the original even while acknowledging and paying (what fans would consider) due homage to both its existence and its rules of existence. Linda Hutcheon has argued that 'in a television series, there is more time available, and therefore less compression of the adapted text is required' (2006: 47). In the case of a film-to-television reboot, not only is compression not required, though, but the compelling expansion of the source is essential for the longevity of the series. Writers must find methods of drawing out themes in ways that interest fans of the original text, but also don't bore them with overwrought exposition and unnecessary details. Such processes aren't unique to television reboots, but are amplified significantly, given the immediate, pressing need to create an ongoing narrative. However, where *Fargo* largely relies upon an audience's close knowledge of the 1996 film, playing with and dancing around expectations created by one or more viewings of the film, and while *The Exorcist* includes a few such moments, *The Exorcist* otherwise builds on a mythos and imagery that is popularly available, and hence that requires little or no close interaction with (or fandom of) the 1973 film.

We examine the pilots of each series, partly to limit our exploration in manageable ways, partly to explore how each series begins and establishes the rules by which it will play. The creators of each series surely knew that their pilots would come under intense scrutiny, both by their own industry bosses and, in due course, by audiences, for what adaptive tone was being set, thereby making the pilots excellent places to look for a statement of adaptive tone. As reboots, these pilots (more so than the rest of the series) become the spaces through which the mythic bedrock of the property is laid most bare, as creators seek to conjure positive memories attached to the originals and demonstrate their proliferative value to those responsible for greenlighting the series. Pilots, in short, must compel viewers to watch the rest of the series, making them especially interesting sites for the examination of what promises are being made, what tone is being struck and what narrative rules are being laid out. Constantine Verevis has suggested of remakes, 'just as adaptations of literary properties often lead viewers back to the source novels for a first reading, remakes lead viewers to seek out original film properties' (2006: 20). Similarly, we consider how both *Fargo* and *The Exorcist* as film-to-television reboots aim in their pilots not to render their predecessors inert, or to correct perceived missteps within the histories of the texts, but rather to reinvigorate interest in, and both renew and extend the value of, the world and mythos created by the source material.

FARGO: 'THERE BE DRAGONS HERE'

Fargo's pilot opens with Carter Burwell's memorable theme music from the film playing over title cards reading 'This is a True Story. The events depicted took place in Minnesota in 2006. At the request of the survivors, the names have been changed. Out of respect for the dead, the rest has been told exactly as it occurred'. The scene is at night, and we can make out a pair of car headlights in the distance approaching us over what appears otherwise to be a barren, snow-filled landscape. As the car nears, the music swells, and we cut to its interior, treated to a driver's-eye view of the road ahead. We begin to hear muffled, panicked noises from the back of the car, before a deer darts in front of the car, causing the driver to swerve off the road and hit a barbed wire fence. As the car settles in the snow, the trunk opens and out jumps a man dressed only in his boxers. He flees into the snowy field, with the driver following him quietly and methodically, before the driver stops to stare at the deer dying in front of him.

This short scene is laden with references that any fan of *Fargo* the film could catalogue while watching, as the film similarly begins with a car approaching us from a distance across a snowy barren landscape, with title cards that are identical but for the year (1987), and accompanied by Burwell's theme music, also beginning on violin. The film's opening occurs in daytime, the screen bathed in white, and yet the pilot's night time invokes a later scene from the film, when Gaear Grimsrud (Peter Stormare) gives chase to two passers-by who witnessed his partner Carl Showalter (Steve Buscemi) dragging a murdered police officer. The film similarly offered a driver's-eye view, until the chased car veered off the road and, upon Grimsrud's arrival, its driver similarly fled into the snowy field before being followed, again laconically, by Grimsrud before Grimsrud shoots him in the back. That scene in the film offered us no barbed wire fence, yet the barbed wire running along the highway proved key to another scene in which Showalter buries some ransom money by the side of the road. In short, the pilot begins with an interesting intermixing of the already-seen and the new. It seems so familiar, and yet is also different – its driver, Lorne Malvo (Billy Bob Thornton), is neither in pursuit nor being chased, the body in the back is of a near-naked man instead of a kidnapped woman, and it's 2006 not 1987. Those title cards serve on one hand as a calling card of *Fargo*, on a par with *Star Wars*' iconic 'A long time ago, in a galaxy far, far away', yet the changed date suggests cosmic repetition, a mythic restaging.

Throughout the pilot, indeed, we see all sorts of semi-familiar elements, yet always with differences, such that Julie Grossman suggests '[t]he film haunts the show' with 'dream-like' repetition (2017: 194). We see Lester Nygaard (Martin Freeman)'s flustering, ineffective insurance salesman trying to upsell a dowdy Midwestern couple in a clear reference to Jerry Lundegaard (William H. Macy)'s flustering, ineffective car salesman trying to upsell a dowdy Midwestern couple. Lester is clearly frustrated, held under the thumb of local bully Sam Hess, and powerless (mocked ruthlessly by his wife) in ways that echo Jerry's frustration and powerlessness at the hands of his father-in-law, who, similar to Sam, is often flanked by his lawyer and who wears his success as a businessman loudly. The film's famous cop, Marge Gunderson (Frances McDormand), finds an apparent match in Molly Solverson (Allison Tolman), with useless deputy Lou (Bruce Bohne) echoed in Bill (Bob Odenkirk) . . . except Molly is neither the Chief nor pregnant, even though our Chief's wife is pregnant, and Bill soon becomes Molly's superior. And beyond specific plot elements, the story is motored by similar engines – whether Lester's or Jerry's frustration, Malvo's or Grimsrud's malevolence, Molly's or Marge's honest, small-town goodness and savvy ability to solve crimes. Those deep mythic values are even embedded in some characters' names – Malvo as force of malevolence, Solverson as the super-cop. Grossman sees this repetition as a 'reimagining' of the film's tone (2017: 199), but that phrase suggests a move away from the film and a 'rerouting' (2017: 195), whereas we suggest it is frequently more of a revisitation, mythic layering and reinstantiation of that tone.

The pilot therefore sets up an interesting game for fans of the film, one that continues throughout the series, no less. Enough plot details, visual references and characterisation are offered to draw strong parallels to events, scenes or characters from the film, in ways that set up clear expectations and anticipated pleasures of repetition that layer almost everything in the pilot. To take the Jerry/Lester pairing, for instance, so much of Jerry's state in the film is of being in over his head, caught up in a plot that unravels in front of him without his control; Jerry watches others take control when he can't. From the outset, then, viewers are invited to assume that Lester is similarly not in control – the dowdy couple won't bite at his sales pitch, Sam belittles him, Malvo plays him. We even hear Lester mutter Jerry's Midwestern 'aw geez' in frustration at times. And yet Jerry is also shown to have a capacity for rage – he attacks his car with an ice-scraper in annoyance, he beats his desk in his office like an impetuous child – in a way that transfers to Lester, such that we are invited to consider Lester capable of anger. Indeed, for all his impotence, Jerry is deceptive and is trying to gain control by underhanded means, so we are invited to expect deception from Lester. Many of Lester's defining features are offered through plot points, but each has a depth and a seeming predictability, even inevitability, to it due to his mythic re-instantiation of Jerry.

Part of this game for the viewer, though, involves never quite knowing when various elements from the film will assert themselves. And thus part of the game also involves being surprised by events or behaviours we did not see coming. Jerry was a bumbling loser, albeit with a temper, but seemed incapable of serious violence, such that when Lester murders his wife by bludgeoning her head with a hammer, the scene is stark for film fans because Lester has done something the Jerry parallels led us to think him incapable of. And yet, very soon thereafter, he gets a bullet wound graze to his hand that, in successive episodes, festers and becomes as key an objective correlative to Lester as Showalter's bullet wound to his face and gushing blood become to Showalter in the latter part of the film. In short, Lester becomes something of an amalgamation of Lester and Showalter, showing increasing signs of Showalter's impatience, heightened anger and yet similar sense of frustration. The mythic resonance of Lester expands to take on this other character we knew, leaving us guessing as to which 'side' will dominate at any point.

Earlier on, in arguably one of the pilot's most tense scenes, Malvo ultimately offers to kill Sam Hess for Lester. Prior to this scene, our only encounter with

Malvo has come in the above-mentioned opening, where his behaviour recalls Grimsrud's. Grimsrud is notoriously quiet, constantly chastised by Showalter for not talking, so when we encounter him sitting stoically in the hospital waiting room, he performs to expectation. But then Malvo engages Lester in discussion, goading him into wanting revenge and capitalising upon Lester's clumsy (or, we may later wonder, planned?) suggestion that Malvo kill Sam. There is still a recognisable malice and violence to Malvo, as he nonchalantly offers of Lester being bullied by Sam, 'I gotta say, if that were me, in your position, I woulda killed that man'. But we now see Malvo as a talker. Indeed, over the course of the pilot, we again see Malvo cause violence with his words alone, as when he later calls one of Hess's sons to tell him his father (who Malvo has since murdered) left his entire estate to Hess's other son, or convinces a motel worker to urinate in the gas tank of his boss's car, only to turn the worker in to said boss mid-act. Malvo, in short, is not entirely Grimsrud, even though his capacity for and inclination towards violence is wholly recognisable.

Similarly, Molly and Chief Vern Thurman's arrival at the scene of the crashed car oscillates between the (famous) scene from the film in which Marge and Lou study Gripsrud's crash, and something altogether new. Lou, who stands to the side holding his and Marge's coffees, is largely a useless simpleton observer to Marge's astute policework, whereas Molly and Vern work in tandem, both clever investigators. Vern then heads home where his endearing banter with his pregnant wife recalls Marge's endearing banter with her husband, leaving us to wonder who is Marge – Molly, the woman cop, or Vern, the Chief with a pregnant wife? When later we meet Bill, Molly and Vern's fellow cop, his clearer parallel to Lou is evident in his comical uselessness (Vern has by this point offered that 'Bill cleans his gun with bubble bath'). This seems to leave Vern unaccounted for, with no clear filmic referent, and his eventual execution by Malvo indeed removes him from the narrative, as if to signal his irrelevance to the larger mythic tale being told.

The multiple mythic resonances come to a point in a traffic stop near the end of the pilot. Malvo has left town and is pulled over for reckless driving by the newly introduced Gus Grimly (Colin Hanks). Given the parallels between Malvo and Grimsrud and between this traffic stop and the one that sets in motion the film's triple homicide, and given that both scenes are washed in the dangerous red lights of the respective police cars' lights, the film's fans would be only too aware of what might happen in the pilot. Malvo's response to Grimly's request for his licence and registration is thus haunted by remembrance of the film's scene in which Grimsrud shoots the policeman in the head. Malvo replies,

> We could do it that way. You ask me for my papers. I tell you it's not my car, that I borrowed it. See where things go from there. We could do that. Or you could go get in your car and drive away.

Billy Bob Thornton's delivery is flat, contributing to a sense of menace, but that danger is amplified significantly by the vivid intertext. Grimly asks why he'd return to his car, leading Malvo to explain "Cause some roads you shouldn't go down. 'Cause maps used to say "there be dragons here". Now they don't, but that don't mean the dragons aren't there', further encouraging Grimly to

> go home to your daughter, and every few years you're gonna look at her face and know that you're alive because you chose not to go down a certain road on a certain night. That you chose to walk into the light, instead of into the darkness.

In later episodes, the mythic play of *Fargo* the television series will become more evident as we hear parables, and as Malvo enacts Biblical punishment upon his victims, but here he comes close to offering a codex for understanding the show. Throughout, its characters are presented with roads that they choose to go down or not, roads we know well from the film. If they are faced with similar choices, and if they meet similar fates, as their filmic counterparts, this is because those roads are precisely mythic, leading into the light or into the darkness, flagging in grand mythic style that 'there be dragons here'. And thus the logic of the reboot is explained by its master manipulator and catalyst of chaos: it is not characters or scenes per se that are being adapted, but a mythic, folkloric repetition. The pilot aims not to reintroduce us to any particular beloved character, nor to reshoot any particular scene, but to find the deeper structures that undergird the fictional world of *Fargo* the film – a land where 'there be dragons' – and to explore what else is built on these structures. From 1987 to 2006, certain forces keep coming back – frustration with a boring life, a sense of male impotence that turns into spewing rage that a woman must clean up, a pattern of crimes that quickly spiral out of control, a battle of good and evil, light and darkness – all set in a remote, barren landscape where everything is either blinding white or dark and red.

Reboots regularly need to justify their existence and to offer audiences reasons why they should return. Towards that end, reboots often build in a logic of and thematic interest in nostalgia and/or revisiting and learning from the past – cf. *The Force Awakens* (Abrams, 2015) and *Casino Royale* (Campbell, 2006) – as if to offer audiences 'insurance' against the idea that they are 'mere' repetition. *Fargo* offers and enacts an interesting alternate strategy by looking to the original not for a set plot or characters per se, but for a deep mythos, archetypes and fictional world. This strategy may be an especially valuable one for film-to-television reboots, as the added time and scope of a television show otherwise risks drawing the filmic story out over many hours, delaying the filmic story interminably by leading up to it with a slow prequel, or offering that filmic story upfront and then venturing into the unknown. Here, instead, it cross-stitches the filmic plot into the very tenor and operating logic of the show, rendering it into myth, instead of focusing on any particular act, line or character.

THE EXORCIST: 'THE POWER IS IN THE REPETITION'

Early in *The Exorcist*'s pilot, in response to Father Bennett (Kurt Egyiawan) checking on Father Marcus's (Ben Daniels) progress, Marcus states, 'Every day is progress. The power is in the repetition'. The quick exchange is hard not to read as a wink to the audience, especially those familiar with the legacy of *The Exorcist* films. It is a subtle reference to one of the most iconic moments from the 1973 film in which two priests continually repeat the phrase 'the power of Christ compels you' as they douse the levitating, possessed child, Regan (Linda Blair), with holy water. The scene and the accompanying phrase have existed in the popular vernacular since the film's release. From Dr. Evil (Mike Myers) chanting the words to an out-of-control automated chair in *Austin Powers: The Spy Who Shagged Me* (Roach, 1999), to uses across shows such as *The Simpsons* (Fox, 1989–) and *Family Guy* (Fox, 1999–), the scene has been parodied and referenced throughout popular culture over the last several decades to the point that even those who have never seen the film are probably familiar with the phrase. By creating a show tied directly to *The Exorcist* property, rather than just a horror show about exorcism, the pilot episode plays with the popular understanding of exorcism, while serving as a reminder that the most iconic images associated with the genre hail from the 1973 film and the William Peter Blatty novel. Images of rotating heads and possessed children who speak in tongues and spew green projectile vomit have circulated with enough consistency and regularity that these elements, at least in the public mind, no longer belong to a specific text but are part of broader exorcism mythology. Exorcism itself, something that had to be explained to the audience in 1973, has become a subset of the horror genre, spawning films outside *The Exorcist* franchise such as *The Exorcism of Emily Rose* (Derrickson, 2005), *The Last Exorcism* (Stam, 2010) and *The Rite* (Håfström, 2011).

The show is not simply a reimagining of *The Exorcist* movie, nor a re-adaptation of the book, but is best understood as a dialogue between both official *Exorcist* texts and exorcism as a myth popularised by those texts. The scene above with Father Marcus references not only the repeated phrase from the movie but also evokes the repetition of the moment within popular discourse and the continued proliferation of exorcism and possession throughout popular culture. But the show's interplay between branded iconography and popular mythology is evident from the opening sequence in which Marcus walks the streets of Mexico City in a brimmed hat and holding a briefcase, loosely recalling the opening of the film, in which Father Merrin (Max von Sydow) navigates the streets of an ancient city in Iraq. Marcus stops at a water spigot to wash his face and have a drink. He is startled by the sound of a dog panting, then looks over to see several dogs barking viciously at each other until they are interrupted by the sound of a child screaming off camera. The priest walks up to a steep set of stairs and faces a tall building. One window has a light on; the child's screams get louder and become mixed with the sound of the dogs barking and the high-pitched drone of the score. As the cacophony of noises reaches a peak, it is abruptly interrupted by a more stylised version of the original film's title card in bold, bright red font.

The opening scenes are similar. In the film, Merrin's motivations are largely unknown to the viewer, involving the investigation into the origins of a small, demonic-looking figurine, which fans of the book might know as the demon Pazuzu. Merrin's search leads him to a human-sized statue of the demon. As he stands across from it, wild dogs begin to attack each other viciously. The growling and snarling of the dogs mix with the uneasy high-pitched tone of the score until the scene fades to a shot of Georgetown, Virginia, where the rest of the story takes place. The pilot reimagines the opening sequence in a way that does not remake the original but rather layers intertextual references in order to appeal to those with varying levels of exposure to *The Exorcist* mythology. Those with a deeper familiarity with the original text might draw connections between the barking dogs in the TV programme and the ones that are outside the statue of Pazuzu in the opening to the film, leading them to speculate that this priest either is Merrin or at the very least is in pursuit of the same demon. The juxtaposition of the barking and the screams might suggest that the suffering child is possessed by not just any demon, but Pazuzu. Directly following the opening credit sequence, we are given what seems to be a point-of-view shot that creeps along a city street. Though it is unclear whose or what's point of view is being represented, those in the know could read the opening as the path of Pazuzu as the demon moves from Mexico City to Chicago in pursuit of his next victim.

However, the opening also incorporates more surface-level intertextual references that play with the popular mythology of the film rather than the nuances of the narrative. For example, every opportunity is taken to show the priest in silhouette, highlighting the brimmed hat and briefcase. We are introduced to the priest in shadow as he walks towards the camera. The lighting casts shadows on the wall as he ascends a long staircase. The shot of a priest in a brimmed hat with a briefcase silhouetted in the fog outside a large house is one of the most iconic scenes not just in *The Exorcist* but perhaps in cinema; it is also an image used on posters and DVD covers and parodied in popular films such as *Scary Movie 2* (Wayans, 2001). The inclusion of this imagery makes the show familiar even to a casual viewer or non-viewer, and juxtaposing it with the extravagant *Exorcist* title card works to reinforce that audiences are variously returning to or finally visiting the world in which the imagery originated. The imagery ascribes to the show a level of recognition and authenticity. The staircase itself and its position at the base of the building recall the now legendary staircase which is the site of Father Karras's (Jason Miller) death in the film and which has become a popular tourist destination in Georgetown.

Many scenes in the show reference no particular moment from the film but rather invite audiences to make use of their working knowledge of general exorcism mythology. When Bennett checks up on Father Marcus's 'progress', he walks and covers his face with a handkerchief. We don't see anything, but hear the rattling of a bed frame and what sounds like the grunts and growls of a large dog. Bennett then threatens to take the child to the hospital because Marcus has gone against 'protocol'. Marcus insists he can help the boy, and the scene escalates until he pulls a gun on Bennett. The tension in the scene is largely derived from the assumption that the audience knows what is at stake. The sequence of events leaves little explained about the boy's condition or Marcus's role therein. The phrase 'exorcism' is never mentioned, and no one references demonic possession. But the sound of a young child breathing heavily in between intermittent guttural growls aims to paint a picture in the viewer's mind. Though the child is revealed moments later, asleep, tied to the bed and covered in sores and sweat, his condition is not revealed. Marcus begins praying over the boy and dousing him with holy water as the child thrashes around on the bed. While the movie spent the majority of its time setting up and explaining exorcism, today exorcism is part of the popular vernacular, allowing it to be presented here, in its televisual form, as procedural.

Though many remakes and reboots require only a vague understanding of previous texts drawn largely from peripheral or paratextual material, as a television series, *The Exorcist* draws heavily from the viewer's expectations not just of the source text, but of procedural television dramas. Even the uninitiated viewer would be unlikely to find the lack of explanation jarring. Reboots are often inclined to subvert or complicate audience expectation. In a television reboot, that inclination is compounded by the affordances of serialised narrative structures that allow for and invite contrivances and underdeveloped narrative threads early on in a series. Providing only bits of information is inherent to modern television's complex narrative structures. The pilot of *The Exorcist* introduces new elements among the familiarity that complicate our expectations or perhaps act as misdirects. Similar to *Fargo*, characters are introduced that seemingly have connections to characters we recognise from the film. We are introduced to two main priests. Though the names and ages might be different, they act as stand-ins for Father Merrin and Father Karras: one is younger and questions his faith, while the other is older and has a history with demons and exorcism. However, the pilot plays with audiences' expectations by offering a new group of characters as the next potential victims of demonic possession. Whereas the film had only one possessed child, the show introduces us to four potential victims – Henry (Alan Ruck), Angela (Geena Davis) and their two children Casey (Hannah Kasulka) and Katherine (Brianne Howey). Even if popular mythology would dictate that a child is the one possessed, we have been presented with two daughters. The narrative heavily pushes us to believe the daughter who we do not meet at church, Kat, is the one who is possessed, and Angela even confronts Father Tomas with her fears that Katherine is possessed. A savvy viewer might be likely to recognise this as a misdirect, which still leaves the father, the other sister and the mother as potential subjects of the eponymous exorcism, with enough evidence offered to support a theory for each. Throughout, the audience must figure out who will eventually require exorcism.

It is not until the final moments of the pilot that the possessed child is revealed as the younger, less moody sister Casey. When Tomas is at the house discussing the possibility of an exorcism for Katherine, he and the mother hear something in the attic. Tomas goes up to investigate. A rat scurries out into the light; the rat is then suspended in the air and crushed, seemingly from nothing. Then Casey, not Kat, emerges from the shadows and approaches Tomas in an unnatural way as if being pulled by strings along the attic floor. The light turns on and Casey is back to normal, seemingly unaware that anything happened. The scene closely resembles one in which Regan's mother (Ellen Burstyn) goes into the attic because she hears what she thinks are rats. When she gets there, she sees nothing but undisturbed rat traps. The show subverts that sequence by giving us both rats and a visual representation of possession that the movie held back.

Inevitably, familiar moments and motifs arise throughout the show, but they are often introduced in ways that distort our popular memory of these events, moving beyond the pop culture cliché to try to instil a sense of gravity and unpredictability to the routine tropes of exorcism stories. When we finally see an exorcism from Marcus it plays out largely as one might expect. The boy is tied to the bed; he is thrashing around and is covered in lesions. Marcus forcefully shouts prayers while holding a crucifix and dousing the boy in holy water, and at the end of the scene, the boy levitates out of bed and says to the priest in a deep, demonic voice, 'Look upon me, Marcus'. This all conforms to the usual filmic portrayal and tropes of exorcism. The boy then begins to rotate his head, the camera zooms in on his neck and, as we see bone begin to emerge, we hear cracking. The priests in the movie, like those in the audience at the time, did not know what was coming, but here, in the rebooted show, Marcus does seem to know what is coming, and the audience probably thinks they do too. The famous scene in the movie in which Regan's head rotates completely around has been valorised for its special-effects wizardry and parodied countless times. However, where Regan's head rotated in one smooth motion, leaving her unharmed, here the boy's head meets real resistance. This is new, and the audience is suddenly met with something that challenges the mythology. The boy's neck snaps and he falls to the floor, dead. Father Marcus holds his limp body and sobs on the floor. We thought we knew the rules of exorcism but now the franchise that made the rules has changed them slightly, and the spinning head is no longer a universal punchline, but a death sentence.

Television offers an especially productive space to reboot a story like *The Exorcist*. Many reboots step back and give the origin story of a character or a group of characters, often spending a majority of the run time putting the pieces into place, before giving us the iconic moments audiences crave only in the closing scenes. The characters, in short, do not become who we want them to be until the story is over. Thus, for instance, in *Solo: A Star Wars Story* (Howard, 2018), Han Solo (Alden Ehrenreich) does not gain possession of his prized Millennium Falcon until the very last scene, while in J. J. Abrams' *Star Trek* (2009), we do not see the flight crew of the *Enterprise* take their position on the bridge until the very end. As is the nature of the reboot, especially as compared to a remake, those moments act more as teasers for a yet-to-be-produced series of films rather than as satisfying conclusions. The expectation is that we will get another movie, and that movie will give us some more of what we want (even if, as in the case of *Solo*, that promise goes unfulfilled if the reboot is judged a failure and no subsequent film is made). However, here television has an advantage, when the 'teasing' can be done by the pilot (in theory, if not always in practice), allowing all future episodes to move onwards. Additionally, the promises offered through the television pilot carry slightly more weight, as we know at least a few episodes have probably already been produced.

The final scene of *The Exorcist* pilot puts all the pieces into place. We know who the possessed child is. As Tomas leaves the house considering what he has just witnessed, he walks the city streets and the iconic, moody piano melody that makes up the intro of Mike Oldfield's 'Tubular Bells' (more popularly known as '*The Exorcist* theme music') begins to play. The sequence is intercut with Marcus gathering his purple shawl, holy water and other items in his old bag, reminding the audience that they are not just watching a show about exorcism, but *The Exorcist*. Like most good film reboots, the pilot aims to generate interest in the future of the series. Viewers are left with a mix of familiar and new elements and little idea of how they might play out in future instalments. However, this excitement and curiosity generated by such moments and imagery take on an amplified significance in the television reboot, if only because it asks for an immediate and more sustained commitment from the viewer as the next instalment is (at most) a week away and the story will unfold over the course of (at minimum) several episodes.

CONCLUSION

In 2001, ABC aired an animated series based on the film *Clerks* (Smith, 1994). The pilot ends with the voiceover teasing, 'Next time on *Clerks*', while the visuals offer a set of colour bars, implying the show will be cancelled. The joke both plays with the sarcastic and self-deprecating humour that launched film director Kevin Smith's career, and engages the viewer's knowledge of televisual narrative forms. *Clerks: The Animated Series* embraced its new medium wholeheartedly, making frequent use of gags like the one above that play with audience expectations about television. Ultimately, ABC only aired two episodes before indeed abruptly cancelling it. But in its brief life, it rendered explicit – and offered meta-commentary on – the peculiar challenges of rebooting film to television, where the known elements of the source must be balanced with the serial and episodic nature of television's narrative structures. Plot lines must be threaded, characters need room to develop and the world of the original text must be expanded beyond what could be captured within the shortened time limit of a film. All reboots suffer from the same existential dilemma of needing to justify their existence. With film-to-television reboots, however, the task is amplified: the reboot must convince fans of the original to return not just once but continuously, starting as early as right now. And thus, whereas a traditional pilot episode is designed to introduce a premise and a set of characters, the television reboot must (also) manipulate and manage previous knowledge of an already established premise and set of characters.

Ultimately, the job of the film-to-television reboot pilot is to move a story beyond the known trajectory and off the map into uncharted territory while, paradoxically, staying on resolutely familiar, comfortable, well-mapped ground. As Lorne Malvo might warn, there be dragons in this challenge, and we shouldn't be surprised to see that many film-to-television reboots are consumed by these dragons. *Fargo* and *The Exorcist* have been comparatively more successful, though, earning multiple seasons and a fair amount of critical acclaim. We have suggested that they do this by engaging with and developing the mythic value of their original texts. Neither *Fargo* nor *The Exorcist* shies away from the repetitious nature of the reboot, rather leaning into the idea that all this has happened before and may happen again, but possibly not as one might expect. It is from this type of mythic repetition that each show creates tension, engages the viewer's curiosity and plays with audience expectations created by the latent memories of previous iterations.

REFERENCES

Cardwell, Sarah (2002), *Adaptation Revisited: Television and the Classic Novel*, Manchester: Manchester University Press.

Grossman, Julie (2017), 'Fargos', in Julie Grossman and R. Barton Palmer (eds), *Adaptation in Visual Culture: Images, Texts, and Their Multiple Worlds*, New York: Palgrave Macmillan, pp. 193–211.

Hutcheon, Linda (2006), *A Theory of Adaptation*, New York: Routledge.

Proctor, William (2012), 'Regeneration and Rebirth: Anatomy of the Franchise Reboot', *Scope: An Online Journal of Film and Television Studies*, 22 (February), 1–19.

Scahill, Andrew (2016), 'Serialized Killers: Prebooting Horror in *Bates Motel* and *Hannibal*', in Amanda Klein and R. Barton Palmer (eds), *Cycles, Sequels, Spin-offs, Remakes, and Reboots: Multiplicities in Film and Television*, Austin, TX: University of Texas Press, pp. 316–34.

Verevis, Constantine (2006), *Film Remakes*, Edinburgh: Edinburgh University Press.

Part III
Politics and Identity

CHAPTER 8

Resistance and Empire: *Star Wars* and the Social Justice Reboot

Derek Johnson

When *Star Wars: The Force Awakens* was released in 2015, its perceived status as a 'reboot' called into question its capacity to deliver innovation and change to a franchise with nearly forty years of history, legacy and nostalgia behind it. As 'Episode VII', the film explored a revised Star Wars universe following the fall of the evil Galactic Empire at the conclusion of 'Episode VI', *Return of the Jedi* (1983). Yet many reviews considered *The Force Awakens* less than a true sequel in its attempts to reboot – and, thus, to re-present, rework and reproduce – the original *A New Hope* (1977) film. At Vice.com, Brian Merchant (2015) called the film 'Star Wars 2.0' in its 'predictable, nostalgia-reliant, repackaged thrills', describing it as a 'pretty unoriginal reboot that adds few, if any, new ideas to our greatest commercial mythology'. Merchant added his voice to reviewers at *Entertainment Weekly* (Sullivan 2015), *Rotten Tomatoes* ('Star Wars' 2015) and *The Verge* (Robinson 2015) who all catalogued various ways in which *The Force Awakens* had paid tribute to, ripped off or even plagiarised the original 1977 film. Such criticisms distinguished the reboot from a sequel that might have pushed the narrative into new, unfamiliar or risky territory; instead, reboots 'hew to the same general megastructure; and they are all increasingly boring'.

However, despite the charge of unoriginality behind this nostalgia, the film was anything but unthreatening in its attempts to reboot the franchise. While the film may have lacked innovation at the level of narrative structures and story beats, changes at a representational level prompted significant anxiety among a number of different audiences who saw its greater inclusion of women and people of colour within this familiar formula alternatively as a means of political progress or the result of so-called political correctness run amok. 'When historically marginalized individuals are given a spotlight that has been traditionally reserved for white, heterosexual men', Antero Garcia (2015) writes of these social-media-fuelled debates, 'a digital shitstorm ensures'. At stake was not just the film itself, but also the franchising of these reboot efforts. Subsequent films, television spin-offs and merchandise surrounding *The Force Awakens* all became battlegrounds for feminists and white supremacist men's rights activists alike to call for change in the way media industries reuse these nostalgic narrative formulae and point the cultural 'spotlights' that come with them.

As a reboot, then, *The Force Awakens* was both aggressively familiar and full of disruptive potential in need of industry management. In that sense, it may be less productive to build a taxonomy of fixed categories in which such reboots are distinguished from sequels and remakes. Instead, it is more useful to consider how, as a form of reproduction within the logics of media franchising (Johnson 2013), reboots like *The Force Awakens* promise potential for change while unfolding in an industrial context that allows change to be managed. The reboot is not just a narrative or aesthetic form, but also a locus of contested claims over the reproduction of popular culture and the disruption or redirection of those processes.

In this sense, the reproduction of the *Star Wars* franchise might best be described as a *social justice reboot* that articulates the industrial management of change with political struggles to transform exigent inequalities of representation, access and privilege within consumer society. The threat (or promise) of change at the levels of casting, marketing and more triggers struggles over cultural privileges of the past, industry priorities in the present and the ongoing dispositions of media franchises inevitably reproduced into the future. In the struggle over the past, present and future represented by the social justice reboot, the ultimate stakes are a question of who will hold, gain or lose cultural power and in what ways as these industrial processes of reproduction unfold.

The significance of these questions extends well beyond the bounds of the *Star Wars* franchise. At the same time as Disney has made *Star Wars* a lightning rod for social justice debates, numerous other rebooted media franchises have become foci for similar political struggles through their industrial reproduction, including, but certainly not limited to, *Ghostbusters*, *Mad Max*, the Marvel Cinematic Universe, *DuckTales*, *Ocean's Eleven*, *She-Ra* and *Star Trek*. It would therefore be a mistake to consider *Star Wars* particularly unique or exceptional in its development of a social justice reboot strategy. Nevertheless, as a franchise subject to continual reproduction – with a new film released every year from 2015 to 2019, as well as new television and merchandising initiatives – the franchise offers a particularly instructive window into the linkages between the reproductive strategies of industry and political struggle over them by producers and consumers alike.

Starting with *The Force Awakens* but moving beyond to include the franchised management of change across other films like *Rogue One: A Star Wars*

Story (2016) as well as transmedia brand extensions like *Forces of Destiny* (2017), it is possible to see the social justice reboot unfolding in tension between activist forces seeking to influence the course of that reproduction and industrial forces seeking to produce a managed form of change through transformation of markets, representations and privileges. First, through analysis of *The Force Awakens* not just at a textual level, but attuned to forces of production and reception that generate meaning from that text, we can see how the franchise reboot can be articulated to discourses of change, diversity and social justice politics. By following that franchising process, we can, secondly, examine how online hashtag activists – primed to consider the *Star Wars* franchise in these politicised terms – confronted the reboot's ongoing promise of industrial change in relation to feminist and alt-right politics alike. Finally, by considering the industrial management of this capacity for change by Disney and Lucasfilm, we can see how this balancing act between familiarity and difference transforms social justice into a manageable media commodity. In this sense, the rebooting of *Star Wars* is significant not because of its divergence from previous narratives (or failure to do so), but instead because of its power to render media franchising a site of political struggle over social justice – one in which social justice is itself rebooted as the commodifiable output of that industrial process.

REBOOTING *THE FORCE*

Although *The Force Awakens* offers nostalgic familiarity, there is no doubt that these pleasures intersect with the cultural politics of change. Daniel Herbert (2017) thus describes this reworking of the *Star Wars* franchise as one attuned to new values of 'diversity'. Whereas the basic outline of *A New Hope* is discernible in *The Force Awakens*, the central narrative is no longer monopolised by white, male, heteronormative characters and character relations. Although her journey mirrors that of Luke Skywalker, Rey (as played by white British actor Daisy Ridley) serves as the franchise's first central female protagonist. Previously, female characters like Princess Leia and Queen/Senator Amidala served as token supporting characters and love interests, standing alone in predominantly male casts. Now, characters like Leia and the newly created Maz Kanata offer female mentorship for Rey, stepping into roles once occupied by male sages like Obi-Wan and Yoda. At the same time, the film tweaks the franchise's racial politics. Although the previous trilogies each centred three white characters (Luke, Han Solo and Leia followed by Anakin, Amidala and Obi-Wan), Rey's companions bring more diversity to the franchise. The Stormtrooper defector, Finn, is played by black British actor John Boyega, while Guatemalan-American actor Oscar Isaac plays ace pilot Poe Dameron. This greater inclusivity extends to background actors, too, with the ranks of the heroic Resistance and evil First Order both proving noticeably more diverse than those of the Rebellion and Galactic Empire that had preceded them (Hayes 2015). Beyond decentring white masculinity, this new triumvirate also troubles the previous films' heteronormative character relations (where Leia, for example, was an object of desire for Han Solo and, more briefly, Luke). *The Force Awakens* does insist upon Finn's romantic interest in Rey; but, at the same time, it encourages viewers to take pleasure in the idea of a relationship between Finn and Poe. In an appearance on the daytime talk show *Ellen* to promote the film, and as reported by E! News (Schnurr 2015), Isaac notes that he was 'playing romance' in the shared between Poe and Finn.

Even if cosmetic, these textual changes caused significant anxiety about the management of *Star Wars* as an ongoing media franchise. On the one hand, feminist critics who took the new representational composition of the franchise as a step forward for empowerment and equality nevertheless expressed serious concern about the failure for that potential to be carried over into the marketing of this film. As media scholar Suzanne Scott (2017) has explored, hashtag activists asked '#WheresRey' to protest the failure of toy manufacturers and Disney's other licensed partners to extend the visibility of the new female protagonist to consumer product offerings. The promise of industry change implied by this reboot thus manifested as a precarious one in need of collective action and intervention to reach its full potential. On the other hand, more regressive forces perceived these shifts in the franchise's representational logics as a catalyst for defending longstanding cultural legacies and privileges. Competing hashtags like #BoycottStarWarsVII aggregated the voices of those who felt threatened by the disruption white heterosexual masculine hegemony represented by black characters like Finn. Even though, as Antero Garcia (2015) points out, the hashtag originally emerged from an attempt to reveal the 'ludicrous' nature of racist outrage online, it nevertheless created a platform for the real backlash that fan cultures 'have been engaged in for years' in opposition to the diversification of science fiction and superhero franchises. In the online spaces of men's right activism and alt-right politics, therefore, the rebooting of *Star Wars* became a genuine topic of concern and point of collective organisation, with sites like *Return of Kings* organising boycotts to mount consumer opposition to this popular feminism (Johnson 2018; Banet-Weiser 2018).

Beyond these reception anxieties, the supposedly minor alterations of this reboot prompted significant industrial negotiation as well. Creative personnel involved in *The Force Awakens* took the shift in representational emphasis as an opportunity to align themselves with the progressive values of social change. At San Diego Comic-Con in 2015 prior to the release of the film, director J. J. Abrams touted his personal commitment to the politics of diversity, insisting that it was 'important people see themselves represented in film' and that the issue was 'a big consideration' in his work with *Star Wars* (Statt 2015).

Presenting a united front, studio franchise steward Kathleen Kennedy positioned these values as guiding management principles for the *Star Wars* brand: 'there is every intention to carry on exactly what J.J. is talking about in all the Star Wars movies that we intend to make'. Thus, the producers twinned the promise of more *Star Wars* product with a creative and corporate social responsibility (Banet-Weiser 2012; Ouellette 2018) to provide stronger points of participation for historically marginalised communities.

Yet, the industrial marketing of *The Force Awakens* continued to hedge this commitment to diversity depending on its value to specific target audiences. In the poster used to promote the theatrical release in the US and UK, for instance, Finn appears to the right of Rey, wielding the blue light sabre that would later become hers. He is the third largest figure on the poster, behind Rey and the helmeted villain Kylo Ren, but significantly larger than Han Solo, Leia or Chewbacca. The poster for the Chinese market, however, diminished the importance of Finn and Poe to the film. Now smaller than Han and Leia, Finn appears beneath them as opposed to his higher position of honour flanking Rey in the US/UK poster (Webb 2015). Although far from prominent in the US/UK poster, Poe disappears altogether. The iterative nature of these marketing materials suggests that as much as creators aligned themselves with the values of representational diversity, Disney was more than willing to temper such ideals depending on the context in which those values might be monetised.

Across the narrative of the film, its reception by consumers and its promotion by creators and marketing materials, the status of *The Force Awakens* as a reboot came to be understood by reference to the values of social identity, diversity and the capacity for change – values that could fluctuate depending on the contexts in which the franchise circulated. As such, this reboot primed critics, fans and creative professionals to engage this franchised entertainment as a site of struggle over the values of diversity and social change. The continued production of the franchise across subsequent films and spin-off products then represented both an opportunity to continue that struggle and deepen the stakes of it.

SOCIAL JUSTICE WAR(RIOR) FILM

In December 2016, the subsequent release of *Rogue One: A Star Wars Story* thus offered even more explicit articulation of the franchise to the activist politics of social change – particularly through this film's intensified focus on the themes of rebellion and struggle against imperialism. As a prequel that told the story of a nascent Rebel Alliance resisting the evil Galactica Empire, the film's themes resonated with critics and activists concerned with rebellion and resistance in the real world. With promotional trailers already in circulation upon the election of Donald Trump to the US presidency in November 2016, *Rogue One* was, even before release, incorporated as part of a culture of resistance to toxic masculinity and white supremacism, particularly as they had taken hold in and reshaped the US electoral landscape.

At *Comic Book Resources*, for example, columnist Brett White (2016) reflected on dialogue from the trailer that resonated as part of a need for activist regrouping after electoral defeat less than a week earlier: 'We have hope. Rebellions are built on hope'; 'Our rebellion is all that remains to push back the Empire'; 'The power that we are dealing with here is immeasurable'. Acknowledging the ways in which the election turned on appeals to popular misogyny and racism and ultimately afforded those politics the institutional power of the state, White noted by contrast that 'If they have hate, then *we* have hope.' For use in everyday politics, he reclaims the position of the rebel who fights the imperialist state. 'When I look at the "Rogue One" trailer', White added, 'I see what I want from America. I see a multicultural group standing strong together led by a rebellious and courageous woman. That's what we are working towards, and what we will continue to work towards no matter what'. Citing the film's female lead, Jyn Erso, as played by white British actor Felicity Jones, with prominent support from Mexican actor Diego Luna, Hong Kong martial artist Donnie Yen, Chinese actor Jiang Wen and British-Pakistani actor/rapper Riz Ahmed, this reading of the film looks to the Rebel Alliance as a model for inclusive politics juxtaposed with an oppressive Empire which 'crushes the rights of others and excludes non-humans from its ranks'. To Erso/Jones's query in the trailer, 'You are rebels, aren't you?', White replies:

> Yes. If being a rebel means being proud of being gay, then yes. If being a rebel means that I believe people of all faiths deserve to be treated with unyielding respect, then yes. If being a rebel means that I believe that human rights are women's rights and women's rights are human rights, then yes. . . . I will rebel by becoming active in my community, by championing diverse voices, by using every skill I have . . . to voice what I know to be right.

Other popular criticism similarly articulated *Rogue One* to contemporary politics. Responding to Disney CEO Bob Iger's insistence that the film was actually not 'in any way' political, David Sims countered by citing the film's 'more forceful edge' compared to previous films while also insisting that 'Declaring that something isn't political is, in itself, political' (2016). In this sense, *Rogue One* could be said to reboot the franchise by dialling up its political relevance, even compared to the valorisation of diversity in *The Force Awakens*.

Given this reception, *Rogue One* and Rebel Alliance imagery served as a resource for activists fighting against the rise of global fascism at the time of the film's release. Opposition to the Donald Trump regime frequently characterised itself as 'the Resistance', inviting identification with the idea of organised political rebellion in terms compatible with those of the *Star Wars* universe. Perhaps most notably, the image of Princess Leia, as portrayed by Carrier Fisher, became a prominent fixture in emerging US political iconography (Loughrey 2017), most visibly the Women's March of 17 January 2017. Leia and Fisher had long served as feminist icons (Caldwell 1983); however, this meditation on the theme of rebellion in *Rogue One*, combined with the presence of a computer-generated Leia in the film to approximate her first franchise appearance, recentred the character as a symbol not just of strong femininity but of even more overt resistance to tyrannical regimes.

In his review of the film for *Los Angeles Review of Books*, media scholar Dan Hassler-Forest (2016) also reads *Rogue One* as a 'politically charged, and even, perhaps, a little bit radical' rejection of global fascism. Although Hassler-Forest does not ignore moments of nostalgia that undercut anti-fascist impulses in their celebration of an imagined past (in this case, the mythology of previous *Star Wars* films themselves), he nevertheless credits the film with giving voice to a leftist political sensibility. More than recognising *Star Wars* as a potential inspiration or allegory for activist action in pursuit of change in the political sphere, Hassler-Forest grapples with the political significance of *Rogue One* as a means of reproducing the *Star Wars* narrative. *Rogue One* represents narrative, creative and industrial change on several fronts in Hassler-Forest's view: not only does the film embrace diversity of casting, it also moves the themes of the franchise into new political territory. Hassler-Forest notes that *Rogue One* is the first *Star Wars* film that 'looks and feels like an actual war film'. This shift is stylistic, but it is also accomplished through narrative and representational focus, where 'anti-fascist struggle is a fundamentally political choice'. Whereas Luke Skywalker fought the Empire in the original trilogy as part of an archetypal hero's journey and Freudian conflict, *Rogue One* trades in 'more-than-symbolic anti-fascism', particularly in its emphasis on 'political choices made at tremendous personal costs' and the representation of those sacrificed lives on-screen 'by ethnic groups that are currently the most vulnerable'. So while seeing *Rogue One* as occasionally 'backward glancing', Hassler-Forest offers it as an 'important step forward' in the political reorientation of storytelling in the franchise.

The effort to situate ongoing reproduction of *Star Wars* within an activist project was undoubtedly fed by the efforts of professionals working behind the scenes to deliver new takes on the legacy franchise. Prior to the release of *Rogue One*, screenwriter Chris Weitz encouraged fans to recognise the film's social relevance following the rise of the alt-right and the acceleration of the politics of hate and oppression, particularly as symbolised by the election of Donald Trump in the US and the Brexit vote in the UK. To signal solidarity with those communities increasingly endangered in this political climate, the safety pin had emerged as a symbol of resistance on the left, a badge that could be worn by allies to communicate that immigrants and refugees could rely on the wearer's concern for their safety. Articulating his work on the franchise to these ally politics, Weitz took to Twitter to suggest that the safety pin could link political action to the symbols and institutions of resistance in the *Star Wars* universe. The image he shared featured the starbird logo of the heroic Rebellion (later called the Resistance) run through with a safety pin, suggesting that followers and fans could be good allies by sharing this image and even wearing Rebel/Resistance logos on their clothes. 'Star Wars against hate. Spread it', Weitz wrote. To make clear the link between his film and safety pin resistance to fascism, Weitz also stated, 'Please note that the Empire is a white supremacist (human) organization', to which fellow writer Gary Whitta added, 'Opposed by a multi-cultural group led by brave women'. While these tweets would later be deleted, publications like the *Hollywood Reporter* documented them and noted their recirculation by other professional participants in the franchise (such as Luke Skywalker actor Mark Hamill, a frequent Trump critic) (McMillan 2016). In this way, *Rogue One* provided a platform not just for 'commodity activism' (Mukherjee and Banet-Weiser 2012) at the level of reception, but also for industry professionals to align themselves with the political project of resistance through their creative reproduction of the franchise.

This professional alignment with social justice politics also made *Rogue One* legible as a symbol of change within the media industries themselves. Identifying a sensibility shared with *The Force Awakens*, Rebecca Sun (2016) of the *Hollywood Reporter* positioned the successive presentation of strong female leads in Rey and Jyn Erso as a 'doubleheader' indicative of changing power dynamics in the executive suite. Sun credited Kathleen Kennedy with having fostered an inclusive creative culture in which women made up more than half the executive team. Despite acknowledging that no woman had (or has, at the time of writing) yet directed a *Star Wars* film, Sun maintained that under the leadership that produced *Rogue One*, Hollywood's 'most storied franchise' had also become 'its most prominent champion of female empowerment'.

However, *Rogue One*'s service to these social justice values presented another opportunity for the alt-right to push against the politics of popular feminism and media progressivism. Claiming that the writers of the new film had equated Trump voters with the fascism of Nazi Germany, alt-right operatives Mike Cernovich and Jack Posobiac called for a boycott of the franchise, rallying around the social media hashtag #DumpStarWars. This threat was welcome news to some opponents on the left, who saw previously ineffectual attempts to dampen the box office success of *The Force Awakens* and the subsequent $71 million dollar opening-day haul for *Rogue One* as indicators of alt-right impotence. 'If their track record is any indication,' wrote blogger Oliver Willis (2016), 'executives at Disney will be rooting for Trump supporters to bash the next film in the Star Wars series, in order to keep the box-office smash record consistent'.

Notably, these efforts to deploy consumer pressure against media industries perceived to be in thrall to social justice warriors were not limited to boycott strategies. They also built on affirmative support for products under the same franchise umbrella that could offer an alternative for competing political identifications. The purchase of licensed merchandise, for example, could figure as a means of continuing to participate in the consumption of a media franchise while shoring up nostalgia and hegemonic privileges compatible with alt-right politics. In one of many journalistic articles meditating on a Reddit discussion called '(((Star Wars))) is Anti-White Social Engineering', Chloe Sargeant (2016) at *Pedestrian* took particular note of the way in which fascist-leaning detractors of the franchise figured licensed toys as a way of subverting the diversity politics of *Rogue One*. While some Reddit users, as she reports, engaged in oppositional readings of the film that allowed them to 'fantasize about being a stormtrooper', others more tangibly considered the potential of the toys offered by Disney and its licensed partners to support such fantasies. 'Kids watching "Star Wars" are going to fantasize about the bad guys and buy toys of the bad guys and the narrative embedded in the film will be totally lost on them', wrote one in Sargeant's account, while another more baldly stated, 'We know which side we prefer. Always buy the Empire Legos. Always root for Hitler. Always retell the story your own way'. In a twisted embrace of Stuart Hall's (1999) encoding/decoding theories, Henry Jenkins' (1992) textual poaching framework and Jonathan Gray's (2010) recognition of toys and other paratexts as powerful gateways for meaning construction, these Reddit users succinctly implicated licensed merchandise as a means of validating fascist fandom. LEGO products become the literal building blocks by which one might construct a fan position to 'root for Hitler' – and where purchase of Galactic Empire products represents a means of fascistic consumer activism. In this logic, the power of the fascist dollar might influence the culture industries to maintain their focus on licensed products that foreground white power.

The efforts of alt-right operatives to mobilise against this reorientation of *Star Wars* towards its newer female and non-white characters had little box office impact. However, their rejection of the reboot's perceived social justice politics nevertheless dovetailed with forms of everyday media fandom invested in the narratives and marketing apparatuses that had previously afforded – and continued to afford – privilege to white masculinity as well as the pleasures of popular misogyny and white supremacism. Notably, it was at the level of consumer products, and not just filmgoing, that struggles over the social justice reboot unfolded. In that sense, we might also consider how Disney and its merchandising partners used reboot logics – and their promise of change – to effect new forms of management over these struggles and their market potential.

PARALLEL DESTINIES

If the #WheresRey? controversy extended from the culture industries' failure to bring the same kinds of representational and marketing changes to the licensed products surrounding *The Force Awakens* that had accompanied the film itself, then *Forces of Destiny* might be considered an attempt to reboot that merchandising plan. Whereas licensed toy manufacturers like Hasbro faced protests for failing to integrate the films' strong female characters into action figure lines too narrowly pitched to boys and men, *Forces of Destiny* put those characters and an imagined consumer base of girls and women front and centre. Announced in April 2017, *Forces of Destiny* was a coordinated transmedia campaign inclusive of toys, animated YouTube shorts, clothing and books which Kathleen Kennedy positioned as being 'for anyone who has been inspired by Leia's heroism, Rey's courage or Ahsoka's tenacity' (Marcotte 2017). The 'centrepiece' of this product array were new 11-inch 'Adventure Figures' the same height as a typical fashion doll but featuring articulation more like that of an action figure, designed to hold blasters and light sabres in dynamic poses. These dolls centred the female characters of the franchise, with the first wave offering Princess Leia, Rey, Jyn Erso and Sabine Wren (from the *Star Wars: Rebels* animated series), as well as non-human characters like BB-8, R2-D2, Chewbacca and Wicket the Ewok.

Although Kennedy pitched these products to 'anyone', in context it was clear that *Forces of Destiny* served as a corrective in a *Star Wars* marketplace that had previously excluded girls and women as a 'surplus' audience (Jenkins et al. 2013: 129; Scott 2013). According to business analysts, Disney and Hasbro were rationally pursuing new market indicators that confirmed demand for more gender-inclusive marketing. As reported in *Forbes*, new consumer data attributed up to 60 per cent of all online sales of superhero merchandise to female consumers (Thompson 2017). Meanwhile, other major entertainment companies had recently profited from marrying their franchised consumer product brands to the values of gender inclusivity. In 2012, the LEGO Group met with a resoundingly positive response for LEGO Friends, a new product line that used feminised colour schemes, svelte 'mini-dolls' and emphasis on themes of friendship and care-giving to create newly gendered points of entry into the otherwise masculine-dominated realm of construction play (Johnson 2014a). Similarly, in 2015, DC Comics introduced a new brand umbrella for marketing characters like Wonder Woman, Batgirl and Harley Quinn called *DC Super Hero Girls* (Tussey and Bak 2019). Creating a coordinated transmedia campaign across books, toys and online video, *DC Super Hero Girls* set the formula that *Forces of Destiny* would adopt. Disney-owned Marvel Comics, too, would launch in 2018 a similar venture called *Marvel Rising* to market its female superheroes to young female consumers. In this sense, the commitment to gender equality and empowerment in *Forces of Destiny* exemplified broader industry trends in which the institutions of media capitalism had assessed the politics of change for their rising market value.

This critical view need not deny measurable change in this reboot of the franchise's merchandising strategy. Although girls and women had long 'made *Star Wars* their own' (Hess 2016) despite the media industries' general refusal to acknowledge their significant participation (Scott 2019), *Forces of Destiny* legitimised female consumers as a desirable target market worthy of service and attention. Moreover, while earlier retail and merchandising endeavors like HerUniverse – a sci-fi-themed fashion outlet launched by *Star Wars* voice actress Ashley Eckstein – had carved out a space to serve female fans as a discrete consumer niche (Johnson 2014b), *Forces of Destiny* took greater steps towards integration and inclusivity for women in highly visible retail centres. As a speciality online retail outlet, HerUniverse stood apart from the merchandising efforts that Disney and Lucasfilm made to reach boys and men in mass market stores, additively creating a new market without disrupting the old ones. To be sure, the creation of a new product line to improve appeals to young girls supported a conservative strategy whereby Hasbro's existing action figure lines could continue to be pitched at boys and men without interruption. However, the integration of *Forces of Destiny* within the 'flow' of retail presentation (Santo 2019) at major US retailers like Target, Wal-Mart and (the now defunct) Toys 'R' Us nevertheless altered the presentation of even existing action figure lines and their gendered values. As shelved by these retailers, *Forces of Destiny* often appeared directly alongside other *Star Wars* toys produced by Hasbro and LEGO. As part of a cohesive, shared retail presentation, *Forces of Destiny* functioned as an integrated part of the marketing of the whole franchise in which the lines between toys 'for girls' and 'for boys' blurred. In this sense, this new franchise sub-brand rebooted not only the merchandising outlook for the *Star Wars* films but also the gendered logics of toy marketing.

However, despite these notable transformations, *Forces of Destiny*'s capacity for market change operated in parallel to assurances of continuity. While space would be made in the franchise and on retailer shelves for new products addressing girls and women as valued consumers, the carefully managed boundaries between product lines allowed masculinised consumer privileges to be preserved as well. This pursuit of inclusivity via the separate-but-equal principles of franchise multiplicity is significant beyond just the persistence of gendered divisions and distinctions in industry marketing strategies. As a means of managing the values of social justice, the reboot logics of franchising enable media industries to endorse change while simultaneously maintaining points of identification with continuity of the hegemonic status quo. Men's rights activists and other alt-right detractors could moan all they wanted about *Forces of Destiny* and what its alterations to consumer privilege might mean, but, as noted in the previous example about white supremacists' embracing Imperial-themed LEGO product, the isolation of different franchise offerings as discrete products with their own varying dispositions to social justice values means that regressive voices could find alternative points of consumer participation and affirmation. In this context, the boycott of one franchise product as part of a social justice struggle can be refigured as a call for intensified consumption of another product in the same franchise. In rebooting the marketing of the franchise, endeavours like *Forces of Destiny* enable media industries to manage their relationships to the values of social justice, playing multiple sides of a political struggle by introducing change in parallel to the maintenance of existing consumer privileges.

CONCLUSION

In exploring the ways in which media institutions like Disney and Lucasfilm figure the continual reproduction of *Star Wars* as part of an attempt to manage the values of continuity and change alongside struggles for social justice, this chapter has revealed the logics of the reboot as an integral component of the politics of popular entertainment. Film reboots – and other logics of franchised reproduction – allow media industries to deliver change, but in a managed way that need not fully disrupt the status quo. Reboots, in this sense, are conservative in nature, even as they might also be celebrated by activists and other forces who see them as a battleground for reimagining familiar images and narratives to be more inclusive. The social justice reboot, in this sense, reveals how the variations in successive entries in a film series (and their accompanying consumer product merchandise) take shape in response to activist pressures (and resistance to them) – but in ways that allow industry to manage that change without disrupting existing power structures.

With that in mind, the term 'social justice reboot' possesses a second meaning. While *Star Wars* might be changed as part of its industrial participation with struggles for social justice, so too might the idea of social justice be transformed through its articulation to the reboot logics of media franchising. When conceived through the film reboot, social justice becomes a commodity to be purchased. In that context, feminist activism comes down to demanding particular interpretations of *Star Wars*, while the counter-activism of white supremacists and men's rights activism means throwing support behind parallel products that express a more nostalgic and hegemonic social order. Social justice rebooted as one offering in an array of commodities transforms it into an industry product shaped by the logics of taste and individualisation rather than collectivity or equality. And, in that sense, the rebooting of social justice through franchise reboots conveys its negotiated management by industry.

While creative executives like J. J. Abrams and Kathleen Kennedy build professional reputations by managing their status as allies of social justice movements, the wider marketing structures of franchising incorporate social justice as merely one choice in a larger, managed array of product offerings. In this way, the social justice delivered by *Star Wars* occurs alongside its denial.

This dynamic is perhaps made most clear by the tension between Rebellion/Resistance and Empire in both the narrative and consumer product merchandising of *Star Wars*. Fan consumers of the franchise are frequently prompted to ask themselves: are they Rebels or Imperials? Do they wish to buy the T-shirt emblazoned with the starbird logo of the Resistance or the six-spoked gear of the Galactic Empire? Although these choices seem as simple as choosing to support a particular sports team – one appears as good as the other, depending on fan preference and fantasy type – in the context of the social justice reboot, those choices accrue additional value through their ongoing implication in activist political struggles.

REFERENCES

Banet-Weiser, Sarah (2012), *Authentic™: The Politics of Ambivalence in a Brand Culture*, New York: New York University Press.

Banet-Weiser, Sarah (2018), *Empowered: Popular Feminism and Popular Misogyny*, Durham, NC: Duke University Press.

Caldwell, Carrie (1983), 'Carrie Fisher: A Few Words on Princess Leia, Fame, and Feminism', *Rolling Stone*, 21 July, <https://www.rollingstone.com/movies/movie-news/carrie-fisher-a-few-words-on-princess-leia-fame-and-feminism-190633/>.

Garcia, Antero (2015), '#BoycottStarWarsVII, Racism, and Classroom Responsibility', *Connected Learning Alliance*, 22 October, <https://clalliance.org/blog/boycottstarwarsvii-racism-and-classroom-responsibility/>.

Gray, Jonathan (2010), *Show Sold Separately: Promos, Spoilers, and Other Media Paratexts*, New York: New York University Press.

Hall, Stuart ([1977] 1999), 'Encoding, Decoding', in Simon During (ed.), *The Cultural Studies Reader*, 2nd edn, London: Routledge, pp. 507–17.

Hassler-Forest, Dan (2016), 'Politicizing Star Wars: Anti-Fascism vs. Nostalgia in "Rogue One"', *Los Angeles Review of Books*, 26 December, <https://lareviewofbooks.org/article/politicizing-star-wars-anti-fascism-vs-nostalgia-rogue-one/>.

Hayes, Britt (2015), '"Star Wars: The Force Awakens" and the Little Casting Choice that Makes a Huge Impact', *Screen Crush*, 16 December, <http://screencrush.com/star-wars-diversity-casting/>.

Herbert, Daniel (2017), *Film Remakes and Franchises*. New Brunswick, NJ: Rutgers University Press.

Hess, Amanda (2016), 'How Female Fans Made "Star Wars" Their Own', *New York Times*, 5 November, <https://www.nytimes.com/2016/11/06/movies/how-female-fans-made-star-wars-their-own.html>.

Jenkins, Henry (1992), *Textual Poachers: Television Fans and Participatory Culture*, New York: Routledge.

Jenkins, Henry, Sam Ford and Joshua Green (eds) (2013), *Spreadable Media: Creating Value and Meaning in a Networked Culture*, New York: New York University Press.

Johnson, Derek (2013), *Media Franchising: Creative License and Collaboration in the Culture Industries*, New York: New York University Press.

Johnson, Derek (2014a), 'Chicks with Bricks: Building Creativity Across Industrial Design Cultures and Gendered Construction Play', in Mark J. P. Wolf (ed.), *LEGO Studies: Examining the Building Blocks of a Transmedia Phenomenon*, New York: Routledge, pp. 81–4.

Johnson, Derek (2014b), '"May the Force Be With Katie": Pink Media Franchising and the Post-Feminist Politics of HerUniverse', *Feminist Media Studies* 14: 6, 895–911.

Johnson, Derek (2018), 'From the Ruins: Neomasculinity, Media Franchising, and Struggles Over the Industrial Reproduction of Culture', *Communication, Culture & Critique* 11: 1, 85–99.

Loughrey, Clarisse (2017), 'Women's March: How Star Wars' Princess Leia Became a Potent Symbol of Resistance', *Independent*, 22 January, <https://www.independent.co.uk/arts-entertainment/films/news/womens-march-on-washington-star-wars-princess-leia-carrie-fisher-a-womans-place-is-in-the-resistance-a7539916.html>.

McMillan, Graeme (2016), '"Rogue One" Writers Subtly Protest Trump with Rebellion Safety-Pin Logo', *Hollywood Reporter*, 11 November, <https://www.hollywoodreporter.com/heat-vision/rogue-one-is-a-political-allegory-tease-writers-946638>.

Marcotte, John (2017), 'Disney and Lucasfilm Launch "Star Wars Forces of Destiny"', *Heroic Girls*, 13 April, <http://www.heroicgirls.com/disney-lucasfilm-launch-star-wars-forces-destiny/>.

Merchant, Brian (2015), '"The Force Awakens" Is the Least Interesting Star Wars Yet', *Vice*, 21 December, <https://www.vice.com/en_us/article/z43v88/the-force-awakens-is-the-least-interesting-star-wars-yet>.

Muhkerjee, Roopali and Sarah Banet-Weiser (eds) (2012), *Commodity Activism: Cultural Resistance in Neoliberal Times*, New York: New York University Press.

Ouellette, Laurie (2018), 'MTV: #ProsocialTelevision', in Derek Johnson (ed.), *From Networks to Netflix: A Guide to Changing Channels*, New York: Routledge, pp. 147–56.

Robinson, Tasha (2015), 'Star Wars: The Force Awakens Shows the Joys – and Limits – of Fulfilled Nostalgia', *The Verge*, 18 December, <https://www.theverge.com/2015/12/18/10543196/star-wars-the-force-awakens-a-new-hope-nostalgia>.

Santo, Avi (2019), 'Shelf Flow: Spatial Logics, Product Categorization, and Media Brands at Retail', in Daniel Herbert and Derek Johnson (eds), *Point of Sale: Analyzing Media Retail*, New Brunswick, NJ: Rutgers University Press, pp. 109–24.

Sargeant, Chloe (2016), 'White Supremacists Are Going to Boycott "Rogue One", Because Of Fkn Course', *Pedestrian* (blog), 12 August, <https://www.pedestrian.tv/entertainment/white-supremacists-are-going-to-boycott-rogue-one-because-of-fkn-course/>.

Schnurr, Samantha (2015), 'Star Wars: The Force Awakens Cast Gets Grilled About Their On Screen Romance by Ellen DeGeneres', *E! News*, 17 December, <https://www.eonline.com/news/724844/star-wars-the-force-awakens-cast-gets-grilled-about-their-on-screen-romance-by-ellen-degeneres>.

Scott, Suzanne (2013), 'Fangirls in Refrigerators: The Politics of (In)Visibility in Comic Book Culture', *Transformative Works and Cultures* 13, <http://dx.doi.org/10.3983/twc.2013.0460>.

Scott, Suzanne (2017), '#wheresrey? Toys, Spoilers, and the Gender Politics of Franchise Paratexts', *Critical Studies in Media Communication* 34: 2, 138–47.

Scott, Suzanne (2019), *Fake Geek Girls: Fandom, Gender, and the Convergence Culture Industry*, New York: New York University Press.

Sims, David (2016), 'Of Course "Rogue One" Is Political', *The Atlantic*, 14 December, <https://www.theatlantic.com/entertainment/archive/2016/12/of-course-rogue-one-is-political/510629/>.

'Star Wars: Episode VII – The Force Awakens Reviews' (2015), *Rotten Tomatoes*, <https://www.rottentomatoes.com/m/star_wars_episode_vii_the_force_awakens/reviews/?page=2&type=user>.

Statt, Nick (2015), 'Director J.J. Abrams Weighs in On Diversity in the Star Wars Universe', *CNET*, 11 July, <https://www.cnet.com/news/director-j-j-abrams-weighs-in-on-diversity-in-the-star-wars-universe/>.

Sullivan, Kevin (2015), 'Star Wars: The Force Awakens, New Hope Similarities', *Entertainment Weekly*, 19 December, <https://ew.com/article/2015/12/19/star-wars-force-awakens-new-hope-similarities/>.

Sun, Rebecca (2016), 'Lucasfilm's Force: Kathleen Kennedy Reveals an Executive Team More Than 50 Percent Female', *Hollywood Reporter*, 7 December, <https://www.hollywoodreporter.com/news/lucasfilms-force-kathleen-kennedy-reveals-an-executive-team-more-50-percent-female-953156>.

Thompson, Luke (2017), 'With "Forces of Destiny," Hasbro Makes Its Biggest Push Yet Towards Female-Skewing Star Wars Toys', *Forbes*, 13 April, <https://www.forbes.com/sites/lukethompson/2017/04/13/hasbro-forces-of-destiny-star-wars-rey-leia-jyn-erso-sabine-celebration/#102300d82438>.

Tussey, Ethan and Meredith Bak (2019), 'Get Your Cape On: Target's Invitation to the DC Universe', in Daniel Herbert and Derek Johnson (eds), *Point of Sale: Analyzing Media Retail*, New Brunswick, NJ: Rutgers University Press, pp. 125–41.

Webb, Sam (2015), 'Star Wars: The Force Awakens Race Row After Black Star SHRINKS in Chinese Poster', *Mirror*, 4 December, <https://www.mirror.co.uk/news/world-news/star-wars-force-awakens-race-6951525>.

White, Brett (2016), 'Rebellions Are Built on Hope: Why Rogue One Matters Now More Than Ever', *Comic Book Resources*, 11 November, <https://www.cbr.com/rebellions-are-built-on-hope-why-rogue-one-matters-now-more-than-ever/>.

Willis, Oliver (2016), 'Trump Supporters' #DumpStarWars Boycott Is a Huge Failure', *Oliver Willis* (blog), 18 December, <http://oliverwillis.com/trump-supporters-dumpstarwars-boycott-is-a-huge-failure/>.

CHAPTER 9

Rebooting the Politics of the Sports Melodrama: *Creed* vs *Rocky*

Chuck Tryon

Franchise reboots have become an essential part of Hollywood's business model. In an era dominated by global, though increasingly fragmented, audiences and intense competition, film franchises provide studios with a layer of certainty, even while providing audiences with cultural narratives that are meaningful and worth revisiting (Johnson 2013: 4–6). Hollywood reboots also allow us to revisit iconic characters within new historical contexts. Ryan Coogler's *Creed* (2015), a reboot of the classic sports melodrama *Rocky* (1976), provides a powerful case study for thinking about how reboots can embrace nostalgia for the original text while also functioning as a critical reading of the original's politics. More specifically, I argue that *Creed* functions as a politically ambivalent but textually reverent reboot of the Rocky franchise, a film that simultaneously celebrates the franchise's skilful deployment of the tropes of male melodrama while also updating the racial and sexual politics of the earlier films. Thus, while the original *Rocky*, in particular, tapped into fears that white masculinity was being threatened both by black athletes who were dominating professional sports, especially boxing, and by declining economic fortunes, *Creed* shifts the focus away from Rocky Balboa as a white, working-class hero, redirecting it to the story of Adonis Johnson Creed, the African-American son of Rocky's rival Apollo Creed. The *Rocky*/*Creed* franchise represents an important limit case for thinking about reboots. In many ways, *Creed* functions more like a sequel or spin-off than a true reboot, in which the previous history of the film's characters is erased. However, *Creed*'s status as an 'origin story', its introduction of a new boxing legend with humble origins in Adonis Creed, help to code it as a type of reboot, one that gives life to a franchise that had reached its limits as Sylvester Stallone's character had aged out of stepping into the ring himself.

This chapter starts with the idea that the early *Rocky* films helped to establish a modern myth, one that was deeply grounded in the politics of racial backlash and class identity in the 1970s. By 'myth', I am loosely borrowing from Roland Barthes' argument that cultural texts present concepts as 'natural', when in fact they are deeply laden with political meanings (Barthes 1972). *Rocky* tapped into post-civil rights fears that blacks were being given preferential treatment over white, working-class men, who were now facing high unemployment and declining job prospects. These themes were foregrounded in the original Rocky, in part through explicit references to the Bicentennial and Apollo's cynical appropriation of the American Dream to promote his bout with Rocky. In many ways the film evoked narratives that Ronald Reagan would later exploit in his run for President four years later, in 1980 (Smith 2018). In fact, as Herman Gray has documented, Reagan's embrace of 'feel-good politics' was part of a larger struggle over definitions of how America was defined (Gray 1995: 15). Thus, Rocky, like Reagan, served to reassure whites that values such as whiteness and individual success would be protected (1995: 16). Revisiting the original text (and the mythos established by it) allowed Coogler to rewrite aspects of the original *Rocky* films and create a new political narrative, one that explicitly challenges stereotypes of African-American athletes. *Creed* exists in an uneasy space between remake and reboot, spin-off and sequel, defying easy categorisation. In part, this status is shaped by *Creed*'s role in contributing to a re-evaluation of the role of authorship in shaping the life of a movie or media franchise. Of course, as Jonathan Gray has powerfully argued, textual authorship is a complex phenomenon, and no single author truly has control over the meaning of a film, much less a sprawling media franchise that has played out over years, if not decades (Gray 2013: 102).

Notably, *Creed* was the first film in the *Rocky* franchise in which Stallone did not receive a screenplay credit (although he did participate in writing the screenplay for *Creed II* (2018)) and the first film since the 1976 original not directed by him, and Stallone's stewardship of the Rocky character has been a defining feature of the franchise. However, Stallone remained involved in the production of the film, reprising his role as Rocky, this time as a secondary character training a younger boxer who becomes a kind of surrogate son that replaces his own absentee child. Coogler repeatedly emphasised the fact that he felt it was crucial to secure Stallone's approval for the new direction of the franchise and to respect the 'legacy' of the *Rocky* films (Whipp 2016). But in addition to maintaining the 'legacy' of the original film, *Creed* also functioned as a launching point for Coogler as an auteur, a rising new cinematic voice capable of moving between small, independent projects and major Hollywood franchises. While Coogler had received critical acclaim for his debut film, *Fruitvale Station* (2013), *Creed* helped to provide the younger director with significantly more visibility.

Fruitvale Station, a retelling of the last hours of Oscar Grant, a young African-American man who was killed by police at a Bay Area Rapid Transit station, served as a key text for representing the ongoing police violence against African-American men, in part by its empathetic portrayal of Grant, a low-level drug dealer, as a loving boyfriend, father and son struggling to find and hold onto work after a brief stint in prison. Similarly, *Creed* faced the challenge of mediating the image of the black boxer, which has historically been entwined with ideas of masculinity and national identity through figures like Joe Louis, who symbolised the superiority of American athletes over their German opponents during World War II, and Muhammad Ali, who became aligned with civil rights and black nationalism (Yasar 2018). Thus, even while *Creed* was promoted as being a continuation of the *Rocky* story, publicity for the film also used Coogler's authorship – and his continued collaboration with *Fruitvale Station* star Michael B. Jordan – as a means for shaping the film's reception. In turn, publicity for the film often emphasised the fact that Coogler explicitly sought the approval of Stallone himself to continue the Rocky story.[1] These promotional materials, as well as other paratexts such as DVD commentary tracks, helped to transform Rocky's cultural significance, specifically by shifting the grounds from which authenticity and outsider status are conferred. Instead of Rocky being defined as an outsider because of his status as a white, blue-collar boxer (who trains, for example, by punching sides of beef in a meat-packing plant), for Adonis, authenticity derives from an innate desire to choose a life in the boxing ring as a way of proving one's worth, a theme that is reflected in both Rocky and Creed's fractured family units. Adonis fights (quite literally, in one sequence) against his dead father's legacy, while Rocky struggles with his role as an absentee father who hardly speaks to his own son.[2] In this sense, Stallone's willingness to relinquish control over his most iconic character becomes a new form of authorship, one in which the entirety of the *Rocky* saga is re-evaluated to rewrite the prior films' racial politics and their representations of masculinity within professional sports.

RETHINKING REBOOT CINEMA

Reboots, remakes and sequels have all, of course, functioned as a central economic strategy of film studios for decades, but there continues to be at least some degree of uncertainty about the definition of what counts as a reboot. Reboots have, as Daniel Herbert points out, allowed studios to dodge some of the negative connotations associated with the term 'remake' (Herbert 2017: 38). William Proctor (2012) has argued that reboots are defined by several key characteristics. First, they must respond to or update a franchise, or series of films, rather than an individual one. When studios revisit a single, stand-alone film, that is considered a remake, but revising a film that is part of series can be seen as a reboot. Second, Proctor argues that reboots typically take us back to a character's origin story, starting again at Year One. Using the metaphor of a malfunctioning computer, Proctor explains that reboots still contain the 'memory' of the prior film cycles but start the 'program', the mode of telling that material, over.

By Proctor's narrow textual definition, *Creed* is not a reboot but a sequel (or perhaps a spin-off, to use an old television term), a continuation of an existing storyline, one that has unfolded over several decades, but following a new set of characters. With that in mind, I have argued that reboots function to mediate the tension between continuity or familiarity, on the one hand, and textual novelty, on the other, that is central to Hollywood production processes (Tryon 2013: 432). *Creed* allows us to learn more about the continuing story of Rocky Balboa, but it also gives us essentially the same story again, although updated for a new era. In fact, the term 'reboot' has been used more colloquially within industry discourse to refer to any film (or TV series) that reinvigorates an existing franchise that has been left dormant for a long period of time. And although the idea of the reboot is sometimes treated pejoratively as a sign of creative exhaustion, it is frequently used neutrally to refer to any series or franchise that is revisited after its original run. These revived movie franchises and TV shows have in some cases exported the themes and settings of the original show to a new era (*Hawaii 5-0, One Day at a Time*) or they can include characters from the original series, continuing their storylines where the series left off when the series or franchise ended (*Roseanne, Gilmore Girls, Arrested Development*).

In the case of the *Rocky* franchise, the most recent film prior to *Creed* had been *Rocky Balboa*, which was released in 2006, nearly ten years prior to *Creed*, but the original cycle essentially ended in 1985 after *Rocky IV*, as the character played by Stallone had aged to the point that it would be implausible for him to continue his boxing career. And while *Creed* continues the storylines of existing characters, the film follows many of the traits of reboots in starting from the beginning of a young, unknown boxer's career at the moment when he gets the opportunity to challenge the light heavyweight champion. Trade industry journalists and film critics also frequently treated *Creed* as a reboot, with *IndieWire* critic Eric Kohn (2015) calling the film a 'reboot worth rooting for' and *USA Today*'s Andrea Mandell (2015) also describing *Creed* as a 'modern reboot'. Thus, one of the aims of this chapter is to advocate for a more expansive concept of what counts as a reboot, to include those serial stories, whether TV shows or film series, that are revived after years of dormancy, and that offer a new creative vision for that series.

With that in mind, I identify four components that help to explain the relationship between *Creed* and the *Rocky* franchise, between the reboot and the source texts it updates. The first component is the centrality of intertextuality. As Constantine Verevis has argued, reboots and sequels invariably engage with the concept of intertextuality, the principle that texts are not self-contained units but are instead infused with relationships with other texts (Verevis 2006: 18–19). *Creed*, of course, contains explicit references to aspects of all the *Rocky* movies, including and, in some cases, rewriting Rocky's career and his relationship with Adonis's father, Apollo, not to mention serving as an implicit reevaluation of the career of Stallone himself. But, like most movies, it contains references to other aspects of the history of cinema, whether the casual quotations of *The Godfather* or visual and stylistic elements, including implicit links between *Creed* and past collaborations between Coogler and Jordan, the actor who plays Adonis. But in more subtle ways, *Creed* acknowledges the changes in how audiences watch boxing, with the matches being filmed in what Ben Travers referred to as the 'HBO style'. Coogler uses splashy graphics to display the heights, weights and records of the boxers competing in the match, opting for a graphic style that emulates HBO's coverage of boxing, an approach that Travers (2015) aligned with new modes of realism. One of Creed's fights is even filmed in a single take, with the camera swooping around, above and even below the boxers, to emulate the mobile camera now commonplace in professional sporting events. This stylisation becomes even more explicit in *Creed II*, in which Adonis is interviewed for an HBO documentary about his upcoming match with Viktor Drago (ironically just months before HBO would stop its boxing broadcasts).

The second component of this relationship is the tension between a franchise's legacy and the desire to disrupt elements of that history. In the case of the Rocky franchise, this tension exists primarily within the franchise's racial and gender politics. While the original film was marked by anxieties about American decline in the post-Watergate era and the related threats to white masculinity, the reboot turns many of these tropes on their head, explicitly adressing the issue of blackness in a cultural moment when Black Lives Matter was dominating news headlines and when the film industry was facing significant critique through campaigns such as the #OscarsSoWhite Twitter hashtag. *Creed* rewrites Apollo, recasting his flamboyant channelling of Muhammad Ali, which is no longer portrayed as a threat, emphasising instead the friendship he shared with Rocky after *Rocky 3*. Adonis's love interest, Bianca (Tessa Thompson), is depicted as having ambitions comparable to the boxer's, as she pursues a career as a successful musician. In addition, a significant plot point portrays Adonis struggling with his own tendencies towards hypermasculinity when he jealously confronts a male musician who could have helped Bianca achieve that dream of a recording contract. At the same time, *Creed* clearly embraces many elements of the original films, using 'call backs' – intertextual references to past films, whether musical cues, plot elements or visual elements – to convey the filmmakers' (and audiences') appreciation of the franchise and its legacy.

This question of legacy is intimately linked to a third, related trait crucial to the franchise and common to reboots in general: the nostalgic engagement with the original text. *Rocky* itself was a nostalgic text, deeply linked with the late-1970s conservative backlash described by Herman Gray, one that longed for an earlier 'golden age' when opportunities were available to working men, who were portrayed as being unfairly victimised by 'social policies such as quotas, affirmative action, and special treatment extended to women, blacks, and other communities of colour' (Gray 1995: 17). While *Rocky*'s nostalgia is built onto a false belief that white working-class men are being supplanted, the film evokes an idealised past in which opportunities for employment, success and even personal connection appeared to be more widely available. Finally, the *Rocky* franchise has for decades functioned as a melodrama. As Jason Mittell has argued, melodrama can be characterised as having a 'commitment to linking morality, emotional response, and narrative drive' (Mittell 2015: 244). While Mittell is primarily discussing serial television, the multi-sequel *Rocky* franchise, which now spans decades in the life of the central character, follows a similar logic, although the underlying moral stance of the franchise changes dramatically in *Creed*, through its complex negotiation of the image of the black professional athlete. This stance is often predicated on the *Rocky/Creed* franchise's careful use of suspense in telling the story of its central characters.

MELODRAMA AND SERIAL STORYTELLING

In her groundbreaking reconsideration of the melodramatic mode, Linda Williams identifies four primary features that manifest themselves in the *Rocky/Creed* franchise. Williams is especially attentive to the ways in which the contemporary (post-*Titanic* (1997)) blockbuster borrows from the tropes of melodrama. She first argues that melodrama is invariably characterised by suspense, whether the quite literal suspension in air of the main characters in James Cameron's *Titanic*, as the boat begins its inexorable collapse into the ocean, or the broader sense of narrative suspense as we seek to discover what happened to the film's key characters (Williams 2012: 536). In the *Rocky* films, suspense is structured primarily around the 'Big Fight' narrative (will the underdog get the opportunity to fight for the title? Will he be able to prove himself?), but it is also structured around the interpersonal relationships that surround the fighter, such as whether the central couple will remain together in a supportive relationship. Second, Williams explains that melodrama is associated with the attempt to achieve 'moral legibility' within the resolution of the suspenseful storyline. In both *Rocky* and *Creed*, moral legibility is achieved in part through narratives of success and opportunity but also of achieving that success fairly and without artificial methods, such as the manufactured superfighter Ivan Drago, who is created by steroids and other technologies in *Rocky IV*. This desire for moral legibility is linked to what Williams describes as a 'space of innocence', an ideal of equality and a lack of cynicism regarding the narratives of success and community, a consistent theme throughout the *Rocky/Creed* franchise, manifesting itself particularly in the constant renegotiations of family and fatherhood, whether Adonis's ambivalence regarding his late father or Rocky's estranged relationship with his own son or even Ivan Drago's attempt to regain legitimacy through his son's boxing career. Finally, Williams attempts to distance modern melodrama from the quality of 'inherent excess'. Excess, she explains, can be expressed through degrees of emotion and aesthetic ornamentation (as in Douglas Sirk's films), and in terms of spectacle. However, while Williams argues that excess is no longer necessary to melodrama, emotional and spectacular excess remain central to the *Rocky/Creed* franchise, in terms of both the dramatic emotional arcs and the visual and sonic flourishes that have dominated the series, whether the dramatic boxing sequences or even the use of iconic symbols, such as the American flag shorts passed down from Apollo to Rocky and eventually to Adonis or the steps of the Philadelphia Museum of Art that provided the culmination of so many training montages.

With these definitions in mind, I want to draw a relationship between the film franchise reboot and the modern melodramatic mode. I am less interested in seeking to rehabilitate the melodramatic mode – Williams, Mittell and other scholars have already effectively done that – but am more interested in exploring how the nostalgic underpinnings of the reboot intersect with melodrama's search for moral legibility, especially as those moral grounds shift over time. In this sense, *Creed* and its sequel, *Creed II*, are defined by their ambivalent nostalgia toward the original franchise, admiring the narrative power of the *Rocky* films while also interrogating their politics.

ROCKY

Rocky and its many sequels offer a textbook illustration of Williams' redefinition of melodrama. The original *Rocky* was linked explicitly to America's Bicentennial and haunted by the Carter-era 'crisis of confidence', in which the United States faced an economic recession, gas shortages and Nixonian political scandals that undermined trust in democracy and opportunity. This political context helped to establish *Rocky* as inherently nostalgic for a golden age of boxing (and of economic opportunity) that no longer seemed to exist, one that concocts a scenario in which a white boxer is transformed into an underdog against an arrogant black boxer who serves as the boxing 'establishment' that seems to control who has access to competing in the sport (Willmore 2015). In fact, the film opens with Rocky Balboa fighting in a bar-room, earning the small sum of $40 for knocking out his opponent despite the serious physical toll that boxing will have on him, in part because Mickey and other trainers do not fully believe in his potential as a fighter. Rocky's early struggles, represented in part by his tiny apartment and by his day job as a bill collector for a shady loan shark, help to convey his status as an underdog. Meanwhile, Apollo is depicted inside his mansion or in luxurious offices where he and his business partners watch from a position of power as they decide how to manage Apollo's career. Rocky's struggles reflect what Kristen Whissel has called, in a slightly different context, the 'thwarted upward mobility' of the film's audience (2006: 25), evoking the real financial hardships that many contemporary viewers of the film faced, even while attributing those struggles, in part, to the threats to a white working class.

The first *Rocky* film was largely structured around a racial backlash narrative, in which Rocky becomes a 'Great White Hope' figure within the world of boxing. This contrast establishes a type of moral legibility, in which the sport of boxing has been corrupted by Apollo's apparent cynicism about the American Dream and by the efforts of publicists to create a spectacle rather than focusing on true competition. Early scenes in the film feature Rocky being supplanted by younger, more athletic (and invariably) black boxers, including one early scene where Rocky's gruff manager, Mickey, removes Rocky's belongings from his locker and gives the locker to a younger, presumably hungrier African-American fighter. Later in the film, Rocky sits in a corner bar and watches a TV sports show featuring Apollo, a character who was explicitly modelled on Muhammad Ali. In fact, Ali himself famously discussed this comparison during a special preview screening of *Rocky II* (1979) with the esteemed film critic Roger Ebert (1979). During the bar scene, Creed mugs for the camera and, using Ali's famous poetic style, encourages children to become educated and to pursue careers as lawyers and teachers rather than going into professional boxing with the Ali-style couplet 'Be a thinker, not a stinker'. In response, a bartender mutters that the world of boxing is dominated by 'jig clowns', setting up the film's efforts to position Rocky as the Great White Hope figure who would save the boxing world from being dominated by black boxers, a fear that Apollo himself cynically exploits when he seeks out a 'lily-white' boxer during his search for an opponent. Stallone's screenplay carefully distances the Rocky character from this overt racism, however, with Rocky defending Apollo as an example of someone who achieved the American Dream, telling the bartender 'he took his shot'. Thus, while Rocky appears from one perspective to be a victim of an unfair system – he is initially prevented from getting an opportunity that he deserves based on his talent and skill – he is unwilling to blame others for his plight, although he avoids directly criticising the bartender's racism. Thus, Rocky is positioned as occupying a space of innocence, in which his sincere desire to compete prevents him from recognising that he is an unwitting participant in Apollo's cynical efforts to exploit the American Dream myth.

The film's suspense is ultimately resolved in the Big Fight, the characteristic climax of all *Rocky* films, where both narrative and moral questions are resolved simultaneously in the ring. It provides a resolution to Apollo's cynical plan for a staged fight that will offer an illusion of opportunity, rather than a real chance at winning the title. Instead, Rocky proves his worth as a fighter, early in the match, holding his own against the heavyweight champion and even becoming the first ever boxer to knock Apollo down in the ring. Rocky therefore demonstrates his strength and determination, winning over an initially sceptical audience within the boxing arena (an affirmation expressed through the 'Rocky!' chants that build to a crescendo as the fight reaches its climax). Rocky both proves his skill as a fighter and restores his relationship with Adrian, who rushes to the boxing ring to meet him as the fight reaches its dramatic conclusion. But, to paraphrase Williams, deserving to win does not mean getting to win. In Rocky's first Big Fight, he loses in a split decision, but the film celebrates his goodness – or innocence – by showing that he was able to compete with integrity against his more famous opponent and by the mutual respect that both fighters share when the final bell rings, with the two fighters clinched together and Apollo telling Rocky, 'ain't gonna be no rematch' (a promise, of course, that lasts until the film's first sequel three years later). But Rocky's inherent goodness is also illustrated through his loyalty to Adrian; even in the midst of the fight's aftermath, he is more concerned about seeking her out than in learning whether he won the heavyweight championship. Adrian herself undergoes a transformation, shifting from a mousy, shy pet shop worker who can barely look Rocky in the eye when he is trying to court her into a more confident and assertive individual who pushes her way through the crowd to embrace him.

Future films in the *Rocky/Creed* franchise trace the evolution of Rocky as a character. While he retains his essential decency and moral code, the *Rocky* films present him with a series of personal and, in some cases, nationalistic motivations for stepping back into the ring and demonstrating his worth as a fighter. This includes the inevitable rematch with Apollo but culminates in his attempt to avenge Apollo's death in *Rocky IV*, when he is killed in the ring by Ivan Drago. The film becomes a personal revenge story and simultaneously allows Rocky to stand up for the United States and, by extension, the individualist ethos during the last years of the Reagan era. These values are expressed through the training montage, in which Rocky is shown working alone in the natural world, the space of innocence, to harden himself for the fight while Drago trains in a facility where he is surrounded by trainers who collectively work to make him stronger and where the Russian fighter develops a machine-like ability to throw and absorb punches. As a result, the character of Rocky becomes a means through which Stallone could explore moral and ethical questions, even as those questions evolve over time.

CREED

Like *Rocky*, *Creed* deploys the elements of melodrama in order to establish grounds through which moral legibility can be achieved. *Creed* deftly takes the original film's racial and sexual politics and subverts them, even while meticulously maintaining the original film's narrative beats. *Creed* reverses the original film's racial politics in part by shifting the point of identification from Rocky to Adonis, Apollo's son from an extramarital affair. This shift allows Coogler to adapt many of the stylistic and melodramatic narrative tropes associated with the original film and to infuse them with a new political perspective that critiques the original films. In true reboot fashion, *Creed* adopts many of the narrative arcs that have made the *Rocky* franchise a multi-generational international success. Like the original *Rocky*, *Creed* opens with a fight scene set in a decrepit, possibly underground boxing ring, presents an unlikely title fight, includes an uplifting training montage, and mixes these elements with personal conflicts: dating relationships, cancer diagnoses, absentee fathers. This careful mix of narrative familiarity with textual novelty helped to position *Creed* as a reboot of a franchise that otherwise seemed to have reached its narrative limits. After a brief sequence establishing Adonis's childhood experiences, in which we learn that Apollo's wife makes the self-effacing gesture of adopting Adonis, *Creed* opens with Adonis fighting in a similar semi-professional setting to the one where Rocky began his career. In this case, Adonis leaves his dreary job as a financial analyst to fight in an underground boxing league in Tijuana, where his superior talent leads him to an easy, if unsatisfying, victory against a less talented opponent.

Creed also follows the logic of the reboot in its careful attention to preserving the legacy of the existing franchise while also introducing the central conflict that will guide the film. After the initial fight, Adonis returns to his apartment, where he watches the Rocky/Apollo rematch from *Rocky II*, now conveniently uploaded to YouTube, on his wall-sized TV set. Initially, the clips evoke nostalgia for the original *Rocky* franchise, but Adonis is haunted by them and leaps from his couch, shadowboxing as the fight plays, the projection of the computer image reflecting on him. During the scene, Rocky has Apollo cornered, and Adonis's punches roughly mirror those being thrown by Rocky, who will of course become his second father (Adonis even refers to him as 'uncle', or 'unc' for short). The scene seems to imply that Adonis is fighting against his father and the legacy he has left for his 'illegitimate' son, evoking the political and textual ambivalence that *Creed* has towards its source film. The scene is also a nod to the fact that in an era of streaming video, the history of cinema – and televised sports – is perpetually available to audiences, potentially altering the ways in which sports media helped to mythologise star athletes.

Intertextual references to past *Rocky* films are sprinkled liberally throughout *Creed* and its follow-up, *Creed II*. Like *Rocky*, *Creed* opens by establishing the boxer's humble origins and by setting up the impediments that prevent him from launching his boxing career. *Creed* also contains callbacks to past *Rocky* films, particularly the iconic training montages. During their early training sequence, Rocky introduces Adonis to the 'old school' methods he learned from Mickey and later from Apollo, requiring Adonis to run behind his van as he drives around the city and then, following a technique he learned in *Rocky II*, directing the younger boxer to try to catch chickens in order to develop better quickness and lateral movement. Similarly, musical cues help to sustain the connection with the *Rocky* franchise, such as the use of Bill Conti's classic score. The training montage culminates with a callback to the famous jogging scene from the original film. In the original movie, Rocky is joined by dozens of supporters running through the city with him, but in *Creed*, Adonis is propelled forward by Meek Mill's 'Lord Knows', a heavy-beat hip-hop song, and by a group of African-American street bikers who push him forward and circle around him as he celebrates the completion of his long run while Rocky looks down at him from a second-floor window. Both films also use the idea of spectacle to portray an idealised image of sports competition. In *Rocky*, Apollo's entrance, in which the champion fighter is dressed as George Washington and then as Uncle Sam, codes him as being insincere and cynical about the American Dream, almost as if he is wearing patriotic drag, while Rocky Balboa's plain white trunks and low-key entrance depict him as more authentic, more focused on proving his individual ability rather than participating in athletic spectacle, even while the film itself revels in its use of those spectacular elements. But unlike the original film, which punishes the black boxer for his hubris, *Creed* reverses this racial narrative, instead depicting Adonis as a heroic figure and Rocky as the guide who will lead a black fighter to greatness (Serwer 2018).

Beyond the boxing ring, *Creed* uses elements of melodrama to develop an emotional storyline that addresses moral, ethical and political issues. Like Rocky Balboa, Adonis develops a love interest, in this case with a musician, Bianca, who happens to be his neighbour when he moves to his tiny, noisy Philadelphia apartment. We learn that Bianca is a rising star musician, but faces progressive hearing loss, a plot point that becomes even more crucial in *Creed II*, when the couple faces the decision of whether or not to have children who might inherit her genetic predisposition toward deafness. Rocky's role as a surrogate father becomes evident during his interactions with Adonis and Bianca. Rocky is able to provide Adonis with answers about his biological father. In fact, just before the big fight, Rocky takes a paternal role towards Adonis and Bianca, gently placing blankets over them after they have fallen asleep on his couch. In turn, Adonis becomes a surrogate son for Rocky, advocating for him at the hospital when he is diagnosed with cancer and pushing him to undergo treatment when Rocky is initially reluctant because chemotherapy failed to save his wife, Adrian. Like the original *Rocky*, the Big Fight in *Creed* culminates with a split decision and, like the original *Rocky*, losing the fight ultimately proves to be beside the point. Although the fight takes place in Liverpool, England, the home of the current champion, 'Pretty' Ricky Conlan, *Creed* ends with Adonis accompanying Rocky as he struggles to walk up the steps of the Philadelphia Museum of Art, the iconic location where Rocky stood at the end of his triumphant training sequence. Now the scene has been rewritten from one that emphasises individual triumph to one in which Rocky and Adonis have developed a supportive and interracial family relationship.

Intertextual references to the Rocky films persisted in *Creed II*, the follow-up to Coogler's reboot while also deepening the issues of legacy and of father-and-son relationships. In the second film in the *Creed* cycle, Adonis ascends to the heavyweight title only to find himself fighting Viktor Drago, the son of Ivan Drago, who beat Adonis's father to death in the boxing ring before losing to Rocky in Moscow in *Rocky IV* and falling into disgrace, putting Adonis in the position not just of avenging his father's loss but also of shoring up his secondary father's legacy as well. Notably, like *Creed*, *Creed II* ends away from the ring, with Rocky travelling from his native working-class Philadelphia to Vancouver to find his biological son and grandson, an image that provides closure to his story while leaving room for Adonis to continue his journey and to carry the boxing franchise forward for a new generation of viewers.

CONCLUSION

Soon after the release of *Creed II*, Stallone announced in an Instagram video that he was retiring the character of Rocky Balboa, even while endorsing the continuation of the *Creed* storyline. The tension between legacy and renewal has been a vital framework for discussions of the *Creed* films, and Stallone made reference to that throughout the video, commenting that 'there's a whole new world that's going to be opening up with the audience, with this generation', and then telling the actor Michael B. Jordan that he would now 'carry the mantle' for the franchise (Sharf 2018). The Hollywood economy has thrived on the reboot as a cultural form. Reboots extend the life of media properties, allowing studios to recalibrate characters and stories for new audiences. However, reboots also offer a unique space for reflecting on and reconsidering the legacy of an existing media property. In the case of the *Rocky/Creed* franchise, Creed adapts many of the tropes of the reboot in order to develop a politically ambivalent reflection on the legacy of the original *Rocky* films. While the Rocky Balboa story, as it plays out over multiple films, is celebrated for its emotional and cultural resonance, *Creed* also gently subverts Rocky's racial politics, even while maintaining reverence for the franchise and its central characters. While the *Creed* films represent a limit case when it comes to defining the idea of a reboot, it also shows the ways in which reboots can allow us to rethink the origin stories of some of our most powerful popular myths.

NOTES

1. See, for example, Staskiewicz (2015). Notably, for *Creed II*, Stallone once again took over screenwriting duties, while Steven Caple, Jr, a classmate of Coogler's, served as director.
2. *Creed II* explicitly picks up on these questions of father-son legacies by reintroducing Ivan Drago, the seemingly robotic Russian boxer who killed Apollo in the ring in *Rocky IV*, who trains his own son to become a boxer and to restore his legacy by fighting Adonis, the biological son of Apollo and the surrogate son of Rocky.

REFERENCES

Barthes, Roland (1972), *Mythologies*, trans. Annette Lavers, New York: Farrar, Straus and Giroux.
Ebert, Roger (1979), 'Watching *Rocky II* with Muhammad Ali', *Roger Ebert*, 31 July, <https://www.rogerebert.com/interviews/watching-rocky-ii-with-muhammad-ali>.
Gray, Herman (1995), *Watching Race: Television and the Struggle for Blackness*, Minneapolis, MN: University of Minnesota Press.
Gray, Jonathan (2013), 'When Is the Author?', in Jonathan Gray and Derek Johnson (eds), *A Companion to Media Authorship*, Malden, MA: Wiley Blackwell, pp. 88–111.
Herbert, Daniel (2017), *Film Remakes and Franchises*, New Brunswick, NJ: Rutgers University Press.
Johnson, Derek (2013), *Media Franchising: Creative License and Collaboration in the Creative Industries*, New York: New York University Press.
Kohn, Eric (2015), 'Review: "Creed" is a "Rocky" Reboot Worth Fighting for', *Indie Wire*, 18 November, <https://www.indiewire.com/2015/11/review-creed-is-a-rocky-reboot-worth-rooting-for-53514/>.
Mandell, Andrea (2015), '"Creed" Casts Rocky as a Familiar Mentor', *USA Today*, 23 November, <https://www.usatoday.com/story/life/movies/2015/11/23/creed-turns-rocky-into-a-mentor/76210594/>.
Mittell, Jason (2015), *Complex TV: The Poetics of Contemporary Television Storytelling*, New York: New York University Press.
Proctor, William (2012), 'Regeneration and Rebirth: Anatomy of the Franchise Reboot', *Scope: An Online Journal of Film and Media Studies*, 22 (February), 1–19.
Serwer, Adam (2018), 'How *Creed* Forever Changed the Rocky Series', *The Atlantic*, 28 November, <https://www.theatlantic.com/entertainment/archive/2018/11/how-creed-forever-changed-rocky-series/576757/>.
Sharf, Zack (2018), 'Sylvester Stallone Says He's Done Playing Rocky Balboa in Emotional Goodbye Video', *IndieWire*, 28 November, <https://www.indiewire.com/2018/11/sylvester-stallone-retires-rocky-balboa-goodbye-video-1202023731/>.

Smith, Kyle (2018), 'How Reagan Used the Movies to his Advantage', *National Review*, 27 March <https://www.nationalreview.com/2018/03/how-reagan-used-the-movies-to-his-advantage/>.
Staskiewicz, Keith (2015), 'How Ryan Coogler Convinced Sylvester Stallone to Make *Creed*', *Entertainment Weekly*, 17 August, <https://ew.com/article/2015/08/17/creed-michael-jordan-sylvester-stallone/>.
Travers, Ben (2015), 'All the "Rocky" References in "Creed" (We Think)', *IndieWire*, 30 November, <https://www.indiewire.com/2015/11/all-the-rocky-references-in-creed-we-think-50291/>.
Tryon, Chuck (2013), 'Reboot Cinema', *Convergence: The International Journal of Research Into New Media Technologies* 19: 4, 432–7.
Verevis, Constantine (2006), *Film Remakes*, Edinburgh: Edinburgh University Press.
Whipp, Glenn (2016), 'For Ryan Coogler, Making "Creed" Was Deeply Personal', *Los Angeles Times*, 5 January, <https://www.latimes.com/entertainment/envelope/la-en-mn-ryan-coogler-creed-director-20160105-story.html>.
Whissel, Kristen (2006), 'Tales of Upward Mobility: The New Verticality and Digital Special Effects', *Film Quarterly* 59: 4, 23–34.
Williams, Linda (2012), 'Mega-melodrama! Vertical and Horizontal Suspensions of the "Classical"', *Modern Drama*, 55: 4, 532–43.
Willmore, Alison (2015), '"Creed" is "Rocky" Without the Racial Insecurity', *Buzzfeed*, 21 November, <https://www.buzzfeed.com/alisonwillmore/creed-review>.
Yasar II, Mustafa (2018), 'The Fleshing Out of Black Masculine Archetypes in Ryan Coogler's Films', *Birth. Movies. Death*, 13 February, <https://birthmoviesdeath.com/2018/02/13/the-fleshing-out-of-black-masculine-archetypes-in-ryan-cooglers-films>.

CHAPTER 10

Ghost Girls: *Ghostbusters*, Popular Feminism and the Gender-Swap Reboot

Claire Perkins

> Every time feminism gains broad traction – that is, every time it spills beyond what are routinely dismissed as niched feminist enclaves – the forces of the status quo position it as a peril, and skirmishes ensue between those determined to challenge the normative and those determined to maintain it.
>
> Sarah Banet-Weiser, Empowered: Popular Feminism and Popular Misogyny (2018)

In 2015, the announcement that a forthcoming remake of *Ghostbusters* would replace the original film's male ensemble with four women prompted a storm of online activity that precisely demonstrated the 'skirmishes' that Sarah Banet-Weiser argues characterise the landscape of popular feminism. As has been comprehensively described, the concerted efforts of online geek discourse quickly made the trailer the most disliked video in YouTube history, in an outpouring of resentful misogyny that has been understood to be as much about the gendered battles of the 2016 US election primaries as the prospective film (Blodgett and Salter 2018). This activity, which largely eclipses the film itself, has been the main focus of commentary on *Ghostbusters*, which is primarily interested in connecting the misogynistic response to changing currents of fandom and broader political trends in online communities (Bryan and Clark 2019; Blodgett and Salter 2018; Proctor 2017). To take Banet-Weiser's logic from above, though, this style of response tends to reinforce a view that the film – at the level of mere concept – does present a feminist challenge to the normative, which is duly positioned and reacted to as a 'peril' by those subscribing to patriarchal belief systems. What has been less considered in this discussion is exactly if and how the film can actually be considered a 'feminist' endeavour. *Ghostbusters* was not a critical or commercial success – for reasons in part attributed to the trolling campaign that plagued it (Ferber 2017) – but its gender-swap premise did lead to a whole cycle of films that have replaced a male ensemble with a female one, including *Ocean's Eight* (Ross, 2018), *Overboard* (Greenberg, 2018), *The Hustle* (Addison, 2019) – a reboot of *Dirty Rotten Scoundrels* (Oz, 1988) and *Life of the Party* (Falcone, 2018) – a reboot of Rodney Dangerfield's 1986 comedy *Back to School*. Seeking to examine how the gender-swap reboot in this way functions as an industrial and political strategy for Hollywood at the end of the twenty-first century's second decade, this chapter will explore how the format, at the levels of concept, narrative and tone, demonstrates what scholars including Banet-Weiser, Rosalind Gill and Catherine Rottenberg theorise as a specifically contemporary form of popular feminism, with a particular interest in how the serial identity of these films – reboots within a discursive cycle – shapes this form of expression.

GENDER-SWAPPING AND POPULAR FEMINISM

The process of interrogating the 'feminism' of popular culture is a key theme across a variety of fields and is, specifically, a keynote of much postfeminist scholarship (McRobbie 2004; Hollows and Mosely 2006; Ferreday and Harris 2017). The notion of popular feminism that I am evoking here presents a specific thread of this work, insofar as it attends to a contemporary moment where pop cultural expression appears to be reacting to, while simultaneously intensifying, some core postfeminist attitudes. If postfeminism is broadly understood as the assumption that historical feminist gains mean equality has been achieved, and feminism is therefore no longer needed, 'a spent force' (McRobbie 2004: 255), contemporary popular feminism marks its emphatic reappearance, in a manner that is signified within the mainstream media as 'cool': 'seemingly moved from being a derided and repudiated identity among young women to becoming a desirable, stylish, and decidedly fashionable one' (Gill 2016: 611). This 'new era' is marked by 'a dramatic increase in the visible expression and acceptance of feminism, and by a similarly vast amount of public vitriol and violence directed toward women' (Banet-Weiser 2018: 5). In Banet-Weiser's evaluation, popular feminism is popular in three senses: it manifests in discourses that circulate in popular and commercial media; it signifies the condition of being liked or admired; and it is a terrain of struggle – 'a space where competing demands for power battle it out' (2018: 1). Most significantly, it is a deeply ambivalent development; important in making feminism as cause and necessity visible but, by way of its operation at the level of visibility, it avoids considering the issue of patriarchy as a social structure, eliding a meaningful engagement with key terms of historical feminist discussion: equal rights, liberation, social justice and intersectionality (Rottenberg 2018: 5). The gender-swap reboot offers a compelling case study of this cultural moment, because discourse around it precisely demonstrates popular feminism as a terrain of struggle. On the one hand, the format is presented and promoted as a type of feminist revisionism; on the other, it provokes widespread critique, not only in the form of misogynistic responses to its very premise, but also from a feminist perspective that judges its 'feminism' to be 'toxic' (Spiers 2018; Hess 2018).

The distinction of the reboot within the broader field of remaking is the objective to restart a franchise: 'to return us to "year one", to the origins of a character, so that the story can be retold in a different format or style' (Tryon 2013: 433). With this goal, the reboot seeks to revive audience interest in a property by 'disavow[ing] and render[ing] inert its predecessor's validity' (Proctor 2012: 4), even while those predecessors – in the form of different filmic iterations of characters and scenarios – are still acutely apparent to viewers. The mere fact of the gender swap promises this 'true' reboot insofar as it implies a new, revisionist perspective from which the story could be told. As I will discuss further in the second part of this chapter, each of the original films in the cycle present an image of masculinity that is highly charged and, from the perspective of the current day, decidedly non-woke – from the womanising swagger of the *Ocean's* series (across both the 1960 and 2000s versions) to the bawdy sexism of *Back to School* and *Dirty Rotten Scoundrels* and the misogynistic themes of *Overboard*. These well-known sexual politics make the strategy of the gender swap in their reboots a high-concept hook – not just in terms of the ready-made premise it presents at a narrative level but as a strategy for Hollywood to advertise an ostensible intervention in its 'woman problem' (Banet-Weiser 2018: 129): the systemic sexism of its industry that has gained mainstream attention in recent years through, amongst other things, the #MeToo and Time's Up movements.

The impression of this 'intervention' is actively encouraged by the narrative image of these films, where all focus is on the gender swap as the primary point of difference for the new property. The official posters for *Ghostbusters*, *Ocean's 8* and *The Hustle*, for instance, all closely reproduce the design and character arrangement of the original posters, tapping into a pure type of high-concept logic in which the novelty of the new film – the original, but with women – can be instantly understood. The straight swap that underpins these narrative images promises, paradoxically, that both nothing and everything will be different. While the trappings and aesthetic of a familiar film world are designed to reassure fans of the original, the presence of the female characters completely disrupts this reassurance to signal a new 'take'.

This promise of revisionism is evident not only in official marketing materials but also in unofficial paratexts. The presence of Feig as director on *Ghostbusters* is important, for instance, because of his profile in making high-budget women-led comedy across three earlier films that all feature the 'unruly' star Melissa McCarthy (Petersen 2017): *Bridesmaids* (2011), *The Heat* (2013) and *Spy* (2015). Feig has always been vocal about his goal to push back against the intractable myth that films featuring women don't sell, and with *Ghostbusters* this became a specific attempt to show that a tentpole could be carried by female leads, three of whom are over forty (Yua 2016). For Feig, this concern with bolstering female visibility in Hollywood takes on specific meaning in the context of rebooting an iconic franchise. His primary goal in making *Ghostbusters*, he claims, was to give women, especially young women, an experience of a property that has always been defined in masculine terms. 'I wanted for little girls to be able to see themselves up on the screen', he declared. 'The original one exists, so you can see boys doing it, but how fun for girls to have this experience!' (Yua 2016).

The dynamics of association and disassociation with the original property that are implied here showcase the mixed messages that the gender-swap reboot presents, as well as how its identity as a remake works against its ostensibly 'feminist' ambition. The swap that defines it works at a high-concept level because it is straightforward and singular: the reboot is presented as a film that changes just one thing. Further details about the process of creating *Ghostbusters* support this impression of continuity, for instance the revelation that Feig and co-writer Katie Dippold rewatched the original two films and made a list of 'everything they'd be bummed not to see if someone else were making a new one, including the Ecto 1 car, ghost traps, the Stay Puft Marshmallow Man and, of course, fan-favorite apparition Slimer' (Yua 2016). In this process, the original franchise – 'sacred canon', as Feig has called it – is firmly kept in place as the legitimate property. The promise of revisionism along the lines of gender is kept deliberately vague, operating purely through the image of women in iconic male roles, with all official communication around the film actually focused wholly on its allegiance to the original franchise. At the level of the film's (high) concept, the act is not revisionist but substitutive, aiming to imply, but ultimately reject, the 'true' reboot's effect of rendering an original property 'inert'. In this way, the paratexts that make up the narrative image of the film work hard to present and sustain an impression that the gender-swap reboot is both feminist and not feminist – a contradiction that is evident not only in its narrative image but, as I will go on to examine, also in its storyline and tone.

Many of these issues come up in popular feminist perspectives that critique the gender-swap format, where the negative mythology of remaking holds particular meaning. The familiar position that the practice demonstrates an indolent aversion to risk-taking takes on the specific charge of sexism in objections that it is 'a safe way for studios to create female-driven content' that actively limits the potential for original storytelling by and featuring women (Saner 2017). From this viewpoint, it is the format's specific identity as a reboot that is understood to be most problematic, though the fact that the films have been overwhelmingly written and directed by men, therefore doing little to address the structural inequality around creative participation in Hollywood, is also heavily criticised. The promise of revisionism signalled in the practice – the sense that the new property will offer a different (gendered) perspective on the story world – is received as a complete fallacy, less about women driving stories than, in Stacy Smith's words, a Hollywood model that '[retrofits] whatever seems to be the idea into existing intellectual property and [assumes] it will be a market success' (Saner 2017).

The 'idea' that is retrofitted here is female empowerment, which, as Banet-Weiser shows, is the concept at the core of all contemporary popular feminist discourses that urge women to be confident, competent and resilient: to 'lean in' to a neoliberal system structured by inequality rather than address the structural causes of that inequality. In this cycle of reboots, the idea finds precise expression: women are framed to be empowered because they are occupying iconic male roles, and, the narrative image promises, fulfilling these as well as or better than their male precursors. The message relies upon the liberal feminist narrative that has dominated mainstream media's presentation of women's progress since the 1970s, and perpetuates the assumption that women in developed nations have gained unprecedented freedoms and choices in the decades since – leading to a reality where gender equality has been substantially achieved (Rottenberg 2018: 7–8). By triumphantly switching out men for women, the gender-swap reboot seeks to give an exact expression of this 'girl power' brand of logic, speaking to embedded cultural knowledge that regards participation and visibility within patriarchal systems as the endgame of feminism.

The manner in which this postfeminist image of achieved equality circulated and was reacted to, by both misogynist trolls and feminist critics, demonstrates the central importance of visibility to contemporary popular feminism. *Ghostbusters* itself was presented to be less important than the mere idea of the film. The narrative image that I have been analysing circulates effortlessly in the economy of visibility that Banet-Weiser argues is the support system for popular feminism: where the imperative to be popular requires 'easy access to grave topics such as discrimination, harassment, racism, and sexual violence' (2018: 140). To be visible means to be accessible to a large audience, and the gender-swap reboot is doubly accessible in this way: its high-concept premise is instantly conveyable and eminently shareable, and its 'feminist' message of achieved equality is readily comprehensible. As part of the liberal narrative described above, it functions quite literally as what Banet-Weiser, citing Joan Scott, calls an 'add women and stir' kind of feminism, bringing more women to the table simply because they are women, and therein assuming that 'the presence of women is sufficient to call feminism into being' (2018: 12). The circulation and traction of this image again performs a kind of double duty. It seeks to attract audiences to the film, using the continuity to the original property to cash in on the growing evidence that female-led narratives do make money, but it also aims to project a 'woke' message that engages with the increasing visibility of gendered disparities in Hollywood, specifically the historical lack of women protagonists in big-budget projects.

It is this strategy, I suggest, that explains the prominence of the gender-swap reboot in the current moment. As Amanda Ann Klein has identified, film cycles differ from film genres in that they are primarily defined not by their images or themes but by how they are used, with the formation and longevity of any individual cycle dependent on an originary film that either draws a large audience or becomes a subject of discussion in the media (2011: 4). The manner in which *Ghostbusters* was discussed in the media is commonly regarded to have had a negative impact, with Feig understanding that the trolling campaign and its backlash turned the film into a 'cause' that tangibly limited its box office returns (Ferber 2017). It is as this cause that the film performed a substantial function for Hollywood, though, with the discourse around its trolling enabling the simultaneous communication of a 'feminist' position – what the trolls were objecting to – and the takedown of that position. As 'cause', the film is a precise example of the intersection of popular feminism and popular misogyny.

REBOOTING REAGANITE ENTERTAINMENT

To this point I have focused on the gender-swap reboot in terms of its narrative image because, as described above, this is the primary way in which it works in popular feminism's economy of visibility. In the remaining part of this chapter, I will consider how the mixed messages that define the format are also readable in the rebooted narrative of *Ghostbusters* and, by extension, in other examples of the cycle. My jumping-off point for this reflection is the fact that many of these contemporary films reboot Hollywood properties that originally appeared in the 1980s as consummate examples of what Andrew Britton and Robin Wood, among others, have theorised as 'Reaganite entertainment' (Britton 1986; Wood 1986). For both, the term defines a cinema of confidence that coincides with the conservative values and free-market success ethic of Reagan's presidency, as well as with the emergence of blockbuster filmmaking as an industrial strategy. Responding tangibly to the alienated and uneasy narratives of the New Hollywood era that encoded the trauma of Vietnam and the challenges to hegemonic white masculinity posed by civil rights advances of the 1960s and 70s, 1980s mainstream American filmmaking overwhelmingly seeks to create an ideologically transparent image of reassurance. High-concept narrative structures present a clearly defined problem that acts of male heroism can unambiguously solve, offering a firm sense of closure that restores patriarchal norms and – via the mechanisms of spectacle and special effects – reduces the audience to a state of wonder (Wood 1986: 165–6). In Britton's well-known evaluation, the critical aspect of this style of filmmaking is the way in which it foregrounds the ideology of entertainment. The repetitiveness of its formulae emphatically tells audiences that they are being entertained, and the films thereby present as forms without significance: 'We are not told not to think, but we are told, over and over again, that there is nothing here to think about' (Britton 1986: 102).

As what Britton termed 'the definitive Reaganite text' (1986: 120), the original *Ghostbusters* foregrounds both these dimensions of reassurance. Its narrative mobilises the ghost metaphor to stage a confrontation between narrowly defined concepts of 'good' and 'evil' in which patriarchal norms are explicitly restored via the spectacle of male heroism. The narrative begins when the initial three members of the team – Peter Venkman (Bill Murray), Raymond Stantz (Dan Aykroyd) and Egon Spengler (Harold Ramis) – are expelled from the psychology department of Columbia University for their disreputable work on the paranormal. Academia is presented here not only as scientifically elite but as an easy and unaccountable option where money is given without the expectation of results – a situation directly opposed to the more 'honest' entrepreneurial pathway the three men take in setting up their own ghostbusting business. Their rise to fame is conveyed in a montage of triumphant trappings overlaid with iconic American magazine covers featuring the three and set to Ray Parker Jr's famous theme song, 'Who Ya Gonna Call?'. Pointedly excluded from this montage is the fourth, black member of the team, Winston Zeddmore (Ernie Hudson), who is hired on the spot in the scene following it with no background or context to his character, and with his only motivation being that he'll believe anything 'if there's a steady paycheck in it'.

Before the team's rise to fame, Dana Barrett (Sigourney Weaver) comes to them after witnessing a fiery portal containing a monstrous demon calling itself 'Zuul' in her apartment's refrigerator. The presence is eventually traced to the building's original architect, who, as a worshipper of a fictive and destructive mythology centred on the sadistic figure 'Gozer', designed the building as a conductor for spiritual turbulence, seeking to bring about the end of the world. Eliminating Zuul is explicitly set up not only as the narrative's central obstacle but as the mechanism by which a romantic union will be secured between Venkman and Dana: 'I'll prove myself to you,' he sarcastically promises. 'I'll solve your little problem'. As the mythology unfolds, Dana's possession by Zuul manifests as aggressive sexual desire, with her seduction of her counterpart in the mythology – possessed neighbour Louis (Rick Moranis) – functioning as the mechanism that calls into being Gozer 'the Destructor', an androgynous, glam-rock inspired female demon played by Slavitza Jovan. It is this figure that the ghostbusting team eventually face off against on the apartment building's roof, expressing an unambiguous punishment of female sexuality and power – 'this chick is *toast*' – when they work together, 'crossing the streams' of their nuclear accelerator weapons to destroy her. Afterwards, amongst the debris, Dana is discovered restored to normal and, whimpering and moaning, is carried away by Venkman, who kisses her extravagantly as the film's end credits come up over the team emerging from the building to the cheers of a gathered New York crowd.

The ideological transparency of this narrative, where anxiety over both nuclear threat and female independence is collapsed into the single metaphor of a ghost who is readily contained by male control, is obscured by the overtly non-serious tone. The performances, most notably Murray's as Venkman, foreground a sense of cynical incredulity towards the fantastic plot, encouraging a celebration of both its absurdity and its specificity that prohibits any meaningful reflection on its real-life connotations. To return to Britton's terms, this style of performance is a convention of the ideology of entertainment – it foregrounds the world on screen as entertainment, nothing more, and promotes a knowing sense of familiarity with the otherness of this 'hermetic, autonomous world . . . which relates to other social practices only by being different from them' (1986: 102).

The revisionist work of the *Ghostbusters* reboot actively addresses these characteristically Reaganite dimensions of narrative and ideological reassurance. While maintaining the overall shape of the original story – New York City is threatened by a large-scale paranormal event that an entrepreneurial team of ex-academic experts successfully solve and foreclose – the 2016 film substantially alters both the narrative terms and comedic tone. At the level of plot, these changes can be read to superficially 'correct' the flagrantly patriarchal and racist values of the original. Most obviously, the source of evil tapped into by the villain seeking to 'cleanse the earth' – here a disgruntled hotel janitor named Rowan North (Neil Casey) seeking revenge for a lifetime of bullying – is not a mythological female deity but a 'natural' phenomenon: a vortex created when currents of supernatural energy that cross the earth intersect. Further, the expulsion of this force is not linked to a heterosexual romantic union; instead, it is female friendship that is asserted in a semi-ironic toast given by one member of the team, Jillian Holtzmann (Kate McKinnon), at the end of the film when she proclaims that, having thought she would never have a friend, the team feel like a family of her own and she loves them. Another pointed correction is evident in the more fully formed characterisation of the fourth member, Patty Tolan (Leslie Jones), a black Metropolitan Transport

Authority worker who leads the team to their second ghost sighting and brings to the scientific expertise of the team an encyclopedic understanding of New York – knowledge that assists in several further trappings.

Beyond these altered plot points, the attempted revisionism of the reboot is evident too in the way the film presents a general acknowledgment of gender inequality. It is self-reflexive about the trolling that plagued its announcement, with the characters seeing sceptical and sexist comments responding to videos of their sightings – 'aint no bitches gonna hunt no ghosts' – and dismissing these: 'you shouldn't be looking at that', Abby Yates (Melissa McCarthy) tells Erin Gilbert (Kristen Wiig). This scepticism towards the team extends to a broader construction of their marginalised status that is held throughout the film, explicitly contrasting with the simplified heroic narrative of the original. Where the male team's first successful trapping leads straight into their fame montage, the women's is followed by a visit to their office from 'famed debunker' Martin Heist, played by Bill Murray, who demands to know why they are 'pretending' to catch ghosts. Desperate to prove their work to this self-reflexive figure of authority, Erin releases the trapped ghost, who promptly throws Heist out the window and flies off. While the expulsion offers tangible satisfaction, this is immediately undermined by the women's agency again being curtailed by male authority. Alongside the police who show up to investigate Heist's death, two suited men from Homeland Security demand they come with them to the mayor's office – the site, in the original film, where the male team are granted full government and military support to proceed with their extermination. In direct contrast, the female team are told that while the mayor (Andy Garcia) and his team believe them, this is only because the government is already aware of and monitoring the paranormal situation, and that the women need to stop drawing attention to it and themselves in order to avoid 'mass hysteria'. To avoid this distinctly gendered prospect, the team are kept anonymous and framed as frauds in the media and, upon further successful captures, privately thanked but publicly shamed by the mayor's assistant (Cecily Strong). Following their final conquest, where they succeed in closing the vortex opened by Rowan, she invites them to – discreetly – continue their study, fully funded, with whatever support they need: 'we need to better prepared', she admits.

While this promise enables a triumphant ending, where the team are reinstated from their dire office above a Chinese restaurant to the now $21,000 per month Tribeca loft space of the original film, the message on the gendering of work is clear. Women's labour is framed to be essential but invisible. This 'joke' is evident too in the modulated tone of the reboot, with its humour deriving primarily from its deflation of the sarcastic, jacked-up heroism of the original film. In a style of satirical performance that is familiar from the tone of *Saturday Night Live* – where all four actresses have appeared, with Jones, McKinnon and Wiig featuring as regular cast members over the past decade – the reboot's comedy arises from the women's understated delivery of non sequiturs. Frequently, the surprising or deadpan effect turns on the distance of their reaction from an expectation cultivated from the original film. When the team arrive at the Mercado Hotel to accost Rowan, for instance, their car screams to a halt directly outside and their suiting up is captured in a montage as they snap on their proton packs. A medium-long shot tilts up from the pavement to frame the four women outfitted in the signature jumpsuits and, as the pumping beat of 'I'm Not Afraid' abruptly cuts out, both Erin and Abby utter 'let's go!' at the same time. 'Oh, I'm sorry,' they both falter, 'did you want to . . .? Next time . . .'. The effect undercuts the heroic grandeur of the montages that precede it, denying an emotionally fulfilling triumph for the women that signifies a broader awareness of how patriarchal systems work to obscure and undervalue female achievement.

This marginalised status is evident too in other ways by which the women are presented as underdogs. When Patty joins the team and asks how they became interested in ghosts, a backstory for the narrative is given that is completely absent from the original film: Erin explains that she saw a ghost when young and was teased and bullied for it and called 'ghost girl', with Abby the only person who believed her. It's not only this exposition that represents a substantial alteration from the first *Ghostbusters*; the gravity with which it is told positions the narrative's genesis as a trauma that its events are actively seeking to overcome. While far from cultivating a sense of realism, the added detail markedly distinguishes the tone of the reboot from the cynicism of the original by suggesting that its action matters in a way that the 'just entertainment' tone of the first film actively discourages. The tone of the reboot in this way creates a comparable, though opposite, ideological effect to that of the original film. Both employ a style of comedy that relies upon a distancing effect, but where the cynicism of the original works to position its fantastic events as immaterial, the reboot uses disaffected satire to carry a message about gender inequality that is sincere, and is designed to frame the film as a cultural product that is not only relatable to but is intervening in real-life gender politics. By repeatedly positioning inequality as the crux of its comedic tone, though, the reboot simultaneously suggests that this issue is not to be taken seriously, which, to return to the ideas from this chapter's first section, works to temper the 'feminism' of its message.

At the level of narrative, this conflicted effect is most apparent in the way that the revisionist work described above is absorbed by a theme of empowerment that manages to simultaneously hark back to the controlling force of the 1980s film and foreground the gendered neoliberalism of the twenty-first century. Both versions of *Ghostbusters* are underpinned by confidence, but where the original presents this as a general keynote for each character and the narrative as a whole, the reboot frames it as a specific quality that the women have to muster and enact in order to overcome their marginalised status. All four women are framed as 'ghost girls', their commitment to the paranormal something for which they are not celebrated but ridiculed and devalued. As such, the ultimate triumph of the narrative is conveyed not as their physical defeat of Rowan and their closing of the vortex, for which they remain anonymous – 'now I know how Batman feels,' quips Erin – but as their psychological resilience in persisting with their work despite the scepticism and condescension they face. If the revisionist aspects of the rebooted narrative can be understood to express a general awareness of gender inequality, then resilience is the strategy by which they overcome this. The scenario precisely communicates popular feminism's belief that confidence is the solution to gender inequality, and also demonstrates how it is a resolution that depends on individuals, not on social and cultural structures (Banet-Weiser 2018: 93–6). The film recognises gendered inequality as a specific injury but, like other resources analysed by Banet-Weiser, Gill and Rottenberg that position confidence as the pathway to women's success, it doesn't point to patriarchal structural forces for this inequality; instead it offers advice on how to join the existing structure through one's individual capacity (Banet-Weiser 2018: 96).

In a manner that links directly back to the film's narrative image, confidence is in this way channelled into the notion that 'feminism' constitutes the capacity to do what men can. To be successful in this, though, women are shown to have to work harder – emotionally, cognitively and physically. The narrative's lead-up to the final battle is presented not as the smooth ascent of the original narrative but as a series of setbacks for the female team. Each of their successful missions is publicly undermined as a publicity stunt by what the mayor's office calls 'these sad, sad women' but, after each, they redouble their efforts and work even harder to prove themselves. This labour is depicted not only in terms of their confidence-building but also as their concerted knowledge, demonstrating Banet-Weiser's argument that the twinned themes of popular feminist discourse are confidence and competence. The reboot carries on the original film's presentation of ghostbusting science in broadly satirical terms but it brings a level of specificity to this that emphasises the women's intelligence and work ethic. Indeed, evidence of this scholarship is what sets the reboot's narrative in motion, when Erin seeks out her estranged friend Abby to have their book – *Ghosts From Our Past: Both Figuratively and Literally: The Study of the Paranormal* – taken offline, seeking to avoid its pseudoscience damaging her tenure case at Columbia University. The book, which Erin tries to dismiss as an old joke between friends, is in fact a 496-page tome with the first sentence 'this is not a joke'. This premise, where the science and achievement of the women's work is rendered in detail, and with obvious sophistication, contrasts pointedly with the introduction of paranormal work in the original film, where Venkman's primitive telepathic human testing is framed as nothing more than a ruse with which to seduce a blonde, female student. The theme is carried throughout the reboot, from the way the women's knowledge of paranormal history enables their understanding of Rowan's plan, to how the scientific inventions of Holtzmann – who is introduced as a particle physicist – are depicted. Following their second ghost sighting, she explains the improvements she has made to their equipment to create a ghost trap: 'I added a booster using microfabricated radio-frequency quadropoles to speed up particles before entering the DLA device . . . then we add the reversible psychokinetic energy sync . . .'. While clearly designed to appear as humorous jargon, the effect nonetheless demonstrates the intersection of the women's confidence and competence, where they redirect the nerdish, derided connotations of being a 'ghost girl' into an expression of empowerment. In the film's final face-off, this superior mental strength pays off by translating seamlessly to physical prowess. The fight sequence is notably amplified from the original film in both length and scale, and concludes with the superhuman feat in which Erin dives into the vortex to rescue Abby from the clutches of the final and largest ghost expelled – an ultimate assertion of female friendship.

The specificity of the women's scientific knowledge is another example of the *Ghostbusters* reboot's popular feminist revisionism, insofar as it pushes back against the marginalisation of women in STEM fields – another theme which is prominent within popular discourse. By demonstrating the team's mastery of obscure science and technology – albeit making this accomplishment extend only to the white women – the film debunks assumptions that women are not suited to the field, a point that is understood to have been central to the toxic responses to the reboot from geek masculinity. For these detractors, the women's demonstration of competence as both action hero protagonists and scientists represents feminism encroaching upon territory that does not belong to women (Banet-Weiser 2018: 132). As with other instances of its attempted revisionism, though, the film's acknowledgement that the 'woman problem' is as prevalent within science and technology as it is within Hollywood is presented in a contradictory manner. Again, this is primarily an effect of how its tone dilutes the potential gravity of its critique. Carrying through the ambivalent stance set up around Erin and Abby's book in the film's premise, the women's mastery of science is presented as something that is at once the result of years of intensive study, but also something casual and non-serious. The latter attitude is especially apparent in the speed and ease with which Holtzmann designs complex devices, and the way these often become the crux of physical jokes that emphasise the team's awkwardness – for instance when Abby's test of the new proton pack sends her whizzing around in the air in what Holtzmann describes as 'a marvellous impression of a deflating balloon'. The trope is further evidence of the reboot's deflation of the heroic and superior qualities of the original film, but the satirical tone that results inevitably undermines the point on women's competence.

This effect is what can finally be understood as the signature achievement of the contemporary Hollywood gender-swap reboot as a format. Its primary function is to strike a balance, at the levels of concept, narrative and tone, between seriousness and non-seriousness; with its revisionist aspects signalling an awareness of gender inequality but its style of presentation positioning this as nothing more than a joke. This use of humour is characteristic of popular feminist media production, where it 'frequently means a distillation of politics, in which words and images are used ironically to create an easy-to-digest critique' (Banet-Weiser 2018: 140). The humorous frame supports the high-concept identity of the gender-swap reboot, where its most impactful work occurs in the mere idea of the film, to situate the format precisely within popular feminism's economy of visibility – rather than a route to politics, 'visibility becomes enough in itself' (Banet-Weiser 2018: 140). I have argued that, as a reboot of an iconic Reaganite film, like many other examples in this current cycle, this visibility for *Ghostbusters* is structured by two key effects. First, its revisionist work at the levels of narrative and characterisation makes over the cinema of confidence particular to the 1980s in terms of a logic of female empowerment that centres the notions of confidence and individuality specific to the gendered neoliberalism of the twenty-first century. This gives rise to easily shareable and consumable images of the team as strong women, and extends to merchandising that is specifically targeted at girls. Second, the reboot transposes the cynical distance of the original into a style of deflating, satirical humour that prioritises self-effacement. This effect works in direct connection with the first. While the revisionism suggests that, unlike the 'just entertainment' identity of the 1986 film, there is something to think about here – namely, gender inequality in Hollywood – the comedic tone undermines this to contradict any meaningful feminist message. This move from 'nothing to think about' to 'something to think about, but not seriously' sums up the mixed messaging that defines the gender-swap reboot as a popular feminist media product: it is a type of filmmaking that presents its rebuke in a palatable way, translating the escapist reassurance of the 1980s to the 'woke' reassurance of the 2010s.

REFERENCES

Banet-Weiser, Sarah (2018), *Empowered: Popular Feminism and Popular Misogyny*, Durham, NC: Duke University Press.

Blodgett, Bridget and Anastasia Salter (2018), '*Ghostbusters* is For Boys: Understanding Geek Masculinity's Role in the Alt-right', *Communication, Culture & Critique*, 11, 133–46.

Britton, Andrew (1986), 'Blissing Out: The Politics of Reaganite Entertainment', in Barry Keith Grant (ed.), *Britton on Film: The Complete Film Criticism of Andrew Britton*, Detroit, IL: Wayne State University Press, pp. 97–154.

Bryan, Peter Cullen and Brittany R. Clark (2019), '#NotMyGhostbusters: Adaptation, Response, and Fan Entitlement in 2016's *Ghostbusters*', *The Journal of American Culture*, 42: 2, 147–58.
Ferber, Taylor (2017), 'Paul Feig Regrets That "Ghostbusters" Remake Was a "Cause"', *Vulture*, 20 November, <https://www.vulture.com/2017/11/paul-feig-regrets-that-ghostbusters-remake-became-a-cause.html>.
Ferreday, Debra and Geraldine Harris (2017), 'Investigating "Fame-inism": The Politics of Popular Culture', *Feminist Theory*, 18: 3, 239–43.
Gill, Rosalind (2016), 'Post-postfeminism?: New Feminist Visibilities in Postfeminist Times', *Feminist Media Studies*, 16: 4, 610–30.
Hess, Amanda (2018), 'The Trouble With Hollywood's Gender Flips', *New York Times*, 12 June, <https://www.nytimes.com/2018/06/12/movies/oceans-8-gender-swap.html>.
Hollows, Joanne and Rachel Mosely (eds) (2006), *Feminism in Popular Culture*, Oxford: Berg.
Klein, Amanda Ann (2011), *American Film Cycles: Reframing Genres, Screening Social Problems and Defining Subcultures*, Austin, TX: University of Texas Press.
McRobbie, Angela (2004), 'Post-feminism and Popular Culture', *Feminist Media Studies*, 4: 3, 255–64.
Petersen, Anne Helen (2017), 'Too Fat: Melissa McCarthy', in *Too Fat, Too Slutty, Too Loud: The Rise and Reign of the Unruly Woman*, New York: Plume, pp. 27–50.
Proctor, William (2012), 'Regeneration and Rebirth: Anatomy of the Franchise Reboot', *Scope: An Online Journal of Film and Television Studies*, 22 (February), 1–19.
Proctor, William (2017), '"Bitches Aint Gonna Hunt No Ghosts": Totemic Nostalgia, Toxic Fandom and the Ghostbusters Platonic', *Palabra Clave*, 20: 4, 1105–41.
Rottenberg, Catherine (2018), *The Rise of Neoliberal Feminism*, New York: Oxford University Press.
Saner, Emine (2017), 'Lord of the Flies to Ocean's Eight: How Hollywood Reboots are Flipping Gender', *The Guardian*, 3 September, <https://www.theguardian.com/film/2017/sep/02/lord-of-the-flies-oceans-eight-hollywood-reboots-flipping-gender>.
Spiers, Emily (2018), 'This Is the Toxic Myth at the Heart of Female Movie Reboots', *The Conversation*, 13 October, <https://theconversation.com/this-is-the-toxic-myth-at-the-heart-of-female-movie-reboots-102125>.
Tryon, Chuck (2013), 'Reboot Cinema', *Convergence: The International Journal of Research into New Media Technologies*, 19: 4, 432–7.
Wood, Robin (1986), *Hollywood From Vietnam to Reagan*, New York: Columbia University Press.
Yua, Jada (2016), 'Who Ya Gonna Troll?', *Vulture*, <https://www.vulture.com/2016/07/paul-feig-ghostbusters-reboot-c-v-r.html>.

Part IV
Fans and Audiences

CHAPTER II

Reboot, Requel, Legacyquel: *Jurassic World* and the Nostalgia Franchise

Kathleen Loock

INTRODUCTION: THE NOSTALGIA-DRIVEN REBOOT

Since the new millennium, Hollywood has increasingly focused on reviving franchises from its immediate past (cf. Loock 2016; Verevis 2017). *Batman Begins* (Nolan, 2005), *Rise of the Planet of the Apes* (Wyatt, 2011) and *The Amazing Spider-Man* (Webb, 2012) are reboots of creatively depleted, too expensive, or dormant film franchises: they disrupt the continuity of the franchise in order to start over with radically redesigned characters and storylines and, hence, an inherent promise of narrative, aesthetic and technological novelty (cf. Proctor 2012; Tryon 2013; Tompkins 2014). This kind of renewal quickly became a common practice in Hollywood, until the arrival of the nostalgia-driven reboot in 2015. Films like *Star Wars: The Force Awakens* (Abrams, 2015), *Terminator: Genisys* (Taylor, 2015) and *Creed* (Coogler, 2015) rely on the return of beloved characters (and actors) as well as on recognisable narrative and aesthetic elements from their respective franchise pasts in order to bind successive generations of viewers to their ongoing, decades-spanning storylines. These films both remake and continue familiar narratives, introduce new characters who appear alongside older ones that viewers already care about, and they are generally invested in evoking the enduring cultural and historical significance of the franchise for the sake of future instalments. *The Force Awakens*, *Terminator: Genisys* and *Creed* certainly succeeded as reboots in the sense that they generated new, long-term interest and revenue, but their nostalgia for the franchise past did not match common understandings of the reboot as a creative (and often critical) intervention whose appeal lies precisely in how it disregards narrative continuity and 'wipes the slate clean' (Proctor 2012) to rewrite the history of a given franchise.

In response to this development, neologisms such as 'requel' (a portmanteau combining reboot and sequel) and 'legacyquel' (blending legacy and sequel) emerged in popular film criticism and academic journals as an attempt to reframe what 'reboot' actually means in the contemporary film and media landscape. These discourses hint at the difficulties of keeping up with the latest trends in Hollywood's constantly evolving large-scale system of cinematic remaking, on the one hand, and of adequately accounting for the cultural work these new films perform at the intersection of popular culture, memory and the formation of generations, on the other.[1] Taking such neologisms as a starting point, this chapter examines the recent move away from reboots that 'seek to disavow any direct narrative or stylistic correlation to the franchise in its previous iterations' (Tompkins 2014: 381; cf. Proctor 2012) to more explicitly serialised, nostalgia-driven reboots that restart their franchise while also revelling in its past. *Jurassic World* (Trevorrow), another 2015 release, belongs to the group of films that are currently redefining the concept of the reboot. Like *Star Wars: The Force Awakens*, *Terminator: Genisys* and *Creed*, *Jurassic World* reboots its franchise as a 'nostalgia franchise': it recalls and exploits the past, blending old and new to launch a string of films that speak to multiple generations of viewers. However, *Jurassic World*'s nostalgic appeal is not derived from reconnecting with familiar characters but from a more abstract fascination of seeing dinosaurs again on the big screen and from the return to the fictional Central American island Isla Nublar and the site of the original theme park from Steven Spielberg's *Jurassic Park* (1993). *Jurassic World* employs nostalgia as a method of renewal that draws its strength from summoning up the past. The film refers to the accumulated history of the *Jurassic* franchise, while simultaneously promising to deliver Hollywood's most thrilling and immersive cinematic dinosaur adventure yet. Nostalgia thus expresses *Jurassic World*'s commitment to franchise continuity and cross-generational shareability without taking away from its promise of narrative, aesthetic and technological novelty.

If nostalgia is commonly understood as the individual or collective longing for an idealised past, for a time and space that no longer exists and presumably never existed in the first place (at least not as it is being remembered in the present), the concept takes on a slightly different meaning in the case of *Jurassic World*. Despite the spatio-temporal dimension of nostalgia that informs the film's theme park setting and the very existence of dinosaurs as its prime attraction, *Jurassic World* is neither a regressive (even destructive) expression of loss and melancholia (cf. Lizardi 2014), nor merely 'a pleasure-seeking yearning for former times that we have not, in fact, lived' (Niemeyer 2014: 9). Instead, conjuring the past of the *Jurassic* franchise and, in extension, Hollywood's long dinosaur legacy turns out to be a highly self-reflexive manoeuvre. Nostalgia serves *Jurassic World* to comment on cinema's technological progress and to position itself in film history, to draw attention to franchise-specific mechanisms of intensification and, ultimately, to construct a temporal experience that also speaks to 'an affective yearning for a community with a collective memory, a longing for continuity in a fragmented world' (Boym 2007: 10). To unfold my argument, I will first situate *Jurassic World* within the discourses surrounding Hollywood's nostalgia-driven reboots and tease out the singularity of the *Jurassic* franchise. Then, I will focus on *Jurassic World*'s serial self-reflexivity, in particular, on how the reboot stages its nostalgic relationship to the past in order to foreground its own achievements in the present. Finally, I will end my discussion by addressing the political implications that arise from the temporal orientation and recursive progression of the nostalgia franchise.

REQUEL, LEGACYQUEL AND THE CASE OF *JURASSIC WORLD*

'No one had anticipated how comprehensively nostalgia, worked integrally into the blockbuster format, could max out interest across multiple generations', *The Guardian*'s Phil Hoad (2015) summed up the record-breaking success of *Jurassic World*. Released twenty-two years after *Jurassic Park*, 2015's spectacular summer blockbuster scored the 'biggest opening weekend in history' (Lang 2015), 'smashed US and international box-office records' (Pallotta 2015) and became the third highest-grossing movie of all time behind *Avatar* (Cameron, 2009) and *Titanic* (Cameron, 1997) (McClintock 2015). By the end of the year, *The Force Awakens* had pushed *Jurassic World* to the fourth rank on that list, but at a budget of $150 million the film had still earned more than $600 million in the North American market and an additional $1 billion worldwide (Box Office Mojo).[2] *Jurassic World* proved that dinosaurs sell. The film's special effects dazzled critics like David Edelstein, whose review of 'one of the most exciting movies about people running away from stuff ever' deliberately ignored *Jurassic World*'s flaws to emphasise its 'movie ride' film aesthetic and 'immersion effect' (cf. Balides 2003). 'It's a ride,' Edelstein (2015) wrote. 'Shell out for the biggest and most kinetic experience'. Other reviewers were less enthusiastic, however, taking issue with the film's conspicuous nostalgia for the first entry in the *Jurassic* franchise. '*Jurassic World* is essentially a retelling of Steven Spielberg's groundbreaking *Jurassic Park* just without any of the originality, heart or soul,' lamented Brandon Katz (2018) in *The Observer*. '[F]rom story structure and marketing to themes and visuals, the former heartlessly swipes everything you loved about the latter, without ever advancing the form' (2018).

A number of reviews and journalistic think pieces on current trends in Hollywood cinema addressed *Jurassic World*'s nostalgic leanings and infatuation with its own franchise past, referring to the film either as a 'requel' or as a 'legacyquel' rather than as a reboot in the traditional sense. In use since the late 2000s, the term 'requel' has become more frequent since around 2015, when film journalists like the *Hollywood Reporter*'s Pamela McClintock diagnosed it as Hollywood's 'latest obsession' (2016: 11). McClintock explains that the requel is different from earlier reboots or remakes in that 'it nods to and exploits goodwill toward the past while launching a new generation of actors and stories' (2016: 11). According to Imax Entertainment CEO Greg Foster, it is a concept that can be compared to 'a mulligan in golf, where a player is informally allowed to replay a stroke' (2016: 11): 'You get to keep the best of both worlds. . . . [Y]ou can cherry-pick and keep what works and what people responded to and cared about' (Foster, quoted in McClintock 2016: 11). And because the combination of reboot and sequel leaves the larger narrative intact, it has come to be regarded as 'an easy way for studios to link generations of fans together and continue to grow an audience, all without having to market and sell a whole new world to ticket buyers', confirms box office analyst Jeff Bock (quoted in McClintock 2016: 12). According to Bruce C. Steele (2015), *Jurassic World* qualifies as a requel since '[i]t simply ignores the previous two *Jurassic* movies – *The Lost World: Jurassic Park* [Spielberg, 1997] and *Jurassic Park III* [Johnston, 2001] – and smartly supersizes *Jurassic Park*'. Put differently, *Jurassic World* thrives on selective memory of the first film of the *Jurassic* franchise, whose defining elements it amplifies according to a serial logic of one-upmanship that drives Hollywood's sequel production more generally (Loock 2017: 98).

Both films are centred around two children and several adults, who are at a theme park that features genetically engineered dinosaurs and who have to fight for their own survival once the creatures break free. Except that the stakes are higher in *Jurassic World* because the theme park is now up and running with 20,000 visitors who are also put in harm's way when the dinosaurs escape. The film easily lends itself to analogy: *Jurassic Park* is the mosquito frozen in amber from which Hollywood extracted DNA to create a genetically modified, pumped-up version of the past in the present. From this vantage point, *Jurassic World* itself is not entirely unlike the theme park's latest attraction, the Indominus Rex, a huge, intelligent and predatory dinosaur hybrid designed in the laboratory by combining the genetic traits of multiple species. This creature is more dangerous than *Jurassic Park*'s T-Rex, posing an entirely new threat because it can camouflage itself and sets traps for the humans. In interviews, director Colin Trevorrow described *Jurassic World*'s Indominus Rex as a product of 'our greed and our desire for profit', which, in turn, propels the consumers' constant longing for 'something bigger and badder and louder' (AFP 2015; see also Dyer 2015: 20). Despite its focus on 'more', *Jurassic World* never strays far from *Jurassic Park*'s success formula. Not only at the level of its subject matter, then, is the film concerned with restoring a long-lost past (by bringing back extinct dinosaurs). In addition, *Jurassic World* nostalgically evokes its own past through the repetition of narrative and aesthetic codes while it fully embraces an intensification-oriented principle of repetition and innovation to tell an already familiar story in an enhanced and therefore potentially new way.[3] It is precisely the combination of nostalgia and intensification that made *Jurassic World* a global box office hit and succeeded in rebooting the *Jurassic* franchise: the sequel *Jurassic World: Fallen Kingdom* (Bayona, 2018) followed and a third (and, at least for the time being, final) instalment, *Jurassic World: Dominion* (Trevorrow), is scheduled for release in June 2021.

The neologism 'requel' certainly captures how *Jurassic World* is having it both ways, as a reboot *and* a sequel. Despite some confusion about the term in recent academic writing, where the 'requel' has been located at the intersection of remake and sequel (e.g. Raya Bravo 2017; Lizardi 2017: 28–9), *Jurassic World* definitely operates as a franchise reboot rather than as a remake of *Jurassic Park*. There is a sense of a new beginning, clearly marked on the level of plot by the renamed, fully operational theme park, a new set of main characters and the innovative science to create the hybrid Indominus Rex. Beyond the fictional world, *Jurassic World* also distinguishes itself from the earlier films with state-of-the-art digital images and 3-D technology.[4] At the same time, *Jurassic World* relies on explicit serialisation strategies to tell an *ongoing* story. By returning to Isla Nublar and, at some point, to the abandoned Jurassic Park visitor centre, by featuring geneticist Dr Henry Wu (B. D. Wong) as a recurring character and by recycling iconic scenes and images, the film establishes meaningful intertextual dependencies to preceding instalments in the *Jurassic* franchise, especially to *Jurassic Park*. Such direct references and allusions function as orienting devices for audiences because they indicate the chronological relationship between the films and affirm their narrative continuity. Since more than two decades have passed between the release of *Jurassic Park* and *Jurassic World*, these references are steeped in nostalgia and expertly employed to trigger media memories and create an aura of cultural legitimacy. In the case of *Jurassic World*, nostalgia thus foregrounds the process of repetition, continuation and intensification that is at play when an amplified follow-up of an already familiar formula from the past is reproduced in the present.

'Legacyquel' is used to describe more or less the same phenomenon but this neologism puts a stronger emphasis on the idea of generational renewal, regarding both franchise characters and audiences. The term was coined by *ScreenCrush* film critic Matt Singer (2015) in order to describe a 'very specific kind of sequel . . . in which beloved aging stars reprise classic roles and pass the torch to younger successors'. Films such as *The Force Awakens*, *Terminator: Genisys* and *Creed*, explains Singer (2015), 'are all about revitalizing old franchises through the notion of legacy', with the ultimate goal of both maintaining excitement among older audiences and passing it on to younger generations. It is the recipe for 'infinitely renewable franchises that burrow ceaselessly into their own mythology' (Hoad 2015) or for what Adam Rogers (2015) has called 'the forever franchise'. In a

Wired piece on *Star Wars*, he predicted that 'You Won't Live to See the Final *Star Wars* Movie', given that Disney, who acquired Lucasfilm for $4 billion in 2012, plans to produce an 'infinite series' of films with a new release every year 'for as long as people will buy tickets' (Rogers 2015).

Drawing on Singer's concept of the 'legacyquel', media and communication scholars César Alberto Albarrán-Torres and Dan Golding (2019) speak of the 'legacy film' as 'a method of franchise nostalgia concerned with inheritance'. They explain that the legacy film offers 'studios a model for redeveloping major properties along contemporary sensibilities, as well as for staging the intergenerational transference of franchise fandom between parents old enough to remember the initial entrants and their children' and describe it as 'an alternative to the reboot' (Albarrán-Torres and Golding 2019; see also Golding 2019: 71–4). However, I contend that the 'legacyquel' or 'legacy film' still serves essentially the same purpose – which is to reboot an already existing franchise. What is new, then, is that the strategies behind the reboot have been refined in order to make the franchise past usable in the present, to weave nostalgia into the new film's fabric and thus create a more inclusive experience that, ideally, appeals to audiences across multiple generations. Where a reboot might alienate older viewers – especially in the case of long-running franchises that have spun their narratives over many decades and whose characters viewers have come to know and love – passing-of-the-torch approaches that take Hollywood's slowly changing representational regimes of race and gender into account promise to be decidedly less risky endeavours for studios with an eye on the bottom line.

How, then, does *Jurassic World* fit into the current reboot trend? Even though the *Jurassic* franchise has occasionally relied on recurring characters, it was always the existence of cloned dinosaurs that served as the storytelling engine, never the lives and loves of the humans that had somehow got in their way. There are no real 'legacy characters' in *Jurassic World*, and yet – just like *Creed*, *The Force Awakens* and *Terminator: Genisys* – the film clearly reboots the *Jurassic* franchise as a nostalgia franchise. I suggest that it does so by exploiting *Jurassic Park*'s cultural legacy and by speaking to a longstanding, near-universal fascination with dinosaurs around which Michael Crichton had already plotted his 1990 novel, namely: 'to see tyrannosaurs or stegosaurs not merely as fossils, but as creatures of flesh and blood' (Holland 2015). *Jurassic World* self-reflexively constructs a nostalgia-tinged version of this longed-for immersion in a fictional world with living dinosaurs.

VERISIMILITUDE, IMMERSION AND *JURASSIC WORLD*'S SERIAL SELF-REFLEXIVITY

Hollywood sequels usually follow quickly on the heels of a box office success and are invested in surpassing their predecessors rather than nostalgically referencing them. Accordingly, nostalgia tends to be limited to the realm of reception where, as Todd Berliner (2001: 109) has shown, the sequel can foster among audiences 'a futile, nostalgic desire to re-experience the original aesthetic moment as though it had never happened' (hence, the familiar discourse of disappointment and loss that often pervades sequel reception). *Jurassic World* incorporates into its plot and visual aesthetics a different kind of nostalgia that is defined by a yearning for the immersive thrill. The film displays an acute self-awareness about its own status as a sequel designed to reboot the *Jurassic* franchise and as a state-of-the-art entry in the rampaging dinosaur genre. It is certainly no coincidence that *Jurassic World* is first and foremost concerned with itself when nostalgically evoking the past. As a derivative film based on existing material, the reboot's claim to originality is widely contested, regardless of its emphasis on introducing novelty. Through nostalgic references *Jurassic World* seeks to secure its place in film history, fabricating its own cultural legitimacy based on the proximity to Hollywood's older dinosaur classics and on its 'genealogical ties' to *Jurassic Park*. Instead of disavowing the past, as reboots are prone to do, *Jurassic World* renders it productive for its own purposes. The film self-reflexively uses nostalgia to indicate how it wants to be watched, and it does so effectively from the very first scene.

Jurassic World opens with two still images of fighting dinosaurs accompanied by soft, melodic music that faintly echoes John Williams' *Jurassic Park* theme. Vintage-style, with their rounded edges and warm, earthy colours, these images do not fill out the entire screen. The first one shows a Tyrannosaurus rex confronting a Triceratops; with a clicking sound, this image is replaced by two fighting Ceratosaurs. Then the scene cuts to a boy, Gray (Ty Simpkins), who is sitting in his room and looking into a View-Master (see Figure 11.1). The View-Master, a 3-D viewing system for the home, was introduced at the 1939 New York World's Fair and became a popular stereoscopic toy in the 1960s. Here, it is a relic of the past among many others in Gray's room. There is a tin model of Robby the Robot from the film *Forbidden Planet* (Wilcox, 1956) on his desk, a poster featuring the pixelated aliens from the *Space Invaders* video game hangs on the blue walls, and numerous tin toys, miniature rocket ships and space shuttles, dinosaur figures and retro cameras populate the shelves. The room itself speaks volumes about *Jurassic World*'s stake in generational transference, and Gray's presence among these nostalgic items makes a promise about the reboot's general attitude towards the past. As the only toy that Gray directly interacts with in this scene, the View-Master takes on a special significance. It becomes an eloquent object, offering a glimpse of *Jurassic World*'s self-understanding as a reboot that is carefully constructed around three interrelated topics: Hollywood's dinosaur legacy, the franchise past and the theme park.

Figure 11.1 Gray's View-Master expresses *Jurassic World*'s (2015) self-understanding as a nostalgia-driven reboot.

First, the 'reel' Gray is looking at establishes a meaningful link to Hollywood's dinosaur legacy. The still images are taken from the 1956 documentary *The Animal World* (Allen), more precisely from the film's ten-minute dinosaur sequence made by stop-motion animator and visual effects legend Ray Harryhausen. They are a nod to the earlier days of dinosaurs on the big screen, a film-historical reference point for viewers to acknowledge the enormous strides cinema has made from Willis O'Brien's stop-motion animation in *The Lost World* (Hoyt, 1925) to the computer-generated 3-D renderings of *Jurassic World*.

Harryhausen occupies an important position in this trajectory because he developed a split-screen technique he called 'Dynamation' that made it possible to combine stop-motion creatures with live-action sequences so that instead of cutting back and forth between a group of archaeologists and a grazing Brontosaurus in the distance or inserting actors into the scene as miniature rear projections, humans and dinosaurs could be seen directly interacting with each other in the same frame (Prince 2012: 33–4). And yet, as Stephen Prince observes, 'because the stop-motion figures do not have motion blur while the live-actors do, the perceptual realism of the sequence is diminished' (2012: 34). In 1993, *Jurassic Park* eventually solves this problem by combining animatronics and digital animation. According to Prince, 'Spielberg's dinosaurs made such a huge impact on viewers in part because they seemed far more life-like than the miniature models and stop-motion animation of previous generations of film' (1996: 28). Even though dinosaurs remain referentially false objects that do not exist outside of *Jurassic Park*'s fiction, there is a 'palpable reality about them . . . due to the extremely detailed texture-mapping, motion animation, and integration with live action carried out via digital imaging' (1996: 34). With the View-Master scene, *Jurassic World* demonstrates its awareness of Hollywood's evolving visual effects and instrumentalises the cinematic past to set the scene for its own enhanced digital imagery and immersive 3-D spectacle.

Second, Gray's View-Master is a model from the 1990s – the decade of the *Jurassic* franchise – when *Jurassic Park* and *Jurassic Park: The Lost World* in fact had their own View-Master 'reels' (and before Mattel released the View-Master VR headset that holds a smartphone and uses an app to show 3-D virtual and augmented reality images). This first scene thus contains a complex web of information, and it says upfront how *Jurassic World* wants to engage with the history of the *Jurassic* franchise. Like the View-Master, *Jurassic World* brings the past into the present, makes the presumably old and obsolete relevant for a younger generation and stirs a nostalgic longing for an adventure with real-life dinosaurs. Indeed, *Jurassic World*'s nostalgic focus on the franchise and Hollywood's dinosaur legacy is so pronounced that the very idea of entertainment and the subjective experience of immersive thrills seem to take precedence over the scientific interest at the heart of the older *Jurassic* films. Gray is glued to his View-Master marvelling at classic, but now outdated representations of dinosaurs, not to the latest book on the extinct creatures like Tim (Joseph Mazzello) in *Jurassic Park*, who excitedly tells palaeontologist Dr Alan Grant (Sam Neill) that he read his book *The Lost World of the Dinosaurs*, or Eric (Trevor Morgan) in *Jurassic Park III*, who also read Grant's follow-up book and says, 'I liked the first one more, before you were on the island. You liked dinosaurs back then'. *Jurassic Park*'s science was remarkably accurate for the time. The film paid close attention to the anatomy and movements of the dinosaurs and integrated contemporary theories about the link between dinosaurs and birds (an argument Grant makes in his book). *Jurassic World*, in contrast, ignores the discoveries of feathered fossils that palaeontology has made since the late 1990s and that have radically changed the visual understanding of dinosaurs.[5] The reboot holds on to the scaly, reptilian creatures viewers already know. Moreover, it trades the cautionary tale of scientific hubris that was associated with the very act of bringing dinosaurs back from extinction through genetic engineering for a story of science gone wrong in the name of corporate greed. The creation of the Indominus Rex in *Jurassic World* follows a capitalist logic in which the necessity for profit to further expand the theme park dictates the production of increasingly spectacular attractions in order to sustain and increase the demand for seeing dinosaurs in the flesh. And yet, the high-concept premise of science, spectacle and mayhem remains as familiar as *Jurassic World*'s T-Rex and Velociraptors.

Finally, *Jurassic World*'s return to Isla Nublar and the site of the original theme park expresses the reboot's desire for franchise continuity and proximity to *Jurassic Park* (both sequels are set on the neighbouring Isla Sorna). Again, the View-Master scene implies as much in the way it anticipates the immersive experience that awaits Gray at the theme park. To be sure, the spectacle of real-life dinosaurs is initially played down by Gray's aunt, Jurassic World operations manager Claire Dearing (Bryce Dallas Howard). In her pitch for the Indominus Rex, she tells potential investors:

> Let's be honest, no one's impressed by a dinosaur anymore. Twenty years ago, de-extinction was right up there with magic. These days, kids look at a Stegosaurus like an elephant from the city zoo. . . . [C]onsumers want them bigger. Louder. More teeth.

Her words certainly encapsulate the serial logic of one-upmanship the reboot itself embraces, even as it takes a more critical stance on the level of plot. Yet, they are proven wrong by Gray, whose face lights up with excitement when the ferry approaches Isla Nublar and who exudes pure joy once he passes through the gates of the Jurassic World theme park and discovers its rides and attractions. Gray shrieks with delight before entering 'Tyrannosaurus Rex Kingdom' and, while his older brother Zach (Nick Robinson) is not as easily impressed, both boys are awestruck at the 'Mosasaurus Feeding Show' (in which the giant water creature eats a great white shark) and during the 'Gyrosphere' ride that lets them roam freely among Apatosaurus, Stegosaurus and Triceratops in a small round vehicle made of glass.

Jurassic Park's theme music links these scenes to similar moments in earlier films: it both reproduces and amplifies a familiar sense of wonder by repeating iconic scenes in a theme park setting that invites viewers to imagine themselves as visitors. In an interview, Spielberg said: 'To see *Jurassic World* come to life is almost like seeing *Jurassic Park* come true' (quoted in Agar 2015), and the reboot deliberately refers back to billionaire John Hammond's (Richard Attenborough) original vision as it exploits the idea of the theme park visit as a (widely relatable) immersive experience that can be shared across generations. The rides and attractions serve *Jurassic World* to showcase its state-of-the-art visual effects as viewers follow Gray and Zach through the theme park. The most exciting ride, however, begins once the two boys take their gyrosphere off the prescribed route and find themselves face to face with the rogue Indominus Rex. Their vehicle is kicked around in a fight between the Indominus Rex and an Ankylosaurus that strangely echoes, yet radically surpasses, Gray's View-Master images and their limited immersive potential (see Figure 11.2).

Figure 11.2 Serial progression: Gray and Zach's 'Gyrosphere' ride echoes and surpasses the View-Master's immersive experience, *Jurassic World* (2015).

Jurassic World abounds with 'movie ride' scenes that achieve powerful immersion effects. According to Constance Balides, such effects work

> through textual strategies such as the placement of the camera in the literal position of a character (a point of view shot) or one associated with a purported character's view as well as special effects zoom shots created with the use of an optical printer and/or involving computer graphic images suggesting movement inward into the image. (Balides 2003: 317).

The experience of immersion is further enhanced by *Jurassic World*'s 3-D technology. The View-Master scene throws immersion in the spectacle of digital technology effects into sharp relief, just as repeating (and renewing) the images of fighting dinosaurs draws attention to the affordances of cinema and the evolution of the medium over time. The past does not become obsolete in this scenario but grounds *Jurassic World* in the present. References to Hollywood's dinosaur legacy, the franchise past and the theme park refer viewers outside of the fictional world of the reboot and suggest a serial progression, a meta-narrative of cinema's technological trajectory towards verisimilitude and immersion that ends triumphantly with *Jurassic World*. Taken together, they do not only anchor the film in time and space but also establish a baseline against which *Jurassic World*'s technical achievements and one-upmanship can be all the more appreciated.

CONCLUSION: THE POLITICS OF THE NOSTALGIA FRANCHISE

In recent years, the concept of the franchise reboot has undergone significant changes. Films like *Jurassic World*, *The Force Awakens*, *Terminator: Genisys* and *Creed* no longer aim 'to nullify history and disconnect stagnant or failed product from a new, cinematic experiment' (Proctor 2012). Instead, they explicitly recall and exploit successful narrative and aesthetic elements in order to reboot their respective franchises as nostalgia franchises. As neologisms like 'requel' and 'legacyquel' are trying to make sense of the recent developments on the reboot front, they attest to the adaptive nature of Hollywood's remaking practice and point towards the film and media industry's growing interest in serialisation strategies that can maintain long-term continuity. Rather than doing away with the past to begin anew, the past is (more or less subtly) integrated into nostalgia-driven reboots, where it tends to foreground the passing of time, the inevitable ageing of familiar characters (and actors), and a diffuse feeling of loss that affects viewers' temporal relationship to the franchise. For, if reboots nowadays also operate as sequels, they 'synchronise the amount of time which has passed in our lives with that of the characters' (Henderson 2014: 166) and encourage older generations to recall their own viewing experiences as well as personal memories associated with the franchise and that particular moment in time.[6] To younger generations, the reboots' references to the past may mean nothing, but they offer entry points to the history of the franchise and thus function as literal materialisations of the 'cultural heirloom' that Will Brooker (2002: 225) mentions when describing how *Star Wars* is being passed down from one generation to the next.

The sequel form, with its emphasis on serialised repetition, innovation and intensification, also preserves a more abstract sense of continuity that extends beyond the fictional world on screen and its entanglement with viewers' subjective experiences and memories. By committing to the franchise past rather than renouncing it, nostalgia-driven reboots certainly function as a stabilising force, 'as a soothing remedy for viewers' increasingly fragmented and disorienting experience of contemporary life' (Loock 2018b: 367), but, at the same time, the backward-gazing temporality of the nostalgia franchise raises pertinent political questions. If reboots make a point of reimagining the white and male-led *Jurassic*, *Star Wars*, *Terminator* and *Rocky* franchises as more diverse and inclusive (Herbert 2017; Golding 2019), they also tend to follow a logic of generational succession in which continuity over many decades and into the future can only be maintained through legacy, inheritance and passing-of-the-torch rituals. As a result, nostalgia-driven reboots almost always promote a conservative politics of 'reproductive futurism' (Edelman 2004) that normalises heteronormative gender scripts and perpetuates traditional notions of family, heterosexuality and biological reproduction (Loock 2019a, 2019b).

Figure 11.3 Backward-gazing temporalities of the nostalgia franchise: *Jurassic World* (2015) privileges ideas of white, middle-class heteronormativity.

Without any 'legacy characters' to speak of, *Jurassic World* is not bound to the generational theme that seems to bring out conservative impulses in most nostalgia franchises. And yet, as Richard Dyer points out, the reboot is not only progressively 'anticapitalist, antimanagerialism, and anti-GM; it is also antifeminist, racist, species-ist, and decidedly not queer' (2015: 19). Once the dinosaurs break loose, Gray and Zach, their aunt Claire and dinosaur handler Owen Grady (Chris Pratt) come to form an unlikely 'family' that, once more, privileges ideas of white, middle-class heteronormativity and male protection (see Figure 11.3). Claire is the character who changes most over the course of the film. She slowly loosens up under the 'manfluence' (Yuan 2015) of her love interest Owen, with whom she tries to escape from the dinosaurs, never once taking off her high heels. In the process, Claire learns to see dinosaurs as more than just 'assets' and children as more than a disturbance. And while those themes strangely resonate with prevalent attitudes in the *Jurassic* franchise, it is not surprising that *Vulture*'s Jada Yuan (2015) asks: 'Was it really necessary for *Jurassic World* to resurrect gender stereotypes along with the dinosaurs?' *Jurassic World* takes a decidedly postfeminist stance with Claire's 'intentional heels' and her assistant Zara's (Katie McGrath) cruel, disproportionately long death scene (which sparked similar online debates to those about Claire's inappropriate footwear). The film's secondary parts – Chinese American chief geneticist Dr Henry Wu, Indian park owner Simon Masrani (Irfan Khan) and Black dinosaur handler Barry (Omar Sy) – may lend *Jurassic World* an air of racial inclusivity. But, as Dyer remarks, 'the roles ensure that they remain subordinate' and even fuel racist stereotypes of 'the inscrutable Oriental, the playboy Indian, the good but incapable Black' (2015: 21). If nostalgia-driven reboots depend on maintaining rather than breaking continuity in order to offer intertextual pleasures, to facilitate the immersion in an ongoing, already familiar story, to fully exhaust the possibilities of serial one-upmanship, and to appeal to multiple generations of viewers, the question remains whether the need to preserve cinematic experiences, memories and sentimental attachments leaves enough room for more than symbolic gestures to inclusion and diversity.

NOTES

1. This is the topic of my book project on Hollywood remaking, in which I define remaking as a process that generates different cinematic forms by repeating, modifying and continuing past renditions in the present. These cinematic forms include remakes, series, sequels, prequels, spin-offs and other films that rely on familiar source material and established fictional worlds in order to sustain or reboot film franchises.
2. In June 2019, *Jurassic World* ranks sixth on that list because of the high-grossing *Avengers: Infinity War* (Russo and Russo, 2018) and *Avengers: Endgame* (Russo and Russo, 2019).
3. On the concept of serial one-upmanship, see Jahn-Sudmann and Kelleter (2012), and Loock (2015, 2017). See also Henderson (2014).
4. *Jurassic Park*, *The Lost World: Jurassic Park* and *Jurassic Park III* were all 2-D films. A 3-D version of *Jurassic Park* was released in 2013 and grossed more than $1 billion worldwide (Box Office Mojo).
5. Starting in 1996, feathered fossils of dinosaurs have been found in China's Liaoning Province, so that palaeontologists today think that large predators like the T-Rex probably had primitive plumage or proto-feathers. See Xu et al. (2012).
6. A similar argument can be made about TV series revivals. See Loock (2018a).

REFERENCES

AFP (2015), 'How the Dinosaurs in *Jurassic World* Came to Life', *News Corp Australia*, 10 June, <https://www.news.com.au/technology/innovation/design/how-the-dinosaurs-in-jurassic-world-came-to-life/news-story/391d003ff3005d31d39cbf5cd6f9012a>.
Agar, Chris (2015), '*Jurassic World*: Steven Spielberg Says It's *Jurassic Park* Come True', *Screen Rant*, 30 April, <https://screenrant.com/jurassic-world-park-steven-spielberg/>.
Albarrán-Torres, César Alberto and Dan Golding (2019), '*Creed*: Legacy Franchising, Race and Masculinity in Contemporary Boxing Films', *Continuum*, doi: 10.1080/10304312.2019.1567684.
Balides, Constance (2003), 'Immersion in the Virtual Ornament: Contemporary "Movie Ride" Films', in David Thorburn and Henry Jenkins (eds), *Rethinking Media Change: The Aesthetics of Transition*, Cambridge, MA: MIT Press, pp. 316–36.
Berliner, Todd (2001), 'The Pleasures of Disappointment: Sequels and *The Godfather, Part II*', *Journal of Film & Video*, 53: 2+3 (Summer/Fall), 107–23.
Box Office Mojo (n.d.), 'All Time Box Office: World Wide Grosses', *Box Office Mojo*, <https://www.boxofficemojo.com/alltime/world/>.
Boym, Svetlana (2007), 'Nostalgia and Its Discontents', *The Hedgehog Review* (Summer), 7–18.

Brooker, Will (2002), *Using the Force: Creativity, Community and Star Wars Fans*, New York/London: Continuum.
Dyer, Richard (2015), '*Jurassic World* and Procreation Anxiety', *Film Quarterly*, 69: 2, 19–24.
Edelman, Lee (2004), *No Future: Queer Theory and the Death Drive*, Durham, NC: Duke University Press.
Edelstein, David (2015), '*Jurassic World* Review: One of the Most Exciting Movies About People Running Away from Stuff Ever', *Vulture*, 12 June, <https://www.vulture.com/2015/06/jurassic-world-review.html>.
Golding, Dan (2019), *Star Wars after Lucas: A Critical Guide to the Future of the Galaxy*, Minneapolis, MN: University of Minnesota Press.
Henderson, Stuart (2014), *The Hollywood Sequel: History & Form, 1911–2010*, London: BFI.
Herbert, Daniel (2017), *Film Remakes and Franchises*, New Brunswick, NJ: Rutgers University Press.
Hoad, Phil (2015), '*Jurassic World* and the "Legacyquel": 2015 Global Box Office in Review', *The Guardian*, 29 December, <https://www.theguardian.com/film/filmblog/2015/dec/29/jurassic-world-star-wars-furious7-avengers-age-of-ultron-minions-2015-global-box-office-in-review>.
Holland, Tom (2015), 'Dinomania: The Story of Our Obsession with Dinosaurs', *The Guardian*, 5 June, <https://www.theguardian.com/books/2015/jun/05/dinomania-dinosaur-obsession-science>.
Jahn-Sudmann, Andreas and Frank Kelleter (2012), 'Die Dynamik serieller Überbietung: Amerikanische Fernsehserien und das Konzept des Quality TV', in Frank Kelleter (ed.), *Populäre Serialität: Narration – Evolution – Distinktion. Zum seriellen Erzählen seit dem 19. Jahrhundert*, Bielefeld: transcript, pp. 205–24.
Katz, Brandon (2018), 'The Dangers of Nostalgia: How *Jurassic World* Took Advantage of Our Memories', *The Observer*, 21 June, <https://observer.com/2018/06/jurassic-world-fallen-kingdom-jurassic-park-movies-nostalgia/>.
Lang, Brent (2015), '*Jurassic World* Scores Biggest Opening Weekend in History, Beats *Avengers* Record', *Variety*, 15 June, <https://variety.com/2015/film/news/jurassic-world-box-office-record-avengers-1201519679/>.
Lizardi, Ryan (2014), *Mediated Nostalgia: Individual Memory and Contemporary Mass Media*, Lanham, MD: Lexington Books.
Lizardi, Ryan (2017), *Nostalgic Generations and Media: Perception of Time and Available Meaning*, Lanham, MD: Lexington Books.
Loock, Kathleen (2015), 'Zwischen Jawsmania und Sequelitis: Die Fortsetzungen von *Jaws*', in Wieland Schwanebeck (ed.), *Der weiße Hai revisited: Steven Spielbergs Jaws und die Geburt eines amerikanischen Albtraums*, Berlin: Bertz+Fischer, pp. 231–44.
Loock, Kathleen (2016), 'Retro-Remaking: The 1980s Film Cycle in Contemporary Hollywood Cinema', in Amanda Ann Klein and R. Barton Palmer (eds), *Cycles, Sequels, Spin-Offs, Remakes, and Reboots: Multiplicities in Film and Television*, Austin, TX: University of Texas Press, pp. 277–98.
Loock, Kathleen (2017), 'The Sequel Paradox: Repetition, Innovation, and Hollywood's Hit Film Formula', in Frank Krutnik and Kathleen Loock (eds), 'Exploring Film Seriality', special issue of *Film Studies* 17.1 (Autumn), 92–110.
Loock, Kathleen (2018a), 'American TV Series Revivals: Introduction', *Television & New Media*, 19: 4, 299–309.
Loock, Kathleen (2018b), '"Whatever Happened to Predictability?": *Fuller House*, (Post) Feminism, and the Revival of Family-Friendly Viewing', *Television & New Media*, 19: 4: 361–78.

Loock, Kathleen (2019a), 'Reproductive Futurism and the Politics of the Sequel', *[in]Transition: Journal of Videographic Film & Moving Image Studies* 6: 3, <http://mediacommons.org/intransition/reproductive-futurism-and-politics-sequel>.

Loock, Kathleen (2019b), 'Retro/Repro: Zur Reproduktionslogik des Retro-Remaking in *Blade Runner 2049*', *Rabbiteye: Zeitschrift für Filmforschung*, 11: 44–60.

McClintock, Pamela (2015), 'Box-Office Milestone: *Jurassic World* Becomes No. 3 Movie of All Time', *Hollywood Reporter*, 22 July, <https://www.hollywoodreporter.com/news/box-office-jurassic-world-becomes-810460>.

McClintock, Pamela (2016), '*Batman v. Superman* and the Rise of the "Requel"', *Hollywood Reporter*, 8 April, 11–12.

Niemeyer, Katharina (2014), 'Introduction: Media and Nostalgia', in Katharina Niemeyer (ed.), *Media and Nostalgia: Yearning for the Past, the Present and the Future*, London: Palgrave Macmillan, pp. 1–23.

Pallotta, Frank (2015), '*Jurassic World* Smashes U.S. and International Box Office Records', *CNN Business*, 15 June, <https://money.cnn.com/2015/06/15/media/jurassic-world-biggest-us-box-office-opening/>.

Prince, Stephen (1996), 'True Lies: Perceptual Realism, Digital Images, and Film Theory', *Film Quarterly*, 49: 3, 27–37.

Prince, Stephen (2012), *Digital Visual Effects in Cinema: The Seduction of Reality*, New Brunswick, NJ: Rutgers University Press.

Proctor, William (2012), 'Regeneration and Rebirth: An Anatomy of the Franchise Reboot', *Scope: An Online Journal of Film and Television Studies*, 22 (February), 1–19.

Raya Bravo, Irene (2017), 'La recuela: entre el remake y la secuela. El caso de *Jurassic World*', *Fonseca: Journal of Communication*, 14: 45–57.

Rogers, Adam (2015), '*Star Wars* and the Quest for the Forever Franchise', *Wired*, December, <https://www.wired.com/2015/11/building-the-star-wars-universe/>.

Singer, Matt (2015), 'Welcome to the Age of the Legacyquel', *ScreenCrush*, 23 November, <http://screencrush.com/the-age-of-legacyquels/>.

Steele, Bruce C. (2015), '*Jurassic, Mad Max* Introduce the "Requel"', *Citizen Times*, 16 June, <https://eu.citizen-times.com/story/entertainment/movies/2015/06/16/movies-jurassic-mad-max-introduce-requel/28801567/>.

Tompkins, Joe (2014), '"Re-imagining" the Canon: Examining the Discourse of Contemporary Horror Film Reboots', *New Review of Film and Television Studies*, 12: 4 (December), 380–99.

Tryon, Chuck (2013), 'Reboot Cinema', *Convergence: The International Journal of Research into New Media Technology*, 19: 4, 432–7.

Verevis, Constantine (2017), 'New Millennial Remakes', in Frank Kelleter (ed.), *Media of Serial Narrative*, Columbus, OH: Ohio State University Press, pp. 148–66.

Xu, Xing, Kebai Wang, Ke Zhang, Qingyu Ma, Lida Xing, Corwin Sullivan, Dongyu Hu, Shuqing Cheng and Shuo Wang (2012), 'A Gigantic Feathered Dinosaur from the Lower Cretaceous of China', *Nature*, 484: 7392, 92–5.

Yuan, Jada (2015), 'There's No Feminism to Be Found in *Jurassic World*'s Genetic Code', *Vulture*, 12 June, <https://www.vulture.com/2015/06/jurassic-world-feminism.html>.

CHAPTER 12

World-building, Retconning and Legacy Rebooting: *Alien* and Contemporary Media Franchise Strategies

James Fleury

November 2019 might come to represent something of a turning point in Hollywood's approach to franchise films – those that use an established intellectual property (IP), or brand. Over three consecutive weekends, three such films failed to attract audiences: Paramount and Skydance's *Terminator: Dark Fate* (Miller, 2019), Sony's *Charlie's Angels* (Banks, 2019) and Warner Bros.'s *Doctor Sleep* (Flanaghan, 2019) (McClintock 2019). That same month, in response to these box office disappointments, Paramount partnered with Netflix to produce the long-gestating third sequel to *Beverly Hills Cop* (Brest, 1984) (Fleming, Jr 2019).

These examples demonstrate how franchise sequels and prequels can also function as 'reboots'. According to Constantine Verevis, 'rebooting' refers to 'the process of restarting, remaking, or re-commercializing a film property or franchise by denying or nullifying earlier iterations in order to "begin again" without requiring any knowledge of those previous works' (2017: 278). While some reboots may take a 'hard reboot' approach of resetting *all* of their respective franchise's narrative, like *Batman Begins* (Nolan, 2005), others take a 'soft reboot' approach of resetting *some* of their respective franchise's narrative, such as *Superman Returns* (Singer, 2006). Each of the above films sought to revive an IP that had either lain dormant (for example, *Charlie's Angels*, whose last film had appeared in 2003 and whose last, short-lived, television series aired in 2011) or experienced diminishing returns (for example, *Terminator: Dark Fate* (Miller, 2019), which picks up from *Terminator 2: Judgment Day* (Cameron, 1991) and ignores its sequels). As Chuck Tryon argues, rebooting 'now functions as a normal part of industry strategy, one that allows studios to generate a sense of textual novelty that will encourage audiences to attend movies in theaters' (2013: 432–3). While it is true that rebooting represents a method by which to drive box office attendance, it – along with other franchising strategies – has also become a method by which to drive streaming-service subscriptions.

The developments of November 2019 therefore show how franchises have had to adapt to a changing media landscape. On the one hand, franchise films increasingly dominate the domestic and global box office. This domination includes not just blockbuster productions but also films with relatively low budgets, like *Halloween* (Green, 2018). On the other hand, franchises also increasingly appear on – and could come to dominate – subscription video on demand (SVOD) services.

For studios and technology-media hybrids (for example, Amazon), acquiring IP represents a means not only to generate licensing revenue but also to supply their SVOD libraries. This dual strategy of licensing and librarying enables companies to recoup their acquisition and development costs and cultivate a unique company brand. While this recalls how studios tended to carry distinct identities in the Classical Hollywood era, the focus today has shifted from specialising in particular *genres*, such as gangster films at Warner Bros., to specialising in particular *brands*: for example, the Disney+ homepage at launch was organised according to content from Disney, Pixar, Marvel, Star Wars and National Geographic (Schatz 1988; Grainge 2008).

In some cases, it seems that studios have turned to SVODs as an alternative distribution platform for franchises deemed unsuitable for theatrical release. Traditionally, studio investment in such franchises has been limited to paratexts: that is, non-theatrical material such as licensed video games, novels and comic books (Gray 2010). For example, following the disappointing theatrical performance of the $150–185 million-budgeted *Blade Runner 2049* (Villeneuve, 2017), Warner Bros.-based Alcon Media Group – which had acquired the *Blade Runner* (1982–present) franchise rights in 2011 – has sought value from the IP through a lower-cost anime series and set of comic books (McClintock 2017; Fleming, Jr 2011; Collis 2018; Petski 2018). Because of streaming, though, franchises that have generated diminishing box office returns can continue to receive film instalments.

At the same time that streaming provides a new revenue stream, franchises have relied on a number of strategies to remain relevant. While some have persisted, like *James Bond* (1962–present) and *Rocky* (1976–present), others have proven difficult to sustain, such as those discussed in the first paragraph. In this chapter, I present 20th Century-Fox's – and now Disney's – *Alien* (1979–present) IP as a case study of how content companies have deployed different franchise management strategies to appeal to new audiences as well as long-time fans. With a particular focus on the films *Prometheus* (Scott, 2012) and *Alien: Covenant* (Scott, 2017) and the video games *Aliens: Colonial Marines* (Sega, 2013), *Alien: Isolation* (Sega, 2014), and *Alien: Blackout* (FoxNext, 2019), I argue that world-building, retconning and legacy rebooting represent strategies by which to maintain the relevance of a franchise in the face of disruptive networked technologies like streaming video and mobile apps.

Across three sections, I analyse how the *Alien* franchise has used extending and rebooting strategies for decades but has especially done so across the films and video games of the 2010s. Each strategy has produced a range of effects. Whereas some franchise entries have generated positive reactions, like *Alien: Isolation*, others have elicited responses that can be described as ambivalent, as with *Alien: Covenant*, or even vitriolic, as was the case with *Alien: Blackout*. This range speaks to the challenges of contemporary franchise management. The chapter concludes with a consideration of how two events from 2019 – Disney's acquisition of Fox and the arrival of Disney+ – will affect not only the future of *Alien* but also other Fox franchises, including, for example, *Planet of the Apes* (1968–present). I base my analysis on media industry trade reports and fan critiques available on online platforms like Reddit and Rotten Tomatoes. This approach therefore combines the top-down perspective of media industries studies with the bottom-up perspective of cultural studies in order to put in dialogue corporate franchise management strategies and audience responses. Through this combination, we can understand how media franchise sustainability often means reconciling technological and cultural changes with industrial traditions.

WORLD-BUILDING IN THE *ALIEN* FRANCHISE

World-building has remained the dominant strategy of the *Alien* franchise. As Mark J. P. Wolf has explained, this practice can take place within a single medium but frequently involves 'world materials, stories, and characters appearing across a range of different media'. In other words, each text expands the 'imaginary world' of a franchise by exploring new situations, characters and locations (Wolf 2018: 141). World-building therefore represents an ongoing, additive form of franchising rather than one that is subtractive (that is, a hard reboot that resets all continuity) or corrective (that is, a soft reboot that resets some continuity).

Unlike *Halloween* (1978–present) or *Spider-Man* (2002–present), *Alien* has yet to receive a hard reboot. Instead, the franchise has extended the same narrative across multiple media since 1979. Broadly speaking, it has followed a series of interactions between a central protagonist (for example, Ellen Ripley, played by Sigourney Weaver in the first four films) and three other character groups: representatives of the Weyland-Yutani Corporation (for example, capitalists like Carter Burke (Paul Reiser) in *Aliens* (Cameron, 1986) or androids like David in *Prometheus*); space marines; and/or the xenomorph aliens. Starting with *Alien* (Scott, 1979), the franchise has expanded out into three sequel films (1986, 1992, 1997), two *Alien vs. Predator* spin-off films (Anderson, 2004; the Brothers Strause, 2007), and two prequel films (Scott, 2012, 2017) as well as numerous comic books, novels, video games and fanworks.

Expansion, however, can lead to tension among stakeholders within a franchise. According to Henry Jenkins, transmedia storytelling refers to a single narrative carried across multiple platforms (2006: 97–8). Clare Parody has specified that transmedia franchises tend to belong to one of two categories: those that begin as cohesively coordinated and those that emerge over time (2011: 211).[1] For Jenkins, the 'ideal' form of transmedia storytelling democratises the contributions of each medium so that a comic book provides equally significant narrative material as a film or TV series (2006: 98). Rüdiger Heinze has argued that expansion tends to create a sense of heterarchy, by which franchises are 'open, dynamic, flexible, and heterogenous' (2015: 76). As the world-building of *Alien* makes evident, heterarchy at once allows for both branching narrative paths – by which audiences can choose their preferred serialised storytelling throughline – and textual hierarchies – by which content companies dictate the preferred path through 'canonising'. Therefore, the significance of elements such as characters and entire texts can be subject to scrutiny and retroactive continuity revision: that is, 'retconning'.

RETCONNING IN THE *ALIEN* FRANCHISE

The world-building of *Alien* has not necessarily followed a systematic, planned path. This has several reasons. First, the original film appeared at an early stage of Hollywood's focus on franchising. For the most part, franchises at the time that began in film, like *Alien*, had relied on a logic of multimedia replication by which other media would function as adaptations; this would include, for example, a novelisation of a screenplay.[2] *Star Wars* (1977–present), however, popularised the notion of transmedia storytelling – by which a single narrative carries across media platforms. Starting in 1978 with Marvel's comic books, Alan Dean Foster's novel *Splinter of the Mind's Eye* (1978) and Steve Binder's *Star Wars Holiday Special* (CBS, 1978), other media contributed original stories to the world established in George Lucas's first *Star Wars* film (Freeman 2017: 63).[3] With transmedia presenting an alternative to multimedia, Fox would shift its franchising approach to *Alien* throughout the 1980s and 1990s.[4] Whereas a novelisation, a comic book arc and a series of video games adapted the narrative of 1979's *Alien*, a line of comic books, starting in 1988, continued the narrative of 1986's *Aliens* even before a third film arrived in 1992.

Beginning with *Alien³* (Fincher, 1992), the franchise splintered into separate narrative paths. This reflects what Matthew Freeman, based on the work of Kristin Fast and Henrik Örnebring, has explained as the tendency for transmedia story worlds to have been 'created over many years by multiple parties and with a lack of certainty over future production plans' (Freeman 2017: 63; Fast and Örnebring 2017: 636–52). Because franchises typically represent the product of several 'authors' across multiple media, hierarchies among these authors and media emerge. In the case of *Alien*, the third film provided a case of retconning – namely, by killing Newt (Carrie Henn) and Corporal Hicks (Michael Biehn), two of the main characters from *Aliens* and its comic book extensions, in the opening minutes. In deference to *Alien³*, the comics renamed these characters as Billie and Wilks. With this retconning, the franchise emphasised the subordinate position of its paratexts. Heinze has argued that retconning and other forms of tension within media franchises can emerge out of the perceived 'bargaining power' or 'cultural capital' of each text; in this case, a film superseded the comic books (2015: 85). Even after adopting a transmedia – rather than multimedia – model, the *Alien* franchise continued to organise its storytelling around the films.

Over the past several decades, the *Alien* films have remained as 'mothership' texts that take narrative precedence over their paratexts. By 2012, the franchise had adopted transmedia storytelling to such an extent that even the marketing campaign for *Prometheus* expanded the narrative. This followed in the footsteps of transmedia marketing efforts for films like *The Dark Knight* (Nolan, 2008) and *Tron: Legacy* (Kosinski, 2010), which Starlight Runner Entertainment, 42 Entertainment, Campfire and other consulting firms supported with alternate reality games, viral videos and branded websites (Hassler-Forest 2016: 682–92). Starlight Runner's *Prometheus* campaign featured a series of promotional videos and websites that added to the film's world and characters. In addition to a video of a TED Talk from Peter Weyland (Guy Pearce), audiences could discover more about his company, Weyland Industries, on 'its' website (Przegalińska 2015: 79–89; Boes 2014). For Fox, the *Prometheus* transmedia marketing campaign functioned to not only deepen fan knowledge of the franchise (for example, learning about the company that would become Weyland-Yutani, a central element in the original four *Alien* films) but also to provide viral content capable of reaching new, online, presumably younger audiences. After all, other promotional material for *Prometheus* framed it as a franchise extension: for example, the editing, sound and title in the teaser trailer resemble those of the trailer for *Alien*. At the same time, this material situated *Prometheus* as a stand-alone film; director Ridley Scott said at the time of the film's announcement, 'The keen fan will recognize strands of *Alien*'s DNA, so to speak, but the ideas tackled in this film are unique, large and provocative' (Fleming, Jr and Finke 2011).

Therefore, the transmedia and traditional marketing material supported the reboot intentions of *Prometheus* as a prequel set about thirty years prior to the events of *Alien* that, seemingly, could stand on its own. These intentions included expanding the franchise's story world, welcoming new audiences and reviving the film series after a pair of critically and commercially lacklustre *Alien vs. Predator* spin-offs.[5] In addition to collecting $403 million worldwide on a budget of $120–130 million, *Prometheus* scored 73 per cent critic and 68 per cent audience ratings on Rotten Tomatoes, and a 64 Metascore from critics and a 6.5 users score on Metacritic (Box Office Mojo 2012; Rotten Tomatoes 2012; Metacritic 2012; Galloway 2012). The franchise, it appeared, had been revived.

Subsequent *Alien* film and video game projects would experiment with retconning but ultimately fail. *Prometheus*'s modest profits and rather ambivalent critical and viewer scores suggested an uncertain cinematic future for the franchise. Audiences had criticised the film's logic, such as a character that could not avoid a rolling spacecraft; other targets of criticism included the film's deliberate pacing and tenuous ties to *Alien*, as only a prototype of the xenomorph creature appears (Deleted account 2016; Shinbrig Goku 2018; Hartwell 2017). As Vivian Sobchack puts it, the film 'hardly lived up to its marketing hype . . . as both a prequel to [Scott's] *Alien* and a "completely original" film' (2012: 32). Sobchack specifies by way of metaphor that 'the film itself is caught between a rock and a hard place', with the rock representing 'the industry franchise and mythology that Scott unknowingly spawned in 1979' and the hard place representing 'an imagined (and possibly unattainable) space freed of its origins and thus open to originality' (2012: 33). Although Scott had announced plans to direct a sequel even before *Prometheus* opened, these plans would remain in flux in light of the mixed reception (Galloway 2012).

In February 2013, less than a year later, the franchise received another high-profile, albeit delayed, reboot with *Aliens: Colonial Marines*. This first-person shooter video game for PC, Microsoft Xbox 360 and Sony PlayStation 3 retconned the events of *Alien³* by revealing Corporal Hicks to have survived that film's opening scene. Despite revising the narrative of *Alien³* in order to align itself more closely with the popular *Aliens*, which holds a 99 per cent critical score and 94 per cent audience score on Rotten Tomatoes, the game proved unpopular with critics and fans, generating critical scores of 43 to 48 per cent on Metacritic, due to its poor gameplay, falsely advertised graphics, underdeveloped characters and deviations from canon (Ogilvie 2013; Sharkey 2013; Sterling 2013; Fleury and Mamber 2019: 31–51). Despite the game's poor reception, its pre-release hype indicated that fans desired a return to the earlier films' continuity, characters and iconography (Totilo 2012).

In 2015, filmmaker Neill Blomkamp revealed via concept art posted on Instagram that he was working on a film that would also use *Aliens* as its foundation. This project would serve as a direct sequel to *Aliens* and would ignore the events of its less renowned sequels. Although the notion of a film retconning other mothership texts – rather than just paratexts – had existed previously, including *Halloween H20: Twenty Years Later* (Miner, 1998), for example, it has recently become a common practice with franchises that have experienced diminishing returns, such as 2018's *Halloween*, 2019's *Terminator: Dark Fate*, and the announced *Robocop Returns* (Kit 2019b). Even though Blomkamp's project was said to arrive after Ridley Scott's *Prometheus* follow-up, it was cancelled before the 2017 release of that film, *Alien: Covenant* (Sneider 2015; Butler 2017). This cancellation reinforced a filmmaker hierarchy within the franchise. According to Scott, the *Aliens* sequel never advanced beyond the concept stage:

> I waited for something like a script to happen because it was done with Fox and I was going to be the producer, and it never really evolved. I don't know what happened, really. It was probably Fox's decision finally, not mine. (Butler 2017)

As Scott frames it, the studio – not him – had chosen to pursue the *Prometheus* sequel over the retconned *Aliens* project. Nonetheless, the decision indicated the power Scott wielded within the franchise, particularly after his 2015 science fiction film *The Martian* had delivered Fox a critical and commercial hit (Box Office Mojo 2016).[6]

Like *Aliens: Colonial Marines*, the *Aliens* retcon concept reflected an audience – and, probably, a studio – desire to pivot away from the more standalone and, therefore, commercially risky nature of *Prometheus* and towards the familiarity of the original *Alien* films. In 2014, Scott had noted that his follow-up would not feature any xenomorphs (Butler 2017). Like he had when announcing *Prometheus*, Scott claimed that its sequel would exist independently within the *Alien* franchise and further deviate from its identifiable elements. By the time the film was released three years later, it would not only include the iconic creature but also emphasise a connection to the franchise through its title, *Alien: Covenant*, posters, which prominently featured xenomorphs, and premise, as it is set eleven years after *Prometheus* and relegates that film's protagonist, Elizabeth Shaw (Noomi Rapace), to a cameo. Scott has admitted that 'the reaction to *Prometheus*' had driven this decision and specified that fans 'were really frustrated' because '[t]hey wanted to see more of the original [monster]' (Butler 2017). Ironically, this frustration did not become evident to Scott or 20th Century-Fox until Blomkamp had unveiled his *Aliens* sequel concept art – three years after *Prometheus* had debuted. By continuing Scott's vision while also trying to appease fans, *Alien: Covenant* represents a hybridised *Prometheus* sequel and *Alien* prequel. Tonally, the film alternates between the existential themes explored in *Prometheus* and the horror of *Alien*. Narratively, it attempts to reconcile the rules established in

Scott's earlier entries. For example, characters play host to the xenomorph in two ways: injection of a virus, the method shown in *Prometheus*, and implantation by a 'facehugger' creature, the method shown in *Alien*. Like Sobchack noted of its predecessor, *Alien: Covenant* found itself stuck between a rock and a hard place. As such, both *Prometheus* and *Covenant* suggest how contemporary franchises struggle to balance authorial and audience control.

Beyond taking control of the franchise away from Blomkamp, Scott used retconning in *Covenant* to assert his authority over the sequels to his 1979 original. Primarily, it posits that an android named David (Michael Fassbender) – rather than the alien 'queen' introduced in James Cameron's *Aliens* – is the creator of the xenomorph species. Furthermore, the film appears to revise the concept introduced in *Alien*[3] that the xenomorph, once hatched, will take on the traits of its host. While Heinze has analysed how the 'bargaining power' or 'cultural capital' of each text can create hierarchies, so can the status of each creator – with privilege reserved especially for filmmakers, like Scott, that have been branded as 'auteurs' (2015: 85). Therefore, *Alien: Covenant* serves as a reboot on two levels: by repositioning *Prometheus* as more of an *Alien* prequel and by reclaiming Ridley Scott as architect of the franchise.

LEGACY STORYTELLING IN THE *ALIEN* FRANCHISE

Retconning and explicit connections to the original film series could not prevent *Alien: Covenant* from receiving an even more ambivalent response than its predecessor. Despite its $97 million budget being $20 million less than that of *Prometheus*, the film earned only $240 million globally – a drop of more than $160 million (Kelley 2017; Box Office Mojo 2017). Additionally, it earned lower scores on Rotten Tomatoes, with 66 per cent from critics and 55 per cent from audiences (Rotten Tomatoes 2017). Like they had with *Prometheus*, audiences took issue with the characters' decision-making and the film's departures from continuity (Mi-16evil 2017). As has become tradition for films with poor advanced-release audience tracking, sequels were announced in the immediate lead-up to *Covenant*'s debut; Scott said at the time, 'I see a really huge franchise here – honestly, as big as *Star Wars*' (Butler 2017; Kelley 2017).[7] Rather than having signaled a sense of confidence in *Covenant*'s ability to generate more films, staking a claim on sequels to a prequel may have actually turned away audiences who felt the franchise lacked a clear narrative path forward.

This path has become more unclear in the time since. In 2019, two years after the release of *Alien: Covenant*, the Walt Disney Company completed its acquisition of 20th Century-Fox. As Disney CEO Bob Iger has explained, the deal took place because of Fox's IP, which – in addition to *Alien* – includes *Planet of the Apes*, *Avatar* (2009–present) and *The Simpsons* (1989–present). With this IP and the 2017 purchase of streaming video company BAMTech, Disney sought to power its Disney+ SVOD that launched in November 2019 (Franck 2019). Despite having bought Fox for its IP, Disney has so far found mixed results with the studio's films, with the true-story *Ford v Ferrari* (entitled *Le Mans '66* in the UK) (Mangold, 2019) out-grossing the *X-Men* franchise entry *Dark Phoenix* (Kinberg, 2019). Due to the box office disappointment of *Dark Phoenix* and other films, such as *Stuber* (Dowse, 2019), Disney cancelled many Fox films that had been in development and announced that some of the newly acquired IP would supply Disney+, including *Home Alone* (1990–present) (Donnelly 2019). While Disney is moving forward with a new, potentially theatrical *Planet of the Apes* film, the fate of a new *Alien* entry remains uncertain – even if a potential *Covenant* follow-up entitled *Alien: Awakening* has been discussed in the press (Kit 2019a).

In the same way as *Aliens: Colonial Marines* had suggested an audience appetite for nostalgia in advance of *Alien: Covenant*, another video game has provided a reboot model for future *Alien* films to follow. Released for multiple platforms in 2014, Sega's *Alien: Isolation* leans into the first film in the franchise through its title and premise. Set fifteen years after *Alien*, the game's main story centres on Amanda Ripley, who leads an investigation into the disappearance of her mother, the film's protagonist, Ellen Ripley. In addition to this campaign, the game includes two downloadable expansions that adapt sequences from *Alien* and feature new voiceovers from the original cast reprising their characters. Whereas *Colonial Marines* and several other video games in the franchise had adopted the action emphasis of *Aliens*, such as *Alien vs. Predator* (Atari Corporation, 1994), *Isolation* borrows the survival horror tone of *Alien*. This anchoring to the first film reflects the more central role its director, Ridley Scott, had taken in the franchise in the years since *Aliens: Colonial Marines* had begun its development back in 2007 (McLaughlin 2013).

By combining nostalgia (for example, extending the narrative and tone of *Alien*) and innovation (for example, Amanda Ripley and a new cast of characters), *Isolation* resembles what Dan Golding has called a 'legacy' franchise text. This type of text, he explains, is the product of franchises from the 1970s to the 1990s having now 'gained significant nostalgic currency' to the extent that they 'have been frequently revived by studios looking for financial dependability and predictability' (Golding 2019: 69). A legacy film like *Creed* (Coogler, 2015) or video game, such as *Gears of War* (Microsoft Game Studios, 2016), will provide old and new elements (for example, in terms of narrative, character and behind-the-scenes talent) in order to appeal to both franchise fans and new audiences. As a legacy text, *Isolation* presents a point of entry for multiple generations into the *Alien* franchise.

In contrast to the critically reviled *Aliens: Colonial Marines*, the game received strong reviews from both critics and audiences.[8] *Isolation* appeared at a time when fewer media-licensed, or tie-in, video games were appearing on home consoles. Instead, studios throughout the 2010s transitioned to mobile devices like smartphones and tablets as the primary platform for tie-ins. This transition has taken place because, compared to console games, mobile apps offer cheaper development costs, a lower barrier to entry for consumers (tie-in apps are often 'free-to-play' but generate revenue through 'in-app purchases') and the ability to be updated in advance of home video and follow-up film releases (Kohler 2013). *Isolation* has gained such a positive reputation that fans have desired a successor for consoles. However, in January 2019, when Fox's in-house video game unit FoxNext announced that a follow-up – entitled *Alien: Blackout* – would release later that month for mobile devices but not home consoles, fans reacted with disappointment (Bankhurst 2019). Although FoxNext assured fans at the time that it was also working with developer Cold Iron Studios on a 'massively multiplayer online shooter' for consoles, this console game's status is uncertain following Disney's January 2020 sale of FoxNext to mobile game company Scopely due to a lack of interest in the video game business (Franzese 2019; Spangler 2020). Although *Isolation* may foreshadow the 'legacy' path that Disney may take the franchise's films down, the lack of updates on a cinematic sequel to *Covenant* and the apparent cancellation of the console project have left the future of *Alien* in stasis.

CONCLUSION: THE FUTURE OF THE *ALIEN* FRANCHISE

A number of potential futures exist for the *Alien* franchise. In terms of paratexts, a series of novels and comic books have appeared since the release of *Alien: Covenant*. Furthermore, despite *Alien: Isolation* receiving only a mobile follow-up and despite Disney's divestment of FoxNext, franchises have gradually been returning to consoles for video game tie-in adaptations and transmedia extensions. These games (for example, *Jurassic World Evolution* (Frontier Developments, 2018) and *Jumanji: The Video Game* (Outright Games, 2019)) allow IP holders to reach the console-gamer audience while also – as the product of small, independent developers – carrying lower-budgets than blockbuster 'AAA' projects like *Red Dead Redemption 2* (Rockstar Games, 2018) (Takahashi 2018a, 2018b). All of these paratexts, then, present low-cost alternatives to another film release as methods to sustain the *Alien* franchise.

Still, Disney might decide to deliver *Alien* to streaming. For the studio, its Disney+ SVOD provides a distribution platform for family-friendly brands. Going forward, Hulu – of which Disney bought control in May 2019 – could function in a manner similar to Touchstone Pictures, which Disney created in 1984 as a banner under which to distribute PG-13 and R-rated films (Lee 2019; Harmetz 1984). This could depend on the commercial performance of the new

Planet of the Apes film – the first Fox IP to be fully developed by Disney for theatrical release. By debuting on streaming, a new *Alien* film could continue the trend of reboots emphasising new technologies, following the 3-D projection for *Prometheus* and FoxNext's *Alien: Covenant In Utero* virtual reality promotion (Tryon 2013: 432–3).[9]

I would like to conclude by returning to a claim I made earlier in this chapter: sustaining a franchise often means reconciling technological and cultural changes with industrial traditions. With *Alien*, this might mean recognising that the franchise is no longer suitable for theatrical distribution while also keeping the franchise anchored to its earlier, favoured films. Adopting a streaming release and a legacy reboot approach could allow Disney to rebirth the *Alien* franchise for fans and new audiences alike.

NOTES

1. Parody explains that franchise storytelling can take the form of either 'a co-ordinated act of transmedia storytelling, the systematic branching and extension of a narrative across multiple media outlets, or a palimpsest of a story world and its inhabitants built-up over time from repeated remakes, reimaginings, and remediations of one or more fictional texts and objects or something in between' (2011: 211).
2. Alternatively, franchises whose films grew out of other media have tended to feature multiple, sometimes competing, narrative threads at any given time (for example, the Warner Bros. *Batman* live-action films (1989–97, 2005–12, 2016–17, 2021) have largely remained independent of the comic books, television series, animated films and video games).
3. As Matthew Freeman reminds us, even *Star Wars* has long been a narrative network 'of contingencies, alternatives, and reboots' (2017: 63).
4. Perhaps not by coincidence, Fox brought a transmedia approach to the *Alien* franchise in light of the commercial success Lucas found with *Star Wars* – the merchandising rights to which Lucas had retained (Fleming, Jr 2015).
5. *Alien vs. Predator* earned 20 per cent critic and 39 per cent audience scores on Rotten Tomatoes and collected $173 million worldwide; the sequel, *Aliens vs. Predator: Requiem* received 11 per cent critic and 30 per cent audience scores on Rotten Tomatoes while making $129 million globally (Rotten Tomatoes 2004; Box Office Mojo 2004; Rotten Tomatoes 2007; Box Office Mojo 2007).
6. *The Martian* received seven Academy Award nominations and earned more than $630 million worldwide.
7. Other films for which sequels were announced immediately prior to release include *The November Man* (Donaldson, 2014), *Independence Day: Resurgence* (Emmerich, 2016) and *Bumblebee* (Knight, 2018) (Coming Soon 2014; De Semlyen 2016; Wakeman 2018).
8. On Metacritic, critic scores across platforms range from 78 to 82 per cent while user scores range from 7.9 to 8.5.
9. As Tryon has argued, reboots often are designed not only to revive interest in a franchise but to showcase technological developments. In the case of *Prometheus*, the film – like Sony's *The Amazing Spider-Man* (Webb, 2012) – provided Fox 'new, but familiar, material not only for selling a transmedia franchise but also for promoting the technological shift to digital projection in theaters' (2013: 432–3).

REFERENCES

Bankhurst, Adam (2019), 'The Internet Isn't Happy that Alien: Blackout Is a Mobile Game', *IGN*, 8 January, <https://www.ign.com/articles/2019/01/08/the-internet-isnt-happy-that-alien-blackout-is-a-mobile-game>.

Boes, Nick (2014), 'Prometheus: Transmedia Campaign', 7 February, <https://www.behance.net/gallery/14357945/Prometheus-Transmedia-Campaign>.

Box Office Mojo (2004), 'Alien vs. Predator', *Box Office Mojo*, 18 December, <https://www.boxofficemojo.com/release/rl776308225/>.

Box Office Mojo (2008), 'Aliens vs. Predator: Requiem', *Box Office Mojo*, 5 March, <https://www.boxofficemojo.com/release/rl793085441/>.

Box Office Mojo (2012), 'Prometheus', *Box Office Mojo*, 13 September, <https://www.boxofficemojo.com/release/rl1063945729/>.

Box Office Mojo (2016), 'The Martian', *Box Office Mojo*, 3 March, <https://www.boxofficemojo.com/release/rl3496969729/>.

Box Office Mojo (2017), 'Alien: Covenant', *Box Office Mojo*, 15 September, <https://www.boxofficemojo.com/release/rl696026625/>.

Butler, Tom (2017), 'Ridley Scott Admits He Got Prometheus "Wrong", Teases Two Alien: Covenant Sequels', *Yahoo! News*, 10 May, <https://www.yahoo.com/news/alien-covenant-ridley-scott-admits-got-prometheus-wrong-teases-two-alien-sequels-exclusive-144721534.html>.

Collis, Clark (2018), 'Blade Runner Universe to Be Explored in Series of Comics and Graphic Novels', *Entertainment Weekly*, 12 July, <https://ew.com/books/2018/07/12/blade-runner-comics/>.

Coming Soon (2014), 'Relativity Announces Sequel to The November Man, Starring Pierce Brosnan', *Coming Soon*, 20 August, <https://www.comingsoon.net/movies/news/122089-relativity-announces-sequel-to-the-november-man-starring-pierce-brosnan>.

Deleted account (2016), 'A Dumb Criticism of Prometheus that I Often Hear and It Drives Me Nuts like Are You Insane?', Reddit, 9 February, <https://www.reddit.com/r/movies/comments/44y8z3/a_dumb_criticism_of_prometheus_that_i_often_hear/>.

De Semlyen, Phil (2016), 'Independence Day 3 Will Be "an Intergalactic Journey" Says Roland Emmerich', *Empire*, 22 June, <https://www.empireonline.com/movies/news/independence-day-3-will-be-intergalactic-journey-says-roland-emmerich/>.

Donnelly, Matt (2019), 'Disney Flushes Fox Film Development, "Redirects" Strategy After Big Q3 Loss', *Variety*, 6 August, <https://variety.com/2019/film/news/disney-fox-xmen-marvel-studio-losses-1203294296/>.

Fast, Kristin and Henrik Örnebring (2017), 'Transmedia World-building: *The Shadow* (1931–Present) and *Transformers* (1984–Present)', *The International Journal of Cultural Studies*, 20: 6, 636–52.

Fleming, Jr, Mike (2011), 'Alcon Plotting "Blade Runner" Prequels And Sequels', *Deadline*, 2 March, <https://deadline.com/2011/03/alcon-plotting-blade-runner-prequels-and-sequels-110722/>.

Fleming, Jr, Mike (2015), '"Star Wars" Legacy II: An Architect Of Hollywood's Greatest Deal Recalls How George Lucas Won Sequel Rights', *Deadline*, 18 December, <https://deadline.com/2015/12/star-wars-franchise-george-lucas-historic-rights-deal-tom-pollock-1201669419/>.

Fleming, Jr, Mike (2019), 'Netflix Licenses From Paramount Rights To Make "Beverly Hills Cop" Sequel With Eddie Murphy & Jerry Bruckheimer', *Deadline*, 14 November, <https://deadline.com/2019/11/beverly-hills-cop-sequel-netflix-eddie-murphy-jerry-bruckheimer-paramount-license-deal-1202785458/>.

Fleming, Jr, Mike and Nikki Finke (2011), 'Ridley Scott Directing "Prometheus" For Fox; Noomi Rapace Locked While Angelina Jolie and Charlize Theron Circling; Damon Lindelof Scripted with Scott from "Alien" DNA', *Deadline*, 14 January, <https://deadline.com/2011/01/ridley-scott-directing-prometheus-for-fox-noomi-rapace-locked-while-angelina-jolie-and-charlize-theron-circling-2nd-female-lead-96773/>.

Fleury, James and Stephen Mamber (2019), 'The (Im)Perfect Organism: Dissecting the Alien Media Franchise', in James Fleury, Bryan Hikari Hartzheim and Stephen Mamber (eds), *The Franchise Era: Managing Media in the Digital Economy*, Edinburgh: Edinburgh University Press, pp. 31–51.

Franck, Thomas (2019), 'Iger Says Disney Bought Fox Because of Value It Adds to Streaming Service: "The Light Bulb Went Off"', *CNBC*, 12 April, <https://www.cnbc.com/2019/04/12/disney-wouldnt-have-bought-fox-assets-without-streaming-plans-iger-says.html>.

Franzese, Tomas (2019), 'Alien Game from FoxNext and Cold Iron Studios Confirmed to be "Massively Multiplayer Online Shooter"', *DualShockers*, 7 January, <https://www.dualshockers.com/alien-mmo-shooter-pc-consoles-foxnext/>.

Freeman, Matthew (2017), 'From Sequel to Quasi-Novelization: *Splinter of the Mind's Eye* and the 1970s Culture of Transmedia Contingency', in Sean Guynes and Dan Hassler-Forest (eds), *Star Wars and the History of Transmedia Storytelling*, Amsterdam: University of Amsterdam Press, pp. 61–72.

Galloway, Stephen (2012), 'Return of the "Alien" Mind', *Hollywood Reporter*, 16 May, <https://www.hollywoodreporter.com/news/ridley-scott-prometheus-alien-324981>.

Golding, Dan (2019), *Star Wars After Lucas: A Critical Guide to the Future of the Galaxy*, Minneapolis, MN: University of Minnesota Press.

Grainge, Paul (2008), *Brand Hollywood: Selling Entertainment in a Global Media Age*, New York: Routledge.

Gray, Jonathan (2010), *Show Sold Separately: Promos, Spoilers, and Other Media Paratexts*, New York: New York University Press.

Harmetz, Aljean (1984), 'Touchstone Label to Replace Disney Name on Some Films', *New York Times*, 16 February, <https://www.nytimes.com/1984/02/16/movies/touchstone-label-to-replace-disney-name-on-some-films.html>.

Hartwell, Chris (2017), 'Why "Prometheus" Remains the Most Misunderstood "Alien" Movie', *Hollywood Reporter*, 19 May, <https://www.hollywoodreporter.com/heat-vision/alien-why-misunderstood-movie-is-prometheus-1005328>.

Hassler-Forest, Dan (2016), 'Skimmers, Dippers, and Divers: Campfire's Steve Coulson on Transmedia Marketing and Audience Participation', *Participations: Journal of Audience and Reception Studies* 13: 1 (May), 682–92.

Heinze, Rüdiger (2015), '"This Makes No Sense At All": Heterarchy in Fictional Universes', *StoryWorlds: A Journal of Narrative Studies* 7: 2, 75–91.

Jenkins, Henry (2006), *Convergence Culture: Where Old and New Media Collide*, New York: New York University Press.

Kelley, Seth (2017), 'Sorry, Ridley Scott: The "Alien" Franchise Is No "Star Wars"', *Variety*, 21 May, <https://variety.com/2017/film/news/alien-covenant-box-office-analysis-ridley-scott-1202439346/>.

Kit, Borys (2019a), 'New "Planet of the Apes" Movie in the Works With "Maze Runner" Filmmaker Wes Ball', *Hollywood Reporter*, 3 December, <https://www.hollywoodreporter.com/heat-vision/new-planet-apes-movie-works-maze-runner-filmmaker-1258816>.

Kit, Borys (2019b), '"Robocop Returns" Lands "Little Monsters" Director Abe Forsythe', *Hollywood Reporter*, 20 November, <https://www.hollywoodreporter.com/heat-vision/robocop-returns-lands-little-monsters-director-abe-forsythe-1256699>.

Kohler, Chris (2013), 'Why Games Based on Movies Disappeared (and Why They're Coming Back)', *Wired*, 13 February, <https://www.wired.com/2013/02/movie-games/>.

Lang, Brent and Justin Kroll (2019), 'How Disney Plus, HBO Max, Peacock Are Banking on Splashy Movies in the Streaming Wars', *Variety*, 29 October, <https://variety.com/2019/film/news/studios-streaming-disney-plus-hbo-max-peacock-apple-tv-netflix-1203385899/>.

Lee, Edmund (2019), 'Disney to Buy Comcast's Hulu Stake and Take Full Control of Streaming Service', *New York Times*, 14 May, <https://www.nytimes.com/2019/05/14/business/media/disney-hulu-comcast.html>.

McClintock, Pamela (2017), '"Blade Runner 2049" Tracking for $40M-Plus U.S. Debut', *Hollywood Reporter*, 14 September, <https://www.hollywoodreporter.com/heat-vision/blade-runner-2049-tracking-40m-us-debut-1039017>.

McClintock, Pamela (2019), '"Charlie's Angels" and When to Put an Expiration Date on Old IP', *Hollywood Reporter*, 20 November, <https://www.hollywoodreporter.com/news/charlies-angels-box-office-bomb-put-an-expiration-date-old-ip-1255570>.

McLaughlin, Rus (2013), 'Origin Stories: How Gearbox Got to Make Aliens: Colonial Marines', *VentureBeat*, 9 February, <https://venturebeat.com/2013/02/09/origin-stories-how-gearbox-got-to-make-aliens-colonial-marines/>.

Metacritic (2012), 'Prometheus', *Metacritic*, 8 June, <https://www.metacritic.com/movie/prometheus>.

Mi-16evil (2017), 'Official Discussion – Alien: Covenant (US Release) [Spoilers]', *Reddit*, 18 May, <https://www.reddit.com/r/movies/comments/6c0sby/official_discussion_alien_covenant_us_release/>.

Ogilvie, Tristan (2013), 'Aliens: Colonial Marines 360/PS3 Review', *IGN*, 12 February, <https://www.ign.com/articles/2013/02/12/aliens-colonial-marines-360ps3-review>.

Parody, Clare (2011), 'Franchising/Adaptation', *Adaptation*, 4: 2 (September), 210–18.

Petski, Denise (2018), '"Blade Runner" Anime Series Inspired by Movie Heads to Adult Swim's Toonami', *Deadline*, 29 November, <https://deadline.com/2018/11/blade-runner-animated-series-inspired-by-movie-adult-swim-blade-runner-2049-1202510982/>.

Przegalińska, Aleksandra (2015), 'Prometheus: A Transmedia Campaign', in Grzegorz Mazurek (ed.), *Management in Virtual Environments: Case Studies*, Warsaw: Kozminski University, pp. 79–89.

Rotten Tomatoes (2004), 'AVP – Alien vs. Predator', *Rotten Tomatoes*, <https://www.rottentomatoes.com/m/alien_vs_predator>.

Rotten Tomatoes (2007), 'Aliens vs. Predator: Requiem (AVP 2)', *Rotten Tomatoes*, <https://www.rottentomatoes.com/m/avp2>.

Rotten Tomatoes (2012), 'Prometheus', *Rotten Tomatoes*, <https://www.rottentomatoes.com/m/prometheus_2012>.

Rotten Tomatoes (2017), 'Alien: Covenant', *Rotten Tomatoes*, <https://www.rottentomatoes.com/m/alien_covenant>.

Schatz, Thomas (1988), *The Genius of the System: Hollywood Filmmaking in the Studio Era*, New York: Pantheon Books.

Sharkey, Mike (2013), 'How Aliens: Colonial Marines Seriously Screws Up Alien Lore', *IGN*, 20 February, <http://pc.gamespy.com/pc/sega-alien-shooter/1227452p1.html>.

Shinbrig Goku (2018), 'Why Did Prometheus Get a Lot of Hate? (Discussion)', *Reddit*, 21 May, <https://www.reddit.com/r/movies/comments/8l1xr7/why_did_prometheus_get_a_lot_of_hate_discussion/>.

Sneider, Jeff (2015), 'Neill Blomkamp to Direct New "Alien" Movie for 20th Century Fox', *The Wrap*, 18 February, <https://www.thewrap.com/neill-blomkamp-to-direct-alien-movie-for-20th-century-fox/>.

Sobchack, Vivian (2012), '*Prometheus*', *Film Comment* 8: 4 (July–August), 30–4.
Spangler, Todd (2020), 'Disney Sells FoxNext Games Unit to Scopely', *Variety*, 22 January, <https://variety.com/2020/digital/news/disney-sells-foxnext-games-scopely-1203475758/>.
Sterling, Jim (2013), 'Review: Aliens: Colonial Marines', *Destructoid*, 12 February, <https://www.destructoid.com/review-aliens-colonial-marines-244276.phtml>.
Takahashi, Dean (2018a), 'How Frontier Leveled up Movie Games with Jurassic World Evolution', *VentureBeat*, 20 June, <https://venturebeat.com/2018/06/20/how-frontier-leveled-up-movie-games-with-jurassic-world-evolution/>.
Takahashi, Dean (2018b), 'How Much Did Red Dead Redemption 2 Cost to Make?', *VentureBeat*, 26 October, <https://venturebeat.com/2018/10/26/the-deanbeat-how-much-did-red-dead-redemption-2-cost-to-make/>.
Totilo, Stephen (2012), 'The Authorized Story of the Next Aliens Video Game Will Change the Way We See Aliens and Alien3', *Kotaku*, 4 May, <https://kotaku.com/the-authorized-story-of-the-next-aliens-video-game-will-5907653>.
Tryon, Chuck (2013), 'Reboot Cinema', *Convergence: The International Journal of Research into New Media Technologies*, 19: 4, 432–7.
Verevis, Constantine (2017), 'Remakes, Sequels, Prequels', in Thomas Leitch (ed.), *The Oxford Handbook of Adaptation Studies*, New York: Oxford University Press, pp. 267–84.
Wakeman, Gregory (2018), 'Will There Be a Bumblebee 2? What's the Future for the Transformers Universe? Here's What its Producer Told Us', *Metro*, 20 November, <https://www.metro.us/entertainment/movies/will-there-be-a-bumblebee-2>.
Wolf, Mark J. P. (2018), 'Transmedia World-Building: History, Conception, and Construction', in Matthew Freeman and Renira Rampazzo Gambarato (eds), *The Routledge Companion to Transmedia Studies*, New York: Routledge, pp. 141–7.

CHAPTER 13

Anticipating the Reboot: Teasing *Top Gun 2*

Paul Grainge

My relation with *Top Gun* (Scott, 1986) has become something of a running joke among friends, family and colleagues. Like others of my generation whose formative film experiences are linked with the phenomenon of high-concept movies in the 1980s (Wyatt 1994), *Top Gun* is both emblematic and nostalgic. Knowing my partiality to the film, I have been given mugs with the *Top Gun* logo, a table mat encasing certified original film stock, a 'Maverick' T-shirt and even dog tags including a personal call sign. In her analysis of the functions of repeat reviewing, Barbara Klinger suggests that familiar movies have the potential to become 'friends' (2006: 154). It is perhaps for this reason that people began pointing me towards various outdoor screenings of *Top Gun* in the UK from the mid-2010s. Tapping into the growing market for outdoor cinema experiences, *Top Gun* has been screened as part of open-air seasons in venues ranging from country parks, castles, botanical gardens and urban rooftops to more context-specific sites such as local airfields. As a 'repeatable classic', *Top Gun* has become ripe for outdoor screenings in its capacity to embody 'karaoke cinema' (Klinger 2006: 181), a nostalgic social event inviting pleasure in the replay of well-known catchphrases, memorable lines, and familiar scenes and songs.

 The status of *Top Gun* as a filmic reference point for Hollywood in the 1980s – stylistically informed by music video, jet-propelling the career of Tom Cruise and portraying naval aviators as 'rock 'n' roll stars of the sky', in the words of director Tony Scott (2004) – heightened anticipation around a potential reboot in the 2010s. As well as friends delighting in sending me promos for open-air *Top Gun* screenings, colleagues would increasingly share social media posts and trade gossip about *Top Gun 2*. Speculation about a sequel began in 2010 when Paramount broached the idea with Scott and the film's original producer, Jerry Bruckheimer. Reflecting on the project before his untimely suicide in 2012, Scott hinted that a new movie would take into consideration developments in military aviation brought about by the shift from dogfights to drones in air warfare. Rumours were sustained by Tom Cruise who commented in different interviews between 2012 and 2015 on his interest in reprising the role of Pete 'Maverick' Mitchell if a suitable story could be worked out. Social media postings intensified rumours, Bruckheimer tweeting a photo of himself with Cruise in January 2016 saying, 'Just got back from a weekend in New Orleans to see my old friend Tom Cruise and discuss a little Top Gun 2'. From 2017, production details began to circulate, Cruise revealing the title *Top Gun: Maverick* in an interview with the American entertainment news programme *Access Hollywood* (2017) and Paramount confirming the director, writers, producers, cast and a provisional release date of summer 2019. Interspersed with official snippets about the film's development was a mixture of fan speculation, movie-site musing and social media cheerleading (and possible job hunting) from original cast members such as Val Kilmer. Having appeared in the original film as Tom 'Ice Man' Kazansky, Kilmer used his Facebook page in 2016 to claim, erroneously, that Gene Hackman and Francis Ford Coppola were involved in the *Top Gun* sequel, and used his Twitter account in 2017 to post images of himself (visibly aged but sporting a T-shirt of his younger self) declaring, 'I'm ready Tom – still got my Top Gun plaque! Still got the moves! Still got it!' (Didymus 2018).

This chapter is less about *Top Gun: Maverick* as a reboot – at the time of writing (mid-2019) the film is still in production with the release date deferred until summer 2020 – than it is about the anticipation of the reboot. Unlike other contributions in this collection, which deal with significant reboots to appear in the last two decades, the chapter is written from a position in which the movie in question does not yet exist. Neither are there, so far, any official trailers, websites or merchandising materials linked to a wider promotional campaign. My focus, quite purposefully, is on the reboot before it has been released or the momentum of advance marketing has begun to build. While Thomas Elsaesser (1998: 16) has likened the arrival of a blockbuster to the turbulence of a weather front, this chapter considers the more gradual changes in atmospheric pressure that precede the Hollywood reboot; it is about the tease, the rumour and the anticipation of the reboot as discursive project. This term points to the pre-emptive forms of industrial and audience talk that give reboots traction in film culture. Using paratexts ranging from DVD bonus features and fan-made trailers to studio-produced imagery, this chapter shifts focus from the reboot as text (what is the reboot?) to the industry and audience relays through which viewers deal with film revivals as prospects (how does the reboot happen?) (Gray 2010: 41). Contributing to work on the paratextual constellations that prefigure media events, I focus on the period in the mid-2010s leading up to the first official publicity still for *Top Gun: Maverick*.

Figure 13.1 Artefacts of *Top Gun* nostalgia, photo by author.

Top Gun: Maverick is not a reboot in the same sense as *Batman Begins* (Nolan, 2005), *Ghostbusters* (Feig, 2016) or numerous other examples where 'a film starts fresh and resets a narrative back to a (new) beginning' (Herbert 2017: 12). The long interval between *Top Gun* and *Top Gun: Maverick* and the reprising of original characters blurs the distinction between sequel and semi-reboot in a strict definitional sense. This blurring was borne out in trade descriptions of the project in the late 2010s which often veered between terms. For example, one article in *Hollywood Reporter* in 2018, headlined '*Top Gun* Reboot Pushed Back a Year', described the project as a 'high-profile sequel' and a 'long-in-the-works follow-up' in the space of a paragraph. Whatever the conceptual slippage between reboot, sequel and follow-up, Paramount's attempt to generate new value from *Top Gun* after thirty years positioned the film as a figurative reboot, a cinematic event marked by the promissory spectacle of supersonic jets.

Rebooting *Top Gun* was part of a wider trend in the 2000s and 2010s for remaking films and television series from the 1980s as high-concept blockbusters. This links to a broader tendency within Hollywood for reworking older media properties as new theatrical features and cross-media platforms. Taking an earlier example, Constantine Verevis (2006) examines the pattern of remaking classic US television series as feature films in the 1990s, ranging from *Maverick* (Donner, 1994) (no relation to *Top Gun*) to the Cruise-starring *Mission: Impossible* (De Palma, 1996). Identifying a different cycle, Kathleen Loock (2016) examines industrial and cultural practices that have given rise to the remaking of 1980s media properties since the turn of the twenty-first century. This ranges from big-screen adaptations of TV series such as *Miami Vice* (Mann, 2006), *Transformers* (Bay, 2007) and *The A-Team* (Carnahan, 2010) to film reboots such as *Tron: Legacy* (Kosinski, 2010), *Footloose* (Brewer, 2011), *The Karate Kid* (Zwart, 2010) and *Mad Max: Fury Road* (Miller, 2015). Describing the cycle as 'retro-remaking', Loock considers the commercial incentives and textual strategies of this cinematic tendency. In business terms, she points out that returning to iconic 1980s movies and TV shows provides studios with opportunities to rejuvenate media properties, selling them anew to cinema's largest target audience, 18 to 24 year olds, while also pitching to the generation for which the films and TV shows are part of 'living memory'. This process can involve using new production technology like computer-generated imaging (CGI) to redefine the look, sense and feel of the story world. However, it can also mean deliberately tapping into the 1980s past of the original as a source of pop-cultural status and value. Retro-remaking, by Loock's definition, often creates a particular temporality that evokes and repackages memories of the 1980s through a movie's codes, music, cameos and so forth, but offers variation in narrative, setting and cast that locates the film in the present. This corresponds with Daniel Herbert's observation that 'reboots try to both remake and extend narratives at the same time' (2017: 39).

Whatever the tone of *Top Gun: Maverick* in its balance of action sensibility and retro repackaging, the prospect of a reboot starring Cruise gave rumours of any such film the status of an event. Analysing the 'paratextual arrays' that form around films and television programmes on the occasion of media anniversaries, Matt Hills (2015) examines the way that media properties are given life as 'unfolding events' at specific milestones. The concept of the unfolding event is useful in thinking about the configuration of 'the tease' beyond discrete textual forms (like the teaser trailer) for it points to the ways in which films and TV programmes are prefigured as discursive projects. Focusing on the proliferation of trailers, merchandise and conventions that accompanied the 50th anniversary of the BBC's flagship science fiction programme *Doctor Who* in 2013, Hills suggests:

> The unfolding event follows a hermeneutic arc which exceeds any one text – it is prefigured via audience expectations, and producer-audience interactions, configured via an array of (para)textual materials, and subsequently refigured by audience understandings and further producer-audience exchanges, as well as forms of cultural recognition (reviews, features and awards). (Hills 2015: 25)

Hills is concerned with the textual and paratextual materials that follow the 'sometimes contingently delayed or rescheduled' release chronologies of films and TV shows as they return, and are recommodified, around anniversaries (2015: 25). *Top Gun 2* went from industry rumour to active development around the time of the film's 30th anniversary in 2016. This was the point when the 'paratextual array' surrounding a reboot intensified and anticipation became marked in a series of conversations, interactions, and studio and fan-produced texts. Developing Hills' concerns with the temporal sequence of paratexts, Carter Moulton examines the Hollywood 'announcement trailer' (a teaser-for-the-teaser-trailer) to consider a specific textual construction and affective sensation that he terms 'speculative nostalgia'. This refers to the way that paratexts 'invite audiences to look forward (anticipate, speculate) while also calling on them, through the deployment of *iconic images*, to look back (nostalgia)' (2018: 3, emphasis in original). In the case of *Top Gun 2*, speculative nostalgia was enacted in a variety of 'pre-textual' forms (Gray 2010: 120), some directly related to the prospect of a reboot and others more discreet in tapping into the memory of the original film.

In previous work on film branding, I examined the increasingly performative role of studio logos in Hollywood film. Focusing on the way that the mountain logo of Paramount was 'brought to life' in various studio films from the 1950s to the 1990s, I argued that studio logos often function at the intersection of recollection and expectation, 'or what might be called the blockbuster's aggregation of memory and hype' (Grainge 2008: 79). Defining Paramount's investment in high-concept film during the 1980s, *Top Gun* used a static version of the studio logo within the original film's opening. Between the film's 20th and 30th anniversaries, however, the Paramount logo underwent substantial digital embellishment. Developments in computer-generated technology provided greater opportunities for movement and narrative integration in the projection of the studio's logo. This was captured in a new digital version of the logo released in 2012 to mark Paramount's centenary. Notable in this case was the dynamic flight of the stars that encircle the mountain. In previous versions of the Paramount logo, the stars enter in the bottom foreground of the frame and fly in a synchronised line towards and around the mountain on the near horizon. In the new version, the stars appear with jet trails from a darkened sky and fly in tight but not identical formation, swooping down and skimming the surface of a lake before propelling upwards to encircle a majestic mountain on the horizon. In this version of the logo, the stars move like fighter jets. Wittingly or not, the digitisation prefigured talk of how the reboot of *Top Gun* – Paramount's quintessential aviation movie – would adapt to a new media, as well as military, context.

Inspired by an article featured in *California* magazine on the 'Top Guns' based at the Miramar Naval Air Station in San Diego, *Top Gun* co-screenwriter Jack Epps Jr (2004) recalled that the original film was initially conceived from a striking point-of-view photograph taken from the cockpit of an F-14. Characterised by co-producer Bruckheimer as '*Star Wars* on Earth', the concept of the movie, Epps Jr explained, was primarily aesthetic: to use real F-14s to give the film 'a look that we haven't seen before'. Production stories often highlight the role of the military in providing hardware and technical expertise. Part of the production folklore of *Top Gun* – worked over in press coverage at the time of the film's release and in subsequent stories about script development and shooting – has coalesced around the use of actual fighter jets and pilots. This folklore is enshrined in a six-part documentary, *Danger Zone: The Making of Top Gun* (2004), made as a DVD bonus feature for a two-disc special edition released around the film's 20th anniversary. Including interviews with cast, crew and military consultants, the documentary proffers 'inside' stories that underline the movie's collaboration with the US military and situates aerial veracity as a distinctive value of the film.

The relation of *Top Gun* to aerial veracity is part of the authenticating discourse of the original film and became a frame for speculation surrounding a reboot. In 2018, the release date of a new *Top Gun* film was put back a year 'in order to provide more time for flight training' (McClintock 2018). While military cooperation was unspecified, the delay, combined with Cruise's reputation for aerial thrill-seeking, hinted that a *Top Gun* reboot would not rely on CGI to re-envision the swooping, skimming and propulsion of aerial combat manoeuvres. The experience of filming in jets while making *Top Gun* became a tested Cruise anecdote in the mid-2010s, sometimes relayed in media interviews for other films. On talk shows around the time of the 30th anniversary of *Top Gun*, ranging from *Jimmy Kimmel Live* (ABC, 2016) to *The Graham Norton Show* (BBC, 2016), Cruise delivered a well-rehearsed story about vomiting during a flight with an F-14 pilot called 'Bozo'. This helped titillate memories of *Top Gun* while promoting action franchises like *Mission: Impossible* where Cruise's aerial stunts became an element of his action star persona. In many ways, the connection of Cruise's star image with real-life aerial stunts began with *Top Gun*. In *Danger Zone: The Making of Top Gun*, Jerry Bruckheimer recounts that Cruise committed to star in the film after being taken up with the Blue Angels, the US Navy's flight demonstration squadron. While Cruise clearly didn't pilot any of the jets in *Top Gun*, his experience of 'barrel-rolls', G-force and other highly physical jet manoeuvres connected Cruise's star image to flying and a sense of cockpit authenticity. *Top Gun* established a discourse of aerial verisimilitude that has continued to function as a promotional feature of action films starring Cruise, and that looped back into the anticipation of a prospective *Top Gun* reboot.

Several months before reports of the *Top Gun* delay, for instance, a series of 'behind-the-scenes' extras for *Mission: Impossible – Fallout* (McQuarrie, 2018) created anticipation for this film's summer release by highlighting Cruise's extensive training for helicopter chase sequences and 'high altitude, low opening' (HALO) parachute jumps. Pointing to the film's aerial set-pieces, digital shorts would authenticate the 'practical action' of *Mission: Impossible – Fallout* and Cruise's skill as a pilot. Paratexts for one Cruise film, in this case, would align with another, reinforcing rumours that *Top Gun*'s deferment was being caused by Cruise insisting on learning how to fly Navy jets (Demerly 2018). Whether or not this story, if true, said more about the ego or commitment of Cruise in wanting to experience (in his words) 'big fast machines' (Access Hollywood 2017), it fed speculation about how a *Top Gun* reboot proposed to work with the legacies of the original film in using fighter jets.

While a *Top Gun* reboot was not confirmed until June 2017, Cruise would coyly admit that 'we're working on it' in interviews through the 2010s, qualifying that 'it's got to be right'. These comments would add to what might be called the 'script tease' playing out in the paratextual array prior to the film's production phase. In developing *Top Gun 2*, for example, screenwriter Justin Marks commented in 2016:

> [W]hen they said they needed a new writer to start to figure out what this movie could be, I really just approached it from that place of, 'Well, what would I not want it to be? What would ruin it for me? What would really, really make me angry if I saw it on screen? How would I start to build a story that would feel like an evolution from the first film, but also feels like something that would very much connect us to why we loved *Top Gun* and Maverick as a character in the first place?' (McKittrick 2016)

For Marks, story 'evolution' turned on developments in aerial combat: how new technologies, from joint strike fighters such as the F-35 to remotely piloted drones, have transformed what *Top Gun* represents in the current era. Military biographer Robert Coram describes the instructors of the Fighter Weapons School (upon which *Top Gun* is based) as 'grand masters of a three-dimensional, high-speed death dance, the most rapidly changing form of combat ever devised' (2002: 72). Since the Gulf War's introduction of 'network-centric warfare' in 1991, however, and the emergence of drones as a tool in the US 'War on Terror', the scope of aerial warfare and the role of the pilot have changed. Talk of a *Top Gun* reboot tapped into these shifts. Commenting on the adaptation of *Top Gun 2* to contemporary military technologies, David Ellison (CEO of Skydance Media, one of the production companies developing *Top Gun 2*) said in 2015: 'When you look at the world of dogfighting, what's interesting about it is that it's not a world that exists to the same degree when the original movie came out . . . so [*Top Gun 2*] is really exploring the end of an era of dogfighting and fighter pilots and what that culture is today' (Campbell 2016). Speculation about *Top Gun 2* would often focus on the extent to which a reboot would render drone technology as part of the 'targeting revolution' transforming air warfare (Kreuzer 2016: 10). However, one anxiety, implied by Marks, was the extent to which drones might ruin the film or disconnect audiences from why they 'loved *Top Gun* and Maverick as a character in the first place'.

In his analysis of the 'sensory assault' of Hollywood action film, Steen Ledet Christiansen suggests that 'contemporary cinema is entering the drone age' (2017: 1). Christiansen uses this term in reference to the production of audiovisual spectacle. He writes: 'Action cinema works through bodily forces that stun our senses, and for more than a decade the genre's audiovisual barrage has taken on an unprecedented intensity and speed, adapting to shifting cultural and technological environments' (2017: 1). While Christiansen is interested in theorising new modes of perception in action cinema, 'acclimatizing audiences for warfare' by the terms of his argument, he considers the way that 'droning' is a modality in many action films, a condition of being terrorised linked in no small part to the 'turbulent sound of drone tones' (2017: 144). Unlike the dogfights of *Top Gun*, memorably set to thrusting rock anthems, Christiansen suggests that drones suffuse a mood of threat and terror via the remoteness of their pilots and the monotony of their pitch. An issue in the speculative nostalgia surrounding *Top Gun 2* became how to update military context without succumbing to the figurative and literal dullness of drones. How, in other words, to reboot the physical presence of the pilot in the 'danger zone' and supercharge the soundtrack in the haptic sensation of the film.

Fan-made trailers circulating on digital spaces such as YouTube became a particular source of imagining narrative and aesthetic scenarios in the context of the drone age. Discussing fan-made trailers as incarnations of audience anticipation and desire, Kathleen Williams considers how recut trailers become performances of knowledge with the Hollywood system, and reveal how audiences actively look forward to a film as prospect, even when hypothetical. She argues that 'recut trailers allow users and audiences to revisit, rework and augment their memory of a feature film, identifying latent story lines, shifting the genre of a film, or allowing a character from a film to exist in a newly imagined film' (2016: 261). Fan-made trailers point to the types of viewer-created paratexts that would come to surround *Top Gun 2* as discursive project. These short-forms would often intercut real footage of stealth fighters with images of drones, or use news clips to establish drones as a potential narrative subject. One fan trailer, for example (with 3.8 million views at the time of writing), recreated *Top Gun*'s opening sequence by showing stealth fighters launching from an aircraft carrier, overlaying Harold Faltermeyer's 'Top Gun anthem' with audio news commentary reporting Freedom of Information Act revelations that 'over 400 military drones have crashed worldwide since 2001' ('Top Gun 2 Trailer' 2015). In other trailers ('Top Gun 2 Trailer' 2018), drones become the projection of enemy power, shifting the reboot away from the original movie's identity as a competition film. In 1980s high-concept mode, aerial combat in *Top Gun* was largely figured as a sporting event (Epps Jr, 2004); the film gave licence to the representation of locker rooms, trophies and beach volleyball scenes that displayed the physicality of flyboys. Fan trailers in the 2010s, meanwhile, recast the reboot in the generic mode of contemporary action cinema, combining aerial footage from the original *Top Gun* with CGI sequences from Hollywood action movies depicting fighter jets in spectacular military conflict.

Many fan-made trailers intermixed footage of Cruise in *Top Gun* with his appearance in more recent action movies (notably the *Mission: Impossible* and *Jack Reacher* franchises and *War of the Worlds* (Spielberg, 2005)) that show him riding motorbikes or wearing military uniform. These juxtapositions were used to signal the interplay of young and mature Maverick. One fan-made trailer (with 2.9 million views at the time of writing) used intertitles to convey the relation between past and present in the character of Maverick, beginning with the potentially parodic 'he used to play volleyball', following with the more sincere 'he then became an instructor' and ending with classic trailer invocation, 'now he's back'. Fan-made trailers comprise part of the textual array that anticipates reboots. Allowing the character of Maverick to exist in a newly imagined military world, these paratexts parse the film's depiction of contemporary aerial combat but also help revisit and rework the presence of Cruise himself. If the dramatic tension of the original film involved the post-traumatic experience of young Maverick overcoming the death of his friend/navigator 'Goose' to prove himself a trustworthy 'wingman', the reboot offered the anticipation of 'afterwardsness' (Sutton 2010) in seeing Maverick as a veteran Top Gun instructor.

The transition in title from *Top Gun 2* to *Top Gun: Maverick* reflected the centrality of Cruise to the project as it developed in the 2010s. The pre-sold title and star presence of Cruise maintained a clear textual relation with the original film, and marked the actor's shift from possible cameo to confirmed lead. The overlay of characters and roles played by Cruise since *Top Gun*, notably in action films, would give the character of Maverick a particular inflection. Adding to the script tease was the gradual confirmation of cast members across 2017 and 2018, a list which mixed seasoned actors like Ed Harris, Jon Hamm, Val Kilmer and Jennifer Connelly with younger actors such as Miles Teller, reportedly playing the role of Goose's son. This aligned with other 'retro' reboots such as *Star Wars: The Force Awakens* (Abrams, 2015) where marketing was built on speculative nostalgia around the 'homecoming' of original characters/actors (Han Solo, Princess Leia, Chewbacca) and the role of a new and more diverse set of main character leads (Rey, Finn) (Golding 2019). Casting information, and the announcement of Joseph Kosinski as director (who worked with Cruise on *Oblivion* (Kosinski, 2013) and directed prior reboots such as *Tron: Legacy*), would point to the film's scale and status within Hollywood's 1980s film cycle.

While retro-remaking often self-consciously activates 'memories of the original and the 1980s past to which it belongs' (Loock 2016: 288), the discursive anticipation of *Top Gun: Maverick* generally eschewed the parody that has developed around certain 'karaoke' features of the original, whether the movie's combat-rock video style or the homo-eroticism of the film's buddy dynamic (Freeman 2015: 120). Listing six things that 'need to happen' in a *Top Gun* reboot, the video blog site Hollywood News (2017) made a plea that the film 'must not be a parody of itself, it must not be intentionally comedic'. This judgement was borne out in the speculative nostalgia of showbiz reporting. Anticipation of a reboot seized on stills and videos from the production set that evoked and echoed the original film. For instance, photos of Cruise astride a motorbike in fighter jacket and shades, taken on set in November 2018, invited forensic examination of the jacket's insignia and curiosity about the prospective love interest riding pillion rather than wry retro commentary.

From 'the need for speed' to 'playing with the boys', *Top Gun* has become a quotable pop-cultural artefact. Speculative nostalgia among producers, audiences and media reporters was linked to the circulation of images that reparsed the film's iconicity. It is here that we might return to Moulton's suggestion that announcement texts 'invite audiences to look forward (anticipate, speculate) while also calling on them, through the deployment of *iconic images*, to look back (nostalgia)' (2018: 3, emphasis in original). In his examination of announcement trailers, Moulton considers short promotional texts, ranging from 10 to 60 seconds in length, that use a 'reveal-conceal structure' to create anticipation by offering cues and clues for upcoming blockbuster movies. He suggests that announcement trailers 'are not merely a part of but *launch* a discursive project, quickly sketching a "horizon of expectations" for the film' (2018: 3). Part of my purpose is to suggest that discursive projects are launched some time before the formalisation of studio publicity and promotion; movies are teased into being, and positioned as prospects, through interplays of trade talk, rumour, and industrial and fan projection. The speculative nostalgia that Moulton associates with the announcement trailer is suggestive, however, and relates to the hermeneutics of reboot return. Pointing to what he calls the 'inter-temporality of Hollywood blockbusters', Moulton writes:

> The intensified recycling and repackaging of blockbuster properties by the entertainment industries directly impacts the way that audiences participate in and make sense of media culture, and in this context, announcement trailers become rich sites for considering how viewing experiences of the past, present and future are made to converge. (2018: 4)

In drawing out this temporal convergence, Moulton suggests that announcement trailers often use iconic images to 'mobilize nostalgia as part of a self-promoting discourse' but juxtapose these with images or sounds that are unfamiliar to create an 'aesthetics of speculation' (2018: 6). On these terms, announcement trailers are significant for how they 'structure popular media consumption as a non-linear movement through personal memory, media history, and affective *time*' (2018: 4, emphasis in original).

This temporal movement is not simply a feature of trailers. It also defined the first publicity still for *Top Gun: Maverick*. Released on 30 May 2018 through Cruise's Twitter account, along with the hashtag 'Day 1', the poster showed Cruise in his flight gear, holding a helmet down by his side, gazing backwards at an F-18 Super Hornet. Evoking one of the key quotes from the original film, the image included the tagline 'Feel the Need' written boldly across the middle of the poster. The speculative nostalgia, in this case, was inscribed through the image of Cruise actually rebooting in military readiness for twenty-first-century aerial combat. While the figure of Maverick gazing at a jet evoked the past – Cruise literally looking backwards – the jet itself, slightly out of focus, invited speculation about which aircraft it was and what fighter and pilot could now do. The temporal construction was vested in details of the image: the backward-facing stance of Cruise, the hint of his Ray-Bans, the presence of a jet and not a drone, the familiarity and weathering of the striped flight helmet bearing the call sign Maverick. However, speculative nostalgia was also established through the image's colour and tinting. While *Top Gun*'s 'air' and 'land' story was distinguished by skies that were either shades of cobalt blue or pastel-orange – the original movie adopting an intensified audiovisual style associated with music video – the announcement poster was sepia, using a palette of yellow-grey. With the classic Paramount logo featured in miniature at the bottom-centre of the image, the 'textual construction and affective sensation' of the promotional image extended forwards and backwards in time. As the visual teaser to the announcement trailer, the poster played with the legacy of *Top Gun*'s high-concept marketing aesthetic, providing a frame that confirmed the reboot was happening and in a style that suggested, per Cruise, that 'it's going to be in the same vein, the same tone as the first one, but a progression for Maverick' (Access Hollywood 2017). 'Feel the need' was not posed as a question in the promotional address of the poster but, rather, as an invocation to audiences in the film's affective coalescing of memory and hype.

Writing this chapter has posed the methodological challenge of how to write about a reboot that has not yet been released. As of May 2019, IMDb lists production and cast information and provides an image (discussed above) but teasingly states 'the plot is unknown at this time' (IMDb 2019). The phrasing 'at this time' suggests further unfolding in the event status of *Top Gun: Maverick*. By considering film as a discursive project, including the kind of rumour and anticipation that swirls before a promotional campaign takes hold, my analysis taps into criticism that explores paratextual temporalities and convergences that occur 'when "the text" has yet to manifest itself as consumable object' (Scott 2017: 139). Moving beyond the isolation of paratext-text relations, this approach throws into relief the temporal flow of paratexts, and the particular challenge for media criticism of ascertaining which flow audiences experience. In this vein, Robert Brookey and Jonathan Gray invite paratextual analysis to ask: 'Which paratexts are loud and which paratexts are quiet? Which are the ones we cannot avoid and which are the ones we are more likely to avoid? And how do different paratexts create different we's there too?' (2017: 105). Accounting for 'anticipation' is variable. My forty-something *Top Gun* fandom may dispose me to a different sequence of paratexts from my slightly younger sister, who first noticed an entertainment story on her Facebook feed, or my teenage son who had to 'ask Alexa' what *Top Gun* was about. For some, anticipation may come with the 'paratextual panic' that Suzanne Scott associates with 'fans trying to infer too much textual understanding about a hotly anticipated film from a limited array of movie trailers, t-shirts and toys' (2017: 139). For others, it may be more routine, part and parcel of Hollywood's promotional churn of Cruise movies and franchise revivals.

To some extent, *Top Gun 2* became a discursive project as soon as the original was released in 1986. An immediate box office hit, the film was also a success in the nascent market of home video, breaking sales records and pioneering commercial video tie-ins when the 'cassette' was released in 1987 (Hunt 1987). Rumours of a sequel first began to circulate in the immediate wake of *Top Gun*'s success, Paramount hoping to release another film by drawing upon leftover flying footage. In the end, the fact that the original movie had used all available frames of the starring F-14s thwarted the studio's commercial need for a speedy *Top Gun 2*. The prehistory of *Top Gun 2* as reboot demonstrates the sometimes fitful way that Hollywood develops projects over time. My concern is the foretelling of promise that attends to film as an unfolding event. As 'prospects', reboots generate hype similar to other blockbusters but the discursivity of anticipation is potentially different in the media temporalities they inscribe. Rather than examine the production history of *Top Gun* as reboot or the promotional campaign surrounding *Top Gun: Maverick*, I have focused on the coalescing of the tease. Revealing the dynamics of speculation and nostalgia that accompany Hollywood reboots, the tease points to a moment of anticipation, levied in paratexts, that helps shape the hermeneutic arc of film and in which 'specific temporal structures are shaped, shared, revised and felt' (Moulton 2018: 1). Situating promotional and paratextual analysis before the Hollywood reboot is filmed, formed or fully known, this chapter proposes the value of studying media properties as prospects and the discursive perambulations that occur before blockbusters 'buzz the tower' at the level of marketing noise.

REFERENCES

Access Hollywood (2017), 'Exclusive: Tom Cruise Reveals the Title for the "Top Gun" Sequel!', *YouTube*, 2 June <https://www.youtube.com/watch?v=O_qJ2ne3OiI>.
Brookey, Robert and Jonathan Gray (2017), '"Not Merely Para": Continuing Steps in Paratextual Research', *Critical Studies in Media Communication*, 34: 2, 101–10.
Campbell, Christopher (2016), 'Will We See Top Gun 2?: Here's What We Know', *Fandango*, 16 May, <https://www.fandango.com/movie-news/will-we-see-top-gun-2-heres-what-we-know-750864>.
Christiansen, Steen Ledet (2017), *Drone Age Cinema*, London: I. B. Tauris.
Coram, Robert (2002), *Boyd: The Fighter Pilot Who Changed the Art of War*, New York: Black Bay Books.
Demerly, Tom (2018), 'Tom Cruise Learning to Fly an F/A-18 and Other *Top Gun: Maverick* Rumors', *The Aviationist*, 10 December, <https://theaviationist.com/2018/11/10/tom-cruise-learning-to-fly-an-f-a-18-and-other-top-gun-maverick-rumors/>.
Didymus, John Thomas (2018), 'Top Gun: Maverick Release Date: Cast, Plot, Soundtrack Details Revealed as Sequel to Tom Cruise's Hit Movie Coming in 2020', *Monsters and Critics*, 31 August <https://www.monstersandcritics.com/movies/top-gun-maverick-release-update-cast-plot-soundtrack-details/>.
Elsaesser, Thomas (1998), 'The Blockbuster: Everything Connects, but Not Everything Goes', in Jon Lewis (ed.), *The End of Cinema As We Know It*, London: Pluto Press, pp. 11–22.
Epps Jr, Jack (2004), interview in *Danger Zone: The Making of Top Gun*, Paramount Home Video.
Freeman, Hadley (2015), *Life Moves Pretty Fast*, London: Fourth Estate.
Golding, Dan (2019), *Star Wars After Lucas*, Minneapolis, MN: University of Minnesota Press.
Grainge, Paul (2008), *Brand Hollywood: Selling Entertainment in a Global Media Age*, London: Routledge.
Gray, Jonathan (2010), *Show Sold Separately: Promos, Spoilers, and other Media Paratexts*, New York: New York University Press.
Herbert, Daniel (2017), *Film Remakes and Franchises*, New Brunswick, NJ: Rutgers University Press.
Hills, Matt (2015), *Doctor Who: The Unfolding Event*, New York: Palgrave Macmillan.

Hollywood News (2017), 'Top Gun 2: 6 Things That Need to Happen in the Sequel', *YouTube*, 22 June, <https://www.youtube.com/watch?v=Gi2MpvFMnX4>.

Hunt, Dennis (1987), 'Top Gun Cassette Breaks Sales Barrier', *Los Angeles Times*, 20 March, H22, <https://www.latimes.com/archives/la-xpm-1987-03-20-ca-8138-story.html>.

IMDb (2019), 'Top Gun: Maverick', <https://www.imdb.com/title/tt1745960/>.

Klinger, Barbara (2006), *Beyond the Multiplex: Cinema, New Technologies, and the Home*, Berkeley, CA: University of California Press.

Kreuzer, Michael P. (2016), *Drones and the Future of Air Warfare*, Abingdon: Routledge.

Loock, Kathleen (2016), 'Retro-remaking: the 1980s Film Cycle in Contemporary Hollywood Cinema', in Amanda Ann Klein and R. Barton Palmer (eds), *Cycles, Sequels, Spin-Offs, Remakes, and Reboots: Multiplicities in Film and Television*, Austin, TX: University of Texas Press, pp. 277–97.

McClintock, Pamela (2018), '"Top Gun" Reboot Pushed Back a Year; "A Quiet Place 2" Will Open in Summer 2020', *Hollywood Reporter*, 29 August, <https://www.hollywoodreporter.com/news/a-quiet-place-sequel-gets-release-date-1138392>.

McKittrick, Christopher (2016), 'King of the Swingers: Justin Marks on *The Jungle Book*', *Creative Screenwriting*, 19 April, <https://creativescreenwriting.com/king-of-the-swingers-justin-marks-on-the-jungle-book/>.

Moulton, Carter (2018), '"Announcement" Trailers and the Inter-temporality of Hollywood Blockbusters', *International Journal of Cultural Studies*, 22: 3, 434–49.

Scott, Suzanne (2017), '#Wheresrey?: Toys, Spoilers, and the Gender Politics of Franchise Paratexts', *Critical Studies in Media Communication*, 34: 2, 138–47.

Scott, Tony (2004), interview in *Danger Zone: The Making of Top Gun*, Paramount Home Video.

Sutton, Paul (2010), 'Prequel: The "Afterwardsness" of the Sequel', in Carolyn Jess-Cooke and Constantine Verevis (eds), *Second Takes: Critical Approaches to the Film Sequel*, Albany, NY: SUNY Press, pp. 139–51.

'Top Gun 2 Trailer' (2015), *YouTube*, 24 September, <https://www.youtube.com/watch?v=x1YZEvuVPoI>.

'Top Gun 2 Trailer' (2018), *YouTube*, 26 June, <https://www.youtube.com/watch?v=8fi7G1s97wA>.

Verevis, Constantine (2006), *Film Remakes*, Edinburgh: Edinburgh University Press.

Williams, Kathleen (2016), 'Extended Attractions: Recut Trailers, Film Promotion, and Audience Desire', in Amanda Ann Klein and R. Barton Palmer (eds), *Cycles, Sequels, Spin-Offs, Remakes, and Reboots: Multiplicities in Film and Television*, Austin, TX: University of Texas Press, pp. 260–76.

Wyatt, Justin (1994), *High Concept: Movies and Marketing in Hollywood*, Austin, TX: University of Texas Press.

CHAPTER 14

A Dark Knight on Elm Street: Discursive Regimes of (Sub)Cultural Value, Paratextual Bonding, and the Perils of Remaking and Rebooting Canonical Horror Cinema

William Proctor

In many accounts, American horror cinema has been in a state of perpetual crisis since the 1970s, a decade that has often been viewed as the cradle of 'New Horror', of a body of 'progressive, exploratory, often radical' (Wood 2018: 400) films 'characterized by countercultural themes and typified by the early work of such filmmakers as George A. Romero, Tobe Hooper, Wes Craven, John Carpenter and David Cronenberg' (Mann 2019: 20). Although there may be at least some degree of legitimacy regarding the ideological health of horror cinema during the period, the way in which this grandest of narratives has been continuously re-ascribed and re-enforced over forty years or so is less about incontestable 'truths' than it is about 'discursive regimes of [sub] cultural value' (Tompkins 2014), discourses that characterise select cult objects as oppositional 'art'.

It is these discursive regimes that feed into the 'rhetoric of crisis' attached to American horror cinema between the 1980s and 2000s, a narrative undergirded by moral dualisms between 'good' and 'bad' objects (Hills 2002), between 'horror-as-art' (Hills 2005) and commercial horror. As Steffan Hantke emphasises, 'it is when measured against this criteria of canonization – transgressiveness coupled with the mystique of rebellion and subversiveness – that contemporary horror films, with their mainstream credentials, fall short' (2010: xviii). Regardless of the fact that 'any characterisation of modern horror or 1970s horror as a totality is bound to be schematic', risking 'a limited one-dimensional account of horror' (Hutchings 2004: 188, 191), it is the discursive force and frequency of these arguments that subscribe to New Horror as existing outside of market forces and commercial, corporate logics. Yet this idea of a mainstream commercial cinema neatly bracketed off from a low-budget, progressive, underground cult cinema remains 'one of the most problematic concepts in film studies'

(Jancovich 2002: 231), one which fails to deal with 'the fact that most of these "other" films were likewise made to maximize profits' (Church 2010: 236). To this, Pierre Bourdieu's assessment of the art/commerce binary seems fitting:

> The opposition between the 'commercial' and the 'noncommercial' reappears everywhere. It is the generative principle of most of the judgements which, in the theater, cinema, painting or literature, claim to establish the frontier between what is and what is not art. (1993: 82)

Applied to American horror cinema, 'the generative principle' that establishes 'the frontier between what is and what is not art' arguably lies in moral dualisms between (good) 'originality' and (bad) 'repetition'. If we accept for a moment that the 1970s produced some of the most sacred and divine texts of the horror film canon, then it is understandable that the 'mindless series of remakes' (Hantke 2007: 91–2) produced between the late 1990s and the first decade of the new millennium would potentially be seen by cultish fan audiences as blasphemy, as a sacrilegious assault on the church of New Horror. In many cases, 'even the potential to ruin an existing film, or the memories associated with it, leads audiences to reject the new versions a priori' (Mee 2017: 202).

During this period, there was arguably no production company that bore the brunt of fan antagonism more than Platinum Dunes. Launched in 2001 by director Michael Bay, Brad Fuller and Andrew Form, the fledgling studio risked baiting a generation of horror fans for whom 'the raw, meat poetry' of films like *The Texas Chain Saw Massacre* (Hooper, 1974) stand as a fortress against 'the sleek high-gloss rhetoric of commercial entertainment' (Lee 2008); fans who cast bids for subcultural capital as a way of shoring up their status as 'real' fans, as connoisseurs and cognoscenti who 'seek to construct identities through the construction of an inauthentic Other' (Jancovich 2002: 306). As online fans are frequently interpellated as buzz-builders and spreaders by production cultures seeking free labour and viral publicity (see Caldwell 2008), the general response to horror remakes and reboots indicates that the producer/fan relationship can just as easily turn sour, which is to say that that fans can quickly become a discursive threat as buzz-killers and anti-fans. In 2009, for example, Platinum Dunes cancelled plans to remake Alfred Hitchcock's *The Birds* (1960) and Roman Polanski's *Rosemary's Baby* (1968) reportedly due to fan backlash (Child 2009). In the grand pursuit of subcultural capital (Thornton 1995), fans often view remakes and reboots as symbolic attacks on totemic objects (Proctor 2017); 'inauthentic horror' dressed in the rotten skin of corporate zombies; and silver bullets shot through the heart of canonical horror cinema.

It is within this fraught, agitated context that Platinum Dunes produced a remake of Wes Craven's *A Nightmare on Elm Street* (1984), a film that sought to reboot the franchise for a new audience and a new millennium, yet ultimately failed to do so despite becoming Platinum Dunes' highest-grossing film at that point. It is important to distinguish between remakes and reboots here given that the terms have been used interchangeably in both press and academic discourse 'despite describing very different products' (Kendrick 2017: 250). In basic terms, a remake is a re-interpretation of a self-contained film, whereas 'what can be said to immediately identify a reboot is the fact that it initiates *a series of texts*' (Gil 2014: 25–6, emphasis added). Put differently, 'a reboot "re-starts" a series of films' by 'beginning again' with a new narrative sequence (Proctor 2012: 4). To complicate matters, a film can be both a remake and a reboot simultaneously: Platinum Dunes' *A Nightmare on Elm Street* (Bayer, 2010) is a remake of Wes Craven's 1984 film, yet it also attempts to reboot the franchise by reactivating the series from year zero. As it did not in the end spark future instalments in the rebooted sequence, however, it is best to view the 2010 Elm Street as both a remake and a 'failed reboot' (Proctor 2012; 2018; forthcoming; see also Verevis 2017: 162).

What is immediately striking is that the healthy economic performance of the Elm Street remake, which accumulated a worldwide gross of $115,664,037 against a production budget of $35 million, seriously undermines the idea that box office performance is the predominant factor undergirding sequel production, as well as complicating the 'pre-sold' and 'instant recognition' philosophy as a transcendental formula for success. However, in this chapter I am less interested in charting the reasons why the film failed to spark a sequel than I am in examining a sample of promotional, 'entry-way paratexts' (Gray 2010) that preceded the release of the film. These paratexts were strategically mobilised to navigate 'the canonical legacy' (Tompkins 2014) of Wes Craven's authorship – for the purposes of this chapter, his 'author-function' (Foucault 1969) – by activating Christopher Nolan's directorial imprimatur, attached to the Batman reboot, *Batman Begins* (2005), and its sequel, *The Dark Knight* (2008). Appealing to what I term a *brand-function* in pre-release interviews, I want to consider the role that directors and their films can have in establishing discursive regimes of (sub)cultural value that are appended to film projects that they were not connected with. We can also witness how Bayer's lack of authorial prestige, in the face of Craven's subcultural weight as horror auteur, is strategically negotiated not through direct confrontation – a discursive struggle that Bayer would undoubtedly lose – but through circumnavigation or valorisation. In this chapter, I will argue that Bayer attempted to bid for distinction, value and belief in the remake by suggesting a paratextual bond between distinct film properties of Batman and Freddy Krueger. In doing so, the *Elm Street* remake/failed reboot serves as a critical lens with which to examine the way in which auteurism may be mobilised in service of promotional rhetorics, and may shift from text to paratext, and from 'author-function' to 'brand-function'.

The chapter is split into two sections. The first discusses film authorship as a 'function of discourse', as Michel Foucault would put it (1969), considering the way in which Christopher Nolan and Wes Craven's directorial prestige operates as an 'author-function'; the second moves on to examine a sample of entry-way paratexts used to promote the *Elm Street* remake/failed reboot.

THE IMPORTANCE OF BEING AN AUTHOR (FUNCTION)

As a discourse, authorship is the product of several arenas colliding and coalescing into a meta-narrative of sorts, a collaboration of fan voices, 'critical industrial practices' (Caldwell 2008), entertainment journalism, academic work and, of course, authors themselves. I am particularly interested in the way in which entry-way paratexts position film directors as auteurs and as brands. As Jonathan Gray explains:

> [a] prime function that authors serve is classificatory. To say that something is the work of a particular author is (a) to offer a certain guarantee of quality predicated on the name value of that author and (b) to frame one's understanding of the current work within the context of meanings and themes from other works to which the author's name is attached. In this regard, authors become genres and brands. (2014)

One of the ways in which the use-value of authors is employed in service of exchange-value is via entry-way paratexts that seek to assign value to a film to mark it as the work of a bona fide auteur in order to bid for consecration as 'art'. However, the auteur/commercial director binary fails to address the way in which auteurs are often activated for commercial purposes and branding opportunities as well. As Timothy Corrigan has argued, 'despite its often overstated countercultural pretensions, auteurism became a deft move in establishing a model that would dominate and stabilize critical reception . . . as a kind of brand-name vision that precedes and succeeds the film', generating 'an artistic (and specifically Romantic) aura' (1991: 102). For Corrigan, the figure of the auteur becomes 'a *commercial* strategy for organizing audience reception, as a critical concept bound to distribution and marketing aims that identify and address the potential cult status of an auteur' (1991: 103, emphasis in original). Foucault's concept of the 'author-function' situates authors as 'projections . . . of our way of handling texts: in the comparisons we make, the traits we exact as pertinent, the continuities we assign, or the exclusions we practice' (1969: 127). An author-function is instead 'a means of classification' that is 'strongly reminiscent of Christian exegesis when it wished to prove the value of a text by ascertaining the holiness of its author' (1969: 127).

In *Hunting the Dark Knight*, Will Brooker draws upon Foucault's author-function concept, charting the construction of Nolan's directorial cachet as it evolved across several stages of meaning-making: 'from posters, previews and press kits through the professional reviews of journalists to the amateur, but no less informed and arguably more invested, public responses of audience members' (2012: 25). Around the time of *Batman Begins*, Nolan was recognised and appreciated as 'an individual artist and stylist', yet 'his name had not yet become commercially useful to the studio, or recognizable to reviewers, as a brand' (2012: 16). At this stage, Nolan 'is almost drowned out by competing discourses' (2012: 25), not least of all by 'the thunder of the "Batman" brand' (2012: 31). Hence, 'the romantic sense of the director as an "homme du cinema" is, therefore, entirely absent' at this juncture and, instead, 'this is Batman's party' (2012: 12).

By the time of the director's next film, *The Prestige* (2006), 'Nolan's brand, bolstered by the success of *Batman Begins*, rose to prominence without the interference of existing, competing discourses' and, consequently, 'began to come into its own as a signifier of quality and a guarantor of certain values' (2012: 25). Although Nolan's newly developed authorial prestige is quietened by the *Batman* brand once more with the release of *The Dark Knight* in 2008, Nolan 'is now a stronger voice, and his 2005 reboot has been judged successful in wiping the slate clean of previous traces' (2012: 29). As *The Dark Knight* became the first billion-dollar film in history at the North American box office and attracted considerable critical praise, Nolan's directorial status continued to evolve, and by the time of the theatrical release of his *Inception* in 2010, 'Nolan's author-function had arrived: it had evolved into a powerful, unambiguous stamp of quality and a guarantor of values' (2012: 34).

In the context of horror cinema, Wes Craven may be recognised nowadays as an auteur, most notably since the director's passing in 2015, but he has been more often pronounced as a 'renowned horror auteur' in academic work (Wee 2006; see also Muir 1998); a 'Master of Horror' in DVD/Blu-Ray paratexts (especially those distributed in boutique editions by cult gentrification specialists Arrow); and a parent of New Horror 'who has thrice pulled cinematic horror up from the flames of self-annihilation' (Muir 1998: 1). Craven's reputation as cultish horror auteur nevertheless encourages bids for distinction through the cult 'art' and mainstream commerce binary. Robin Wood (2018) may have argued that Craven's first film, *The Last House on the Left* (1972), is cinematic art, but the critical establishment was not so kind. Indeed, the negative reception of the film, which led to protests calling for the film's removal from cinemas, demonstrated that Craven was not considered an auteur, but 'the party who wrote this sickening tripe and also directed the inept actors', as Howard Thompson wrote for *The New York Times* (1972). Evidently, there is a difference between a ('good') bona fide auteur and a ('bad') cult and/or horror auteur, at least within certain interpretative communities. However, what is important is that a 'bad' horror auteur may be deified (and reified) within fan cultures as an 'Author-god', as 'good' cultish object, and testament to further cultural distinctions and hierarchies. As creator, writer and director of *A Nightmare on Elm Street*, however, Craven's author-function began to steadily transition from obscure cult director to popular, well-known brand name. It was 'the film that finally propelled Wes Craven into the big league' (Robb 1998: 61).

The diachronic passage of Craven's author-function has been given extra oxygen through critical and academic considerations of the *Elm Street* sequels as 'bad' objects. Craven himself had publicly denounced the franchise on many occasions, decrying the trajectory of the series as 'a little more commercial', and 'like making cheeseburgers': 'You get a formula for something that satisfies the appetite, and then you make it over and over again and make a business out of it' (Wells 2000: 93). Here, Craven essentially 'self-fashions' himself as a non-commercial, cult auteur standing in protest against an egregious fast food cinema, which is flipped and sold without intellectual nourishment. (Incidentally, Craven's ideological and artistic posturing did not prevent him from producing four films in the highly commercial *Scream* franchise.) Yet whereas Craven may be forever attached as the towering auteur of the first *Elm Street* film – as in Wes Craven's *A Nightmare on Elm Street*, an appellation branded on film posters in 1984 (see Robb 1998: 61, 77) – it is less likely that Jack Sholder, Chuck Russell, Renny Harlin, Stephen Hopkins or Rachel Talahay are recognised as auteurs of their *Elm Street* sequels. As Karra Shimabukuro states, the *Elm Street* series 'moved from [Craven's] auteur film to *just another cog in the studio system*, with specific goals of making the series a more commercial piece' (2015: 58, emphasis added). As such, these discursive regimes of (sub) cultural value and oppositional taste, ultimately construct an auratic barrier that sequels, remakes and reboots struggle to breach. Given the sonic boom of Craven's horror auteur-function, his prestige as creator of dream demon Freddy Krueger, and the canonical legacy of *A Nightmare on Elm Street*, perhaps Bayer's remake was always fated to fail.

FROM AUTHOR-FUNCTION TO BRAND-FUNCTION

Platinum Dunes' original remit – to remake canonical horror films from the 1970s and 1980s – was likely to be contentious from the start. Although many of Platinum Dunes' remakes and reboots were box office triumphs, arguably serving to encourage the company to continue raiding the cult archives, the online fan backlash gained significant traction as the 2000s progressed. It seems that Platinum Dunes was not aware of the minority horror fan audiences' cult proclivities, but rather that the idea of remaking the seminal slasher movie [*The Texas Chainsaw Massacre*] was in part motivated by research showing that 90 per cent of the film's anticipated core audience (eighteen-to-twenty-four-year-old males) knew the title of Tobe Hooper's original but had never seen it. (Verevis 2006: 146).

Laura Mee's suggestion that fannish 'rhetoric [which] implies that the remaking process changes, challenges, or damages the earlier text, aesthetically, emotionally, or even economically' is 'inaccurate' (2017: 202), but such a viewpoint takes fans' complaints far too literally, as opposed to symbolically and affectively. For horror fans who cast bids for subcultural capital by demonising remakes as blasphemous 'Others', which, in turn, (re-)commemorates and (re-)establishes the originals as sacred and holy, the 'earlier text' *is* 'damaged' at the symbolic level (see Proctor 2017). While not entirely 'wrong' per se, Mee's cold rationality fails to understand the discursive regimes of (sub)cultural value that underscore fan discourses of this type: not as literal, but as metaphorical enactments.

By the same token, it is not only the holy 'aura' of the canonical horror film that is threatened by remakes and reboots, but the figure of the anointed horror auteur as well. It is plausible that hiring a director with subcultural capital of his or her own might lessen the potential for backlash, at least to some extent. For instance, the remake of Wes Craven's *The Hills Have Eyes* (1977) seems to have repelled at least some backlash by involving Craven as producer, and by hiring Alexandre Aja to direct; prior to the remake of *The Hills Have Eyes* (2006), Aja had accumulated a degree of subcultural capital in horror circles with his 'New Wave of French Horror' film *Haute Tension/Switchblade Romance* (2003). Conversely, Platinum Dunes' remakes 'were helmed by directors with a track record in video and television commercials' (Heffernan 2014: 61), a strategy that would keep costs as low as possible. However, hiring Marcus Nispel to direct the remake of *The Texas Chainsaw Massacre* (2003) would force negative comparisons not only between the original and the new version, but between the two directors as well. Essentially, Nispel's career as a director of music videos and commercials, with *The Texas Chainsaw Massacre* being his debut feature film, was a match neither for the canonical legacy of the film itself nor for Tobe Hopper's reputation as horror-auteur *par excellence*. In other words, Nispel did not possess enough of an authorial reputation with which to brand the remake, and perhaps symbolically defend it against criticism from the horror fan culture.

Like Nispel, Samuel Bayer began his career as a music video director, and the *Elm Street* remake was his first and, at the time of writing, his last feature film. Although Bayer may have accumulated at least some (sub)cultural capital as the director of Nirvana's 'Smells Like Teen Spirit' music video (1991) and, to a lesser extent, Green Day's 'Boulevard of Broken Dreams' (2004) – both of which are invoked in the *Elm Street* remake's electronic press kit (EPK) – he did not, like Nispel, possess a level of directorial prestige that could negotiate the power of Craven's authorship. As such, Bayer pointed away from Craven as much as possible, although not invariably, by mobilising the 'Nolan Function' (Brooker 2012) as a way to discursively promote the film. It did this not by confronting the canonical legacy of the 'Craven Function', but by suggesting a paratextual bond with Nolan's first two *Batman* films, the superhero origin story and the reboot concept as narrative template:

> I like what Christopher Nolan did with Batman. I think Tim Burton is an amazing director, but I think that Christopher Nolan reinvented, to a certain degree, the superhero genre. Heath Ledger's portrayal made people forget about Jack Nicholson. The new Batmobile made me forget about the old Batmobile . . . That's the way we're approaching Nightmare. (McCabe 2010: 36)

At the core of Bayer's narrative lie the concepts of memory and 'forgetting' (Harvey 2015), both of which are central to the reboot concept: memories of Tim Burton, the old Batmobile and Jack Nicholson as the Joker. Just as Nolan's *Batman Begins* 'forgets' Burton's *Batman* films – and more pointedly, Joel Schumacher's *Batman and Robin* (1997), the film that sent the *Batman* film series to cultural purgatory for almost a decade – Bayer is seemingly advocating that his *Elm Street* remake will 'make people forget' Craven's *Elm Street*. Suggesting that 'the way we're approaching Nightmare' by encouraging a paratextual bond with *Batman Begins*, and *The Dark Knight*, is also to suggest that the source material for the remake is not Craven's original, but rather the narrative blueprint of the reboot concept; or, more accurately, the blueprint specifically advocated by Nolan and his co-writer, David S. Goyer, who, in turn, drew upon the concept from its origins in superhero comics (Proctor 2018; forthcoming). Arguably, Bayer attempts to stave off comparisons with Craven's *Elm Street* by articulating that the remake is better viewed as a conceptual adaptation of the reboot principle, with the 'Nolan Function' and Nolan's *Batman* pulled into service as a brand-function. Simply put, Bayer wants nothing more than to hope that some of that Nolan magic will rub off and guide the reception of the *Elm Street* remake, perhaps to challenge, or at least address, the *a priori* 'bad' object status of canonical horror remakes and reboots.

Moreover, Bayer implies an analogy between Jack Nicholson and Robert Englund, and Heath Ledger with Jackie Earle Haley, the new Freddy. As the only actor to portray Freddy Krueger at this point, Englund's shadow haunts the text despite his absence (which is always already present at the symptomatic level). Having played Freddy for over two decades across multiple media – eight franchise films, the *Freddy's Nightmares* TV series (1988–90) and a raft of other appearances, the most recent of which was in an episode of US sitcom *The Goldbergs* in 2018 – Englund's cultish synonymy with the role suggests that Craven is not the only 'auratic' figure that requires negotiation (which also implies that actors can possess author-functions and canonical legacies as well). Yet, whereas Ledger's appointment as the Joker was received poorly upon announcement – until of course the release of *The Dark Knight* in theatres put paid to fan criticisms – the hiring of Haley as Krueger was applauded by fans, not least because of his turn as Rorschach in Zack Snyder's (2009) adaptation of Alan Moore and David Gibbons' seminal *Watchmen* comic series. In interviews, Haley recognised that Englund's star persona as Freddy remained such a commanding presence that he required negotiation, but rather than mobilise Englund as 'bad' object, Haley instead wholeheartedly embraced the actor's canonical legacy. Haley declared he was:

> perfectly fine with being Freddy number two. Because you know what? Robert Englund has done an amazing job with this character. He's done it for two decades in numerous films and he's made the character iconic. He's in all our minds even if we haven't seen the movies. And rightfully so. (Ryan 2010)

Yet in order to append value, belief and authenticity onto the *Elm Street* remake, and hence construct the film as 'good' object, discursive regimes of (sub)cultural value require a 'bad' object with which to compare and contrast. Clearly, then, Craven, Englund and the original *Elm Street* film are untouchable entities, so Haley and Bayer shift focus to construct the Elm Street sequels as 'bad' objects that the remake seeks to redress by going 'back to the origins of *Nightmare on Elm Street* . . . when it was scary [. . .] Back when it was less comedic [and] more serious' (Ryan 2010). Said Bayer: 'Freddy became a vaudevillian, comedic character that you're not really scared by, and I don't think that's what [original director and franchise creator] Wes Craven intended' (Yarm 2010, square brackets in original). On the few occasions when Craven is mentioned directly, Bayer does not seek to struggle with his author-function nor the canonical legacy of his *Elm Street*, but instead, substantiates his aura, and his directorial intent, with Bayer suggesting that he is operating as a directorial surrogate for Craven's original authorial intentions. Thus, the remake will return Freddy 'back to his origins' as 'scary' dream demon rather than comedian with one foot in the camp tradition:

> They needed to make *Batman Begins* before they made *The Dark Knight* . . . [They] had to go back to the mythology of the character; they had to reintroduce the character to audiences as if he had never existed before. That's the way we've approached Freddy Krueger (Yarm 2010).

Bayer continues:

> In fact, I told all my cast and crew that we must do with Freddy what Christopher Nolan did with Batman. I'm trying to make a dark and serious film, and I hope I'm achieving that. One of the most extraordinary aspects of Dark Knight is the way it integrates Batman into a believable world, and I want to do the same with Freddy. That doesn't mean the classic elements of the mythology will be absent from our Nightmare on Elm Street. (Rosales and Sucasas 2010)

It is striking that the promotional discourses that surrounded *Batman Begins* enacted similar rhetorical flourishes: a 'back-to-basics' approach, 'back to the origins', 'back to the mythology', a 'dark and serious' reinvention. As Brooker writes, 'the idea of realism was central to the promotion and distribution of Nolan's Batman – particularly *Batman Begins*' (2012: 89). This discursive thrust sought to strategically erect aesthetic and generic boundaries between Batman as 'Dark Detective' and as 'Camp Crusader', thus furnishing moral dualisms between 'good' and 'bad' iterations of the character; between Nolan's 'stripped-down tough' Batman and Schumacher's 'swishy, showy form of camp' (2012: 93). In this light, both the Batman and Freddy Krueger brands are seen to have been damaged in some way by camp and comedy, with the respective reboots being anchored to this idea of 'realism' as a mode of repair, as a corrective mechanism with which to transform franchise brands from 'bad' to 'good' objects once more to extend their shelf-life (or 'brand-life').

At the same time, however, there can be such a thing as too much 'reinvention'. Rather than wiping the slate clean and beginning again from scratch, then, both Nolan and Bayer sought to link their respective (re)iterations with 'good' canonical objects from the archives, which along with claims about 'roots', and 'origins', suggests that Nolan's *Batman Begins* and Bayer's *Elm Street* are not 'reinventions' exactly, but *uninventions*: films that promote the notion of rewinding the clock to a time when the characters were generically 'pure'. Yet, neither Nolan nor Bayer sought to sketch out their reinventions on a blank slate, but frequently summoned support from historical 'good' objects, as well as retaining 'some contrasting traces of the bad old one in the production discourses; and rather than erasing it, they in fact made the bad object visible again, as a point of comparison' (Brooker 2012: 106). The difference between *Batman* and *Elm Street*, however, is that the former has an eighty-year mythos to draw from, comprising thousands of comics and an armada of transmedia ventures in radio, television, animation, computer games and so on, while the latter is a comparatively short-lived film franchise consisting of eight films, a spin-off TV series and non-canonical comics. Both properties might very well include transmedia expressions, but for *Elm Street* there is arguably only one 'good' object: that is, Wes Craven's *A Nightmare on Elm Street*, which for Bayer remains 'the best one, and the one I really looked at' (Yarm 2010).

Bayer clearly recognises the difficulties related to reinventing Freddy Krueger in a way that overly interferes with the canonical legacy of the franchise. In a sense, Bayer seems to be working from an academic understanding of genre theory, most notably the delicate balance between formula and invention. The *Elm Street* remake will be 'a dark and serious' film, cut from the same cloth as Nolan's *Batman Begins* and *The Dark Knight*, but one which also aims to return to the scary world envisioned by Craven. For Bayer, this was a world where Freddy was terrifying, before he became a 'vaudevillian, comedic character', and yet it '[d]idn't mean the classic elements of the mythology [would] be absent from our Nightmare on Elm Street' (Yarm 2010):

> You certainly couldn't make Freddy Krueger without the striped sweater, the hat, the glove – those are like Batman's cape and his utility belt. If you look at images of burn victims, it is really is frightening what happens to the skin, the features that get burned off: your eyelids, your nose, your lips, your ears. I don't think the original character looked like a burn victim. I always thought he looked like a witch. (Yarm 2010)

Like Batman, Freddy has 'classic' elements that should not be erased. Yet Bayer also argues that the original Freddy make-up fails to live up to the 'realism' mantra, which in a way partially constructs Englund's 'look' as failing to meet the generic aspirations of the remake. On the one hand, Craven's *Elm Street* is the ultimate 'good' *Elm Street* object – 'the best one' – whereas on the other, the original Freddy make-up doesn't capture the reality of burn victims effectively. In essence, 'the striped sweater, the hat, the glove' are the immovable accoutrements of Freddy's design, but the burned visage is not; that is up for reinvention in order to fit the character in with Bayer's realistic aesthetics ('the way we're approaching Elm Street'). Here, Bayer runs the risk of tampering with the canonical legacy of Freddy Krueger by suggesting that Craven's *Elm Street* contains a 'bad' element that requires reinvention.[1]

CONCLUSION

Paratexts of this type, then, put in play multiple contradictions. They are employed 'either to deflect readers from certain texts or to inflect their reading when it occurs' (Gray 2010: 36), whereas they also wrestle with the dialectics of reinvention and 'the classic elements of the mythology'. Too much reinvention runs the risk of Freddy becoming unrecognisable; not enough, and the remake becomes a 'pointless' victim of remake and reboot culture (Mee 2017).

By seeking to navigate and negotiate the canonical legacy of the 1984 film, the prestigious aura of the 'Craven Function' and Englund's star persona as Freddy Krueger, Bayer summoned Nolan and Nolan's *Batman* as a brand-function, to such an extent that audiences were primed to think of the *Elm Street* remake as aesthetically and generically in communion with Nolan's *Batman Begins* and *The Dark Knight*. In drawing upon similar ideologies related to 'realism', 'reinvention', 'origins' and 'roots', perhaps 'Freddy Begins' would have been a more appropriate title for Bayer's purposes. In doing so, Bayer actively constructed Nolan's *Batman* films not as cinematic texts specifically, but, rather, as brands and entry-way paratexts. In so doing, Nolan's *Batman* becomes the lens with which audiences should view Bayer's remake of Wes Craven's *A Nightmare on Elm Street*, a strategy that indicates the perils of remaking and rebooting canonical horror cinema.

NOTE

1. It is worth considering that way that Nolan's brand-function has also been mobilised in the service of other films, such as the James Bond reboot, *Casino Royale* (Campbell, 2006), Rob Zombie's *Halloween* (2007), *Terminator: Salvation* (McG, 2008), *Rise of the Planet of the Apes* (Wyatt, 2011) and more besides (see Proctor 2012; and forthcoming).

REFERENCES

Bourdieu, Pierre (1993), *The Field of Cultural Production: Essays on Art and Literature*, New York: Columbia University Press.
Brooker, Will (2012), *Hunting the Dark Knight: Twenty-First Century Batman*, London: I. B. Taurus.
Caldwell, John Thornton (2008), *Production Culture: Industrial Reflexivity and Critical Practice in Film and Television*, Durham, NC: Duke University Press.
Child, Ben (2009), '*The Birds* and *Rosemary's Baby* Remakes Killed by the Wrath of Fans', *The Guardian*, 17 June, <https://www.theguardian.com/film/2009/jun/16/the-birds-remake-michael-bay>.
Church, David (2010), 'Memory, Genre, and Self-Narrativization; or, Why I Should Be a More Contented Horror Fan', in Steffan Hantke (ed.), *American Horror Film: The Genre at the Turn of the Millennium*, Jackson, MI: University Press of Mississippi, pp. 235–43.
Corrigan, Timothy (1991), *Cinema Without Walls. Movies and Culture After Vietnam*, New Brunswick, NJ: Rutgers University Press.
Foucault, Michel (1969), *Language, Counter-Memory, Practice*, ed. Donald F. Bouchard, New York: Cornell University Press.
Gil, Stephen (2014), 'A Remake by Any Other Name: Use of a Premise Under a New Title', in Carlen Lavigne (ed.), *Remake Television: Reboot, Reuse, Recycle*, Toronto: Lexington Books, pp. 21–36.
Gray, Jonathan (2010), *Show Sold Separately: Promos, Spoilers, and Other Media Paratexts*, New York: New York University Press.

Gray, Jonathan (2014), 'The Use Value of Authors', <https://spreadablemedia.org/essays/gray/#.XbWEey10e9s>.
Hantke, Steffan (2007), 'Academic Film Criticism, the Rhetoric of Crisis and the Current State of American Horror Cinema: Thoughts on Canoncity and Academic Anxiety', *Literature*, 43: 4, 191–202.
Hantke, Steffan (2010), 'They Don't Make 'Em Like They Used To: On the Rhetoric of Crisis and the Current State of American Horror Cinema', in Steffan Hantke (ed.), *American Horror Film: The Genre at the Turn of the Millennium*, Jackson, MI: University Press of Mississippi, pp. vii–xxxii.
Harvey, Colin B. (2015), *Fantastic Transmedia: Narrative, Play and Memory Across Science Fiction and Fantasy Storyworlds*, London: Palgrave.
Heffernan, Kevin (2014), 'Risen from the Vaults: Recent Horror Film Remakes and the American Film Industry', in Richard Nowell (ed.), *Merchants of Menace: The Business of Horror Cinema*, New York: Bloomsbury, pp. 61–75.
Hills, Matt (2002), *Fan Cultures*, London: Routledge.
Hills, Matt (2005), *The Pleasures of Horror*, London: Continuum.
Hutchings, Peter (2004), *The Horror Film*, London: Routledge.
Jancovich, Mark (2002), 'Cult Fictions: Cult Movies, Subcultural Capital and the Production of Cultural Distinctions', *Cultural Studies*, 16: 2, 306–22.
Kendrick, James (2017), 'The Terrible, Horrible Desire to Know: Post 9/11 Horror Remakes, Reboots, Sequels and Prequels', in Terence McSweeney (ed.), *American Cinema in the Shadow of 9/11*, Edinburgh: Edinburgh University Press.
Lee, Nathan (2008), 'Return of the Return of the Repressed!: Risen from the Grave and Brought Back to Bloody Life: Horror Remakes from *Psycho* to *Funny Games*', *Film Comment*, 44: 2, 24–8.
McCabe, Joseph (2010), 'Recurring Nightmare', *Horror: SFX Edition*, 42, 36–9.
Mann, Craig Ian (2019), 'The Beast Without: The Cinematic Werewolf as a (Counter)Cultural Metaphor', *Horror Studies*, 10: 1, 7–25.
Mee, Laura (2017), 'The Horror Remake Massacre: Adaptation, Reception and Value', in Colleen Kennedy-Karpat and Eric Sandberg (eds), *Adaptation, Awards Culture, and the Value of Prestige*, London: Palgrave, pp. 193–209.
Muir, John Kenneth (1998), *Wes Craven: The Art of Horror*, Jefferson, NC: McFarland.
Proctor, William (2012), 'Regeneration and Rebirth: Anatomy of the Franchise Reboot', *Scope: Online Journal of Film and Television Studies*, 22 (February), 1–19.
Proctor, William (2017), 'Bitches Ain't Gonna Hunt no Ghosts: Totemic Nostalgia, Toxic Fandom and the *Ghostbusters* Platonic', *Palabra Clave*, 20: 4, 1105–41.
Proctor, William (2018), 'Reboots and Retroactive Continuity', in Mark J. P. Wolf (ed.), *The Routledge Companion to Imaginary Worlds*, London: Routledge, pp. 224–36.
Proctor, William (forthcoming), *Reboot Culture: Comics, Film, Transmedia*, London: Palgrave Macmillan.
Robb, Brian (1998), *Screams and Nightmares: The Films of Wes Craven*, New York: Overlook Press.
Rosales, Luis M. and Angel Sucasas (2010), 'Dreams Don't Die', *Fangoria*, 292, 26–32.
Ryan, Mike (2010), 'Jackie Earle Haley: "I'm Perfectly Fine Being Freddy Number Two"', *Vanity Fair*, 30 April, <https://www.vanityfair.com/hollywood/2010/04/jackie-earle-haley-im-perfectly-fine-being-freddy-krueger-number-two>.
Shimabukuro, Karra (2015), 'I Framed Freddy: Functional Aesthetics in the A Nightmare on Elm Street Series', in Wickham Clayton (ed.), *Style and Form in the Hollywood Slasher Film*, London: Palgrave Macmillan, pp. 51–67.
Thompson, Howard (1972), 'Last House on the Left', *New York Times*, 22 December, <https://www.nytimes.com/1972/12/22/archives/last-house-on-left.html>.

Thornton, Sarah (1995), *Club Cultures: Music, Media and Subcultural Capital*, Cambridge: Polity Press.
Tompkins, Joe (2014), '"Re-imagining" the Canon: Examining the Discourse of Contemporary Horror Film Reboots', *New Review of Film and Television Studies*, 12: 4, 380–99.
Verevis, Constantine (2006), *Film Remakes*, Edinburgh: Edinburgh University Press.
Verevis, Constantine (2017), 'New Millennial Remakes', in Frank Kelleter (ed.), *Media of Serial Narratives*. Columbus, OH: Ohio State University Press, pp. 148–69.
Wee, Valerie (2006), 'Resurrecting and Updating the Teen Slasher: The Case of *Scream*', *Journal of Film and Popular Television*, 34: 2, 50–61.
Wells, Paul (2000), *The Horror Genre: From Beezlebub to Blair Witch*, New York: Wallflower Press.
Wood, Robin (2018), *Robin Wood on the Horror Film: Collected Essays and Review*, Detroit, MI: Wayne State University Press.
Yarm, Mark (2010), 'A Nightmare on Elm Street Director Samuel Bayer on Rebooting the Franchise', *Vulture*, 29 April, <https://www.vulture.com/2010/04/a_nightmare_on_elm_street_dire.html>.

Index

Abaius, Cole, 38
ABC, 49, 50, 51–3, 123
Abrams, J. J., 33, 36, 40, 130–1, 139
Access Hollywood, 206
action figures, 136–7
'Adventure Figures', 136
Adventures of Superman (1952–8)
    see Superman
aesthetic collaboration, 88–90
Ain't it Cool News, 37
Aja, Alexandre, 225
Alamo Drafthouse, Austin, Texas, 37–40
Albarrán-Torres, César Alberto, 178
Alcon Entertainment, 66
Alcon Media Group, 190
Ali, Muhammad, 145, 147, 150
Alien franchise, 9, 189–204
  Alien (Scott, 1979), 192
  Alien: Awakening (potential new film), 197
  Alien: Blackout (FoxNext, 2019), 191, 198
  Alien: Covenant in Utero (virtual reality), 199
  Alien: Covenant (Scott, 2017), 190–1, 195–6, 197
  Alien: Isolation (Sega, 2014), 190–1, 197–8
  Alien vs. Predator (Atari Corporation, 1994), 197
  Alien vs. Predator: Requiem (Strausse, 2007), 199n
  Alien vs. Predator (spin-off films), 192, 194, 199n
  Alien^3 (Fincher, 1992), 193, 194, 196
  Aliens (Cameron, 1986), 191, 192, 194–5, 196
  Aliens: Colonial Marines (Sega, 2013), 190–1, 194, 195, 197
  Prometheus (Scott, 2012), 9, 190–6, 199, 199n
The Amazing Spider-Man (Webb, 2012)
    see *Spiderman* franchise
American Dream, 144, 150–1, 153
American Movie Classics, 50
Anderson, Douglas, 103
The Animal World (1956 documentary), 180
'announcement trailer', 209, 214–5
anti-auteur reboot, 90–1
anticipating the reboot, 205–18
AOL-Time Warner, 58
Archie Comics, 22
Arrow, 223
AT&T, 59–60
Atkins, Barry, 71
Australia, 39–40
auteurism, 99, 102, 104, 107, 108, 222–4
  anti-auteur reboot, 90–1
  auteur-reboot, 85–8
'author function', 221–9
Avatar franchise, 196
  Avatar (Cameron, 2009), 175

INDEX

B movies, 49, 85
Back to School (Dangerfield, 1986), 158
Bale, Christian, 58
BAMTech, 197
Banet-Weiser, Sarah, 23–4, 160–1, 167
  Empowered: Popular Feminism and Popular Misogyny, 157, 158
Barthes, Roland, 74, 144
Bass, Saul, 87
Batman franchise, 47–63
  Bat-books, 57
  Batman (Burton, 1989), 54, 57–8, 226
  The Batman (Hillyer, 1943), 49
  Batman (TV show, 1960s), 47, 49, 51–3
    camp crusader, 51–3
    Catwoman (character), 52
    Holy Batmania: Special Collector Bat Video (1989), 53–4
    Robin (character), 52
  Batman, Columbia serials, 49–50
  Batman and Robin (Bennet, 1949), 49–50
  Batman and Robin (Schumacher, 1997), 57, 226
  Batman Begins (Nolan, 2005)
    'author function', 221
    'back to basics', 227–9
    franchising, 50
    'hard reboot', 9, 173, 189, 226
    Nolan's brand, 223, 230
    as 'quintessential reboot', 3
  Batman comic books, 47–9
  Batman Forever (Schumacher, 1995), 57
  Batman Returns (Burton, 1992), 57
  Batman TWI's films, budget and revenues, 58t
  Batman v Superman: Dawn of Justice (Snyder, 2016), 59
  Batman WCI's films, budget and revenues, 57t
  Brooker, Will, *Hunting the Dark Knight*, 223
  The Dark Knight (Nolan, 2008), 193, 221, 223, 226–30
  Elfman, Danny, *Batman: The Original Movie Picture Score*, 57
  Joker (character), 52, 58, 226–7
  Justice League (Snyder, 2017), 59
  Penguin (character), 52
  Suicide Squad (Ayer, 2016), 59
Bates Motel (A&E, 2013–17), 111–12
Battlestar Galactica (1978–9), 55
Bay, Michael, 26–8, 220, 227–8
Bayer, Samuel, 221, 225–6
Berliner, Todd, 179
Beverly Hills Cop (Brest, 1984), 189
Big (Marshall, 1988), 92, 94n
Binder, Steve, *Star Wars Holiday Special*, 192
The Birds (Hitchcock, 1960), 220
Black Lives Matter, 147
Blade Runner franchise, 65–80, 190
  Blade Runner 2019 'trilogy', 66, 71
  Blade Runner 2022: Black Out, 65–6, 69–70
  Blade Runner 2036: Nexus Dawn, 65–6, 69–70
  Blade Runner 2048: Nowhere to Run, 65–6, 69–70
  Blade Runner 2049 (Villeneuve, 2017), 65–6, 68, 76, 77, 190
  Blade Runner Director's Cut (Scott, 1992), 65, 71–2, 74–5
  Blade Runner Final Cut (Scott, 2007), 65, 71–2, 74–5
  Burroughs, William, *Blade Runner: A Movie* (1979), 71
  Deckard, Rick (character), 65–9, 68, 72–7, 77
  Dick, Philip K., *Do Androids Dream of Electric Sheep?* 65, 66, 71–2, 75
  Jeter, K. W., 65, 66, 72
  'K' (character), 65–9, 73–6
Blatty, William Peter, *The Exorcist*, 118
Blomkamp, Neill, 194–5, 196
Bock, Jeff, 176
Bourdieu, Pierre, 220
box office
  Alien: Covenant (Scott, 2017), 196
  Alien vs. Predator (spin-off films), 199n
  Batman films, 57–9, 57t, 58t
  Blade Runner 2049 (Villeneuve, 2017), 77
  Dark Phoenix (Kinberg, 2019), 197
  The Force Awakens (Abrams, 2015), 134–5
  Ghostbusters (Feig, 2016), 162
  Jurassic Park 3-D, 186n
  Jurassic Park (Spielberg, 1993), 175
  Jurassic World (Trevorrow, 2015), 175, 176–9

INDEX

A Nightmare on Elm Street (Bayer, 2010), 221
   Platinum Dunes, 224
   rebooting, 189–90
   Rogue One: A Star Wars Story (Edwards, 2016), 134–5
   Star Trek franchise, 35–6
   Superman WCI's films, 56–7, 56t
   Top Gun (Scott, 1986), 216
boxing coverage, 147
brand-function, 224–9
Brexit, 133–4
Bridesmaids (2011), 159
Britton, Andrew, 162–3, 164
Brooker, Will, 77, 228
   Hunting the Dark Knight, 223
Brookey, Robert, 216
Bruckheimer, Jerry, 206, 210, 211
Bukatman, Scott, 70, 73
Burger King, 40
Burroughs, William, *Blade Runner: A Movie* (1979), 71
Burton, Tim, 226
Burwell, Carter, 113–14
Butch Cassidy and the Sundance Kid (Hill, 1969), 89

California magazine, 210
Cameron, James, 148
Cannon Group, 56–7
'canonical legacy', 221
Caple Jr., Steven, 155n
Cardwell, Sarah, 112
Carter, President, 149
Cartoon Network, 24
Casetti, Francesco, 99
Casino Royale (Campbell, 2006), 117
Catch-22 (Nichols, 1970), 88–9
Cernovich, Mike, 134
CGI, 208, 210, 213
Charlie's Angels (Banks, 2019), 189
children's media, 111
Christiansen, Steen Ledet, 212
Clerks (Smith, 1994), 123
Clerks: The Animated Series, 123
Clinton, Hillary, 59
CNN, 59–60
Coen brothers, 88–9
Cohen, Anne, 92
Cold Iron Studios, 198

collaborative production, 90–1
Columbia Pictures, 49–50
Comic Book Resources, 132
comic books
   Alcon Media Group, 190
   Alien franchise, 192–3, 198
   Batman, 47, 57
   Proctor, William, 7–8
   Superman, 1
   Teenage Mutant Ninja Turtles, 21, 23
   Teenage Mutant Ninja Turtles Adventures, 22
   Watchmen, 227
Comic-Con 2017, 69
Conti, Bill, 153
Coogler, Ryan, 143, 147, 152–4
Coppola, Francis Ford, 102, 206
Coram, Robert, 212
Corrigan, Timothy, 222
Craven, Wes, 220–30
'Craven Function', 226, 230
Creed franchise *see Rocky* franchise
Crichton, Michael, 178
Crisis on Infinite Earths comic book series, 7
cross-media platforms, 208
Cruise, Tom, 205–6, 208, 210–16

Daily Beast, 36
Darabont, Frank, 90
The Dark Crystal: Age of Resistance (TV show, 2019), 7
The Dark Knight (Nolan, 2008) *see Batman* franchise
Dark Phoenix (Kinberg, 2019), 197
DC comics, 50, 56, 57, 136
DC Extended Universe (DCEU), 58–9
DC 'hyperdiegesis', 7–8
DC Super Hero Girls, 136
DC universe, 7–8, 47
De Palma, Brian, 89
Dell Publishing, 48
Department of Justice (DoJ), 59–60
Detective Comics, 47
Dick, Philip K., *Do Androids Dream of Electric Sheep?* 65, 66, 71–2, 75
digital technologies, 6–7
Dippold, Katie, 159
Dirty Rotten Scoundrels (Oz, 1988), 158
'discontinuity', 102–4

236   INDEX

Disney, 55–6, 128–38, 178, 190–1, 196–9
Disney Jr, 19
DISNEY XD, 24
Disney+, 190–1, 197–8
'diversity', 129–35, 184; *see also* gender; race
Doctor Sleep (Miller, 2019), 189
Doctor Who franchise, 209
Dovemead Limited (DL), 56
Dozier, William, 49, 51–7
DreamWorks, 57
'drone age', 212–13
DVD
    Bat-serials, 50
    bonus features, 206, 210
    commentary, 86, 88–90, 93n, 145
    'A Heist in Heels', 93
    Holy Batmania: Special Collector Bat Video (1989), 54
    Ocean's franchise, 81
    Danger Zone: The Making of Top Gun, 210–11
DVD/Blu-Ray, Craven, Wes, 223
Dyer, Richard, 185
'Dynamation', 180

E! News, 130
Eastern Colored Printing, 48
Eastman, Kevin, 21
Ebert, Roger, 150
Eckstein, Ashley, 137
Eco, Umberto, 1, 8
Edelstein, David, 175
electronic press kit (EPK), 226
Elfman, Danny, *Batman: The Original Movie Picture Score*, 57
Ellen (TV show), 130
Ellison, David, 212
Elsaesser, Thomas, 206
encoding/decoding theories, 135
Englund, Robert, 226–7, 229–30
Entertainment Weekly, 127
Epps Jr, Jack, 210
Erin Brockovich (Soderbergh, 2000), 89
Ewins, Michael, 106
The Exorcist franchise
    Blatty, William Peter, *The Exorcist*, 118
    The Exorcist (Friedkin, 1973), 112, 118–22

The Exorcist (TV show), 112–13, 118–22, 123
Oldfield, Mike, 'Tubular Bells', 122

Facebook, 206
'failed reboot', 221–2, 224
Fallis, Jeffrey, 103
Faltermeyer, Harold, 213
'fanagement', 39
Fancher, Hampton, 65
fandom, reimagining, 33–46
fan-made trailers, 206, 212–13
Fantastic Fest, 38
Fargo franchise
    Fargo (Coen, 1996), 112, 113–18
    Fargo (TV show), 112–18, 123
Fast, Kristin, 193
Feig, Paul, 158–9, 162
female
    empowerment, 165–6
    fans, 42–3, 136–8
    friendship, 164
    'girl power', 160
    independence, 164
    merchandising, 136–8
    #MeToo, 65–6
    Women's March 17 January 2017, 133
    see also gender
feminism, 127–8
    popular, 158–62
    postfeminism, 158, 160–1
La Fille sur le pont (Leconte, 1999), 89
Film Crit Hulk, 101
Film School Rejects website, 38
film-to-television reboots, 111–25
Finger, Bill, 48
Fisher, Carrie, as political iconography, 133
Forbes, 136
Forbidden Planet (Wilcox, 1956), 179
The Force Awakens (Abrams, 2015) *see* *Star Wars* franchise
Ford, Harrison, 65–6
Ford v Ferrari (Mangold, 2019), 197
'forever franchise', 177–8
Form, Andrew, 220
Foster, Alan Dean, *Splinter of the Mind's Eye*, 192
Foster, Greg, 176
Foucault, Michel, 222–3
    The Archaeology of Knowledge, 5

Fox, Megan, 27
FoxNext, 198, 199
franchising, 8–9, 21
  anti-franchising discourses, 97–110
  contemporary media strategies, 189–204
  'forever franchise', 177–8
  intellectual property (IP), 189
  logics, 104–7
  media, 97–110
  see also individual film franchises
Freddy's Nightmares (TV show), 226–7
Freeman, Matthew, 193, 199n
Frost, Mark, 107
  The Final Dossier, 105
  The Secret History of Twin Peaks, 105
Fruitvale Station (Coogler, 2013), 144–5
Fuller, Brad, 220
The Funnies comic strip collection, 48

Gallagher, Mark, 91
Garcia, Antero, 128, 130
Gears of War (Microsoft Game Studios, 2016), 197
Geffen, David, 57
Geffen Film Company, 57
gender, 81–96
  'diversity', 129–35, 184
  inequality, 164–6, 169
  politics, 147
  rebooting film history as film herstory, 92–3
  stereotypes, 185
  swapping reboots, 157–71
  'woke' message, 162, 169
  see also female; masculinity
genres, 81–96, 190
Gerstel, Shirley, 35
Ghostbusters franchise, 157–71
  Ghostbusters (Feig, 2016), 157–71
  Ghostbusters (Reitman, 1984), 157–71
G.I. Joe: The Rise of Cobra (Sommers, 2009), 26–7
Giant-Baum-Kaye, 'Edge of Reality', 65
Gibbons, David, 227
Gill, Rosalind, 167
The Godfather (Coppola, 1972), 147
Golan-Globus Productions, 56–7
The Goldbergs (sitcom), 227
Golden Harvest, 22
Golding, Dan, 178, 197

Goldner, Brian, 26
Goldsman, Akiva, 57
Goyer, David S., 226
The Graham Norton Show (TV show), 210–11
Gray, F. Gary, 92
Gray, Herman, 144, 148
Gray, Jonathan, 19, 34, 72, 135, 144, 216, 222
Green Day, 'Boulevard of Broken Dreams,' 225–6
The Green Hornet, 54
Greenway Productions, 50
Griffin, Ted, 89
Grossman, Julie, 114–15
The Guardian, 175

Hackman, Gene, 206
Hadas, Leora, 37
Haley, Jackie Earle, 226–8
Hall, Stuart, 135
Halloween franchise, 191
  Halloween (Green, 2018), 190, 195
  Halloween (Zombie, 2007), 4
  Halloween H20: Twenty Years Later (Miner, 1998), 195
Hamill, Mark, 134
Hanna, Erin, *Only at Comic-Con*, 36
Hannibal (NBC, 2013–15), 111–12
Hantke, Steffan, 219
'hard reboot', 189, 191
Harryhausen, Ray, 180
Hasbro, 26, 27, 136, 137
Hassler-Forest, Dan, 133
Haute Tension/Switchblade Romance (Aja, 2003), 225
'HBO style', 147
The Heat (Kruhlik, 2013), 159
Heinze, Rüdiger, 192, 193, 196
Hendershot, Heather, 24
Herbert, Daniel, 4, 8, 129, 145, 208
HerUniverse, 137
Hess, Amanda, 86
Hills, Matt, 39, 71, 209
The Hills Have Eyes (Aja, 2006), 225
The Hills Have Eyes (Craven, 1977), 225
Hitchcock, Alfred, 220
Hoad, Phil, 175
Hollywood News video blog site, 214
Hollywood Reporter, 134, 176, 208

Home Alone franchise, 197
Hooper, Tobe, 225
horror cinema, 4, 219–32
House of Representatives' Special Subcommittee on Investigations, 51
Hulu, 198–9
The Hunger Games (Ross, 2012), 90–1
Hunting, Kyra, 19
The Hustle (Addison, 2019), 158
Hutcheon, Linda, 112

Iger, Bob, 132, 196–7
Image Comics, 23
Imax Entertainment, 176
immersion, 178–183, 183
Inception (Nolan, 2010), 223
IndieWire, 146
Instagram, 154, 194–5
intellectual property (IP)
    Alien franchise, 190–1, 196–9
    Batman franchise, 49–50, 55–6, 59
    comic books, 8
    franchising, 189
    Star Trek franchise, 33
    Teenage Mutant Ninja Turtles franchise, 20, 23–4, 30
    Twin Peaks franchise, 100, 102
International Film Productions (IFP), 56
intertextuality, 26, 146–7, 152–4
    industrial, 2–3, 19–20
    transmedia, 21
io9, 39
Isaac, Oscar, 129–30
The Italian Job (Gray, 2003), 92

Jack Reacher franchise, 213
James Bond franchise, 190
Jenkins, Henry, 21, 135, 192
Jeter, K. W., 65, 66
    Blade Runner 2: The Edge of Human, 72
Jimmy Kimmel Live (TV show), 210–11
Johnson, Broderick, 66
Johnson, Derek, 8–9, 21, 34, 100, 101
Jordan, Michael B., 145, 147, 154
Jumanji: The Video Game (Outright Games, 2019), 198
Jurassic franchise, 174–82
    Jurassic Park III (Johnston, 2001), 176, 181
    Jurassic Park (Spielberg, 1993), 174–82

Jurassic World Evolution (Frontier Developments, 2018), 198
Jurassic World: Fallen Kingdom (Bayona, 2018), 177
Jurassic World (Trevorrow, 2015), 173–88, *180*, *183*, *185*
    serial self-reflexivity, 178–83
    View-Master, 179–83, *180*
    white, middle-class heteronormativity, *185*
The Lost World: Jurassic Park (Spielberg, 1997), 176, 181

Kane, Bob, 48
Katz, Brandon, 175
Keller, James, 90–1
Kelley, Katie Martin, 37
Kennedy, Kathleen, 131, 134, 136, 139
Kilmer, Val, 206
Kinder, Marsha, 19–2, 24–5, 29
King, Kyle T., 103
Kinney Services, 56
Kitt, Eartha, 52
Klein, Amanda Ann, 162
Klinger, Barbara, 205
Knowles, Harry, 37, 44n
Kohn, Eric, 146
Kosinski, Joseph, 214
Kosove, Andrew A., 66
Kurtzman, Alex, 37, 38

Laird, Peter, 21
The Last Airbender (Shyamalan, 2010), 24
The Last House on the Left (Craven, 1972), 223
League, Tim, 37, 38, 44n
Leconte, Patrice, 89
Ledger, Heath, 226–7
Lee, Bruce, 54
'legacy', 144, 147–8, 154–5, 155n, 189–204
'legacy film', 178
'legacy franchise', 197
'legacyquel', 2, 173–88, 174, 184
LEGO, 135–8
Lethal Weapon franchise, 82
Lichtenstein, Roy, 52
Lindelof, Damon, 37, 38
Logan Lucky (Soderbergh, 2017), 84, 86, 88
London Cannon Group, 56–7

Loock, Kathleen, 208
Los Angeles Review of Books, 133
The Lost World: Jurassic Park (Spielberg, 1997) *see Jurassic* franchise
The Lost World (Hoyt, 1925), 180
Louis, Joe, 145
Lowry, Elizabeth, 106
Lucas, George, 192, 199n
Lucasfilm, 129, 137, 138, 178
Lynch, David, 97–110
'Lynchverse', 97, 100

McAvoy, David, 104
McCarthy, Donald, 105
McCarthy, Melissa, 159
McClintock, Pamela, 176
Magic Mike (Soderbergh, 2012), 87
Mandell, Andrea, 146
Le Mans '66 (Mangold, 2019), 197
Marks, Justin, 211–12
The Martian (Scott, 2015), 195, 199n
Marvel, 190, 192
Marvel Comics, 136
'Marvel films', 102
Marvel Rising, 136
Marx Company, 48–9
masculinity, 158
    men's rights activism, 127–8, 130, 135, 137–8
    patriarchy, 164–5
    white, 162–3
    see also female; gender
Masters, Kim, 36
The Matrix franchise, 21
Maverick (Donner, 1994), 208
Mee, Laura, 225
Meehan, Eileen, 35
melodrama and serial storytelling, 148–9
men's rights activism, 127–8, 130, 135, 137–8
merchandising
    Alien franchise, 199n
    Batman franchise, 48–9, 56–8, 199n
    female, 136–8
    Star Wars franchise, 130, 135, 199n
    Teenage Mutant Ninja Turtles franchise, 21–2, 25, 27, 29–30
Merchant, Brian, 127
Meredith, Burgess, 52
Metacritic, 194, 199n

#MeToo, 65–6
MeTV, 54–5
    'Super Sci-Fi Saturday Night', 55
Milestone, Lewis, 81
Mill, Meek, 'Lord Knows,' 153
Miller's Crossing (Coen, 1990), 88–9
Mirage Studios, 21, 23
Mission: Impossible franchise, 211, 213
    Mission: Impossible (De Palma, 1996), 208
    Mission: Impossible - Fallout (McQuarrie, 2018), 211
Mittell, Jason, 5, 66–7, 70–1, 148
mobile apps, 198
montage, 89, 90
    trans-filmic, 91
Moore, Alan, 227
Moulton, Carter, 209, 214–15
movies as 'friends,' 205
MTV, 40, 57
Murdoch, Rupert, 50
music videos, 225–6
'myth', 144
mythic repetition, 111–25

National Geographic, 190
National Periodicals, 47
Navarro, Peter, 59–60
Netflix, 7, 189
New Hollywood, 36, 162–3
'New Horror', 219–20, 223
New Line Cinema, 22
'new millennial remakes', 20
'New Wave of French Horror', 225
The New York Times, 223
Newgard, Bob, 35
Newmar, Julie, 52
Newsweek, 36
Nicholson, Jack, 226
Nickelodeon, 23–5
Nickelodeon Animation Studio, 25, 27, 30
Nielsen Company, A. C., 51
Nielsen television ratings, 51, 53
A Nightmare on Elm Street franchise, 219–32
    Freddy's Nightmares (TV show), 226–7
    Krueger, Freddy (character), 221, 224, 226–30
    A Nightmare on Elm Street (Bayer, 2010), 220–1, 224–30
    A Nightmare on Elm Street (Craven, 1984), 220–1, 224, 226–30

Nimoy, Leonard, 33, 38–9
Ninja Turtles: The Next Mutation (TV show, 1997–8) *see Teenage Mutant Ninja Turtles* franchise
Nirvana, 'Smells Like Teen Spirit', 225–6
Nispel, Marcus, 225–6
Nixon, Richard, 149
Nochimson, Martha, 99
Nolan, Christopher, 58, 221–3, 226, 228–30, 230n
'Nolan Function,' 226
'non-fans', 34
nostalgia, 117, 209, 214–15
nostalgia franchise, 102–3, 127–8, 148, 173–88, 197

Oblivion (Kosinski, 2013), 214
O'Brien, Willis, 180
The Observer, 175
Ocean's franchise, 81–96, 158
  numbering of, 82–4
  Ocean's 8/Eight (Ross, 2018), 81–4, *84*, 86, 88, 90–3, 93n, 158
  Ocean's 11 (Milestone, 1960), 81, 86, 87, 93n, 94n
  Ocean's Eleven (Soderbergh, 2001), 82, *83*, 86–90, 93, 93n
  Ocean's Thirteen (Soderbergh, 2007), 81, 82–3, 86, 88, 93n
  Ocean's Twelve (Soderbergh, 2004), 82–3, 86–8, 91, 93n
Oldfield, Mike, 'Tubular Bells', 122
Orci, Roberto, 37, 38
Örnebring, Henrik, 193
#OscarsSoWhite, 147
Overboard (Greenberg, 2018), 158

Paramount Pictures
  intellectual property (IP), 189
  logo, 209–10, 215–16
  Star Trek franchise, 34, 37–40, 42, 43
  Teenage Mutant Ninja Turtles franchise, 24, 27, 30
  Top Gun 2, 205–6, 216
Paramount Studios, 26
Paramount Television, 34–5
paratexts, 71, 206, 216
'paratextual arrays', 208–9
paratextual bonding, 219–32

paratextual framing, 107–8
'paratextual panic', 216
Parker Jr, Ray, 163
Parody, Clare, 192, 199n
Pedestrian, 135
pilots, 113–18, 120–1, 123
Pinkerton, Nick, 100
Pitt, Brad, 89
Pixar, 190
Planet of the Apes franchise, 191, 196
  Planet of the Apes (potential new film), 197, 199
  Rise of the Planet of the Apes (Wyatt, 2011), 173
Platinum Dunes, 220–1, 224–5
Playmates Toys, 21, 25, 29–30
Pleasantville (Ross, 1998), 90
Polanski, Roman, 220
pop art, 51–2
popular feminism, 158–62; *see also* feminism
Posobiac, Jack, 134
posters, 131, 158, 195, 224
postfeminism, 158, 160–1
The Prestige (Nolan, 2006), 223
Prince, 'Batdance,' 57
Prince, Stephen, 180
Proctor, William
  action-genre reboots, 84
  feminine visibility, 92
  intertextuality, 19
  narrative continuation, 100
  reboot as restart, 97, 111
  reboot characteristics, 145–6
  reboot definitions, 3
  reboot genealogy, 6
  reboot rising from the ashes, 38
  role of audiences, 85–6
  studio economy, 93n
Prometheus (Scott, 2012) *see Alien* franchise
Puig, Claudia, 93

Les Quatre cents coups (Truffaut, 1959), 89

race
  'diversity', 129–35, 184
  politics, 147, 150–1
  racism, 164–5
  stereotypes, 185

INDEX 241

white masculinity, 162–3
white supremacists, 127–8, 138
'woke' message, 162, 9
Reagan, Ronald, 144, 151–2
Reaganite entertainment, 162–9
Red Dead Redemption 2 (Rockstar Games, 2018), 198
Reddit, 135, 191
Reeve, Christopher, 56
repetition, 114–15, 118–22
'reproductive futurism', 184
'requel', 2, 100, 173–88
retconning, 189–204
'retro' reboots, 214
'retro-remaking', 208, 214
Return of Kings website, 130
Return of the Jedi (Marquand, 1983) see *Star Wars* franchise
Riefenstahl, Leni, 88–9
Rise of the Planet of the Apes (Wyatt, 2011) see *Planet of the Apes* franchise
Rise of the Teenage Mutant Ninja Turtles (TV show, 2018) see *Teenage Mutant Ninja Turtles* franchise
Robocop Returns (new film), 195
Rock Band game, 40
Rocky franchise, 143–56, 190
   Creed (Coogler, 2015), 143, 152–4, 173, 177, 178, 184, 197
   #OscarsSoWhite, 147
   Creed franchise, 143–56
   Creed II (Caple Jr, 2018), 147, 149, 153–4, 155n
   Rocky (Avildsen, 1976), 143, 149–52
   Rocky Balboa (Stallone, 2006), 146
   Rocky II (Stallone, 1979), 150, 152–3, 153
   Rocky IV (Stallone, 1985), 146, 149, 151–2, 154
Roddenberry, Gene, 35, 37
Rodgers, Adam, 177–8
Rogue One: A Star Wars Story (Edwards, 2016) see *Star Wars* franchise
Romero, Cesar, 52
Rosemary's Baby (Polanski, 1968), 220
Ross, Gary, 81, 82–4, 86, 87, 90–3, 94n
Rotten Tomatoes, 127, 191, 194, 199n
Rottenberg, Catherine, 167

San Diego Comic-Con 2015, 130
Sargeant, Chloe, 135
Saturday Night Live (TV show), 164–5
Scahill, Andrew, 111–12
Schumacher, Joel, 57, 226, 228
Scorsese, Martin, 102
Scott, Joan, 160–1
Scott, Ridley, 9, 70, 71, 193–7
Scott, Suzanne, 42, 130, 216
Scott, Tony, 205–6
Scream franchise, 224
ScreenCrush, 177
Section Eight, 91
self-reflexivity, 178–83
'sequel hook', 85–6
serial continuity, 66–70
Shapiro, Howard, 54
Shatner, William, 33
The Shawshank Redemption (Darabont, 1994), 90
Shimabukuro, Karra, 224
The Shining (Kubrick, 1980), 75
Showtime, 97–110
'side-quel', 72
Sight and Sound, 98, 106
The Simpsons franchise, 196
Sims, David, 132
Singer, Matt, 177–8
Sirk, Douglas, 149
Skydance Media, 189, 212
Smith, Stacy, 160
Snyder, Zack, 227
Sobchak, Vivian, 194, 196
social justice reboot, 127–42
Soderbergh, Steven, 82–4, 86–91, 93, 93n
'soft reboot', 189
Solo: A Star Wars Story (Howard, 2018) see *Star Wars* franchise
Sontag, Susan, 51–2
Sony, 189, 199n
Space Invaders, 179
'speculative nostalgia', 209, 214–15
Spiderman franchise, 191
   The Amazing Spider-Man (Webb, 2012), 4, 173, 199n
Spielberg, Steven, 174, 175, 180–1, 182
sports melodrama, 143–56
Spy (2015), 159
Stallone, Sylvester, 143–7, 152, 154, 155n

Star Trek franchise, 33–46
  letter writing campaigns, 34
  Star Trek (Abrams, 2009), 9, 34, 36, *41*, 43, 122
    Kirk, James T. (character), 40–2, *41*, 44n
    Spock (character), 40–2, 44n
    Uhura (character), 40–2, *41*
    younger audience, 40–3
  Star Trek: Discovery (2017–), 43
  Star Trek II: The Wrath of Khan (Meyer, 1982), 33, 37–9, 44n
  Star Trek: Into Darkness (Abrams, 2013), 44n
  'Star Trek Lives!' convention, 34–5, 36, 39
  Star Trek: Picard (2020–), 43
  Star Trek: The Animated Series, 35
  Star Trek: The Motion Picture (Wise, 1979), 35, 39, 40
  Star Trek (TV show, 1960s), 34–5, 55
Star Wars franchise, 9, 82, 127–42, 178, 184, 190, 192, 196, 199n
  The Force Awakens (Abrams, 2015), 127–36
    #BoycottStarWarsVII, 130
    #DumpStarWars, 134
    #WheresRey, 130, 136
    box office, 175
    franchising, 9
    'legacy,' 177–8
    nostalgia franchise, 117, 173, 184, 214
  Forces of Destiny transmedia campaign, 136–8
  Princess Leia (character), as political iconography, 133
  Return of the Jedi (Marquand, 1983), 127
  Rogue One: A Star Wars Story (Edwards, 2016), 131–5
  Solo: A Star Wars Story (Howard, 2018), 122
  Star Wars: A New Hope (Lucas, 1977), 35, 127, 129, 192
  titles, 114
Starlight Runner, 193
Steele, Bruce C., 176
Sterling Entertainment Group, 53
stop-motion, 180
streaming, 190–1, 197, 198–9
Stuber (Dowse, 2019), 197
studio logos, 209–10
subscription video on demand (SVOD), 190, 197, 198–9
Suicide Squad (Ayer, 2016), 59
Sullivan, Kevin P., 83
Sun, Rebecca, 134
Superman franchise, 1, 8, 48, 56–7
  Adventures of Superman (1952–8), 48
  Batman v Superman: Dawn of Justice (Snyder, 2016), 59
  Man of Steel (Snyder, 2013), 1, 58–9
  Superman (Donner, 1978), 56
  Superman IV (Furie, 1987), 56–7
  Superman Returns (Singer, 2006), 189
  Superman WCI's films, budget and revenues, 56t
'Supersystem', 19–32

teasing, 205–18
TED Talk, 193
Teenage Mutant Ninja Turtles franchise, 19–32
  Ninja Turtles: The Next Mutation (TV show, 1997–8), 23
  Rise of the Teenage Mutant Ninja Turtles (TV show, 2018), 30
  Teenage Mutant Ninja Turtles Adventures comic book, 22
  Teenage Mutant Ninja Turtles (Barron, 1990), 22
  Teenage Mutant Ninja Turtles (Liebesman, 2014), 25–30
  Teenage Mutant Ninja Turtles: Out of the Shadows (Green, 2016), 29–30
  Teenage Mutant Ninja Turtles (TV show), 21–2, 25
  TMNT (Munroe, 2007), 27
  'Turtlemania', 22
  Turtles Forever (Burdine, 2009), 23
television-to-film reboot, 208
Terminator franchise, 81
  Terminator 2: Judgment Day (Cameron, 1991), 189
  Terminator: Dark Fate (Miller, 2019), 189, 195
  Terminator Genisys (Taylor, 2015), 173, 177, 178, 184
  Terminator Salvation (McG, 2009), 81

The Texas Chain Saw Massacre (Hooper, 1974), 220, 225
textual poaching, 135
Thompson, Howard, 223
Thomson, Luke Y., 83–4, 90
3-D, 4, 25, 177, 179, 180–1, 183, 199
Time, 36, 50, 58
Time Inc., 58
Time Warner, 87
  Comedy Channel, 50
Time Warner Incorporated (TWI), 56, 58–60
Time's Up movement, 158
Titanic (Cameron, 1997), 148, 175
title cards, 113–14, 120
Tompkins, Joe, 4, 19, 20
Top Gun franchise
  Top Gun 2/Maverick, 205–18
  Top Gun (Scott, 1986), 205
    Danger Zone: The Making of Top Gun, 210–11
    nostalgia, *207*
Touchstone Pictures, 198
toys and merchandise
  Batman franchise, 48–9, 56–8
  Star Wars franchise, 130, 135
  Teenage Mutant Ninja Turtles franchise, 21–2, 25, 27, 29–30
Toys 'R' Us, 25, 137
trailers
  'announcement trailer', 209, 214–5
  fan-made, 206, 212–13
  recut, 212–13
Transformers franchise, 26–27
Transformers (Bay, 2007), 26–27
Transformers: Revenge of the Fallen (Bay, 2009), 26–27
transmedia
  franchise, 35–6
  intertextuality, 21
  marketing, 193–4
  storytelling, 21, 192, 192–6, 199n
Travers, Ben, 147
Travers, Peter, 83
Trevorrow, Colin, 176
Triumph of the Will (Riefenstahl, 1934), 89
Tron: Legacy (Kosinski, 2010), 193, 214
Truffaut, François, 89
Trump, Donald, 59–60, 132–5, 157
Tryon, Chuck, 4, 189, 199n

Turner Broadcasting System, 50
Turner Classic Movies, 50
Turtles Forever (Burdine, 2009) *see Teenage Mutant Ninja Turtles* franchise
TV Guide, 34–5, 39
TV Tropes, 85
20th Century-Fox
  Alien franchise, 190–1, 196–7, 199n
  Batman (TV show, 1960s), 49, 55–6
  Planet of the Apes (potential new film), 199
  Prometheus (Scott, 2012), 193, 195
20th Century-Fox Television, 50
Twin Peaks franchise
  Frost, Mark, 105, 107
  Twin Peaks: The Return (TV show), 97–110
Twitter, 134, 147, 206, 215

UHF, 54
United American Video Company (UAV), 53–4
US elections 2016, 59–60, 132–5, 157
USA Today, 146

Vangelis, 'Memories of Green', 75
Variety, 35, 40
Verevis, Constantine, 5–6, 113, 146–7, 189, 208
The Verge, 127
VHF, 54
VHS tape, 50
Viacom, 23–5, 27, 30, 40
Vice.com, 127
video games, 190–1, 192, 194, 197–8
videos, 216
View-Master, 179–83, *180*
Villeneuve, Denis, 65–6, 77
virtual reality, 199
Visual Thesaurus, 85
Vulture, 101, 185

Walmart, 53
War of the Worlds (Spielberg, 2005), 213
Ward, Burt, 52, 55
Warner Bros., 54, 56, 66, 86–7, 189, 190
Warner Brother Records, 57
Warner Communications Incorporated (WCI), 56–8
Watchmen (Snyder, 2009), 227

WCIU, 54–5
Weigel, John J., 54
Weigel Broadcasting Company (WBC), 54–5
Weitz, Chris, 133–4
West, Adam, 52
Weyland, Peter, 193
Whissel, Kristen, 150
White, Brett, 132
Whitta, Gary, 134
Williams, John, 179
Williams, Kathleen, 212–13
Williams, Linda, 148–9, 151

Willis, Oliver, 134–5
Winson, Joan, 35
Wired, 178
'woke' message, 162, 169
Wolf, Mark J. P., 191
Wonder Woman franchise, 48
 Wonder Woman (TV show, 1975–9), 55
Wood, Robin, 162, 223

X-Men franchise, 197

YouTube, 50, 54, 157, 212–13
Yuan, Jada, 185

EU representative:
Easy Access System Europe
Mustamäe tee 50, 10621 Tallinn, Estonia
Gpsr.requests@easproject.com

www.ingramcontent.com/pod-product-compliance
Lightning Source LLC
Chambersburg PA
CBHW071831230426
43672CB00013B/2812